A
GREEN
HISTORY
OF THE
WORLD

By the same author

The Right to Know:
The Inside Story of the *Belgrano* Affair

Whitehall: Tragedy and Farce

Breach of Promise:
Labour in Power 1964–1970

Whitehall: Changing the Old Guard

Secrecy in Britain

1940: Myth and Reality

CLIVE PONTING

A GREEN HISTORY OF THE WORLD

SINCLAIR-STEVENSON LTD

First published in Great Britain by
Sinclair-Stevenson Limited
7/8 Kendrick Mews
London SW7 3HG, England

British Library Cataloguing in Publication Data
A CIP catalogue record for this book is available for the British Library.
ISBN: 1 85619 050 1

Typeset by Rowland Phototypesetting Limited
Bury St Edmunds, Suffolk
Printed and bound in Great Britain by
Clays Ltd, St Ives plc

To

PATRICK AND SHIRLEY RIVERS

CONTENTS

Maps xi

Tables and Charts xi

Preface xiii

1 The Lessons of Easter Island 1

European discovery – Polynesian colonisation – rise and decline – the 'mystery' explained

2 The Foundations of History 8

Influence of the physical world – significance and role of ecosystems – effect on human history

3 Ninety-nine per cent of Human History 18

Way of life among gathering and hunting groups – spread of human settlement – variations in subsistence techniques – impact on the environment

4 The First Great Transition 37

The slow transition to agriculture – three 'core areas', South West Asia, China and Mesoamerica – social and political consequences – emergence of complex societies across the world – link with culture and warfare

5 Destruction and Survival 68

Environmental impact of agriculture – strain imposed by artificial environments – self-inflicted decline of Sumer and Indus valley societies – degradation of the Mediterranean area – fall of the Maya – contrasting stability of agriculture in the Nile valley

6 The Long Struggle 88

The persistent problem of feeding the world's population – limitations of the agricultural base in the history of China and Europe – influence of climate –

causes and effects of malnutrition and famine – the diffusion of crops and animals – the European solution

7 The Spread of European Settlement 117

Internal colonisation and transformation of the landscape – the expansion of Europe – impact on the native peoples and cultures throughout the world

8 Ways of Thought 141

Influence of classical, Jewish and Christian thought on the European view of the world – the relationship between humans and the natural world – the idea of progress – alternative traditions – impact of classical economics and Marxist theory – the pursuit of economic growth

9 The Rape of the World 161

Early examples of the destruction of wildlife – extinctions – impact of the introduction of alien species – studies in the history of exploitation: fishing – fur trade – sealing – whaling – the idea of conservation

10 Creating the Third World 194

The Atlantic Islands in the fifteenth century as a microcosm of colonial development – slavery and indentured labour – towards a world economy – plantation agriculture – spread and development of cash crops – exploitation of timber and minerals – consequences for the Third World

11 The Changing Face of Death 224

Causes, impact and spread of infectious diseases – the story of bubonic plague – the influence of agriculture, trade, sanitation and poverty – rise of the 'diseases of civilisation'

12 The Weight of Numbers 240

Different patterns of population explosion – expansion of agricultural land – changes in farming technology – rise of the food industry – the 'green revolution' – world food problems – impact of agriculture – deforestation, soil erosion, salinisation, desertification – ecological disasters across the world

13 The Second Great Transition 267

Sources of energy – human, animal, water and wind power – the first energy crisis – transition to fossil fuels – growth of energy sources and consumption

14 The Rise of the City 295

Pre-industrial cities – urban growth – the role of suburbs and transport – the conurbation and the metropolis – Third World cities – environmental problems

15 Creating the Affluent Society 315

Poverty of agricultural societies – impact of industrialisation – growth in consumption and retailing – cars and tourism – problems of affluence – distribution of the world's wealth – problems of the Third World

16 Polluting the World 346

Early city pollution – water supply – waste disposal – smoke – early industrial pollution – effects of industrialisation – acid rain – industrial diseases – new chemicals – problems of toxic waste – nuclear pollution – traffic – mixing new cocktails – CFCs and the ozone layer – global warming

17 The Shadow of the Past 393

Ecological interpretation of human history – stability and sustainability of human societies – lessons of the past

Guide to Further Reading 408

Index 415

MAPS

1 The Settlement of the World   25
2 South-West Asia   45
3 China   48
4 Mesoamerica   50
5 Mesopotamia   56
6 Map of the World   118

TABLES AND CHARTS

1 Climate Change   111
2 Food Chains   13
3 The First Great Transition   53
4 World Population 10,000 BC–200 AD   90
5 World Population AD 200–1700   92
6 Annual Temperatures in England AD 900–2000   99
7 The Worldwide Diffusion of Crops and Animals   110
8 World Population 1700–2000   241
9 Energy   289
10 Urbanisation   308
11 Pollution   384

PREFACE

As some people climb mountains because they are there, others find themselves writing books because they are not there. In his preface to *The Normans in the South* John Julius Norwich explains how, after a holiday on the island, he badly wanted to understand the background to Sicily's fascinating mix of civilisations. He found only a few specialised texts and realised that if he wanted a complete history of Norman Sicily for the general reader, he would have to write it himself. However diffident he felt about his qualifications he felt strongly enough about the interest and significance of his subject to launch himself into the task. This work owes its conception to that sort of experience. There are many books about the current state of the environment and the prospects for the future but few probe very far into the past or explore the extent to which the environment has shaped human history and none covered the ground and asked the questions that seemed to me to be important. I feel strongly that there is a need for a book that looks at world history from a 'green' perspective.

This book makes no claims to original scholarship. In the twenty years that I have been thinking and reading about the subjects covered in this history, and during the time that I was actively engaged on research, I have incurred a great debt to the many hundreds of historians, archaeologists, anthropologists, scientists of various disciplines, economists and others who have written about the different topics that are embraced. Much of what they wrote was not undertaken with any specifically 'green' perspective in mind and, therefore, I hope they will, if necessary, excuse the use that has been made of their work. In a general work of this kind it has not been possible to include detailed footnotes and specific accreditations and I have to resort instead to a generalised, but nonetheless sincere, expression of gratitude.

This book does not pretend to be a complete history of the world. It does not deal with political, military, diplomatic or cultural history. These aspects are already well covered elsewhere. Most of the so-called great historical figures either do not appear at all in these pages or, at best, rate only a passing mention. Instead I have tried to concentrate on what I believe are some fundamental issues that have perhaps not always received the attention they deserve in previous accounts. I am convinced, after nearly twenty years of supporting 'environmental' causes, that 'green' issues are not simply about the state of the natural world but have to include central problems such as the use of resources and energy, the distribution of poverty and wealth, how people treat other people, and the way people think about the world they inhabit. But these issues are addressed in a historical context. *This book does not attempt to propose solutions.*

I have tried to write a *world* history. But I would accept that the coverage of every area of the globe is not equal. A history of the world's people that reflected the experience of the majority would require the bulk of attention to be focused on the history of China, India and the rest of Asia. On this basis the history of Europe and the United States receives more than its fair share of this book, but this bias can, I believe, be justified because of their overwhelming importance in influencing what has happened in world history and to the global environment in the last five hundred years. I have not deliberately neglected Africa – I can only plead a lack of relevant material. All dates are AD unless otherwise indicated.

The research for this book involved consulting many hundreds of books and articles, often of only marginal relevance to my subject matter. Rather than give a comprehensive but completely unwieldy list of sources I have opted instead to give a guide to particularly valuable books that illuminate an important area or which would be useful reading for those who feel they would like to investigate a topic in more detail than the space available here allows.

In the course of writing this book I have incurred two particular debts of gratitude. First, to my editor Christopher Sinclair-Stevenson without whose enthusiasm and support it would never have been written. Second, as always, to my wife Sally whose own interest in the subject and perceptive criticisms of successive drafts have been invaluable. I am also grateful to the London Library for its eclectic and sometimes helpfully eccentric collection, to the staff of the Main and Natural Sciences libraries and, not least, the inter-library loan section at University College, Swansea for helping to find often slightly obscure texts. Part of Chapter 5 was given as a paper at the annual conference of the British Association in 1990 and I am grateful for their interest in the subject and for contributions from participants in the conference.

CLIVE PONTING

1

THE LESSONS OF EASTER ISLAND

Easter Island is one of the most remote, inhabited places on earth. Only some 150 square miles in area, it lies in the Pacific Ocean, 2,000 miles off the west coast of South America and 1,250 miles from the nearest inhabitable land of Pitcairn Island. At its peak the population was only about 7,000. Yet, despite its superficial insignificance, the history of Easter Island is a grim warning to the world.

The Dutch Admiral Roggeveen, onboard the *Arena*, was the first European to visit the island on Easter Sunday 1722. He found a society in a primitive state with about 3,000 people living in squalid reed huts or caves, engaged in almost perpetual warfare and resorting to cannibalism in a desperate attempt to supplement the meagre food supplies available on the island. During the next European visit in 1770 the Spanish nominally annexed the island but it was so remote, underpopulated and lacking in resources that no formal colonial occupation ever took place. There were a few more brief visits in the late eighteenth century, including one by Captain Cook in 1774. An American ship stayed long enough to carry off twenty-two inhabitants to work as slaves killing seals on Masafuera Island off the Chilean coast. The population continued to decline and conditions on the island worsened: in 1877 the Peruvians removed and enslaved all but 110 old people and children. Eventually the island was taken over by Chile and turned into a giant ranch for 40,000 sheep run by a British company, with the few remaining inhabitants confined to one small village.

What amazed and intrigued the first European visitors was the evidence, amongst all the squalor and barbarism, of a once flourishing and advanced society. Scattered across the island were over 600 massive stone statues, on average over twenty feet high. When anthropologists began to consider the history and culture of Easter Island early in the twentieth century they agreed on one thing. The primitive people living in such poverty-stricken and backward conditions when the Europeans first visited the island could not have been responsible for such a socially advanced and technologically complex task as carving, transporting and erecting the statues. Easter Island therefore became a 'mystery'and a wide variety of theories were advanced to explain its history. Some of the more fantastic ideas involved visits by spacemen or lost civilisations on continents that had sunk into the Pacific leaving Easter Island as a remnant. The Norwegian archaeologist Thor Heyerdahl, in his popular book *Aku-Aku* written in the 1950s, emphasises the strange aspects of the island and the mysteries that lay hidden in its history. He argued that the island was first settled from South America and that from there the people inherited a tradition of monumental sculpture and stone work (similar to the great Inca achievements). To account for the decline he introduced the idea that at a late stage other settlers arrived from the west and began a series of wars between the so-called 'long-ears' and the 'short-ears' that destroyed the complex society on the island. While this theory is less extravagant than some of the others that have been put forward it has never been generally accepted by other archaeologists.

The history of Easter Island is not one of lost civilisations and esoteric knowledge. Rather it is a striking example of the dependence of human societies on their environment and of the consequences of irreversibly damaging that environment. It is the story of a people who, starting from an extremely limited resource base, constructed one of the most advanced societies in the world for the technology they had available. However, the demands placed on the environment of the island by this development were immense. When it could no longer withstand the pressure, the society that had been painfully built up over the previous thousand years fell with it.

The colonisation of Easter Island belongs to the last phase in the long-drawn-out movement of human settlement across the globe. The first people arrived sometime in the fifth century at a period when the Roman empire was collapsing in western Europe, China was still in chaos following the fall of the Han empire two hundred years earlier, India saw the end of the short-lived Gupta empire and the great city of Teotihuacan dominated most of Mesoamerica. They were Polynesians and part of a great process of exploration and settlement across the vast expanse of the Pacific Ocean. The original Polynesians came from south-east Asia and they reached the islands of Tonga and Samoa about 1000 BC. From there they moved further east to the Marquesas Islands about 300 AD and then in two directions, south-east to Easter Island and north to Hawaii in the fifth century. The last phases of the movement were to the Society Islands about 600 and from there to New Zealand about 800. When this settlement was complete, the Polynesians were the most widely spread people on earth encompassing a huge triangle from Hawaii in the north to New Zealand in the south-west and Easter Island in the south-east – an area twice the size of the present continental United States. Their long voyages were made in double canoes, joined together by a broad central platform to transport and shelter people, plants, animals and food. These were deliberate colonisation missions and they represented considerable feats of navigation and seamanship since the prevailing currents and winds in the Pacific are against west to east travel.

When the first people found Easter Island, they discovered a world with few resources. The island was volcanic in origin, but its three volcanoes had been extinct for at least 400 years before the Polynesian settlers arrived. Both temperatures and humidity were high and, although the soil was adequate, drainage was very bad and there were no permanent streams on the island; the only fresh water available was from lakes inside the extinct volcanoes. Because of its remoteness the island had only a few species of plants and animals. There were thirty indigenous species of flora, no mammals, a few insects and two types of small lizard. The waters around the island contained very few fish. The arrival of the first humans did little to improve the situation. The Polynesians in their home islands depended on a very limited range of plants and animals for subsistence: their only domesticated animals were chickens, pigs, dogs and the Polynesian rat and the main crops were yam, taro, breadfruit, banana, coconut and sweet potato. The settlers on Easter Island brought only chickens and rats with them and they soon found that the climate was too severe for semi-tropical plants such as breadfruit and coconut and extremely marginal for the usual mainstays of their diet, taro and yam. The inhabitants were, therefore, restricted to a diet based mainly on sweet potatoes and chickens. The only advantage of this monotonous, though nutritionally adequate, diet was that cultivation of the sweet potato was not very demanding and left plenty of time for other activities.

It is not known how many settlers arrived in the fifth century but they probably numbered no more than twenty or thirty at most. As the population slowly increased the forms of social organisation familiar in the rest of Polynesia were adopted. The basic social unit was the extended family, which jointly owned and cultivated the land. Closely related households formed lineages and clans, each of which had its own centre for religious and ceremonial activity. Each clan was headed by a chief who was able to organise and direct activities and act as a focal point for the redistribution of food and other essentials within the clan. It was this form of organisation and the competition (and probably conflict) between the clans that produced both the major achievements of Easter Island society and ultimately its collapse.

Settlements were scattered across the island in small clusters of peasant huts with crops grown in open fields. Social activities were centred around separate ceremonial centres, which were occupied for part of the year. The chief monuments were large stone platforms, similar to those found in other parts of Polynesia and known as *ahu*, which were used for burials, ancestor worship and to commemorate past clan chiefs. What made Easter Island different was that crop production took very little effort and therefore there was plenty of free time which the clan chiefs were able to direct into ceremonial activities. The result was the creation of the most advanced of all the Polynesian societies and one of the most complex in the world for its limited resource base. The Easter Islanders engaged in elaborate rituals and monument construction. Some of the ceremonies involved recitation from the only known Polynesian form of writing called *rongorongo*, which was probably less a true script and more a series of mnemonic devices. One set of elaborate rituals was based on the bird cult at Orongo, where there are the remains of forty-seven special houses together with numerous platforms and a series of high-relief rock carvings. The crucial centres of ceremonial activity were the *ahu*. Over 300 of these platforms were constructed on the island, mainly near the coast. The level of intellectual achievement of at least some parts of Easter Island society can be judged by the fact that a number of these *ahu* have sophisticated astronomical alignments, usually towards one of the solstices or the equinox. At each site they erected between one and fifteen of the huge stone statues that survive today as a unique memorial to the vanished Easter Island society. It is these statues which took up immense amounts of peasant labour. The statues were carved, using only obsidian stone tools, at the quarry at Rano Raraku. They were fashioned to represent in a highly stylised form a male head and torso. On top of the head was placed a 'topknot' of red stone weighing about ten tons from another quarry. The carving was a time-consuming rather than a complex task. The most challenging problem was to transport the statues, each some twenty feet in length and weighing several tens of tons, across the island and the then erect them on top of the *ahu*.

The Easter Islanders' solution to the problem of transport provides the key to the subsequent fate of their whole society. Lacking any draught animals they had to rely on human power to drag the statues across the island using tree trunks as rollers. The population of the island grew steadily from the original small group in the fifth century to about 7,000 at its peak in 1550. Over time the number of clan groups would have increased and also the competition between them. By the sixteenth century hundreds of *ahu* had been constructed and with them over 600 of the huge stone statues. Then, when the society was at its peak, it suddenly collapsed leaving over half the statues only partially completed around Rano Raraku quarry. The cause of the collapse and the key to understanding the 'mysteries' of Easter Island was massive environmental degradation brought on by deforestation of the whole island.

When the first Europeans visited the island in the eighteenth century it was completely treeless apart from a handful of isolated specimens at the bottom of the deepest extinct volcano crater of Rano Kao. However, recent scientific work, involving the analysis of pollen types, has shown that at the time of the initial settlement Easter Island had a dense vegetation cover including extensive woods. As the population slowly increased, trees would have been cut down to provide clearings for agriculture, fuel for heating and cooking, construction material for household goods, pole and thatch houses and canoes for fishing. The most demanding requirement of all was the need to move the large number of enormously heavy statues to ceremonial sites around the island. The only way this could have been done was by large numbers of people guiding and sliding them along a form of flexible tracking made up of tree trunks spread on the ground between the quarry and the *ahu*. Prodigious quantities of timber would have been required and in increasing amounts as the competition between the clans to erect statues grew. As a result by 1600 the island was almost completely deforested and statue erection was brought to a halt leaving many stranded at the quarry.

The deforestation of the island was not only the death knell for the elaborate social and ceremonial life it also had other drastic effects on every day life for the population generally. From 1500 the shortage of trees was forcing many people to abandon building houses from timber and live in caves, and when the wood eventually ran out altogether about a century later everyone had to use the only materials left. They resorted to stone shelters dug into the hillsides or flimsy reed huts cut from the vegetation that grew round the edges of the crater lakes. Canoes could no longer be built and only reed boats incapable of long voyages could be made. Fishing was also more difficult because nets had previously been made from the paper mulberry tree (which could also be made into cloth) and that was no longer available. Removal of the tree cover also badly affected the soil of the island, which would have already suffered from a lack of suitable animal manure to replace nutrients taken up by the crops. Increased exposure caused soil erosion and the leaching out of essential nutrients. As a result crop yields declined. The only source of food on the island unaffected by these problems was the chickens. As they became ever more important, they had to be protected from theft and the introduction of stone-built defensive chicken houses can be dated to this phase of the island's history. It became impossible to support 7,000 people on this diminishing resource base and numbers fell rapidly.

After 1600 Easter Island society went into decline and regressed to ever more primitive conditions. Without trees, and so without canoes, the islanders were trapped in their remote home, unable to escape the consequences of their self-inflicted, environmental collapse. The social and cultural impact of deforestation was equally important. The inability to erect any more statues must have had a devastating effect on the belief systems and social organisation and called into question the foundations on which that complex society had been built. There were increasing conflicts over diminishing resources resulting in a state of almost permanent warfare. Slavery became common and as the amount of protein available fell the population turned to cannibalism. One of the main aims of warfare was to destroy the *ahu* of opposing clans. A few survived as burial places but most were abandoned. The magnificent stone statues, too massive to destroy, were pulled down. The first Europeans found only a few still standing when they arrived in the eighteenth century and all had been toppled by the 1830s. When they were asked by the visitors how the statues had been moved from the quarry, the primitive islanders could no longer remember what their ancestors had achieved and could only say that the huge figures had 'walked' across the island. The Europeans, seeing a treeless landscape, could think of no logical explanation either and were equally mystified.

Against great odds the islanders painstakingly constructed, over many centuries, one of the most advanced societies of its type in the world. For a thousand years they sustained a way of life in accordance with an elaborate set of social and religious customs that enabled them not only to survive but to flourish. It was in many ways a triumph of human ingenuity and an apparent victory over a difficult environment. But in the end the increasing numbers and cultural ambitions of the islanders proved too great for the limited resources available to them. When the environment was ruined by the pressure, the society very quickly collapsed with it leading to a state of near barbarism.

The Easter Islanders, aware that they were almost completely isolated from the rest of the world, must surely have realised that their very existence depended on the limited resources of a small island. After all it was small enough for them to walk round the entire island in a day or so and see for themselves what was happening to the forests. Yet they were unable to devise a system that allowed them to find the right balance with their environment. Instead vital resources were steadily consumed until finally none were left. Indeed, at the very time when the limitations of the island must have become starkly apparent the competition between the clans for the available timber seems to have intensified as more and more statues were carved and moved across the island in an attempt to secure prestige and status. The fact that so many were left unfinished or stranded near the quarry suggests that no account was taken of how few trees were left on the island.

The fate of Easter Island has wider implications too. Like Easter Island the earth has only limited resources to support human society and all its demands. Like the islanders, the human population of the earth has no practical means of escape. How has the environment of the world shaped human history and how have people shaped and altered the world in which they live? Have other societies fallen into the same trap as the islanders? For the last two million years humans have succeeded in obtaining more food and extracting more resources on which to sustain increasing numbers of people and increasingly complex and technologically advanced societies. But have they been any more successful than the islanders in finding a way of life that does not fatally deplete the resources that are available to them and irreversibly damage their life support system?

2
THE FOUNDATIONS OF HISTORY

Human history cannot be understood in a vacuum. All human societies have been, and still are, dependent on complex, interrelated physical, chemical and biological processes. These include the energy produced by the sun, the circulation of the elements crucial for life, the geo-physical processes that have caused the continental land masses to migrate across the face of the globe and the factors regulating climatic change. These constitute the essential foundations for the way in which the various types of plants and animals (including humans) form complex, interdependent communities. Although scientific knowledge about some of these areas, especially climatic change, is still sketchy, research in a wide variety of disciplines is increasingly making it clear that life on earth and all human societies depend on the maintenance of a number of delicate balances within and between a whole series of complex processes. The findings help us to understand the way in which the environment has influenced the development of human societies and, just as important, the human impact on the earth.

Human history has been affected by the action of large scale geo-logical and astronomical forces over long periods of time. Although the amount of land on the globe has remained broadly constant its distribu-tion has altered radically. The rocks a few miles below the earth's surface are molten and flow in convection currents caused by the heat rising from the earth's core. This flow causes movements in the earth's crust in the form of large 'plates' which move across the surface of the globe. The convection currents from the core of the earth well up in ridges under the oceans and then flow outwards forcing the plates further apart so that the north Atlantic is currently widening at about half an inch a year and the east Pacific by about four inches a year. Material flows back down into the earth in the deep oceanic trenches. Where the plates meet there is major instability causing earthquakes and volcanoes.

These movements are manifested in the natural disasters that have punctuated human history – volcanic eruptions such as Thera, which may have overwhelmed Minoan society on Crete, the eruption of Vesuvius that destroyed Herculaneum and Pompeii or major earthquakes such as that in Shensi province in China in 1556 that killed over 800,000 people or those affecting Lisbon in 1755 and Tokyo in 1923 that killed tens of thousands. The impact in the long term is even greater. About 400 million years ago the earth had two supercontinents – Laurasia (north America, Europe and Asia) and Gondwanaland (south America, Africa, India, Australia and Antarctica) divided by the Tethys Sea. When this massive land mass broke up, the southern continents were situated over the south pole, causing glaciers in what is now Brazil and South Africa, and Laurasia was in the tropics. What is now North America broke away from Europe about 200 million years ago, although the major drift apart to form the Atlantic ocean has only occurred in the last 80 million years, Gondwanaland began to break up into separate continents about 160 million years ago but the formation of most of the Indian Ocean and the break between Australia and Antarctica occurred in the last 60 million years. Africa and South America split apart 100 million years ago.

The drift of the continents across the globe has had a profound impact on human history. It has determined the distribution of resources, and it accounts for the differing flora and fauna of the continents. Material welling up from the earth's core formed part of the continental land masses and determined the location and concentration of the world's mineral resources. The position of the continents at an earlier stage of their history explains the distribution of fossil fuel reserves in the modern world. Coal, oil and natural gas come from the decomposition of the vast tropical forests present about 250–300 million years ago. Continental drift has also been a major influence in determining the current distribution of plants and animals. Some have evolved in isolation and others been driven to extinction by competitors when suddenly brought into contact with other parts of the world. For example, marsupial mammals had a worldwide distribution about 80 million years ago. As the continents drifted apart marsupials were replaced in Eurasia by placental mammals. They survived in South America until it joined North America about 30 million years ago and they live on in Australia, which has remained isolated. The evolution of animals in different parts of the world has also had major effects on human history. The isolation of the Americas from the Eurasian landmass meant that animals domesticated in Europe and Asia such as sheep, goats, cattle and horses were not present. This influenced both their agriculture and their transport – domesticated animals were relatively unimportant and, although societies in the Americas were aware of the principle of the wheel, they could not utilise it because no draught animals were available.

Climate has been a fundamental force in shaping human history. Year to year variations in the weather influence crop yields but more significantly major, long-term trends have affected the ability of humans to settle parts of the globe, influenced the way plants and animals are distributed and placed limits on the crops that can be grown. The distribution of the continents has also been one of the factors determining climate. The ice ages, which have dominated the world's climate for the last two-and-a-half million years, depend for their effect on the current distribution of the land masses of the northern hemisphere. Large scale ice sheets could not develop, and move further south when the climate deteriorated, without the continents clustering towards the north pole and the formation of a land-locked Arctic Ocean about three million years ago.

The position of the continents is only one factor influencing the world's climate. Apart from the steadily increasing energy output of the sun and the levels of gases such as carbon dioxide and methane in the atmosphere, the major factor determining climate is a series of astronomical cycles affecting the earth and its orbit round the sun. In the 1920s a Yugoslavian scientist, Milhankovic, put foward this theory but he was largely ignored. Only in the last thirty years, with the scientific analysis of cores taken from ocean sediments and ice sheets giving information on climate stretching back over hundreds of thousands of years, have his theories been accepted. Over a period of 90–100,000 years the earth's orbit varies from being nearly circular to more elliptical. At present the orbit is becoming more circular and reducing the difference between the times when the heat from the sun falling on the earth is at its maximum and minimum. The second cycle, the timing of the earth's closest approach to the sun, is completed every 21,000 years. At the moment the earth is nearest to the sun during the northern hemisphere winter. This reduces the impact of seasonal climatic change in the north whilst increasing it in the southern hemisphere. The third cycle affects the 'tilt' of the earth, which varies over a period of about 40,000 years. At the moment the tilt is decreasing, which again reduces the difference between the seasons. Although there are other short-term cycles, such as minor variations in the sun's output over a 22–23 year period (linked to sunspot activity and reversals of the solar magnetic field), it is the combination of the three long-term cycles that largely determines the earth's changing climate.

The long term cycles alter the distribution of the sun's energy falling on the earth. The current closeness of the continents in the northern hemisphere to the pole is of crucial importance because only a 2 per cent drop in heat from the sun during the northern summer can initiate glaciation. Cool summers allow winter snow and ice to survive to the next winter and the growing snow cover causes further cooling by increasing the reflectivity of the earth's surface. This further reduces the temperature in the northern hemisphere leading to a rapid increase in the extent of ice sheets and glaciers. The same process cannot work in the southern hemisphere when changes in the earth's orbit produce cool summers there. Apart from Antarctica there is insufficient land near to the pole and too much water (which moderates the temperatures) to allow continental ice sheets to form. For the last two-and-a-half million years a cycle of ice ages has affected the earth's climate; the interglacial periods have normally been short, a total of about 250,000 years out of the last two million. The warmest interglacial was the one about 120,000 years ago (with temperatures about 2°C warmer than today).

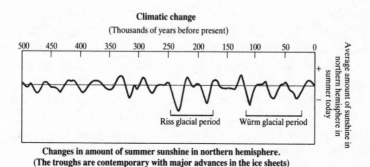

Climatic change
(Thousands of years before present)

Riss glacial period   Würm glacial period

Average amount of sunshine in northern hemisphere in summer today

Changes in amount of summer sunshine in northern hemisphere.
(The troughs are contemporary with major advances in the ice sheets)

The various forms of life on earth, including humans, do not exist independently, they are part of ecosystems – a term which is used to refer to a community of organisms and their environment. There are many different types of ecosystem such as a tropical forest, a grassland prairie or a coral reef but the foundation of all of them, and therefore the basis for all life on earth, is photosynthesis – the process by which the energy of sunlight is used by plants and certain types of bacteria to create the chemical compounds essential for life. It is the only way that energy is introduced into the system. Very little of the sun's energy is, in fact, converted into matter (often as low as 0.2 per cent) and there is no way in which this efficiency can be improved since it depends on the amount of light falling on the earth, the laws of physics and the amount of carbon dioxide in the atmosphere. (Selective breeding of plants does not increase the efficiency of photosynthesis, it simply makes plants put more of their effort into producing those parts that humans find useful at the cost of other parts).

Within an individual ecosystem photosynthesisers (such as plants, trees and grasses) provide the basic energy input. They are at the bottom of a food chain which links together all the different organisms. When photosynthesisers die they are broken down in the soil by decomposers such as funguses and their essential elements become available for other plants to use. (The pattern is similar in a marine environment.) Photosynthesisers are also eaten by animals (herbivores) which are able to extract essential nourishment from the plant. Herbivores are in turn eaten by other animals (carnivores) which are capable of extracting their food from animals. Some animals, known as top carnivores, can eat both herbivores and other carnivores. When all these animals die their carcasses rot and the essential elements are recycled. Most ecosystems have complex food chains with numerous interrelationships between the various parts. However behind this complexity there is an iron rule. The higher an animal is in the food chain, the rarer it will be. Each step up the food chain is further removed from the primary production of the photosynthesisers and therefore less energy efficient – consequently the numbers that can be supported get smaller. A cow for example is only able to store 0.6 per cent of the primary production of the grass in a field. This is why only a very small number of carnivores can exist within an ecosystem compared with the number of primary producers. In the case of a deciduous wood in southern England, 88 per cent of the primary production by photosynthesisers (in this case trees, plants and grasses) eventually falls to the ground and decomposes on the woodland floor and another 8 per cent is stored as dead wood, which eventually decomposes. Only about 3 per cent is available for herbivores to eat and even less for the carnivores who have to live off the herbivores.

Ecosystems are not static. Over time they develop through an orderly and predictable series of changes resulting from the modification of the environment by the plants and animals themselves to culminate in a climax system which has the maximum possible number of plants and animals for the available energy input. It takes thousands of years to

Food chains

GENERALISED FOOD CHAIN

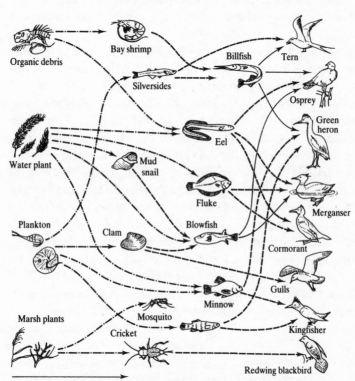

Energy flow (thickness of arrows shows relative importance of food source)

PART OF THE FOOD CHAIN IN A LONG ISLAND ESTUARY

move from bare rock through lichens and mosses to ferns, plants and eventually trees to create a climax forest that can survive for very long periods – provided there is no human interference. The original pioneer species that colonise the rock are adapted to coping with poor soils or with none at all. Slowly, as decayed matter is accumulated, a better soil is created, capable of sustaining annual plants and successively perennials, grasses, shrubs and trees. As the ecosystem develops and changes, so do the plants and animals that can be supported. This development of an ecosystem has occurred countless times during the earth's history – for example the retreat of an ice sheet after a glacial period exposes bare rock, which within a few thousand years is converted into a climax temperate forest. Where a climax ecosystem is destroyed (as is often the case through human intervention to clear forests) then the subsequent process of change is speeded up because good soil already exists. For example arable land (the result of forest clearance at an earlier stage in its history) left uncultivated in England will, through a succession of arable weeds, grasses, and shrubs such as hawthorn and mixed scrub, revert to an oak and ash forest within 150 years.

The different types of ecosystem depend to a large extent on the temperature and level of rainfall. They are therefore found in broad bands between the poles and the equator. Changes in the earth's climate cause these bands to change location, often by hundreds of miles over a period of several thousand years, as well as producing major local variations. At present, near the poles, low rainfall, low temperatures and permafrost produce tundra (poorly drained, acidic soils covered in low scrub). Further away from the pole in the northern hemisphere (though not in the southern because there is no land in the right place) are the great coniferous forests known as the taiga. Further away still from the poles are the temperate forests with their rich secondary flora, better soils, high leaf drop and a correspondingly large quantity of decomposers. Then there are the grasslands, which have less rain than the temperate forests and where the soils are poorer. In two bands sited about 30°N and 30°S of the equator are large areas of desert – a product of the global weather system which concentrates large masses of very dry air in these latitudes. Finally in the tropics, around the equator, with both high rainfall and temperatures, are the vast, tropical rainforests. There are of course many local variations within this overall picture such as the tropical savannas of grassland with scattered thorny trees and the temperate rain forests of north-west America and southern New Zealand.

The productivity of the different ecosystems varies greatly. In the tundra the level of primary production is low because of the cold and lack of sunshine. This means fewer species can be supported and then not in large numbers. The food chain is therefore short and relatively simple. The open oceans are virtual deserts whereas coral reefs and estuaries teem with life, reaching levels equivalent to the most productive of all terrestrial systems – the tropical forests. These forests, which cover about 6 per cent of the world's land surface, produce about

40 per cent of all terrestrial primary plant production and contain about half of all the plants and animals on earth. Rainforests are remarkable not just for the quantity of life found there but also for the diversity. A typical four square mile patch of forest will contain the following species (not individuals) – 1,500 flowering plants, 750 trees, 125 mammals, 400 birds, 100 reptiles, 60 amphibians, 150 butterflies and probably over 50,000 insects. (In total in the tropical forests there are probably 20 million species of insect). Tropical forests are, however, very different in their structure from temperate forests, which have rich soils. Three-quarters of all the nutrients are held in the plants and trees and only 8 per cent in the soil. Very little rain water runs off into the soil – over half is evaporated and most of the rest absorbed directly by the plants and trees. The soil itself is thin, acidic and of poor quality with very little humus. If the ecosystem is destroyed through forest clearance most of the nutrients are destroyed too; there is little available in the soil to support crops or grass and the exposed ground can quickly turn into a hard, baked clay.

Soil is the product of an ecosystem – it has been created by living plants and animals and it continues to rely on them to remain fertile and productive. Before the earliest forms of life emerged from the sea there was no soil; all the land on the earth was bare, eroded rock and deserts. Soils build up over thousands of years through physical, chemical and biological processes as rock is weathered into minute fragments and incorporated together with the remains of dead plants and animals to form a medium that supports bigger plants and trees as the ecosystem develops to a climax. Fertility is built up and maintained as an active process through the interaction of the plant cover, the existing soil, the work of decomposers and other environmental factors such as rainfall and temperature. All of these processes make the various types of soil found in different parts of the globe one of the most complex living systems on earth. Just one acre of good soil from a temperate region will contain about 125 million small invertebrates, and thirty grams of that soil will contain 1 million bacteria of just one type, 100,000 yeast cells and 50,000 fungus mycelium. Although soils are created over time this process is, on a human timescale, so slow that the soil is in effect a non-renewable resource. It is also a highly fragile one. Ecosystems develop naturally in a way that protects the soil on which they depend. On the dry grasslands it is the roots of the grass that hold together a poor soil and in the temperate forests it is the whole process of extensive leaf drop in the autumn, combined with a large number of decomposers living off the dead material, which maintains a highly fertile soil. In tropical forests, where the soils are generally poor in nutrients and potentially vulnerable to the high rainfall and temperatures, the ecosystem has developed in such a way as to protect the soil. Once the trees and plants of an ecosystem are destroyed or badly damaged then the underlying soil is very quickly subjected to severe strain and can be easily destroyed or eroded away by wind and rain leaving only a degraded remnant.

To fully understand the individual parts of an ecosystem, it is necessary to see them as part of a bigger whole. All the parts of an ecosystem are interconnected through a complex set of self-regulating cycles, feedback loops and linkages between different parts of the food chain. For example, the fertility, stability and texture of a soil depend on an interaction with the other parts of the ecosystem which have produced it. If one part of an ecosystem is removed or disrupted there will be knock-on effects elsewhere in the system. The extent of the reverberations will of course vary depending on the nature, scale and duration of the initial disruption; on the relative significance of the part or parts affected; and on the resilience of the ecosystem. For example, if one species of animal is wiped out (by disease or by being hunted to extinction) then there will be ramifications up and down the food chain. The population of those plants and animals that formed its diet will increase, while those that previously hunted it for food will decrease, and these changes will then bring further secondary disruption at other levels in the food chain. A form of disruption which destroys the primary producers (as with a forest fire or deliberate clearance) will constitute an attack on the base of the food chain and it will have disastrous effects on all parts of the chain.

Just as the plants and animals in an ecosystem are part of a greater whole so ecosystems themselves are part of a greater whole – the earth itself. For all practical purposes the earth is a closed system. Although sunlight gets in to provide the necessary energy for life all the other resources are finite. The fact that the earth is a closed system also means that nothing can get out. All waste products must go somewhere. This fact, combined with the limited resources available to all living things, means that the recycling of the materials necessary for life is an essential function of all ecosystems and the other physical and chemical processes on earth. Problems can arise though when artificial wastes are 'disposed of' in ecosystems, for example by dumping at sea or discharging into the air. Many of these products cannot be recycled at all by natural systems or not in the concentrations in which they are found as a result of human activity and they remain as pollutants somewhere in the system. All pollution is, therefore, bound to affect natural processes and ecosystems, whether on land, in the oceans or in the atmosphere.

Humans too are part of the earth's ecosystems, whether or not they are always conscious of this fact and its implications. All plants and animals tend to modify the environment as they compete and co-operate with others to survive and flourish. In their relationship to the ecosystem, two factors distinguish humans from all other animals. First, they are the only species capable of endangering and even destroying the ecosystems on which they depend for their existence. Second, humans are the only species to have spread into every ter-restrial ecosystem and then, through the use of technology, to have dominated them. (They have even been able to develop ways of heavily exploiting marine ecosystems too.)

The most important task in all human history has been to find a way of extracting from the different ecosystems in which people have lived enough resources for maintaining life – food, clothing, shelter, energy and other material goods. Inevitably this has meant intervening in natural ecosystems. The problem for human societies has been to balance their various demands against the ability of the ecosystems to withstand the resulting pressures.

3
NINETY-NINE PER CENT OF HUMAN HISTORY

For all but the last few thousand years of their two million years existence humans have obtained their subsistence by a combination of gathering foodstuffs and hunting animals. In nearly every case people lived in small, mobile groups. It was without doubt the most successful and flexible way of life adopted by humans and the one that caused the least damage to natural ecosystems. It enabled them to spread across the face of the globe into every terrestrial ecosystem and to survive not just in favourable areas with easily obtained food but also in the rigorous conditions of the Arctic, the tundra of ice-age Europe and the marginal dry lands of Australia and southern Africa.

The origins and earliest development of humans and their immediate ancestors have to be deduced from scanty evidence, usually the fossilised remains of partial skeletons, sometimes as little as a jaw bone or a tooth, and therefore interpretation is difficult. Not surprisingly, the topic arouses great controversy between experts and numerous conflicting schemes have been put forward to explain the nature of particular fossils and their relationship to each other. The fact that the remains have, so far, only been found in a few areas of the world, mainly east and south Africa, has naturally heavily influenced explanations of the likely geographical origins of human ancestors and their development.

Fossils found from about 2–1.5 million years ago and called *Homo erectus* are recognised as being the direct ancestors of modern humans. But much earlier fossil remains reveal evidence of certain 'human traits', notably upright posture (as early as 3.5 million years ago) and toolmaking linked to the first stone tools about 2 million years ago. The distinguishing characteristic of *Homo erectus* is a large brain size of about 1,100cc (about three-quarters of modern human capacity). They probably emerged in Africa, although if a skeleton from Java is correctly dated at about 1.9 million years ago this theory might need to be revised and it is certainly the case that far less archaeological work on human origins has been done in south-east Asia than east Africa. The available archaeological evidence suggests that they survived until about 100,000 years ago when the first anatomically modern skeletons, named in a piece of immense self-flattery *Homo sapiens*, are found in east and southern Africa. By about 30,000 years ago fully modern human types (*Homo sapiens sapiens*) were widespread throughout the world.

The earliest humans appear to have inhabited a variety of habitats within a belt of tropical and semi-tropical country stretching from Ethiopia to southern Africa. The population was small, thinly spread, living in groups which probably depended mainly on the gathering of nuts, seeds and plants, which they would have supplemented by scavenging dead animals killed by other predators and perhaps the hunting of a few small mammals. It was this basic form of subsistence – gathering and hunting – that was to last as the human way of life until the development of agriculture about 10,000 years ago.

Gathering and hunting as a way of life is now restricted to a handful of groups in the world such as the Bushmen of south-west Africa, some pygmy groups in the equatorial forests of Africa, the Hadza of east Africa, a few groups in India and south-east Asia, some Aborigines in Australia, some Inuit in the Arctic and the native inhabitants of the tropical forests of South America. These groups now occupy essentially marginal habitats, having been gradually pushed aside by the advance of agriculture. Two-thirds of the Inuit originally lived in a much more benign climate south of the Arctic Circle, while the Aborigines used to live mainly in the productive regions of eastern Australia not in the central and northern deserts. The commonly accepted view of gathering and hunting is that it produces a life which is, to quote Thomas Hobbes, 'nasty, brutish and short'. In the last thirty years new anthropological studies of existing gathering and hunting groups have provided a fascinating insight into how humans lived for the overwhelming majority of their history and how they were integrated into the environment. These studies have emphasised the relatively easy way in which sufficient food could be extracted from what would have been much more productive ecosystems than those now occupied by such groups. In parallel with these findings there has been a revolution in archaeological thinking and techniques for investigating early human remains. Instead of collecting large numbers of stone tools and trying to classify them into different 'cultures' on the basis of marginal differences in the way in which they were made or by comparing the different types of tools found at different sites, archaeologists have adopted a much more sophisticated approach. This emphasises trying to understand, often using contemporary groups as examples, what tools were made to do, what activities were carried out at the different sites, how human groups exploited their environment in different ways to obtain food and how their seasonal movements were integrated into this overall pattern.

What emerges from these new approaches is a much more positive view of gathering and hunting groups. In general, gatherers and hunters do not live under the constant threat of starvation. Rather they have a nutritionally adequate diet selected from a wide range of the available food resources. This wide variety of food is normally only a small proportion of the total amount of food available in the environment. Obtaining food and other forms of work take up only a small proportion of the day, leaving a large amount of time free for leisure and ceremonial activities. Most groups survive with very few goods because their wants are few and because they would find extra goods a hindrance to their mobile way of life. Items such as hunting tools or cooking utensils have no great value because they can be easily replaced from locally available materials. The pattern of life varies during the year depending on the seasonal availability of different types of food. Most of the time they live in small groups of about 25–50 people and come together in larger groups for ceremonial purposes, marriage and other social activities at a time when food supplies allow a larger population to gather in one place. Within the group there is no concept of food ownership and food is treated as available to all. Food is not stored because that would interfere with mobility and because their experience dictates that some food will always be available even if certain items are occasionally in short supply.

The bushmen of south-west Africa illustrate how easily gathering and hunting groups can obtain sufficient food. The mainstay of their diet is the highly nutritious mongongo nut obtained from a drought-resistant tree. It is a very reliable source which keeps for over a year. It contains 5 times the calories and 10 times the amount of protein of an equivalent amount of cereal crops and half a pound (about 300 nuts) has the calories of two-and-a-half pounds of cooked rice and the protein of almost a pound of beef. In addition 84 different species of food plants are available although the bushmen normally only use twenty-three of them. There are 54 edible animals available although only 17 are hunted regularly. Compared with modern recommended levels of nutrition the diet of the bushmen is more than adequate: calorie intake is higher, protein consumption is about a third higher and there are no signs of any deficiency diseases. The amount of effort required to obtain this food is not very great – on average two-and-a-half days a week. The work involved is steady throughout the year (unlike agriculture) and apart from at the height of the dry season the search for food rarely involves travelling more than six miles in a day. Women and men devote about the same amount of time overall to obtaining food but the women, who are responsible for gathering, bring in about twice as much food as the men are able to hunt. The women tend to work about one to three hours a day and spend the rest of the time in leisure activities. Hunting, which is carried out by the men, is more intermittent involving perhaps a week of hunting followed by no activity at all for two or three weeks. About 40 per cent of the group play no part in the work of obtaining food. About one in ten are aged over sixty and treated as honoured members and the young are not expected to provide food until they marry at about the age of twenty for women and twenty-five for men. Similar patterns have been found amongst the Hadza of east Africa and the Aborigines of Australia.

All of these groups have now been pushed into marginal subsistence areas and so it is safe to assume that when similar groups were able to live in locations with more abundant resources food gathering would have been even easier. Indeed many contemporary groups fail to see the attractions of agriculture with its much greater workload. As one bushmen told an anthropologist, 'Why should we plant when there are so many mongongo nuts in the world?' Leisure time is valued very highly and preferred to increasing food supplies (which are already more than adequate) or producing more material goods (which can be a hindrance). Earlier this century the Siane tribe in New Guinea adopted modern steel axes instead of their traditional stone tools. This reduced the amount of time needed to provide an adequate level of subsistence by about a third. The new spare time was not spent in increasing output but was devoted to ceremonies, leisure and warfare. Similarly in sixteenth-century Brazil the Portuguese found that the Indian tribes, if not enslaved, would only work for them until they had earnt enough to buy metal tools and then they wanted to enjoy their extra leisure.

In general, gathering and hunting groups live largely by gathering. Hunting is a difficult and hazardous activity with only intermittent rewards at best. Studies of top carnivores in ecosystems (which is the role humans are trying to adopt when hunting) show that they only make a kill about once in every ten attempts. Humans, even with some help from technology, are much less well adapted to this role than lions or tigers and are likely to achieve even lower rates of success. In early gathering and hunting groups, operating with fairly primitive spears

and bows and arrows, most of the meat in their diet is likely to have
come from scavenging animals killed by other predators. In the equatorial and tropical areas hunting rarely contributes more than a third of
a group's diet. Ecosystems further away from the equator are less
productive and therefore the available plant food needs to be supplemented – often through the more time-consuming task of fishing.
The great grasslands pose major problems for these groups in finding
food because of their lack of suitable plants for human consumption and
the difficulty of hunting the large herds of grazing animals. It is only in
the Arctic areas, with their almost total lack of suitable plant food, that
hunting dominates subsistence. In these areas finding sufficient food is
not easy and survival requires a great deal of skill and effort to make use
of the limited resources available.

In order to obtain the necessary subsistence, gathering and hunting
groups depend on a deep knowledge of their local areas and in particular
an awareness of what types of food will be available at different places
and at different times of the year. Their way of life revolves around
major seasonal changes in methods of subsistence and patterns of social
organisation are integrated into these changes. Contemporary gathering and hunting peoples again illustrate how historical groups would
have adapted to their particular conditions. The bushmen of south-
west Africa live in a relatively homogeneous environment, moving
camp about five or six times a year but never moving on more than
about ten or twelve miles at a time and making longer trips only for
social occasions such as marriage. The Gidjingali Aborigines of northern Australia have a clear seasonal round of varying exploitation. In the
wet season, when the swamps are full, they eat waterlilies – the stalks
are eaten raw, the seeds made into unleavened cakes and the corms
cooked. In the early dry season they move to an area where large yams
are found since the tubers are easy to locate at this time of the year when
the tendrils are still green. Later they move to the edge of the wetlands
where the men hunt geese and the women dig up spike rush corms. At
the height of the dry season subsistence depends on cycad nuts which,
although difficult to prepare, are plentiful and can support the large
groups of people who gather together at this time for ceremonial,
religious and social events. Only in a brief period before the rainy
season is there any shortage of suitable food when subsistence depends
on less favoured roots and plants.

An example of an extreme form of adaptation to a harsh environment
influencing all forms of economic and social life is provided by the
Netsilik Inuit living north and west of Hudson's Bay in Canada, who

were studied in the 1920s before they had any real contact with modern technology. Their way of life depended on careful exploitation of every part of their environment. Houses and storage facilities were made from the snow and ice. Clothing, kayaks, sledges and tents came from the skins of animals and the bones provided tools and weapons. Cooking utensils were made out of stone. The seasonal round of subsistence activity was highly varied. In the winter the Netsilik were totally dependent on seal hunting. A huge number of hunters had to cover the numerous holes in the ice used by the seals for breathing. This was therefore the time of the year when extended social groups gathered together in great igloo communities and took part in the major religious and ceremonial activity of the year. The large winter camps broke up into small groups living in tents from June when it was possible to hunt the seals on the ice. By July the groups moved inland fishing and occasionally hunting caribou. In August they constructed stone weirs across streams in order to catch the plentiful supply of salmon trout moving upstream to spawn. At the end of the month they again came together in large groups for the communal activity of hunting from kayaks as the caribou crossed the rivers during their annual migration. In October smaller groups of Inuit would fish for salmon before reassembling in larger groups for the winter seal hunt. In each of the phases of communal hunting there were social customs to ensure that everybody was fed and that nobody was penalised because of poor luck or lack of skill.

These modern examples of gathering and hunting groups tell us a good deal about the way in which historical groups would have operated in the various environments they inhabited around the world. All gathering and hunting groups, both contemporary and historical, seem to have tried to control their numbers so as not to overtax the resources of their ecosystem. This was achieved through a number of accepted social customs. The most widespread was infanticide involving the selected killing of certain categories such as twins, the handicapped and a proportion of female offspring. (Studies in the 1930s showed that Inuit groups killed about 40 per cent of their female children.) In addition, protracted weaning of infants probably provided a form of birth control and some of the old people may have been abandoned if they were ill and a burden on the group. In such ways the demand for food and, therefore, the pressure that gathering and hunting groups placed on their environment was reduced. Population densities were generally low (although the numbers would vary according to the type of environment and its natural level of productivity). The best estimate for the total population of the world about 10,000 years ago, just before the adoption of agriculture in a few areas, was not more than about four million and in earlier periods it would have been considerably less than that.

The gradual development of human societies and the spread of settlement across the globe into different environments can be traced to four basic traits that distinguish humans from other primates. Fundamental to all advance was an increase in brain size. A bigger brain seems to have been important in achieving the power of abstract thought so vital in the development of technology. A second vital breakthrough (made as early as three-and-a-half million years ago) was the ability to stand fully upright on two feet. This was important not just in increasing mobility but also in freeing the hands to undertake other tasks such as using and making tools. The third trait was the use of speech. Not surprisingly there is absolutely no evidence as to when speech was adopted but it is generally assumed to have been at an early date and the ability to communicate would have opened the way to increased group co-operation and more elaborate social organisation in general as well as aiding the spread of different cultural advances. The fourth trait was fundamental to the human settlement of the world – the adoption of technological means to overcome difficulties imposed by hostile environments. Although other animals use tools, humans are the only ones to make them. Stone toolmaking began about two million years ago with the first crude stone choppers from pebbles, although other less durable tools that have not survived would probably have been used earlier.

Apart from stone tools, the artefacts and technologies used by the earliest humans were wooden spears (about 400,000 years ago), bolas stones for entangling animals (about 80,000 years ago), the use of wood and skins and also fire. Since fires also happen naturally, the exact date at which fire was first deliberately used is a matter of considerable controversy. There are ambiguous indications from the site of Chesowanja in east Africa dated to about one-and-a-half million years ago but the first definite, and widely accepted, evidence comes from about 500,000 years ago. Traces of the use of fire are first found in association with animal kill sites, suggesting that it was brought to the sites in order to cook the meat, as well as at camps where it would have been used for heat and light and possibly protection. At this early stage, it is unlikely that it was used to drive animals into suitable killing sites, although this technique certainly was used at much later dates. But for at least two million years the principal technology used by humans was the stone tool. For about the first one-and-a-half million years of tool

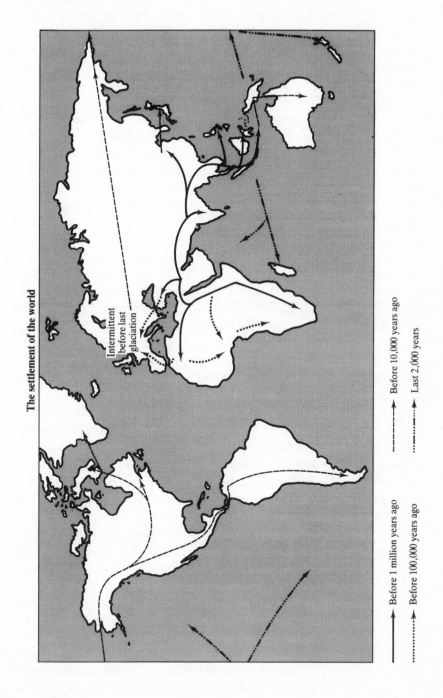

The settlement of the world

Intermittent before last glaciation

Before 1 million years ago

Before 100,000 years ago

Before 10,000 years ago

Last 2,000 years

making the dominant types were a chopper like tool made from pebbles and a hand axe with a working edge round most of the perimeter. These tools were relatively easy to make and are found in huge quantities. For example, the disarticulated skeleton of a hippopotamus found at Olduvai Gorge in East Africa was surrounded by 459 blunted hand axes and choppers.

It was with this primitive tool kit that the first humans were able to move from Africa into the frost-free zones of the Middle East, India, south China and parts of Indonesia, although the use of clothing from the skins of animals would have been necessary too. The exact chronological framework is difficult to establish because of the lack of archaeological work in many areas, but it is clear that *Homo erectus* had spread outside Africa by about one-and-a-half million years ago, very soon after the first skeletons of this direct ancestor of modern humans were found. But the areas occupied were still restricted. With the skills that they possessed at this time humans could only adapt to those ecosystems found in the semi-tropical areas where there was a considerable variety of vegetable material that could be gathered easily and a wide range of small and easily hunted animals to supplement this diet. The equatorial rain forests were not penetrated and the settlement of Europe posed formidable difficulties. These problems were not solved for a very long time and so the settlement of Europe is a comparatively late phenomenon in human history despite its relatively easy access from the Near East and Africa. European ecosystems made it very difficult, even in interglacial periods, to extract enough subsistence with only a limited technological base: the plant life was less rich and the scope for gathering more limited. The hunting of medium and large-sized game was therefore vital, but difficult. Even if they were only scavenging and killing the sick and old members of the herds the groups would have needed to move over large areas when following the seasonal movements of the animals and they would have found it difficult to keep in touch for social and cultural activities. The first evidence of human occupation is dated to about 730,000 years ago and most areas of Europe had seen human settlement by about 350,000 years ago. But this settlement was intermittent and confined to interglacial periods when the climate of Europe would have been equable enough to support gathering and hunting with a limited tool kit. The conditions during glacial periods, when the great northern ice sheets advanced and the climate of even southern France deteriorated into semi-arctic conditions producing a type of tundra, would have been too severe.

It was not until the last, long, glacial period that began about 80,000 years ago and lasted till about 12,000 years ago that the first permanent occupation of Europe took place. It marked a major advance in the ability of humans to adapt to a harsh ecosystem. During this period the whole of Scandinavia, north Germany, Poland, north-west Soviet Union and most of Britain were covered in ice and at the height of the glacial period, about 20,000 years ago, the ice sheets moved even further south. The area to the south of these ice sheets was one of permafrost and a tundra type vegetation. But this tundra was richer than that now found in northern Europe because of the longer summers. It supported a wide variety of animal life dominated by large herds of reindeer, woolly mammoth, bison and wild horse together with smaller numbers of woolly rhinoceroses, giant elk and saiga antelope. Given the low level of plant life and therefore the limited role that gathering could play in the subsistence base, humans were dependent on these large animal herds for their existence. This challenging environment produced a highly developed and sophisticated culture to control the available food supply and it stimulated a much greater degree of social integration than ever before achieved by human groups.

The conventional picture of the ice-age inhabitants of Europe is that they were hunters preying randomly on the herds of reindeer and other large animals. But pure hunting is a high risk strategy: the rate of success is very low and continual hunting only frightens the herds, making them more difficult to follow and attack. A much more sophisticated approach to obtaining subsistence in a difficult environment was in fact employed. This was based on managing the herds with the minimum of disturbance. In eastern and central Europe it involved following the migrating herds between their winter ranges on the Hungarian plain and the edge of the Black Sea to their summer grazing areas in the Jura, southern German highlands and the Carpathians. Human habitation sites are found along the natural migration routes and on the edges of the natural grazing grounds of the reindeer. The herds were not hunted at random but culled on a selective basis to remove the sick and the old. Enough animals to provide meat for the season were herded away from the main group, driven to areas such as natural basins and killed as required. The numbers of humans that could be supported in this way though were very small. A herd of about 1,500 reindeer would perhaps be sufficient for only about three families or fifteen or so individuals. These groups would also have been forced to be highly mobile, coming together in larger numbers, essential for ceremonial and social activities, for only short periods of the year.

A very different way of life developed in south-west France and northern Spain at the height of the last glaciation about 25–20,000 years ago. When the climate was at its most severe, northern Europe seems to have been partially abandoned and a relatively dense population developed further south. Subsistence was based on the large herds of reindeer and red deer that passed through the Dordogne area and northern Spain. Within this region it was possible for a moderately dense human population to sustain a reasonable level of food supplies without undertaking long migrations following the herds. They were able to utilise different parts of the area at different times of the year and food from the herds was supplemented by a plentiful supply of salmon and other fish in the rivers. In these semi-settled conditions a highly integrated society emerged that produced the great cave paintings found at sites such as Lascaux in south-west France and Altamira in northern Spain (roughly contemporary paintings and rock art have also been found at the Apollo cave in South Africa and in Australia). The exact function and meaning of the European cave paintings is still unclear but their religious and ceremonial nature is not in dispute and there was almost certainly some magical element involved in seeking to control the herds on which the way of life of the community depended. When the ice slowly retreated the herds gradually moved north. They fell in size as the increasing bands of forest also moved north, eliminating the tundra as the climate improved. The whole subsistence base of the humans in the area slowly collapsed and a series of major adjustments was required in order to obtain food from a radically different environment. There was a greater emphasis on gathering from the richer ecosystem produced by the milder climate, and on the use of smaller animals living in the wooded conditions, on fishing and on marine resources such as shellfish.

Europe was also one of the areas to see a significant development in human technology involving the development of new techniques in the production of tools and also the use of new materials. They constitute one of the most significant changes made by humans and the greatest burst of innovation before the invention of pottery and the use of metal. They began about 40–30,000 years ago and appear to be linked to the spread of fully modern humans, *Homo sapiens sapiens*. The number of different types of stone tools manufactured rose from six to eighty and the nature of the tools changed significantly. Before about 40,000 years ago tools tended to be large – mainly hand axes or flakes from a prepared core – with only a minimal investment of time and effort in their preparation. After this date the emphasis changed to the production of very thin, parallel-sided blades from the core and later still, after about 20,000 years ago, small light blades used as points for projectiles. These new tools required different and more complicated manufacturing techniques involving heat treatment and pressure flaking from the core. Mastery of these techniques not only needed higher motor abilities and co-ordination but also greater mental skills to cope with the number of separate stages needed to manufacture these artifacts.

For the first time, previously available materials such as bone, antler and ivory were worked into tools, some of them extremely complex to make, such as barbed harpoons. Spears were improved through the use of bone or ivory points to replace stone and by the use of the spear thrower to increase range. Hunting was also made easier and less manpower intensive by the invention, about 23,000 years ago, of the bow and arrow and the likely use about this time of snares, traps and nets, which would have widened the resource base available for human exploitation. Although clothes had been made from skins for hundreds of thousands of years, life in Europe, at the height of the last glaciation, required major improvements in survival techniques. Hoods, gloves and foot mittens were produced and by 20,000 years ago eyed needles and fine thread (a product of fur trapping) were being used. Good insulation from the cold provided by warm clothing meant that the level of calorie intake necessary for survival in the harsh conditions was kept low enough to be extracted from the environment. The development of new techniques was probably accompanied by a greater degree of specialisation within the gathering, hunting and herding groups and the use of increasingly high quality materials that could only be found in a small number of locations led to the creation of regional networks for their exchange.

The permanent settlement of Europe at a time of extremely severe climatic conditions was a major human achievement and a sign of increasing human control over the environment. It was made possible by a combination of the adoption of new technologies and more sophisticated animal management. The settlement of Australia did not require such elaborate adaptations because of the relatively benign climate in the eastern part of the continent and the ease with which gathering and hunting groups could find food. It could only have come about, however, after one major invention – the boat – because Australia, although joined to New Guinea at the height of the glaciation, was never linked to the Asian mainland. Australia was settled about 40,000 years ago at a time when sea levels were at their lowest and when a voyage of about sixty miles would have been needed. Tasmania was linked to Australia until about 15,000 years ago (it was settled about 20,000 years ago) and New Guinea became an island about 8,000 years ago. The initial settlement was probably by a small group, perhaps as few as twenty-five people, but the population grew rapidly in what had been an undisturbed environment to reach about 300,000 – the same level as when Australia was first reached by Europeans. The society which developed in Australia did not lead to the development of more complex social organisations as happened in almost every other area of the world.

The settlement of America was almost the last stage in the movement of humans across the globe. This was because it depended on the ability of human groups first to survive in the harsh climate of Siberia and then to advance eastwards to the Bering Strait. The crossing to Alaska was made at the height of the last glaciation when the reduced sea levels turned the Bering Strait into a land bridge. The climate in the area is likely to have been less severe than now with reasonable opportunities for hunting and herding the large animals of the area. But movement south out of Alaska could only have taken place at a slightly warmer stage when the two major ice sheets of north America, centred on the Rocky mountains and the Laurentian shield, would have retreated and separated enough to open up the passes to the south east. This could have taken place at one of two periods – either 30–23,000 years ago or about 13,000 years ago. Although this is a matter of great controversy in early American archaeology, the latter date is the more likely. Once the first human settlers were able to move through the passes to the south they found an enormously rich environment that provided plenty of opportunities for relatively easy subsistence. The human population multiplied rapidly and within a few thousand years had spread to the tip of South America.

A whole series of adaptations were required in order to extract food from the wide variety of ecosystems found in the Americas. On the plains of North America, given the lack of a large variety of plants for gathering, subsistence depended on exploiting large herds of bison and other animals. These were often killed in a crude and highly wasteful way by driving them into narrow canyons or over cliffs. At Caspar in Wyoming about 10,000 years ago a single kill involved at least seventy four animals and in a roughly contemporaneous kill in south-east Colorado hunters appear to have set off a stampede into a canyon and ended up with about 200 corpses most of which could not be used because they were squashed at the bottom of a large pile of bodies. In eastern North America the spread of the forest after the ice sheets retreated changed the ecosystem and removed most of the large animals suitable for hunting. Societies adapted to these new conditions in much the same way as those in post-glacial Europe – by exploiting smaller animals such as deer, by fishing, by placing a greater emphasis on gathering. Further north in the Arctic areas settlers were attracted by the abundant meat from caribou, arctic foxes and hares and only later moved on to exploit marine resources, especially the seals. The deserts of the south-west required a different adaptation with the emphasis on mobility so as to exploit a wide range of plants and animals in a difficult environment. In the tropical areas of central and south America a way of life based on the widely available plant resources supplemented by a small amount of hunting was possible.

Perhaps the most extraordinary development though took place on the north-west Pacific coast with its abundant marine resources of seals, sea lions, sea otters and in particular the salmon that came to spawn in the rivers. This relatively plentiful supply probably involved more effort in storage than in procurement. The various animals were dried during the summer or smoked in the autumn and the fat was rendered down to oil to provide sufficient food for the winter. Although there were, naturally, fluctuations the supply of food was sufficiently reliable to avoid the need for mobility and this area produced one of the few examples of a settled society not based on agriculture. Villages developed each with a population of about 1,000 living in long, communal houses with village chiefs, considerable social stratification and specialisation of labour together with complex mechanisms for barter and gifts of food as a way of obtaining prestige and ensuring adequate subsistence was available for all. This complex society even produced a hereditary caste of slaves. Extensive food storage meant that winter was a time when the effort required for subsistence was minimal and elaborate ceremonial activities took up most of the spare time. This proved to be a highly stable way of life that survived until Europeans arrived in the area.

By about 10,000 years ago, with the movement of the human frontier through the Americas, nearly all parts of the globe had been settled. The final phase in the human settlement of the world took place relatively late in the Pacific and Indian Oceans. This settlement was carried out not by pure gatherers and hunters but by groups that obtained their subsistence through a primitive form of agriculture although they still relied on stone tools and supplemented their diet through occasional hunting. In the Pacific, the Micronesian people settled islands such as the Marshalls and Carolines but it was the

Polynesians who carried out the most extensive voyages. From New Guinea they reached Tonga and Samoa about 1000 BC and moved further east to the Marquesas about 300 AD. From there they sailed to Easter Island and Hawaii about a century or two later. The last two major islands of the world were settled by humans about 800 AD in the Pacific and the Indian Oceans at a time when Charlemagne's empire was at its peak in western Europe and the Vikings were beginning their epic voyages, when Islam dominated the Mediterranean and the Near East and China was ruled by the T'ang dynasty. The Polynesians reached New Zealand and people moving west from Indonesia settled the small island groups in the Indian Ocean together with Madagascar.

Every major area of the world (except Antarctica) had now been settled by humans. Gathering and hunting groups had, over hundreds of thousands of years, adapted to every possible environment in the world from the semi-tropical areas of Africa to ice-age Europe, from the Arctic to the deserts of south-west Africa. The subsistence techniques used in these differing environments varied widely from dependence on gathering and the hunting of small animals to the herding of reindeer, hunting of bison and the highly complex mixture of strategies required in the Arctic. It is often assumed that these groups lived in close harmony with the environment and did minimal damage to natural ecosystems. The gathering of food did require very detailed knowledge and considerable understanding of where resources could be found at different times of the year so that the annual round of subsistence activity could be organised accordingly. The herding and hunting of animals similarly required close study of their habits and movements. There is also evidence that some of these groups did try to conserve resources in the interest of maintaining subsistence over a long period. Totemic restrictions on hunting particular species at certain times of the year or a pattern of only hunting an area every few years would have helped to maintain population levels in the hunted animals. Some groups had sacred areas where hunting was forbidden and others, such as the Cree in Canada, used a form of rotational hunting, only returning to an area after a considerable length of time, which allowed animal population levels to recover from the bouts of slaughter. Apart from specific cultural restrictions one of the main reasons why gathering and hunting groups, in many instances, avoided over-exploiting the available natural resources was that their numbers were small and therefore the pressure they placed on the environment limited.

However, gatherers and hunters are by no means passive in their acceptance of ecosystems and many of their activities do alter the environment considerably and cause damage. The modern Hadza of east Africa are known to destroy wild beehives in order to obtain a small amount of honey and other groups often destroy many of the wild plants on which they depend by carelessly uprooting large numbers. Moreover, gathering and hunting groups do alter the conditions in which wild 'crops' grow, intervening in order to benefit some favoured plants at the expense of others that they do not require. One of the most effective ways of doing this is by burning and the use of fire for such purposes was widespread among gathering and hunting groups. Fire alters the habitat significantly, by favouring annual plants that grow well in new ground and by increasing nutrient recycling. The Aborigines used fire regularly to encourage an edible bracken on Tasmania and the Maoris on New Zealand used the same technique to increase the spread of an edible bracken the rhizome of which formed a substantial part of their diet. In New Guinea from about 30,000 years ago, not long after it was first settled, there is widespread evidence of forest clearance by felling, ring barking and the use of fire. This opening up of the forest cover was to encourage food plants such as yams, bananas and taro to grow and to provide room for the sago tree. In post-glacial Britain patches of woodland were cleared by burning in order to encourage the growth of forage for red deer. Most groups also tended wild plants by transplanting and sowing in their natural habitats and by removing competing plants. Some even used techniques such as irrigation on a small scale to improve the habitat of favoured plants. Although these interventions in a natural ecosystem are very different from agriculture, which involves *replacing* the natural system with an artificial one, they reveal humans modifying the environment if only on a small scale and in limited locations.

The most dramatic impact that gathering and hunting groups had on their environment though was through hunting animals. It is much easier to damage this part of an ecosystem because the numbers are smaller and populations, particularly of larger animals or carnivores at the top of the food chain, usually take a long time to recover from any overhunting. Although there is some evidence of attempts by groups not to overhunt, there is far more of uncontrolled hunting and even the extinction of species. We have already seen how the great bison hunts on the plains of north America could kill hundreds of animals in one drive even though only a few were required. The bison population was huge (about 50–60 million) so that even a large number of kills a year on this scale would not significantly reduce numbers. Smaller populations though could be badly affected. The effect of hunting was made worse by the tendency of hunters to concentrate on one species to the exclusion of others. On the Aleutian Islands in the north Pacific the population concentrated on killing the sea otter for over a thousand years after the settlement of the islands about 500 BC until it was virtually extinct and the subsistence base of the community destroyed. Then the islanders had to alter their way of life substantially and accept a lower level of subsistence from the diminished resources that remained.

The impact humans could have on animal numbers is well illustrated by the examples of Madagascar, Hawaii and New Zealand, previously isolated islands with unique fauna suddenly subjected to severe stress. Because no large mammals had been able to reach such isolated spots large flightless birds had evolved, in the absence of major predators, to become the dominant animals. They were defenceless against human predation. Within a few hundred years of the settlement of Madagascar many of the larger animals, including a big flightless bird and a pygmy hippopotamus, were extinct. On Hawaii within a thousand years of human settlement thirty-nine species of land birds had become extinct. In New Zealand the Maoris were faced with a temperate environment where many of their traditional crops such as banana, breadfruit and coconut from the sub-tropical Polynesian islands could not be grown and even yams and taro could only be grown on the North Island. This forced a radical shift in their normal subsistence pattern towards wild plants such as bracken fern and the leaf heads of the cabbage tree together with marine resources. Hunting also became more important. The large number of flightless birds such as the kiwi, weka and the many species of moa (most of them about six feet high though one type was over twelve feet tall) were hunted ruthlessly and their eggs were eaten too. Within 600 years of the first settlement twenty-four species of moa were extinct together with twenty other types of bird.

Gathering and hunting groups could even have had an impact on animal populations on a continental scale. A number of species became extinct around the end of the last glaciation at a time when climatic change and the consequential shift in vegetation types were adversely affecting the large mammals that had inhabited the tundra of northern and central Europe. In Eurasia five large animals – the woolly mammoth, woolly rhinoceros, giant Irish elk, musk ox and steppe bison – together with a number of carnivores became extinct within a period of a few thousand years as the ice sheets retreated and the tundra was replaced by forest. The changing environment put the greatest strain on these large animals but hunting by humans would have had a devastating impact on a population already in decline and may have tipped the balance between extinction and survival.

The extinction of species in Eurasia was on a relatively small scale. Elsewhere in the world it was massive. In Australia, over the last 100,000 years, 86 per cent of the large animals have become extinct in an area where the climatic impact and therefore the effect on animal habits of the ice ages was minimal. The most likely explanation is hunting by Aboriginal groups in the last 40,000 years. Even if the largest animals were not themselves hunted on a large scale, disruption of the ecosystem as a result of human intervention – by destroying habitats or killing the smaller herbivores on which the carnivores depended – could easily lead to extinction. Equally remarkable is the 80 per cent loss of large animals in South America and the 73 per cent loss suffered in the north of the continent. Unlike Eurasia, where only the animals on the steppe tundra were affected, the extinctions in the Americas involved every type of ecosystem. Although some occurred at the end of the last glaciation, climatic changes had not produced such massive extinctions in the past and there is little doubt that they were the outcome of human intervention in some form. As the first settlers in America moved south out of Alaska and the Rocky Mountains they would have found a rich, undisturbed environment and their number would have risen quickly, thanks to the easily obtained resources. These first American settlers left a trail of destruction across the continent. Two-thirds of the large mammals present when humans first arrived were driven to extinction. Some of these were archaic types, such as the plains camel (found only in North America because of its isolation), others were giant species particularly sensitive to both climatic change and overhunting. Overall the extinctions included three genera of elephant, six of giant edentates (armadillos, anteaters and sloths), fifteen of ungulates and a large number of giant rodents and carnivores.

By about 10,000 years ago humans had spread over a period of about two million years from their original area of southern and eastern Africa to every continent. The slow expansion of human settlement depended upon a number of linked developments. Growth in brain size gave increased capacity for abstract thought and conceptualisation and an ability to provide increasingly sophisticated cultural and technological solutions to the challenges posed by a wide range of difficult and even hostile environments. These solutions included the use of fire and clothing to enable humans to live in harsher climates and the adoption of increasingly elaborate subsistence strategies. In the benign sub-tropical areas gathering and hunting groups could rely mainly on the wide variety and large quantity of plant food available supplemented by only a small amount of hunting. As human groups moved away from the tropics this way of life had to be drastically modified and a whole variety of different techniques adopted. These ranged from more intensive hunting to herding of large animals to the highly complex seasonal round of activities practised by the Inuit of the Arctic. Technological changes were vital in allowing human settlement around the globe and they occurred on several different fronts, starting with the production of increasingly sophisticated stone tools and the introduction of new weapons such as the bow and arrow but also including the use of furs and skins for clothing, the construction of shelters from a wide variety of materials and the adoption of more complex food processing techniques – cooking in pit hearths rather than open fires and grinding nuts and seeds.

The rate of development was of course very slow and also patchy. Not until about 40,000 years ago did the pace of technological change increase rapidly, at least in comparison with earlier periods. But taken together, these developments were of fundamental importance for the rest of human history and the future of the earth. Humans had become the only animals to dominate and exploit every terrestrial ecosystem. Yet at this stage the overall impact of the gathering and hunting groups on the environment was small because of the low, thinly spread population and their limited technology. Even so they were already making their presence felt as a number of animals were hunted to extinction and the environment was modified in subtle ways. The gathering and hunting way of life was highly stable and very long lasting. For hundreds of thousands of years it was the only way in which humans were able to extract the necessary subsistence from the environment. The number of people that could survive in any one area was constrained by their position at the top of the food chain. Only in exceptional cases such as the Pacific coast of North America were resources so abundant that settled populations could develop in sizeable villages.

Then, about 10,000 years ago, after two million years of a highly stable and well-adjusted way of life, the methods humans used to obtain their food began to change in a number of locations across the globe. The pace of change was still slow but far faster than in the past. Its consequences were far more radical than anything that had gone before. It brought about the most fundamental alteration in human history – and one which made possible all the subsequent developments in human society.

4

THE FIRST GREAT TRANSITION

For about two million years humans lived by gathering, herding and hunting. Then in the space of a few thousand years a radically different way of life emerged based on a major alteration to natural ecosystems in order to produce crops and provide pasture for animals. This more intensive system of food production was developed separately in three core areas of the world – south-west Asia, China and Mesoamerica – and it marked the most important transition in human history. Because it was capable of providing much greater quantities of food it made possible the evolution of settled, complex, hierarchical societies and a much faster growth in human population. About 10,000 years ago, before the evolution of agriculture, the population of the world was approximately four million and rose very slowly to about five million by 5000 BC. Then, in the crucial period as settled societies developed on a major scale after 5000 BC, it began doubling every millennium to reach 50 million by 1000 BC and grew to 100 million within the next 500 years and to 200 million by 200 AD. The upward trend has continued ever since, though not at a steady rate and often interrupted by the consequences of famine and disease, so that agriculture now supports a world population of just over five billion.

The combined phenomena of the transition to agriculture, the growth of settled societies, the emergence of cities and craft specialisation and the rise of powerful religious and political elites, are often referred to as the 'Neolithic Revolution'. However, although the consequences of all these changes were clearly revolutionary – both in their impact on the way of life and on the environment – it is misleading to describe the process itself as a revolution. The timescale over which these changes took place was long, at least four or five thousand years, and the contribution of any one generation would probably be very small. Moreover the idea of a revolution implies action undertaken with the aim of bringing about change, and what we can see in retrospect as a 'process' would not have been embarked on in such a self-conscious or deliberate way. Human societies did not set out to invent 'agriculture' and produce permanent settlements. Rather a series of marginal changes were made gradually in existing ways of obtaining food as a result of particular local circumstances. The cumulative effect of the various alterations was important because they acted like a ratchet. Adjustments in subsistence methods to a more intensive form enabled a larger population to be supported but meant that it became impossible to go back to a gathering and hunting way of life because the larger number of people could not then be fed. Over this long period there was no straight line of development from 'gathering and hunting' to 'agriculture'. Many different ways of obtaining food from plants and animals would have been tried in various permutations and with changing balances between plant and animal foods. Some of these strategies would have failed and others would only have been partly successful. Only slowly and unconsciously did a radically new solution to the human problem of extracting food from different ecosystems emerge.

This long transition can best be understood by abandoning any idea of a clear distinction between gathering and hunting on the one hand and agriculture on the other. They should be seen as parts of a spectrum of human activities of different degrees of intensity designed to exploit ecosystems. Gathering and hunting groups are not passive in their acceptance of the environment: they carry out a wide variety of activities that involve interfering with natural ecosystems for the benefit of humans. In terms of animal exploitation there is a clear gradation between random hunting of a herd, controlled predation, herd following, loose herding, close herding and finally modern intensive factory farming. Gathering and hunting groups carry out the first three or four processes but not the last two. In utilising plants there is a range of intensity from foraging of wild plants, tending wild plants through cultivation, domestication of genetically distinct crops some of which can only propagate through human intervention and finally genetic engineering to create new species unknown to nature. Gathering and hunting groups did practise certain forms of cultivation (and some still do): they alter habitats by burning to clear ground and improve nutrient recycling, they engage in replanting and sowing plants in the wild, weeding and even small-scale irrigation. Preparing artificial habitats specifically for growing and tending plants and gradually selecting and domesticating certain types is only an intensification of this process of intervention.

Gathering and hunting groups in glacial Europe had already demonstrated an ability to exploit herds of reindeer and deer in quite sophisticated ways in order to extract subsistence from a hostile environment. Such relatively intensive exploitation of animals does not require settled agricultural communities, as is demonstrated by present day groups of nomadic herders such as the Sami (reindeer), Masai (cattle), or various peoples of central Asia (horse). There are other examples too of varieties of exploitation techniques that adopt some but not all of the processes that are to be found in modern agriculture. In the Levant as early as 18,000 BC humans were herding gazelles in a semi-domesticated environment: at sites such as Abu Hureyra in Syria and Nahal Oren in Israel over 80 per cent of the animal bones recovered were those of gazelles even though many other species were available to both herd and hunt. At the same time these groups were also harvesting wild forms of plants such as einkorn, emmer and barley that were to be domesticated 10,000 years later. The use of wild grains was not necessarily an inferior way of obtaining food. Recent experiments using stone sickles to harvest the large stands of the wild ancestors of current crops that still grow in the Near East have shown that such techniques could be highly productive and the wild grains are often far more nutritious than the domesticated varieties. Wild emmer in Israel has produced yields of 2,500–4,000 pounds an acre, a rate as good as that of wheat in medieval England. In Mexico, teosinte, a wild form of maize, has been found to be highly productive with three-and-a-half hours' gathering providing enough food for one person for ten days. The effort involved in obtaining food from these wild 'crops' is also far less than with domesticated crops since no sowing, weeding and tending is required.

The identification of domesticated plants and animals from archaeological remains is very difficult. It is for, example, impossible to tell the difference between the remains of plants and grain gathered in the wild and those that come from the same plants and grain in fields where they have been planted and cultivated by humans. It is usually possible to distinguish the characteristics of plants during the domestication process as they gradually alter from their wild progenitors to fully domesticated varieties but the changes take place over a considerable period of time. The difficulties encountered by archaeologists are compounded by the problems associated with tropical and semi-tropical sites, where plant remains are rarely well preserved in the warm, wet climate. Many plants, particularly roots and tubers such as yams and potatoes, and also trees such as coconut and sago, show almost no changes when domesticated and therefore pose immense problems in trying to date changes in subsistence techniques. Similar problems apply to working from animal bones. It is almost impossible to identify directly from the archaeological record whether wild animals were being herded. The best indirect method is to look for findings such as a large percentage of bones from young animals, which suggests that highly selective predation techniques were being used. The morphological changes that take place on domestication are subject to dispute although it is generally agreed that animals become smaller and retain more of their juvenile characteristics. But this process again can only take place over long periods of time, which makes it very difficult to use changes in physical characteristics to identify changes in animal husbandry techniques in the short term.

There is also no clear distinction, and a great deal of continuity, between the tool kits and artifacts of gathering and hunting groups and the first agricultural communities, particularly in south-west Asia (the area where the earliest moves towards agriculture took place). The first grinding slabs and stones are found in the Near East about 15,000 BC and were probably used to crush nuts (particularly acorns) and berries but possibly gathered seeds as well. Other tools such as mortars and sickles, which would seem to be 'agricultural' are found among the remains of groups that did not practice agriculture. Conversely, many tools associated with gathering and hunting groups (such as burins and scapers) are also found in the deposits of settled communities that practised agriculture. Villages are not solely associated with agriculture as the Indian settlements of the north-west coast of North America demonstrate with communities of 1,000 people dependent mainly on fishing and other marine resources. Neither is pottery confined to agricultural societies. The Jomon culture in Japan made pottery for thousands of years before the adoption of agriculture.

This more complex picture reinforces the view that a fundamental distinction between agriculture and gathering, herding and hunting should not be drawn. No radically new techniques or relations between humans and plants and animals developed in the period beginning about 10,000 years ago. Humans had been involved in obtaining subsistence from the various ecosystems of the earth for many hundreds of thousands of years. Over that time the methods adopted had evolved. The techniques available to a group living in late glacial Europe or at a similar period in the Near East were far in advance of anything used by the earliest hominids in East Africa. Previous subsistence strategies had used different solutions depending on what was economically favourable at the time, including intensive reliance on selected plants, dependence on one type of animal or a broad spectrum of resource use involving both gathering and hunting. Each of the methods that characterise agriculture had been adopted by one or more groups at some time in the past, though usually in isolation. What was new was the combination and intensification of techniques that began to emerge in a few areas of the world about 10,000 years ago. It was here that the methods adopted by humans to obtain their food slowly amounted to more than just a variation on the theme of gathering and hunting.

It is difficult to explain why agriculture was adopted. Gathering and hunting groups had developed an extensive repertoire of methods for obtaining subsistence, in most cases, and in all but the most marginal areas, without needing to expend large amounts of time and effort. By exploiting a wide range of resources they were also able to reduce the risks involved by guarding against the failure of any one plant or animal. Agriculture is most definitely not an easier option than gathering and hunting. It requires far more effort in clearing land, sowing, tending and harvesting crops and in looking after domesticated animals. It does not necessarily provide more nutritious food, nor does it offer greater security because it selects and depends on a far smaller range of plants and animals. The one advantage agriculture has over other forms of subsistence is that in return for a greater degree of effort it can provide more food from a smaller area of land.

Many of the earliest explanations for the adoption of agriculture were based on the view that agriculture offered such obvious advantages that it was adopted as soon as human knowledge and cultural achievements had reached a sufficiently advanced level. This approach, following recent research into the way gathering and hunting groups operated and obtained their food, has now largely been abandoned. Another theory has linked the adoption of agriculture to the climatic changes taking place at the end of the last glaciation. Improvements in the climate would certainly have produced major changes in vegetation belts and therefore in the resources available for humans to exploit. In north-west Europe the replacement of the tundra by temperate forest completely destroyed the subsistence base of the reindeer herders and forced a shift to radically different methods of obtaining food. But climatic changes had happened before without producing any fundamental alterations in subsistence patterns and they were spread over thousands of years giving plenty of time for humans to adopt alternative gathering and hunting strategies. The effects of climate change in the three core areas of south-west Asia, China and Mesoamerica would also have been very different and therefore unlikely to elicit a similar response. In addition the plants and animals that were eventually domesticated had existed in the same areas for thousands of years, and had often been utilised short of full domestication.

The explanation that best fits modern knowledge is based on increasing population pressure. Although gathering and hunting groups take a number of measures to limit their population to a level the environment can support without strain, they are not always successful. The usual solution is for the excess population that cannot be supported by the existing territory of the group to separate, form a new group and exploit a new area. If, in the case of prehistoric groups, this process continued over a long time then eventually all the suitable territories would be occupied. It is possible that a human population of around four million (the level reached about 10,000 years ago) or even less, was about the maximum that could readily be supported by a gathering and hunting way of life. If population growth continued beyond this point, especially in areas that were relatively crowded, groups would be forced into ever less favourable habitats where they would have to depend on lower quality plants and animals or where ecosystems were less rich and therefore more effort would be required in order to obtain sufficient food. Over thousands of years a continuation of this displacement process and the need for more effort in obtaining food would drive groups towards much more intensive and time-consuming ways of exploiting the environment, eventually resulting in what is now recognised as full-scale agriculture. Once some of these groups had reached a point where they were prepared or had no alternative but to adopt agricultural techniques, they would have been subject to a ratchet effect. Food production would rise and more people could be fed. In the absence of population control, this higher population would then increase the pressure towards even more intensive cultivation. The changes from one generation to the next would have been slight but the cumulative effects would have been great.

The changes now acknowledged as the emergence of agriculture, took place initially in south-west Asia, China and Mesoamerica over a period of several thousand years. The similarities between the three areas are such that a common process can be identified but the end results showed significant differences. The crops that could be cultivated and the animals which could be domesticated were determined by the local ecosystems which, in their turn, were determined by the climate and the way continental drift had separated the various continents and allowed plants and animals to evolve in isolation. The different forms of

agriculture that emerged were to have a profound effect on the development of human societies in these different areas and therefore on the
course of world history.

The first area to experience these changes was south-west Asia, a
crescent-shaped region stretching from what is now Palestine and Syria
through the southern parts of Anatolia to the Zagros mountains of Iran.
This area had long been occupied by gathering and hunting groups and
there is no major discontinuity between them and the later agricultural
communities. The wild progenitors of the crops that were domesticated
in the area have now been clearly identified. Wheat comes from two
wild forms still found in the region – emmer and einkorn – and barley
from a wild form of the plant. Wild forms of legumes such as lentils,
chickpeas, and peas have also been found. These wild plants still exist
in the region in large stands and their distribution gives a good
indication of where domestication is likely to have taken place.
Although their ranges overlap, emmer has a very limited distribution in
the wild (largely confined to the upper Jordan valley), whereas einkorn
and chickpeas are found in south-east Anatolia and wild barley is fairly
widely distributed in Palestine and the Zagros mountains. Recent
experiments have shown that emmer and wild barley can be easily
cultivated but genetic studies suggest that modern wheats, peas and
lentils come from only a very limited part of the wild stock and that
domestication may therefore have occurred on only a small number of
occasions. The way in which wild characteristics such as seed dispersal
mechanisms have been lost again points to only a limited number of
domestications. These biological considerations suggest that domestication may have happened only because a small number of groups
were forced to exploit what were seen at the time as less favourable
resources.

Other characteristics of these early cultivated plants influenced the
course of domestication. The wild ancestors of the plants domesticated
for their seeds tend to be weedy types well adapted to growing in
disturbed and open sites. Before cultivation they survived in poor thin
soils in areas lacking much competition and subject to marked wet and
dry seasons. They produced large seeds, were able to germinate easily,
grow quickly and survive dry summers – all characteristics which would
have been useful to human cultivators. Continual harvesting would
unconsciously select those seeds with less effective dispersal mechanisms because they would be easier to gather and this process would lead
to a slow loss in natural dispersal ability. Deliberate sowing of specially
selected seeds would increase this selection pressure. Both wild and

cultivated wheats and barley are predominantly self-pollinating (unlike the majority of plant species which are cross-pollinated). The advantage of this characteristic for human cultivators was that the cultivated forms would easily have become independent and not subject to swamping by the more numerous wild plants. Occasional cross-pollination would provide just enough genetic flexibility for the cultivated forms to spread, adapt and produce new characteristics.

In parallel with the increasing cultivation and domestication of wild plants the relationship between humans and animals was also becoming more intensive. The first fully domesticated animal was the dog. The Aborigines of Australia and New Guinea domesticated it possibly earlier than anywhere else in the world and the same process took place over most of the northern hemisphere from North America to Japan in the late glacial and early post-glacial periods, although the Near East was comparatively late in this development. Its agricultural significance was slight – it seems to have been done mainly for reasons of companionship and possibly protection rather than to add dog meat to the diet. The first animal to be domesticated and exploited economically was the sheep. This occurred in south-west Asia about 1,000 years before the first fully domesticated crops of einkorn, emmer and barley and it raises the intriguing question of whether some of the first seed plants were gathered as feed for animals and only later transformed into human food. Certainly wild lentils grow in thin, small stands and have a low number of seeds per plant, which would make them uneconomic to harvest for their seeds but by using the whole plant they could still be suitable for animal feed. The great advantage of animals such as sheep and goats (which were domesticated about 8000 BC) and later cattle is that they do not compete directly with humans for food. Indeed they convert what would otherwise be material unsuitable for human consumption such as grass into usable products such as meat and therefore greatly extend the range of food available to humans. Animals such as pigs do compete directly for human food sources and they were not domesticated until 6500 BC at the earliest, when food supplies would probably have been more extensive.

It is possible to trace the gradual transformation of human subsistence, and as a consequence human society, across the south-west Asian region as new techniques were adopted. Again there is no clean break or sudden shift from gathering and hunting to agriculture but an evolving mix of strategies with a slow transition towards more intensive forms of exploitation over a long period of about 3,500 years after 10,000 BC. In Khuzistan on the slopes of the Zagros mountains in the earliest semi-

South-West Asia

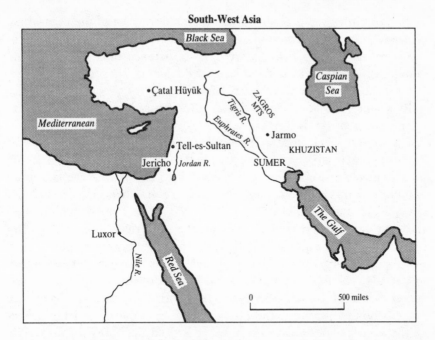

agricultural phase people fed themselves by a combination of hunting (mainly for gazelle and onager), the herding of goats and a few sheep and the extensive reaping of a wide variety of wild plants. This pattern supported a mixture of settlements – small villages of about 100 people (but not necessarily occupied permanently) to exploit the wild cereals and legumes, together with seasonal camps and caves for hunting. In the next phase, plant gathering became much less important and was overtaken by cereal cultivation combined with herding of goats. This more intensive system allowed bigger houses and villages to be built. By 8500 BC, in the Zagros mountains, sheep were being herded (but probably not domesticated in this region), wild grains reaped and hunting remained important. By 7500 BC the inhabitants of Jarmo, a village of about 25 houses, depended on a fairly intensive system of mixed farming, growing domesticated barley, emmer and peas combined with herding sheep and goats while hunting provided only about 5 per cent of their total food. In Palestine and Syria the Natufian culture, which flourished in the 1,500 years after 9000 BC, was based originally on a combination of harvesting wild grains and herding gazelle and goats without full domestication but again with hunting playing only a minor role. The domestication of emmer and einkorn and some legumes enabled them to produce a much higher food output and led to the first large settlement of about 2,000 people at Tell es-Sultan but it was probably only inhabited for part of the year when crops were being harvested. At the end of this long transition a fundamental change had occurred – subsistence now depended on cultivating domesticated varieties of wild plants in special fields and controlling herds of domesticated animals.

By about 7000 BC, as settled agriculture was slowly adopted, there were a series of small farming villages scattered across the south-west Asian region. Communities across the whole of south-west Asia were becoming increasingly sedentary as intensive exploitation of a small area for growing crops and feeding animals meant that a seasonal round of mobile camps was no longer necessary. Then, when food production in some areas was sufficient to sustain a larger, permanent population, the first towns appeared. By 6500 BC, at Jericho, a small town, surrounded by a defensive wall, and covering almost ten acres, had developed. A larger town spreading over about thirty-two acres grew up at Çatal Hüyük in southern Anatolia. It was dependent on the cultivation of wheat and other cereals together with domesticated sheep and goats although hunting for ox, pig and deer remained important. Most of the villages contained only a few hundred people with perhaps a handful of craft specialists but otherwise little social differentiation. Pottery was invented about 6000 BC but technology remained, as with gathering and hunting groups, based on stone tools with metals such as copper only utilised for ornamental purposes. Neither Jericho nor Çatal Hüyük were true cities in that they lacked significant social stratification and both were dependent on particular local conditions – the well at Jericho and the exploitation of obsidian deposits at Çatal Hüyük, which were traded over a large area – for their expansion. The development of true cities did not begin for about another 1,500 years.

By 6000 BC the first stage of the transformation of human society in south-west Asia was complete and settled life was becoming the norm. All the region's major crops and animals had been domesticated and no major new types were added for thousands of years. The crops and animals domesticated in this region were crucially important because they formed the basis for the adoption of agriculture in other areas. The great transition that had occurred in south-west Asia was transferred to other regions, spreading by a combination of new groups adopting agriculture and settlers who already practised it moving into new areas. A way of life based on domesticated wheat and barley and herds of sheep and goats (and later cattle) spread to central Asia and the Nile valley almost unchanged and then also to Europe, where difficult adaptations were necessary. Apart from one type of einkorn all the plants used in the formative stages of European agriculture came from south-west Asia as did the animals – sheep and goats were not native in post-glacial Europe. Even the European reaping knife and the quern (hand-mill) were of the same design as those in Asia. Despite these common features it is not necessary to visualise a wave of agricultural settlers spreading across Europe. In many places agriculture was clearly taken up by existing gatherers and hunters although central Europe was undoubtedly colonised by new groups of agriculturalists. In the eastern Mediterranean the adoption of agriculture posed few problems because the climate was not very different from that of south-west Asia and between 6000–5000 BC Greece and the southern Balkans shifted their subsistence base to agriculture. Cattle were probably first domesticated here at this time and then spread back into south-west Asia (although they were not milked for about another 3,000 years).

The movement of agriculture into central and north-west Europe took about three millennia after its adoption in Greece, and this long period gives an indication of the difficulties involved in adapting what were originally crops and techniques suited to long hot dry summers to the different ecosystems and climates found in the region. By 4000 BC agriculture was predominant in coastal zones round the whole of the Mediterranean, though not in a continuous band, and had moved onto the easily worked soils of central Europe in the Rhine/Danube and Vistula/Dnestr areas. Between 3000–2000 BC it had been adopted in north-west Europe and a thousand years later it reached Denmark and southern Sweden. Beyond this area gatherers and hunters continued their old way of life. Over most of Europe fields and pasture could only be created by clearing parts of the climax temperate forests, which was still a difficult task with the resources available – stone axes and burning. (In the Near East much of the land would have been covered by a more open type of vegetation.) After clearing the trees, crops were planted in the newly exposed, ash enriched soil until yields began to fall. In a form of 'slash and burn' or swidden agriculture new areas would then be cleared and the abandoned plots allowed to revert to grass and through secondary succession to brambles, shrubs and woodland for further clearance decades later. Because of the difficulty of sustaining fertility with the limited amount of manure available it was not until population pressure increased still further that permanent fields and pastures would be cleared and maintained. Other changes were also induced by the different conditions in Europe. The climate forced a shift in crops. Oats and rye originally grew as weeds in the first cultivated cereal fields of south-west Asia but they flourished in the cooler, wetter climate of north-west Europe and became crops in their own right. Apart from such changes the early European agriculturalists adopted much the same pattern as in south-west Asia – small villages of peasant farmers obtaining their subsistence from mixed farming.

A few extra crops and animals were domesticated in southern Europe and Asia after about 6000 BC. In the Mediterranean, olives, vines and figs were cultivated by about 4000 BC but only the vine moved into northern Europe and then quite late, being introduced into many areas by the Romans in the first centuries AD. The dromedary and the Bactrian camel were domesticated between 2000–1500 BC but the most important new animal to be introduced was the horse shortly after 3000 BC. Use of the horse not only revolutionised warfare in the Near East by changing the role of the chariot and developing cavalry, it also enabled a whole new culture to develop on the plains of central Asia. Thereafter for thousands of years the history of the Near East, China, India and Europe was to be heavily influenced by successive waves of nomadic horsemen such as the Huns and Mongols descending on settled societies.

The second core area that saw the development of agriculture was

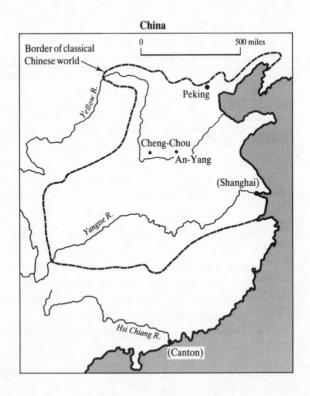

China

China. The modern picture of farming in China is of wet rice production in paddy fields but the origins of agriculture lie in a very different
environment among the semi-arid loess plains of the north of the
country. Loess is a wind-borne soil of fine particles that is very easy to
work even with primitive digging sticks. The soils in this area were
thick and not heavily weathered and therefore had a high mineral
content. There was only a light wood cover and although the area is
semi-arid most of the rain falls in the summer, which makes crop
cultivation possible. The area also originally contained a large number
of wild grasses, some of which would have been suitable for cultivation
and domestication. The crops domesticated in China differ markedly
from those of south-west Asia. Wheat and barley are not indigenous
(they need some winter rain): wheat was not introduced until about
1300 BC and barley slightly later. Instead agriculture was based on
millet and rice grown as a dry land crop rather than in special paddy
fields. For a long period millet remained the primary crop and the basis
for peasant agriculture with rice a luxury food for the elite. It was only
later that rice was adapted to growing further south in wet field
conditions. The earliest millennia of Chinese agriculture differed from
both south-west Asia and Mesoamerica in one important respect. In the
other two regions a nutritionally balanced agricultural regime based on
a starchy cereal seed and legumes rich in protein developed. Although
soybeans are native they were domesticated very late – about 1100 BC on
the north China plain – and then spread rapidly but until then Chinese
agriculture was dominated by seed crop production. Pigs and poultry
were the main animals to be domesticated followed much later by sheep
and goats.

The earliest habitation sites are found not in the flood plain of the
Yellow river, an area of very dense settlement later, but on elevated
terraces and mounds along tributaries of the river. Millet was first
domesticated about 6000 BC and the first settled communities developed at about the same time. Within a thousand years a number of
small villages practising agriculture had developed in the same way as in
south-west Asia but the process took place some three or four thousand
years later and developed independently. Farming further south in the
Yangtse valley, using rice and clearing ground through the swidden
system, was known by shortly after 5000 BC and again was soon followed
by the development of small villages. China was not the only area of the
world where rice was domesticated. It seems to have been subject to
multiple domestication (of more than one type) in India and across
south-east Asia in a broad belt from the southern foothills of the

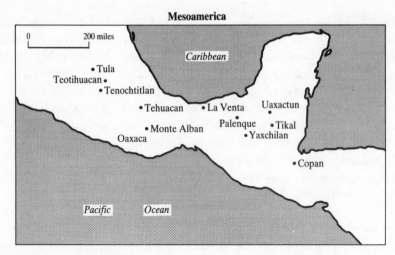

Himalayas through upper Burma, north Thailand to Vietnam and the far south of China.

Mesoamerica (an area that encompasses the modern states of Guatemala, Belize, parts of Honduras and San Salvador and, most important, Mexico south and east of 24°N) was the last of the three core areas to develop agriculture. Most of the evidence about the process comes from the highland areas of Mexico – Tehuacan and Oaxaca – where the climate is dry enough to preserve plant remains. As late as about 6000 BC (when agriculture was widespread in south-west Asia) the area was still occupied by groups dependent on a very wide variety of food sources. They hunted small game such as rabbit and deer, harvested nuts and beans and collected wild grasses, an early type of maize and various squashes. These groups still led a mobile life utilising seasonal resources and a wide variety of animals such as grasshoppers, snails, mice, lizards and snakes. During the dry season they lived in small groups but came together in larger groups of about a hundred in the wet season when food was more plentiful. About this time, or a little earlier, the first steps towards agriculture were taken, not with the cultivation of wild cereals but by creating small garden plots to grow a wide variety of plants that had previously been gathered from the wild (although the work involved in tending these plots did not involve them giving up their mobile way of life). About thirty plants were grown not just for food but also for dyes, medicines and (in the case of gourds) as containers. The list included chili peppers, tomatoes, avocados, papaya, guava, five types of squash, gourds and beans. Some of the earliest of these plants may have been domesticated about 7000 BC but many such as maguey, prickly pear and mesquite show no changes on domestication and so dating is particularly difficult. The uses of the plants also changed over time. Pumpkins were originally grown for their seeds but cultivation gradually changed their bitter flesh into a sweet, more palatable variety.

Development of full scale agriculture in Mesoamerica was delayed by two factors. The first was a lack of suitable animals for domestication. The geographical isolation of the Americas meant that unlike Europe and Asia there were no sheep, goats or cattle. This meant that hunting animals remained a vital activity in order to provide sufficient meat in the diet. Of even greater importance though was the role of maize, the main grain to be domesticated. The exact origins of maize are still a matter of great dispute, especially its relationship to a wild grass called teosinte. It may be descended from teosinte, or from a different but unknown ancestor, or it may be of hybrid origin possibly involving teosinte. Maize was being cultivated from about 5000 BC but it was still a very small grain. The earliest cobs were no bigger than a human thumb and for at least 2,000 years they were chewed rather than being ground into flour. For genetic reasons it was difficult to cross maize with other wild grasses and produce better, higher yielding varieties. The earliest cultivated maize was virtually identical with wild material and was only slightly bigger in size because of better growing conditions. Not until about 2000 BC were the first higher-yielding varieties developed and modern maize cobs are about seven times the size of the earliest domesticated varieties. This low productivity during the early stages of Mesoamerican agricultural development meant that for a long time it was more economic to gather food from wild plants than depend on maize. Even after 2,000 years of domestication cultivated plants made up only about a quarter of the diet. Not until about 2000 BC was productivity great enough to support village life, which then developed fairly rapidly across Mesoamerica. But this long transition to settled communities had a profound effect on world history. It meant that the evolution of complex societies in Mesoamerica began some 4,000 years after Europe and Asia. Thus when the first Europeans arrived in the Americas in the sixteenth century they found a society that was in many ways comparable to those of Mesopotamia in about 2000 BC.

A subsidiary area to Mesoamerica in the development of agriculture was Peru which, in archaeological terms, includes large parts of present day Bolivia and Ecuador. Maize spread south from Mesoamerica to reach the Andean highlands about 1000 BC and the coastal regions about 150 years later. Other plants such as chili peppers and beans were domesticated in both areas but from different wild progenitors. A major

Peruvian crop, which was unique to the Andean highlands until the sixteenth century AD, was the potato. The exact date of domestication is unknown but it could only have taken place when selection of tubers had reduced the naturally high, poisonous, glycoalkaloid levels. Selection of wild tubers for greater size is likely to have helped. In the Andean highlands the potato was the central element in a food complex that included oca, ulluco, anu and a grain – quinoa.

The development of agriculture in other parts of the world is much more difficult to trace, partly because far less archaeological investigation has been carried out but also due to the fact that plant remains are not well preserved in the sites and because many of the plants show few changes when domesticated. Domestication of roots and tubers may well have taken place in south-east Asia and New Guinea by about 7000 BC using taro and yams, which would have needed little more than the cultivation of wild varieties in specially tended plots. Taro and yams formed the basis for agriculture in this area and were normally combined with other plants such as breadfruit, bamboo, coconut, bananas and sago and associated with animals such as poultry and pigs, which were independently domesticated in the region. This agricultural complex also formed the agricultural basis for the Polynesian people as they spread out across the Pacific. Yams were also domesticated in the tropical areas of west Africa but the date is unclear. In the period between 7000–3000 BC the lowlands east of the Andes produced a different tropical complex from the plants available in the area – manioc, sweet potato and arrowroot (and possibly peanuts). These then spread into other tropical areas of south and central America and the Caribean.

By about 2000 BC all the major crops and animals that make up the contemporary agricultural systems of the world had been domesticated. However, for thousands of years there were separate streams of agricultural development as a result of lack of contact between Eurasia and the Americas and even between different parts of Europe and Asia. Then, in two waves, the various separate systems were brought together. From the seventh century AD Islamic traders brought many of the semi-tropical crops of south-east Asia to the Near East and the Mediterranean. Then, much later, in the sixteenth century American crops were brought to Europe (and eventually Asia) and European plants and animals were taken to the Americas and Australasia.

The adoption of agriculture was the most fundamental change in human history. Not only did it produce settled societies for the first time, it also radically changed society itself. Gathering and hunting

THE FIRST GREAT TRANSITION

DATE BC	SOUTH WEST ASIA/MESOPOTAMIA	CHINA	MESOAMERICA
9000	Domestication of sheep		
8500	First semi-permanent settlements		
8000	Fully domesticated einkorn/emmer/barley Domestication of goats		
7500	Village of Jarmo flourishing		
7000	Towns of Jericho/Çatal Hüyük flourishing		
6500	Domestication of pigs		
6000	Domestication of cattle in Europe First pottery	Domestication of millet	Domestication of peppers/ tomatoes/ squash/gourds etc.
5500	First irrigation in Khuzistan	Development of first villages in Yellow River area	
5000	First settlements in Mesopotamia	Domesticated rice/first villages in Yangtse area	Cultivation of maize
4500	Large scale temple construction in Sumer Use of wheel		
4000			
3500	First script in Sumer		
3000	Large cities/stratified society/secular rulers in Sumer		
2500	Akkadian Empire in Sumer		
2000		First cities/stratified society	First high yield varieties of maize Development of first villages
1500			
1000			First ceremonial centres
500			Olmec culture
BC/AD			Development of major city at Teotihuacan

groups were essentially egalitarian, but sedentary communities, almost from the beginning, resulted in increasing specialisation within society and the emergence of religious, political and military elites and a state with the power to direct the rest of society. At the root of these social changes was a new attitude to the ownership of food. Gathering and hunting groups generally regard plants and animals not as things 'owned' by individuals but as available to all. Plants and animals are taken from the wild and there are normally strong social conventions on how food must be shared between all members of the group. Agriculture introduced the idea of ownership of food either by individuals or larger organisations. The move to growing crops in fields and the practice of herding and breeding flocks of animals opened the way to viewing the resources used and the food produced as 'property' and the far greater degree of time and effort involved compared with gathering and hunting encouraged this trend.

The main advantage of agriculture as opposed to gathering and hunting is that in return for greater effort it enables a much higher output of food to be obtained from a smaller area. Once that greater effort has been made there is normally a surplus of food over and above the immediate requirements of the cultivator's family. This surplus can then be used to support and feed individuals not engaged in the production of food. The first non-farmers were probably craftsmen producing pottery, tools and other specialised items for the community. But ruling groups, probably religious at first and then political, rapidly took over the distribution functions. Societies emerged with large administrative, religious and military elites able to enforce the collection of food from peasant farmers and organise its distribution to other parts of society. In parallel, unequal ownership of land, and therefore of food, rapidly emerged.

In its broadest sense human history in the 8,000 years or so since the emergence of settled agricultural societies has been about the acquisition and distribution of the surplus food production and the uses to which it has been put. The size of the surplus available to a particular society has determined the number and extent of other functions – religious, military, industrial, administrative and cultural – that the society can support. Without a food surplus it would be impossible to feed priests, an army, industrial workers, administrators and intellectuals. The link may have been more obvious in earlier, simpler societies but it is still present in contemporary societies. In medieval Europe, and many other feudal and quasi-feudal societies, there was a direct relationship between the amount of land owned and the provision of military service and the church obtained food either through the direct ownership of land or through the extraction of tithes. The redistribution of food has occurred both within individual societies and between societies. All societies have to have a mechanism for the allocation of the food surplus to non-farmers. This may be through direct ownership of land by rulers, elites and religious organisations, as in most pre-industrial societies, a market mechanism (aided by huge subsidies), as in modern western industrialised countries, religious mechanisms, probably backed up by the threat of force, as in many ancient societies or by the use of naked force as the Soviet Union demonstrated in the early 1930s during the collectivisation and industrialisation drives. The development of larger states and empires made it possible to extract a surplus of food from dependent territories by inducing them, by various means, to grow crops intended for the dominant power. The Roman empire achieved this in the Mediterranean region by turning Egypt and North Africa into grain producing areas for Italy and Rome in particular. European states carried out much the same policy from the sixteenth century in their colonial territories and spheres of influence by introducing new crops and production methods and making the dependent territories turn from subsistence farming to large scale production for the European market.

The development of widespread and effective mechanisms for the extraction of surplus took time to emerge. The first settled communities in south-west Asia, China and Mesoamerica were small villages made up almost entirely of peasant farmers with only a limited amount of specialisation. But the pressure of rising population, which had slowly forced the adoption of more intensive food production did not cease with the evolution of agriculture and settled communities; indeed it intensified. This forced the development of even more intensive forms of food production from less favourable environments as groups of people were edged into even more marginal areas.

The earliest agriculture in south-west Asia was dry farming – it depended on rainfall for crop production. The emergence of irrigation, about 5500 BC in south-west Khuzistan (on the eastern fringes of Mesopotamia), is another illustration of the same combination of pressures that produced agriculture. The advantage of irrigation is that in return for even more effort than dry farming (in digging and maintaining irrigation channels) it enables a higher output of food to be obtained from an even smaller area. Between 7000 and 6000 BC the agricultural population of south-west Asia was confined primarily to the highland zone but in the next thousand years or so population seems to have increased rapidly so that nearly every area suitable for dry farming was occupied. It was at this point that some communities were forced to exploit the more difficult environment of Mesopotamia – an area lacking adequate rainfall, stone and timber and which required the

Mesopotamia

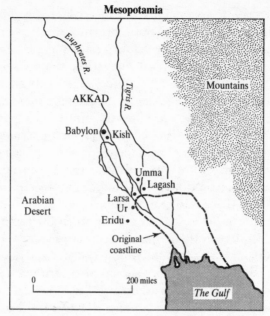

adoption of irrigation techniques. At first, settlement was confined to the easily worked areas of northern Mesopotamia and only slowly did it move into southern areas where more extensive irrigation works were necessary. The land was initially fertile and produced abundant crops and high levels of surplus food. However only a small part of the available land could be irrigated because of technical problems in building and maintaining the canals and therefore considerable organisation and control was required to ensure the most productive use of limited resources. As population continued to rise, settlements became more dense because of the limited room available for expansion. All of these factors had important effects on developments in Mesopotamia.

In the period after 5000 BC Mesopotamia was occupied by communities with a fairly uniform culture; people established settlements along river banks so that irrigation was confined to relatively small scale, simple schemes. These settlements were nearly all small towns or villages scattered at roughly equal distances across the landscape. Although agriculture was vital for basic subsistence, hunting and fishing in the surrounding marshes were still important sources of supplementary foods. Archaeological investigation of the very earliest towns has revealed a considerable degree of internal social organisation from the beginning of settlement in the area. Nearly all had large temples as the focus of urban life and they played a fundamental part in the redistribution of resources among farmers, the religious elite and specialist craftsmen, by controlling food production and distributing rations to all members of the community. An intensification of this process of developing control within society took place in the south of Mesopotamia from about 4500 BC. At Uruk huge temples were constructed (including one 225 feet long, 200 feet wide and 40 feet high) and they were regularly rebuilt. This would have required the organisation of large amounts of labour and illustrates the degree of control already exercised by the main religious organisations. By 3500 BC Uruk was already a substantial ceremonial centre with only small settlements in the surrounding region. Five hundred years later the population of Uruk had grown rapidly to about 50,000 and the number of local settlements had fallen from 146 to 24 in what appears to have been a process of increasing political control and forced resettlement in the chief town of the area. Similar processes, though on a less drastic scale, can be detected at other cities in the region such as Ur, Kish, Lagash and Umma, all of which had populations of about 10–20,000. In parallel with this major burst of urbanisation, irrigation works became more extensive, complex and remote from the rivers; canals were built over large areas which had no natural watercourses in order to increase the area available for food production as population continued to grow.

By about 3000 BC the southern area of Mesopotamia known as Sumer was dominated by eight large cities. Within these cities major social changes were taking place. Producing a surplus of food involves far more than merely growing an excess above the needs of the cultivator. The surplus has to be transported, stored and re-allocated and this requires institutions able to organise the process. Control of the surplus also involves determining who owns and works the land and who has rights to the food. From the start the temple played a key role in the organisation of society in Mesopotamia. In the earliest settlements the temple seems to have owned all the land and its priests and administrators were responsible for collecting food, storing it and then distributing it, often in uniform rations. Other agricultural resources were also held centrally – at Shuruppak the temple owned and accounted for 9,660 donkeys – and ploughing was organised through labour gangs. The amount of power wielded by the religious elite was not static and large scale feedback mechanisms operated. Those in authority sought to increase control and extract a greater surplus and achieve more power through their ability to direct more resources. A bigger surplus created the ability to maintain more non-farmers, and the longer this process continued the greater the degree of social differentiation until separate classes with markedly different access to wealth and power emerged.

This more powerful state structure offered religious benefits in return for the bulk of the population providing food, labour and eventually military service as the rivalry between the city states mounted.

Within the cities of Sumer, by about 3000 BC, strongly stratified, class societies had developed: there were slaves at the bottom of the hierarchy, the bulk of the population were peasant farmers and above were craftsmen and then an administrative, religious and military elite. Growing rivalry between the cities led to increasing militarism, fortifications and the organisation of militias. Uruk built a huge city wall about six miles in circumference, twelve to fifteen feet thick with large defensive towers. The increasing importance of war led to the emergence of temporary military leaders, who rapidly transformed themselves into permanent, hereditary, secular rulers. Large palaces with staffs of several thousand (plus large numbers of slaves) rose alongside and then replaced the temples as the main buildings in the city. The increased importance of warfare reinforced trends to greater internal control and direction over society. By about 2500 BC, land was owned not by the temple or the city but by private individuals, thereby completing the full development of a class society with ruling families wielding political power and controlling large estates with their dependent labour force. At a later stage, by 1800 BC when southern Mesopotamia was part of the Babylonian empire, there were legally separate classes of nobles, commoners and slaves.

In parallel with these developments, and increasing the pressure for greater specialisation and stratification within society, were a number of technological advances which occurred in the early stages of the settlement of Mesopotamia. Smelting of copper had begun in Anatolia shortly before 6000 BC and was in use in Mesopotamia about a thousand years later, and the wheel was first developed for making pottery about 4500 BC. Both of these new processes required trained specialists, who had to be fed by other members of society. Although metal tools were more durable than stone tools, they were not much more effective and much of the earliest metal work took the form of luxury items for the elite. The wheel was soon adapted for vehicles drawn by domesticated animals. But the most important development of all was the invention of writing, stimulated by the need to keep accounts in the temples of all the complex transactions involved in obtaining, storing and redistributing the food surplus. The first baked clay tablets using a fully developed script come from the Eanna sacred precinct in Uruk, where over 4,000 have been found dating from about 3100 BC. They form part of the temple's administrative archives and 85 per cent of them deal with economic matters such as allocating resources for agriculture and providing food to the population in what appears to be a fairly strict rationing system. These tablets illustrate once again the overwhelming importance of centralised controls within a society attempting to wrest subsistence from a difficult environment.

The first steps towards stratified, hierarchical societies with a large degree of state control were taken in Mesopotamia from about 5000 BC. Similar but independent developments took place in Egypt, only slightly later than in Mesopotamia, and then were repeated in the Indus valley, China, Mesoamerica and Peru. Like Mesopotamia, the Nile valley was not one of the original core areas for the domestication of plants and animals: both took over the agricultural system that had evolved in south-west Asia and adapted it to meet their local conditions. The Nile valley had been occupied by gathering and hunting groups existing on a plentiful supply of wild foods and game for some 20,000 years before the first agricultural settlements appeared about 5500 BC. Agriculture based on sheep, cattle and emmer wheat had been well established in North Africa for hundreds of years before farmers moved into the Nile valley. The long, narrow and fertile valley provided an excellent environment for agriculture – much better than Mesopotamia. The annual flood came at the right time of the year for crop growing and was normally sufficient to provide a crop over two-thirds of the immediate valley area. Artificial irrigation was only necessary on a small scale and this could be accomplished by dredging the river's natural overflow channels, making small breeches in natural levees and creating small earth dams to retain water. These measures helped even out a very variable natural flood level, retained water in basins for later use, and allowed planting on newly irrigated ground at the edge of the flood plain and the cultivation of a second crop in intensive garden plots.

Egypt developed in different ways from Mesopotamia. The easier environment and the lower intensity of irrigation meant that there was less pressure on land compared with Mesopotamia and therefore highly structured cities did not emerge. The two great Egyptian cities of Memphis and Karnak-Luxor were essentially local markets, cult centres and the residence of officials rather than populous cities on the scale of Uruk (which had a resident population of nearly 50,000). Most Egyptians were peasants living in villages and the system for regulating the annual Nile flood remained a local rather than a central state responsibility. Nevertheless an elite class of priests, administrators, warriors and rulers did emerge, as in Mesopotamia, through the appropriation of the agricultural surplus. This strongly centralised political superstructure continued though to rely on a much more decentralised administration of agriculture and flood control based on the ancient nomes or divisions of the valley. The unification of Egypt into a single state is conventionally dated to about 2950 BC and the emergence of the First Dynasty. This is roughly contemporary with the period in Mesopotamia when secular rulers had become dominant, although Egypt was probably unified for about ten rulers before the First Dynasty. This dynasty seems a radically new departure only because it is contemporary with the emergence of writing, invented independently of Mesopotamia and a few hundred years later. Here too the function of writing was essentially administrative – allocating resources and food – and it did not feature in a continuous text for another 300 years.

The Indus valley was settled by migrating farmers, almost certainly moving eastwards from south-west Asia, about 3500 BC, cultivating wheat and barley in the comparatively dry climate of the area and relying on domesticated sheep and goats together with a few humped cattle. As in Egypt the water control system was essentially small scale but the appropriation of the food surplus to feed non-producers led to the emergence of a highly stratified society by about 2300 BC. The main characteristic of Indus valley society was its cultural uniformity over a very wide area. There is little evidence of the sort of organic growth of settlements and the evolution of cities that took place in Mesopotamia. The two main cities – Harappa and Mohenjo-Daro – though nearly 400 miles apart were built to similar plans and were dominated by huge citadels (1,200 feet long and 600 feet wide built on artificial platforms 40 feet above the flood plain) where all the major public buildings were situated. All of the cities had large central granaries for the storage and redistribution of food. It is not known whether the central authority in society was religious or secular but what is clear is that it was authoritarian and capable of mobilising a large amount of labour and imposing a more rigid uniformity across a bigger area than the first two complex societies to emerge in the world.

The development of such societies in China was a much slower process than in Mesopotamia, Egypt and the Indus valley. The exact reasons are not clear but they may be linked to the slow development of irrigation systems and consequently the longer period before substantial food surpluses emerged. The precise sequences and chronology of early Chinese cultures is difficult to establish. The earliest farming communities following the domestication of millet about 6000 BC were small villages of about 200 people with only very limited social stratification and the farmers followed a swidden system of cultivation, clearing fields for a few years and then abandoning them when fertility levels declined. As population grew and the amount of unused land declined, settlements became permanent with farmers adopting a form of rotation and fallowing in an attempt to maintain fertility. The use of the potter's wheel and other craft techniques led slowly towards a more stratified society. Irrigation though remained on a very small scale and millet was still a far more important crop than either wheat or rice. The first urban, stratified society emerged from this background about 1750 BC at the beginning of the Shang period when the whole of the north China plain came under a single secular ruler. In the two main cities – Cheng-Chou and An-Yang – a central ceremonial and administrative area was surrounded by a massive defensive earth wall. Unlike Mesopotamia secular rulers appear to have dominated from the beginning of settled communities although they were strongly supported by the religious elite whose functions helped to integrate society. Both written records and archaeological investigations confirm that the Shang period saw the development of distinct classes. Burials show a huge range in wealth between different parts of society and while the rulers lived in large palaces the peasants lived in semi-subterranean huts. Like similar complex societies in Mesopotamia, Egypt and the Indus valley there were central mechanisms for storing grain (in this case in huge pits) and redistributing it. There was also strong central control of labour not just for agriculture but also for other state work such as constructing palaces and temples.

The development of a highly organised society in Japan came extremely late in world terms. Japan was partly dependent on external developments in China but the history of its social changes clearly demonstrates how changes in food production were necessary preliminaries for the emergence of stratified, specialised societies. Although hand-pressed pottery making began about 10,000 BC (the earliest in the world), for a long period settlements were small, about fifteen huts, with the population dependent on hunting deer and pigs and on fishing. Not until about 1400 BC did the Japanese begin to cultivate their first crops (barley and rice, probably from Korea, which itself obtained them from China). However the scope for farming on a large scale in Japan was limited because over three-quarters of the land was unsuitable for cultivation. In its earliest form agriculture, as in many other areas of the world, was based on a swidden system and population densities were low. Animals played little part because the shortage of land meant that priority had to be given to crop production and fish remained a major source of protein. Not until rice became the main basis for subsistence in north Kyushu about 300 BC and spread gradually over the whole of the western half of Japan was there a basis for higher levels of food production. Increased food supply brought more craft specialisation including pottery (now made using wheels) and bronze production. With more intensive cultivation a more complex society could be supported yet development remained slow until the emergence of a recognisable Japanese state after the adoption of writing, introduced from China in the sixth century AD.

In the Americas the historical development of this type of society was heavily influenced by a number of environmental factors. The difficulty, for genetic reasons, in producing high-yielding varieties of maize compared with the relative ease with which domesticated wheat and barley could be crossed with other types to improve output, meant that settled communities did not emerge in Mesoamerica till about 2000 BC. The Americas also lacked animals suitable for domestication (apart from the llama and the alpaca in Peru). Although the principle of the wheel was known it was not developed for transport because there were no draught animals available. Metal working was also restricted mainly to gold and silver goods for the elite because of the lack of easily worked deposits and stone tools remained the norm until the European conquest. Despite these handicaps, sophisticated, hierarchical societies did develop and achieve significant, cultural progress equal to, and in some areas in advance of, developments in similar societies elsewhere in the world. Indeed the astronomical knowledge and calendrical systems of the Maya in the sixth to eighth centuries AD were probably the most advanced in the world at that time.

The development of more productive varieties of maize about 2000 BC was the basis for the first settled Mesoamerican communities. These were still small and people depended for part of their food on gathering from the wild and hunting. Within a thousand years the first small towns and ceremonial centres emerged as maize became an increasingly important part of the diet. As in Mesopotamia, huge temples were a feature of these settlements from the start and they acted as centres for redistributing the food surplus to a growing number of craftsmen, priests and administrators. Large ceremonial centres developed such as La Venta on the Gulf coast of Mexico (a major Olmec site) with pyramids 400 feet long, 200 feet wide and 100 feet high. Such ambitious architectural projects would have involved the direction of vast quantities of human labour. The pace of development was heavily influenced by a further leap in the productivity of maize about 400–300 BC when the length of the cob doubled. This formed the basis for the huge increase in social complexity and organisation found in the Classic period in Mesoamerica lasting from 300–900 AD.

The centre of this development was the city of Teotihuacan. Situated in the valley of Mexico, it covered an area of about ten square miles with a population of about 100,000 and with its enormous pyramids, ceremonial avenues and large plazas was far grander in conception than any city in Mesopotamia. Its rise illustrates yet again the way in which increases in food production led to highly structured societies organised around strong central institutions responsible for food production and distribution. The city was highly planned, there was probably no clear distinction between political and religious authority and the population lived in strictly separate areas. The elite lived near the temples and the adjacent parts were occupied by craftsmen and traders making or dealing in goods for the elite. Large numbers of peasants lived in densely settled compounds, probably organised on a clan basis, within the city. The highly concentrated population was supplied with food (fruit and vegetables as well as the ubiquitous maize) from diverse sources. Irrigation in the valley and a system of highly productive chinampas, or 'floating' gardens, in the swamps and on the lakes, provided a highly intensive system of agriculture. Further away from the city, but still under its political control, more peasants produced yet more food from the terraced hillsides in a semi-intense system while on the borders of the territory farmers still relied on low-intensity swidden agriculture. The overwhelming impression of Teotihuacan is one of an immense central power able to develop and dominate a highly unified city and also enjoying strong powers of direction over the whole of a rigidly organised society. The Teotihuacan empire, which, at its height, influenced all of Mesoamerica, collapsed about 700 AD. It was replaced, in much the same way as Sumer was conquered by the Akkadians, by the military empire of the Toltecs based on Tula (also in the valley of Mexico) and they in their turn were supplanted by the Aztecs with their capital at Tenochtitlan (the current Mexico City). These later societies were dependent on the same sort of agricultural base, especially the chinampas, and structurally, apart from their greater military element, were remarkably similar to Teotihuacan and exercised equally strong central control.

The way in which, across the world, increasing food production and growing population gradually gave rise to more highly organised societies is illustrated on a smaller scale in the islands of Hawaii. Because the islands were settled comparatively late, social developments were still at an early stage when the first Europeans arrived in the eighteenth century and wrote accounts of what was happening, noting down oral traditions about the recent past. These accounts give an idea of how other societies in the world might have developed in their early stages. The Hawaiian islands were first settled about 500 AD by the Polynesians, probably by a group no more than fifty strong. They brought with them the normal Polynesian social organisation based on hereditary chiefs who monopolised religious rituals and received offerings from those under their authority. In Hawaii it was the position of the chiefs that was to change as numbers rose and society became more complex. By about 1100 all the islands in the group had been settled, although the villages were almost entirely confined to the coasts, and the population had grown to about 20,000. But society remained simple and largely unstratified. The situation began to change after 1100 with a more rapid rate of population growth, accompanied by the expansion of settlement inland, so that by about 1400 all the available land on the islands had been taken up and had come under the control of the various chiefs. This situation produced major social problems. In the past, conflict within chiefly lineages had been resolved by younger sons splitting off from the main group and setting up their own groups in the unsettled areas. This was no longer possible and so conflict increased, with disgruntled members of the chiefly families leading revolts of commoners.

The response to these growing social and political problems, exacerbated by crop failures as agriculture was forced on to ever more marginal land as numbers rose to around 300,000 by the end of the eighteenth century, was increasing central control. By about 1440 on the island of O'ahu individual chiefdoms were replaced by a single ruler and other islands rapidly followed the same path. This central, political control brought social changes as the chiefs drew further away from the rest of society (marrying only into the families of chiefs from other islands), enforced tribute to themselves rather than the traditional gods, took over what had previously been commonly-held land and made the peasants into their tenants. Warfare broke out as chiefs tried to control more territory so as to exact more tribute. The result was growing inter-island warfare until in 1795 the islands were conquered and united under a single ruler. Not long afterwards the society and culture of the islands began to disintegrate as Europeans started to exploit the Pacific.

The development of agriculture, bringing with it intensive forms of food production and settled societies, had essentially the same effect all over the world. Surplus food was used to feed a growing religious and political elite and a class of craftsmen whose main role was to supply and service that elite. The redistribution of surplus food required extensive control mechanisms for transport, storage and reissue leading to powerful central institutions within society. These processes became self-reinforcing as the elites with political and social power took an ever greater degree of control and imposed greater discipline through enforced labour and service, first in labour gangs for major social projects such as temples or irrigation works and then in the rapidly growing armies. Societies that were broadly egalitarian were replaced by ones with distinct classes and huge differences in wealth. These changes had two further consequences of great significance, one generally seen as positive and the other as negative, but both have helped to shape the rest of human history.

The development of organised societies and the increasing ability, as agriculture became slowly more productive, to support a growing number of people not engaged in the direct production of food formed the basis for all subsequent human cultural and scientific advances. The demands of the religious and secular elites produced the great temples, palaces, state buildings, theatres and other structures that make up the great ancient sites of the world and are the main memorials of past societies. At the same time, craftsmen produced exquisite works of art that are still admired. Settled societies also made possible the great developments in religious and spiritual thought. Gathering and hunting groups, certainly in their later stages, seem to have had systems of religious belief to integrate humans into their environment – as is still the case with the Aborigines of Australia for instance. Indeed religion acted as one of the main motivating and organising forces behind the development of complex societies, particularly in areas like Mesopotamia, as humans moved to exploit new and difficult environments. The development of writing and its evolution into the highly flexible modern scripts was fundamental for all the later advances in human knowledge. The earliest societies also quickly developed extensive astronomical knowledge, notably among the Babylonians and the Maya and many sites from Mesoamerica to China and bronze age Britain are aligned towards significant solar, stellar and lunar positions. None of the major human cultural and intellectual achievements would have been possible without the development of agriculture, and a food surplus capable of supporting artists, builders, architects, priests, philosophers and scientists.

The other side of the coin is the parallel development of increasing coercion within society and warfare. The great buildings and monuments of ancient societies could only be constructed using huge amounts of human labour. The ability to mobilise labour on this scale demonstrates very clearly the enormous power and authority wielded by the religious and secular elites. Although there may have been, particularly in the early phases of organised societies, a degree of voluntary participation in a common endeavour, this was replaced fairly rapidly by coercion. One of the reasons why internal organisation and discipline within society grew was the developing external threat and increasing warfare. The place of warfare in the earliest phases of human history is controversial but there is evidence of fighting between gathering and hunting groups about 20,000 years ago with the development of the bow and arrow, a far more effective weapon than the spear. Some of the cave paintings in France and Spain from the last glaciation appear to show humans under attack and evidence from cemetry 117 at Jebel Sahaba in Nubia from the pre-neolithic Qadan culture gives an idea of what this sort of fighting might have involved. Of the fifty nine burials over forty per cent had extensive wounds caused by arrowheads and one young adult female was found with twenty-one arrowheads in her body including several shot into the mouth.

The development of settled societies undoubtedly increased the reasons and the potential for warfare by instituting defined territories and clear ownership of resources. From the start the earliest settled communities had to defend themselves. By about 7500 BC Jericho was surrounded by a wall almost half a mile long, ten feet thick and over thirteen feet high, with a least one tower thirty-three feet in diameter and twenty-eight feet high. Çatal Hūyūk in Anatolia was built as a series of interconnected houses with common walls accessible only through a hole in the roof and a series of blank walls facing outwards from the village to provide some protection. Hacilar was constructed on similar principles with an outside wall as well. Societies rapidly became militarised and formed their own armies. In pre-dynastic Egypt there was continual warfare between the cities and the unification of upper and lower Egypt was accomplished by force. In Mesopotamia battles between Lagash and Umma lasted for 150 years over a dispute about fields along the boundary between the two cities. The development of metal technologies was quickly followed by the use of metal battle axes, arrowheads, shields and helmets. The invention of the wheel led to the development of the chariot about 2800 BC in Mesopotamia, originally drawn by asses until the domestication of the horse.

Armies and militias increased in size and by 1285 BC Egypt was able to deploy an army 20,000 strong (larger than many in Europe before the late eighteenth century) at the battle of Kadesh. The development of iron weapons, first used by the Assyrians in the early part of the first millennium BC, only increased these trends towards more destructive and extensive warfare. It frequently involved mass killing and the destruction of crops, animals, villages and cities. In the 300 years of the militaristic Assyrian empire about four-and-a-half million people were forcibly deported in the Near East in an attempt to establish political control. Such inhumanity was easily exceeded by the gruesome record of the Aztecs of Mesoamerica, who ritually slaughtered huge numbers of prisoners of war (sometimes 20,000 at a time) by ripping out their still beating hearts on the steps of the great temple at Tenochtitlan.

By about 3000 BC in Mesopotamia and Egypt, a few hundred years later in the Indus valley, a millennium or so later in China and another two millennia later in the Americas, hierarchical, militaristic societies ruled by religious and political elites with immense powers of control over their populations were established. Despite the development of more sophisticated metal technologies in Eurasia there was no fundamental change in the human way of life for several thousand years. The overwhelming mass of the population remained peasants, landless labourers or slaves, and subject to extensive expropriation of their produce, forced labour and the risks of highly destructive warfare. Only a very small minority within each society could be supported in a more affluent or a more intellectually rewarding, style of life. Various states and empires rose and fell (often as a result of changing fortunes in warfare, revolts or the unexpected deaths of rulers but also because of important changes in their vital agricultural base) without fundamentally altering this way of life.

Despite the variations in cultural achievements, none of these empires and states altered the way in which humans obtained their subsistence once settled agriculture had been adopted. Nevertheless their impact on their immediate environment was often far-reaching. They provide the first examples of intensive human alteration of the environment and of their major destructive impact. They also provide the first examples of societies that so damaged the environment as to bring about their own collapse.

5

Destruction and Survival

The adoption of agriculture, combined with its two major consequences – settled communities and a steadily rising population,
placed an increasing strain on the environment. That strain was
localised at first but as agriculture spread so did its effects. Some areas
such as the temperate forest ecosystem of north and west Europe with
its moderate temperatures, high rainfall and rich soils, were able to
withstand the strain reasonably well. Other areas with more easily
damaged ecosystems and with a higher population density began to be
affected within a thousand years of the adoption of agriculture and a
settled way of life.

Agriculture involves clearing the natural ecosystem in order to create
an artificial habitat where humans can grow the plants and stock the
animals they want. The natural balances and inherent stability of the
original ecosystem are thereby destroyed. Instead of a variety of plants
and permanent natural ground cover a small number of crops make only
part-time use of the space available. The soil is exposed to the wind and
rain to a far greater extent than before, particularly where fields are left
bare for part of the year, leading to much higher rates of soil erosion
than under natural ecosystems. Nutrient recycling processes are also
disrupted and extra inputs in the form of manures or fertilizers are,
therefore, required if soil fertility is to be maintained. The adoption of
irrigation is even more disruptive since it creates an environment that is
even more artificial than dry farming, which relies on rainfall. Adding
large amounts of water to a poor soil may allow the farmer to grow his
preferred crop but it can have catastrophic longer term effects. The
extra water drains into the underlying water table and will, over
differing lengths of time depending on local conditions, cause water
levels to rise until the soil becomes waterlogged. The additional water
also alters the mineral content of the soil: it increases the amount of salt,
and may eventually, especially in hot areas with high evaporation rates,

produce a thick layer of salt on the surface which makes agriculture impossible. The only way in which this process can be avoided is by very careful use of irrigation, not overwatering, and leaving the ground fallow for long periods.

The spread of sedentary societies also increased pressures on the environment in other ways. The overall impact of gathering and hunting groups, with their mobile way of life and low level of demand for goods, had been light and comparatively diffuse. But the emergence of villages and towns (and an increasing population) meant that the demand for resources was now more concentrated, and efforts to increase supply would inevitably impose significantly greater strains on smaller areas. New demands arose, especially for construction materials for permanent houses and also for new and more varied goods. Forests suffered most as the requirement for wood to build houses, heat homes and cook food rose steadily. Local deforestation leading to increased soil erosion became a problem around settled areas. Recent evidence from central Jordan suggests that as early as 6000 BC, within about a thousand years of the emergence of settled communities, villages were being abandoned as soil erosion caused by deforestation resulted in a badly damaged landscape, declining crop yields and eventually inability to grow enough food.

The creation of artificial environments to grow food and the rise of communities not only concentrated the environmental impact of human activities but also meant that it was far more difficult for human societies to escape the consequences of their actions. In particularly sensitive ecosystems and where the impact of human modifications to the environment was particularly concentrated in its effects, the foundations of society could be so damaged as to cause its collapse. These early societies were dependent on the production of a food surplus in order to feed and support the growing number of priests, rulers, bureaucrats, soldiers and craftsmen. If food production became more difficult and crop yields fell, and with them the surplus available for distribution within society, then the very basis of the early city states and empires was undermined. It is perhaps not surprising that the first signs of widespread damage emerged in Mesopotamia, the area where the most extensive modifications to the natural environment had first been made.

When, in 1936, one of the excavators of the earliest cities of Sumer, Leonard Woolley, wrote a book about his work entitled *Ur of the Chaldees* he was puzzled by the desolate, largely treeless landscape of contemporary southern Mesopotamia.

'Only to those who have seen the Mesopotamian desert will the
evocation of the ancient world seem well-nigh incredible, so complete is the contrast between past and present . . . it is yet more
difficult to realise, that the blank waste ever blossomed, bore fruit for
the sustainance of a busy world. Why, if Ur was an empire's capital,
if Sumer was once a vast granary, has the population dwindled to
nothing, the very soil lost its virtue?'

The answer to Woolley's question is that the Sumerians themselves
destroyed the world they had created so painstakingly out of the
difficult environment of southern Mesopotamia.

The valley of the twin rivers, the Tigris and Euphrates, posed major
problems for any society, especially in the south. The rivers were at
their highest in the spring following the melting of the winter snows
near their sources and at their lowest between August and October, the
time when the newly planted crops needed the most water. In the north
of Mesopotamia the problem was eased by the late autumn and winter
rains but rainfall was very low, and often non-existent further south.
This meant that in the Sumerian region water storage and irrigation
were essential if crops were to be grown. However, a combination of
local conditions meant that these processes involved both costs and
benefits. At first the advantages would have outweighed the disadvantages but slowly a series of major problems would have become
apparent. In summer, temperatures were high, often up to 40°C, which
increased evaporation from the surface and as a consequence the
amount of salt in the soil. Water retention in the deeper layers of the soil
and hence the risk of waterlogging was increased by two factors. The
soil itself had very low permeability. This was exacerbated by the slow
rate of drainage caused by the very flat land, itself made worse by the
amount of silt coming down in the rivers, probably caused by deforestation in the highlands, which added about five feet of silt every millennium and caused the delta of the two rivers to extend by about fifteen
miles a millennium. As the land became more waterlogged and the
water table rose, more salt was brought to the surface where the high
evaporation rates produced a thick layer of salt. Modern agricultural
knowledge suggests that the only way to avoid the worst of these
problems is to leave land fallow and unwatered for long periods to allow
the level of the water table to fall. The internal pressures within
Sumerian society made this impossible and brought about disaster.
The limited amount of land that could be irrigated, rising population,
the need to feed more bureaucrats and soldiers and the mounting

competition between the city states all increased the pressure to intensify the agricultural system. The overwhelming requirement to grow
more food meant that it was impossible to leave land fallow for long
periods. Short-term demands outweighed any considerations of the
need for long-term stability and the maintenance of a sustainable
agricultural system.

About 3000 BC Sumerian society became the first literate society in
the world. The detailed administrative records kept by the temples of
the city states provide a record of the changes in the agricultural system
and an insight into the development of major problems. In the Early
Dynastic period, which lasted just over six hundred years until 2370 BC,
the major city states – Kish, Uruk, Ur and Lagash – were militaristic,
organised societies using the food surplus produced by irrigation to
feed both the bureaucracies that ran the states and the armies with
which they continually competed for domination of the area. All these
states were dependent on their agricultural base for the large-scale
production of wheat and barley and that was being slowly undermined
by environmental degradation brought about by irrigation. About 3500
BC roughly equal amounts of wheat and barley were grown in southern
Mesopotamia. But wheat can only tolerate a salt level of half a per cent
in the soil whereas barley can still grow in twice this amount. The
increasing salinisation of the soil can be deduced from the declining
amount of wheat cultivated and its replacement by the more salt
tolerant barley. By 2500 BC wheat had fallen to only 15 per cent of the
crop; by 2100 Ur had abandoned wheat production and overall it had
declined to just 2 per cent of the crops grown in the Sumerian region.
By 2000 the cities of Isin and Larsa no longer grew wheat and by 1700 BC
salt levels in the soil throughout the whole of southern Mesopotamia
were so high that no wheat at all was grown.

Even more important than the replacement of wheat by barley was
the declining yield from crops throughout the region. In the earliest
phases of Sumerian society when areas went out of production because
of salinisation they were replaced by newly cultivated fields. Rising
population, and the demand for a greater food surplus to maintain an
army as warfare became more frequent, reinforced the demand for new
land. But the amount of new land that could be cultivated, even with
the more extensive and complex irrigation works that were becoming
common, was limited. Until about 2400 BC crop yields remained high,
in some areas at least as high as in medieval Europe and possibly even
higher. Then, as the limit of cultivatable land was reached and salinisation took an increasing toll, the food surplus began to fall rapidly. Crop

yields fell 42 per cent between 2400 and 2100 BC and by 65 per cent by
1700 BC. Dating from 2000 BC there are contemporary reports of 'the
earth turned white', a clear reference to the drastic impact of salinisation. The consequences for a society so dependent on a food surplus
were predictable. The size of the bureaucracy, and perhaps even more
important, of the army that could be fed and maintained, fell rapidly,
making the state very vulnerable to external conquest. What is remarkable is the way that the political history of Sumer and its city states so
closely follows the steady decline of the agricultural base. The independent city states survived until 2370 BC when the first external conqueror
of the region – Sargon of Agade – established the Akkadian empire.
That conquest is contemporary with the first serious decline in crop
yields following widespread salinisation. For the next six hundred years
the region saw the Akkadian empire conquered by the Guti nomads
from the Zagros mountains, a brief revival of the region under the
Third Dynasty of Ur between 2113–2000 BC, its collapse under pressure from the Elamites in the west and Amorites in the east, and about
1800 BC the conquest of the area by the Babylonian kingdom centered
on northern Mesopotamia. Throughout this period, from the end of the
once flourishing and powerful city states to the Babylonian conquest,
crop yields continued to fall making it very difficult to sustain a viable
state. By 1800 BC, when yields were only about a third of the level
obtained during the Early Dynastic period, the agricultural base of
Sumer had effectively collapsed and the focus of Mesopotamian society
shifted permanently to the north, where a succession of imperial states
controlled the region, and Sumer declined into insignificance as an
underpopulated, impoverished backwater of empire.

The artificial agricultural system that was the foundation of
Sumerian civilisation was very fragile and in the end brought about its
downfall. The later history of the region reinforces the point that all
human interventions tend to degrade ecosystems and shows how easy it
is to tip the balance towards destruction when the agricultural system is
highly artificial, natural conditions are very difficult and the pressures
for increased output are relentless. It also suggests that it is very
difficult to redress the balance or reverse the process once it has started.
Centuries later, when the city states of Sumer were no longer even a
memory, the same processes were still at work in Mesopotamia.
Between 1300–900 BC there was an agricultural collapse in the central
area following salinisation as a result of too much irrigation. Around
Baghdad in the seventh and eighth centuries AD, both before and after
the Arab conquest, the area was flourishing with high crop yields from

irrigated fields supporting a wealthy and sophisticated society. But the same pressures seem to have been apparent as in Sumer over 3,000 years earlier. To boost food production four major new irrigation canals were dug between the Tigris and Euphrates, which, in turn, led to waterlogging, a rapidly rising water table and salinisation. At this time the population of Mesopotamia was probably about one-and-a-half million but the agricultural collapse brought about through intensive irrigation and the Mongol conquest in the thirteenth century caused a massive decline in population to about 150,000 by 1500 and brought about the end of the sophisticated society that had survived in the area for centuries.

Many of the same forces that brought about the collapse of the first settled societies in Mesopotamia seem to have been at work in the Indus valley too, although it is not possible to identify the trends in such detail because the script used by the inhabitants has not been deciphered. As in Mesopotamia what was once a flourishing society and a rich and productive area has been turned into a desolate region through over-exploitation of a delicate environment. The complex, hierarchical, highly centralised society which emerged about 2300 BC lasted less then 500 years. The settlers in the Indus valley faced one major problem – the tendency of the river to flood over wide areas and change its course. Extensive works were built to contain the river and to irrigate the fields to produce the food that supported and fed the ruling elite, priests and the army. In the hot climate of the valley, irrigation would have had the same effect as in Sumer – raising the water table, increasing water-logging, producing progressive salinisation of the soil and eventually a layer of salt on the surface, which would have led to the gradual decline of crop production.

The other factor undermining the environment of the Indus valley was deforestation. The area that attracted the first settlers was richly forested country with a plentiful supply of wildlife. Part of this forest was cleared to provide fields for agriculture. More important though was the construction technique used by the inhabitants. To build their huge temples and palaces Mesopotamian societies used mud bricks dried by the sun. The people of the Indus valley also used mud bricks but they dried them in ovens, and the process required enormous quantities of wood. Very rapidly the trees in the area were cut down. This exposed the soil to the elements and caused rapid erosion and decline in soil quality. About 1900 BC the Indus valley society came to a sudden end. The immediate cause was probably external conquest following a period of internal decline. The extent of the environmental degradation through salinisation and deforestation suggests a substantial reduction in the available food surplus may have led to a reduction in the size of the army and increased vulnerability to external conquest – in much the same way that Sumer collapsed.

Extensive deforestation has been a problem for a number of societies throughout history. A larger human population put an increasing strain on local environments generally and in particular supplies of wood – the one readily available resource for heating, cooking and in many cases construction. Forests were cleared to make room for fields to feed the steadily growing number of people. It is the slow, steady, and in many ways unspectacular, destruction of the woods and forests around all settled communities that forms the background to the development of human societies. These early societies lacked the technology for large-scale clearance but between them the metal axe, ring barking and fire would have been very effective ways of obtaining wood or clearing a section of the forest. No one generation would have been conscious of making any dramatic changes. Generally people seem to have accepted the process as a natural way of obtaining the resources humans needed. As settlements moved into new areas so the whole process of attrition would start again. There is little evidence of any attempt at major planting or replanting, although coppicing was practised in many parts of Europe as a way of obtaining a sustainable crop of wood. Over hundreds of generations the scale of destruction could be massive. Huge areas that had once been dense forests would become treeless or retain only isolated pockets of woodland in the least accessible places.

In China the development of agriculture and the rise of the first settled societies had been based on the cultivation of millet on the easily worked loess soils in the north of the country. Although the soil was rich it was very easily eroded once the natural grass cover had been removed in order to make way for fields of millet. Very rapidly huge gullies and canyons developed as the soil was blown away by the wind or washed away by the rain. At the same time hillsides were cleared of trees for fuel and construction. Steadily the deforested area increased until, by about two hundred years ago, nearly all the original forests of China had been cleared. The wholesale loss of trees in the highlands of China was one of the main causes of the often disastrous flooding of the Yellow river (so-called because of the amount of soil it carried from erosion upstream), which regularly resulted in major changes of course by the river in the lowlands and huge loss of life. The same sequence of events can be seen in Japan. The scale of forest destruction, particularly following the great rebuilding of castles and towns at the beginning of the Tokugawa period (shortly after 1600 AD) was such that it led to the imposition of strict government controls in the form of licences for further tree felling. The same problems can be identified in the great medieval Christian kingdom of Ethiopia. The original centre of the state was in the northern area – Tigre and Eritrea. Continual deforestation produced a badly degraded environment of poor soils and eroded hillsides, some in such a ruined state that they could no longer support shrubs or even grass. By about 1000 AD the damage was so great that the focal point of the state had to shift to the south and a new capital in the central highlands. However, the same process was repeated, again leading to major environmental damage in this area. Just how quickly and completely people could transform the area surrounding a new or expanding settlement is illustrated by what happened around Addis Ababa after it became the capital of Ethiopia in 1883. Within twenty years a zone stretching for 100 miles around the town had been devastated – stripped of its trees by charcoal burners producing fuel for the capital.

The effects of the steady and continual cutting down of trees can be seen at their clearest in the Mediterranean region. Modern visitors regard the landscape of olive trees, vines, low bushes and strongly scented herbs as one of the main attractions of the region. It is, however, the result of massive environmental degradation brought about not by the creation of an artificial system such as irrigation but by the relentless pressure of long-term settlement and growing population. The natural vegetation of the Mediterranean area was a mixed evergeen and deciduous forest of oaks, beech, pines and cedars. This forest was cleared bit by bit for a variety of reasons – to provide land for agriculture, fuel for cooking and heating, and construction materials for houses and ships. Other activities ensured that it did not regenerate. Overgrazing by sheep, cattle and particularly goats meant the young trees and shrubs were eaten before they could grow and mature. Gradually the flocks of animals reduced the vegetation to a low scrub of largely inedible plants. Removal of the tree cover, especially on steep slopes, led to large scale soil erosion which ruined agricultural land (already short of manure because the farmers practised transhumance, moving the flocks of animals to different areas for summer and winter) and the large amount of silt brought down in the rivers blocked water courses and caused large deltas and marshes to form at river mouths.

This process of long-term environmental decline can be traced around the Mediterranean and the Near East in every area. Overall it is now estimated that no more than ten per cent of the original forests that once stretched from Morocco to Afghanistan even as late as 2000 BC still exist. One of the first areas to suffer was the hills of Lebanon and Syria. The natural climax forests here were particularly rich in cedars, and the cedars of Lebanon became famous throughout the ancient Near East for their height and straightness. They were prized by the states and empires of Mesopotamia as building materials and control of the area or trade with its rulers was a high priority. Later the cedars became one of the mainstays of Phoenician commerce and were traded over a wide area. Gradually the trees were cut down until the renowned cedars of Lebanon were reduced to a pathetic remnant in a few places – there are now just four small groves of cedars left in the region – maintained as a symbol of former glory.

In Greece the first signs of large-scale destruction began to appear about 650 BC as population rose and settlements expanded. The root of the problem here was overgrazing on the eighty per cent of the land that was unsuitable for cultivation. Although the Greeks were well aware of techniques for preserving soil such as the use of manuring to maintain the structure of the soil and of terracing to limit erosion on hillsides, the pressure from a continually rising population proved too great. The hills of Attica were stripped bare of trees within a couple of generations and by 590 in Athens the great reformer of the constitution, Solon, was arguing that cultivation on steep slopes should be banned because of the amount of soil being lost. A few decades later the tyrant of Athens, Peisistratus, introduced a bounty for farmers to plant olives, the only tree that would grow on the badly eroded land because it had roots strong enough to penetrate the underlying limestone rock. Many of the writers of ancient Greece such as Herodotus, Xenophon and Aristotle were aware of the problem but the most graphic description of the effects of deforestation and soil erosion was left by Plato in his *Critias:*

'What now remains compared with what then existed is like the skeleton of a sick man, all the fat and soft earth having wasted away, and only the bare framework of the land being left . . . there are some mountains which now have nothing but food for bees, but they had trees not very long ago . . . there were many lofty trees of cultivated species and . . . boundless pasturage for flocks. Moreover, it was enriched by the yearly rains from Zeus, which were not lost to it, as now, by flowing from the bare land into the sea; but the soil it had was deep, and therein it received the water, storing it up in the retentive loamy soil, and . . . provided all the various districts with abundant supplies of springwaters and streams, whereof the shrines still remain even now, at the spots where the fountains formerly existed.'

The same problems can be identified in Italy a few centuries later as population rose and Rome grew from a small city into the centre of an empire encompassing the Mediterranean and most of the Near East. About 300 BC Italy and Sicily were still well forested but the increasing demand for land and timber resulted in rapid deforestation. The inevitable consequence was much higher levels of soil erosion, and as the earth was carried down in the rivers, the gradual silting up of ports in the estuaries. The port of Paestum in southern Italy silted up completely and the town decayed while Ravenna lost its access to the sea. Ostia, the port of Rome, only survived by constructing new docks. Elsewhere large marshes developed around river mouths built with the soil eroded in the hills. The Pontine marshes were created about 200 BC in an area which had supported sixteen Volscian towns four hundred years earlier.

The creation of the Roman empire increased the pressure on the environment in other areas of the Mediterranean as the demand for food increased. Many of the provinces of the empire were turned into granaries to feed the population of Italy, particularly after 58 BC when the citizens of Rome started to receive free grain for political reasons. North Africa, for example contains a whole series of impressive Roman remains, such as the great city of Leptis Magna in Libya, from what were once some of the most flourishing and highly productive provinces of the empire. But they now lie surrounded by vast deserts, a memorial to widespread environmental degradation brought about by human actions. The area continued to flourish even after the final destruction of Carthage in 146 BC but the growing Roman demand for grain pushed cultivation further into the hills and onto vulnerable soils that were easily eroded when deforested. There is no single date that marks the decline of the North African provinces – it was a long drawn-out process of increasing strain and deterioration in the environment as soils eroded and the desert slowly encroached from the south. The process was intensified after the fall of Rome as tribes such as the Berbers moved into the cultivated areas bringing with them their large flocks of grazing animals, which completed the work of removing the remaining vegetation cover. Similar pressures can be identified in Asia Minor where the interior of the old Roman provinces of Caria and Phrygia was completely deforested by the first century AD. A few decades later the emperor Hadrian had to restrict all access to the remaining forests of

Syria because of the amount of deforestation. Some regions in the area were less seriously affected and continued to prosper as food exports to the main imperial cities and towns such as Antioch and Baalbeck flourished until the early Byzantine period. But both are now ruins, some of the limestone hills of the area have lost up to six feet of soil and Antioch is under twenty-eight feet of water-borne silt from hillsides ravaged by deforestation.

The causes of the decline and fall of the Roman empire are still a subject for debate by historians. But most would agree that it was the result of the interaction of a number of factors causing internal political decay and vulnerability to external pressure. It would, therefore, be too simple to see environmental degradation as the single, or even the main cause, of the decline and fall. But there is no doubt that it was an important contributory factor and that the difficulties in extracting the food surplus needed to feed both the population of Rome and large standing armies was one of the causes of internal weakness in the empire. The deterioration of the environment of the Mediterranean region did not end with the fall of Rome. Freed from some of the demands of the imperial system some areas may have recovered enabling secondary forests to develop as population fell. The recovery in population levels by around 1000 AD followed by a steady rise, meant that deforestation continued until the present day. As more forests were cleared, more soil was eroded away. The same trends can be identified in Spain where overgrazing by the huge flocks of sheep kept by the *Mesta*, the most powerful of the medieval guilds, permanently degraded the environment of large parts of central Spain, in particular La Mancha and Extremadura, producing vast expanses of poor quality grass and scrub.

The development of settled societies in the Americas produced the same sequence of events as in Eurasia – the clearance of land for agriculture, deforestation and soil erosion. There is a strong suspicion that the collapse of the great city of Teotihuacan in the valley of Mexico and some of the early city states in the coastal area of Peru in the first centuries AD were linked to problems arising from the overuse of irrigation and the consequent failure of the agricultural base leading to an inability to maintain the superstructure of the state. But the clearest case of environmental collapse leading to the demise of a society comes from the Maya – who developed in what are now parts of Mexico, Guatemala, Belize and Honduras – one of the most extraordinary societies of its type found anywhere in the world. Some of the first

explorers to find the 'lost cities', the Americans John Stephens and
Frederick Catherwood in the late 1830s, were as much at a loss as
Leonard Woolley in Mesopotamia to explain what had happened. At
Copan and Palenque they mused on a vanished society:

'We . . . strove in vain to penetrate the mystery by which we were
surrounded. Who were the people that built this city? . . . architec-
ture, sculpture, painting, all the arts which embellish life, had
flourished in this overgrown forest; orators, warriors and statesmen,
beauty, ambition, and glory, had lived and passed away, and none
knew that such things had been or could tell of their past existence. . . . In the romance of the world's history nothing ever
impressed me more forcibly than the spectacle of this once great and
lovely city, overturned, destroyed and lost; discovered by accident,
overgrown with trees for miles around, and without even a name to
distinguish it.'

The main obstacle to understanding what really happened is that the
Mayan script has still been only partially deciphered. However archaeological research since the sites were rediscovered and the use of
increasingly sophisticated techniques in the last three decades or so
have brought new insights.

Mayan society was a remarkable achievement in that it developed in
dense lowland tropical jungle. The earliest settlements in this area,
which posed major problems for human exploitation in terms of
obtaining enough food, date from about 2500 BC. Population rose
slowly and settlements grew in size and complexity so that by about 450
BC it is possible to identify separate ceremonial areas and buildings
within the settlements. Two hundred years later at Tikal in Guatemala
a complex, hierarchical society had emerged (easily identified by the
large differences in status between the burials of different groups) and
steep pyramids over 100 feet high with temples on their summits were
being built out of the local limestone rock in the north acropolis of this
major centre. Over the next two or three centuries this process was
repeated throughout the area until a whole series of major settlements
had developed with a remarkably uniform culture displayed in the
architectural styles and common script. The considerable intellectual
achievements of the Maya were reflected, in particular, in their astronomy (where they made detailed and accurate calculations not just about
the phases and positions of the sun and moon but also planets such as
Venus) and in their highly complex and extremely accurate calendar,

based on a fifty-two year cycle counting from a fixed date in the past equivalent to 3114 BC (although the significance of this date remains unknown). All the Mayan sites have a large number of stone stelae inscribed with a series of dates, which can be translated, and texts, which, very largely, remain undeciphered. The main phases of Mayan history though are clear. By the first centuries AD a large number of elaborate ceremonial centres had developed throughout the region. For about a couple of centuries after 400 there was strong influence from the city of Teotihuacan in central Mexico but when that declined after 600 the Maya entered their most spectacular period. Huge pyramids, often aligned towards significant astronomical points, were built at all the centres and large numbers of stelae erected. Then, within a few decades after 800, the whole society began to disintegrate. No stelae were erected, the ceremonial centres were abandoned, population levels fell abruptly and the cities were soon covered by the encroaching jungle.

Until the 1960s it was believed that the Maya were virtually unique in the world in that they were peaceful and governed not by secular rulers and a military elite but by a religious caste obsessed by the intricacies of their calendar and astronomical observations. Since only the dates on the stelae could be understood it was assumed that these recorded various events associated with astronomical and calendrical cycles. The way in which the Maya obtained their food and supported the priestly elite in a lowland jungle environment remained a puzzle. Studies of the twentieth century Maya suggested that the only viable strategy would have been a swidden system, involving clearing a patch of jungle with stone axes during the dry season between December and March and then setting fire to the area just before the start of the rainy season when maize and beans would have been planted with a digging stick to be harvested in the autumn. The cultivated patch would have been abandoned after a couple of years as weeds reinvaded and made clearance too difficult. This agricultural system is widely used in tropical areas and highly stable in the long-term but it can only support a small population in any area because of the need to have a large amount of land for each farmer – the cleared patches cannot be re-used for about twenty years or more until the jungle has regrown (the task of clearing jungle is far less laborious than that of clearing grass and scrub). It was, therefore, assumed that the Maya lived in small, shifting settlements scattered throughout the jungle only coming together at the ceremonial centres, where the small priestly caste lived permanently, for part of the year.

In the last thirty years these assumptions about Mayan society have been abandoned and a radically different picture of the Maya adopted which helps to explain why the society collapsed so abruptly. The most important change has stemmed from a new understanding of the texts engraved on the stelae. It is now clear that these do not represent religious texts but rather they are monuments to the different secular rulers of the cities, setting out the dates of their birth, accession and death together with the major events of their reign. All the rulers at Tikal between 376 and about 800 when the site was abandoned have now been identified, as have the rulers of Palenque from 603–799 and those of many other cities. The signs on the stelae indicating the different cities have been deciphered and, although the texts still cannot be read in full, the conquest of one city by another, and hence the existence of warfare, can be deduced. The picture of a peaceful, religious society has been replaced by a view of Mayan society as dominated, in the same way as other early societies, by a secular elite supported by armies and engaged in fairly continuous warfare between the different cities. Recent archaeological work has also made the nature of these cities much clearer. They were not merely ceremonial centres occupied by a small elite but true cities with a large permanent population. At the centre were the huge ceremonial areas with magnificent temples and palaces built around a plaza. Beyond were complexes of thatched huts on platforms grouped around courtyards where most of the people lived in extended family groups. They provided the labour force that constructed the public buildings and residences for the elite. Excavations in the outer areas of Tikal suggests that, at its height, the population was at least 30,000 and possibly as high as 50,000 (of the same order as the great cities of Mesopotamia). Other cities, though not quite so large, would have followed the pattern of dense urban settlements and it seems likely that the total population in the Maya region at its peak might have been near to five million in an area that now supports only a few tens of thousands.

This new knowledge about the nature of Mayan society has been complemented by new information about the way the Mayans obtained their food. Obviously a swidden system could not be productive enough to support such a large population. Not enough land was available between the cities, which in some cases were no more than about ten miles apart, to make this feasible. Hunting and fishing would have provided no more than useful supplements and although the ramon, or breadnut tree, whose nuts can be ground to make flour, grows in profusion in the Mayan area, studies of the current day Maya suggest that it would only be used as a food of last resort. Archaeological fieldwork in the 1970s disovered that a much more intensive agricultural system was in fact used by the ancient Maya. On the hillsides they would clear jungle and make fields using extensive terracing to try to contain the inevitable soil erosion. Equally important though was the construction of raised fields in swampy areas. These followed the same principle as the chinampas of central Mexico except that they were not built out into lakes. Grids of drainage ditches were dug in the swamps and the material from the ditches was used to form raised fields. Traces of the huge areas once covered with these fields have now been found in the jungle from Guatemala across to Belize. In the fields crops such as maize and beans were grown for food together with others such as cotton and cacao.

This intensive cultivation system was the foundation for all the achievements of the Maya. However, when too much was demanded of it, it could not withstand the strain. The crucial period came after the waning of Teotihuacan influence about 600. It was marked by increasing warfare between the Mayan cities and a much greater emphasis by the elite on the construction of more and larger ceremonial buildings taking up huge amounts of labour. Population continued to rise steadily and a higher proportion lived in the cities where they were available to man the armies and work on construction projects. Cultivation became more intense. However the ecological basis to support such a massive superstructure was simply not there. The soils in tropical forests are easily eroded once the tree cover is removed. Mayan settlements clustered, not surprisingly, around the areas of fertile soil but three-quarters of the fertile soil in the area occupied by the ancient Maya is today classified as highly susceptible to erosion. Around Tikal for example 75 per cent of the soil is classed as highly fertile but nearly 60 per cent is highly vulnerable to erosion once it is cleared of trees. Clearing the forest, therefore, ran the risk of bringing about soil deterioration and declining crops yields and this would be exacerbated by the lack of domesticated animals to provide manures to maintain soil structure and fertility. The forest was cleared not just to provide land for agriculture but also for fuel, construction materials and for making the huge amounts of lime plaster that coated the ceremonial buildings. Population pressure pushed fields and terraces into ever more marginal areas which were even more vulnerable to erosion. Across the Maya area the vulnerable soils were increasingly exposed to the wind and the rain and eroded away.

Soil erosion caused by deforestation would have reduced crop yields in the affected areas and the associated higher levels of silt in the rivers would have seriously damaged the extensive raised fields in the marshy areas by altering the delicate balance between water levels and the fields and making the ditches much more difficult to keep clear. The first signs of declining food production are evident in the period before 800, when the skeletons from burials of the period show higher infant and female mortality and increasing levels of deficiency diseases brought about by falling nutritional standards. A reduction in the food surplus on which the ruling elite together with the priestly class and army depended would have had major social consequences. Attempts were made to increase the amount of food taken from the peasant cultivators, leading to internal revolt. Conflict between the cities over the declining resources would have intensified, leading to more warfare. The fall in food supplies and the increasing competition for what was available led to very high death rates and a catastrophic fall in population, making it impossible to sustain the elaborate superstructure the Maya had built upon their limited environmental base. Within a few decades the cities were abandoned and no more stelae were erected to commemorate rulers. Only a small number of peasants continued to live in the area. The deserted fields and cities, buried under dense jungle, were not found again until the nineteenth century.

By using the natural resources readily available to them, by finding ways of exploiting these more fully and, in some cases, by creating artificial environments, the Maya were able to build a complex society capable of great cultural and intellectual achievements, but they ended up destroying what they had created. Perhaps the more complex the superstructure, the more difficult it was to retain an awareness of the connections or to alter course. But success or failure also depended to a large extent on the resilience of the ecosystem concerned. Some ecosystems, such as those in the temperate climate of north and west Europe, were better able to withstand continued human occupation. The ecosystems themselves were less easily disrupted and continued human occupation (though at a lower population density than in the Mediterranean or China) and partial clearance of the forests resulted in only a low level of environmental damage during the first millennia of settled, agricultural societies. In this area none of the societies came under the threat of a major environmental collapse.

The most striking example of a society establishing a sustainable balance between the natural environment and its demand for food is Egypt. For about seven thousand years after the emergence of settled societies in the Nile valley about 5500 BC the Egyptians were able to exploit the annual flood of the river as the basis of a succession of states from the various dynasties of the Pharaonic era, through the Ptolomies to the period of the Roman empire, and under the Arabs and the Mamluks, until new technology in the nineteenth century began to undermine the system.

Each year the river Nile would flood the vast length of its lower valley depositing huge quantities of silt from its twin sources in Ethiopia and Uganda. To some extent the Egyptians happened to be the beneficiaries of somebody else's environmental problems. Much of the silt was the result of deforestation and soil erosion in the highlands and although, at present, it is estimated that the Nile carries about a hundred million tons of silt a year, it was probably less in earlier periods. The heaviest rainfall in the highlands occurred in June and the flood reached Egypt, nearly 2,000 miles away, in September. Here it spread out over the narrow valley (no more than twelve miles wide in places) through natural overflow channels into flood basins to produce the rich, permanently renewed soil of Egypt. The flood ended by November but this short period was exactly right for the sowing of autumn crops.

The great stability of the agricultural system originally adopted by the ancient Egyptians and used (without major changes) by their successors lay in the fact that what they did was to exploit a natural process, with only minimal human interference, and then only at a low technological level. The whole water control system was built upon regulating the natural flow of the river to provide the right amount of water at the right time together with the silt to fertilise the land, rather than producing an artificial environment. In some places they breached natural levees to ensure that the water reached the maximum possible area and in others they built artificial banks to provide semi-natural basins to enable water to be retained for longer. The natural irrigation of the flooded area made it both impractical and unnecessary to build artificial canals. Because of its underlying geological structure and essentially natural irrigation system the Nile valley suffered none of the problems and unwanted and damaging side-effects of Mesopotamia's artificial irrigation system. Within a month of the flood the water table was more than ten feet below the surface and so waterlogging was not a problem and there was no build-up of salts in the surface layers. This eliminated the need for the long, fallow periods essential, but not adopted, in Mesopotamia if the twin disasters of waterlogging and salinisation were to be avoided. The silt, rich in nutrients and regularly renewed, also eliminated the need for heavy manuring and ensured the continuing fertility of the soil. The level of this fertility can be judged by the fact that in the eighteenth century AD crop yields in the Nile valley were about twice as high as in France. The absence of salinisation is demonstrated by the increasing importance in Egyptian agricultural output of wheat, a crop more sensitive to salt levels, compared with barley – the exact opposite of what happened in Mesopotamia.

Although there were some changes in the agricultural system over the centuries, it showed a remarkable degree of continuity. In the Pharaonic period Egyptian farmers planted wheat, barley, beans and chick peas as their main winter crops together with flax, the main textile fibre, in the flood basins. Vegetables, particularly onions, lentils and also fodder crops, were planted in those areas where water was still available in the spring. On the higher land date palms flourished. Sorghum, which was resistant to semi-drought conditions, was introduced as a main summer crop in the Ptolemaic period and crops such as sugar, cotton and rice were cultivated for the first time in the Islamic period. The technology involved in utilising the annual flood was, like the rest of the system, basically simple. For the first four thousand years or so the fields were watered from the channels by buckets moved by hand. About 1340 BC the shaduf (or bucket and pole system) was brought into use and its greater efficiency increased the amount of cultivated land by about ten per cent. A similar increase was again achieved about 300 BC when the animal-drawn water wheel was introduced. After that there were no technological changes of importance until the nineteenth century.

The long term stability of the Egyptian agricultural system was maintained as long as there were only limited modifications to the natural flood regime. However, there were problems stemming from the fact that there could be major fluctuations from year to year in the flood level of the Nile and from a tendency for there to be sustained periods of especially high or low floods. In the short term the results for both Egyptian farming and society could be disastrous and these fluctuations had a major influence on the course of Egyptian history, particularly under the Pharaohs. Very high floods destroyed many settlements and the artificial works for containing water. Very low floods left some areas dry and lacking in silt. For example, although the 1877 flood was only about six feet below normal, it still left about a third of the valley without water and silt. Either extreme reduced crop yields with severe social implications.

In general the overall trend has been towards a fall in flood levels, probably caused by declining rainfall in the highlands that are the source of the Nile, but with major fluctuations within that trend. After about 3000 BC flood levels fell by about a quarter but it was the long series of extremely low floods in the period from 2250–1950 BC that brought about major social disruption and the end of the Old Kingdom in Egypt. These low floods drastically reduced crop yields, leading to mass starvation, death of livestock, lack of seeds for the next planting season and abandonment of marginal land. This happened at a time when the demands of the state (huge construction projects and support of a growing bureaucracy, army and priesthood) were imposing an ever heavier burden on a weakened agricultural base. The result was the political and social collapse of the Pharaonic state in the wake of a full-scale revolt by the peasantry. There followed two centuries of disunity before Egypt was reunited at the beginning of the so-called Middle Kingdom. This period was marked by a series of very high floods (those between 1840 and 1770 BC were nearly thirty feet higher in places than the modern average) which, although destructive, at least ensured adequate water and silt for crop production. A substantial decline in flood levels after about 1150 BC again caused major political and social problems. The fall in food production made it more difficult to support a large number of non-producers, especially the army, at a time when the Egyptians were under considerable external pressure, from a wave of what their records refer to as 'sea-peoples', attempting to settle in the Nile delta. The powerful Egyptian state under the Ramessid dynasty that had built the great temples at Abu Simnel collapsed. Egypt was once again disunited and was only reunited about two hundred years later under external conquerors.

Despite these vicissitudes that had such a major impact on Egyptian history, the Nile flood continued to provide a stable way of supporting a large population and a complex society in Egypt until the nineteenth century. Only then were major changes made which, within a relatively short space of time, began to have widespread effects. In the 1840s the first artificial irrigation systems were built to provide more irrigated land to grow extra crops, not for food but other items such as cotton for sale in Europe. Within a few decades permanent irrigation had pro-duced widespread salinisation and waterlogging in the newly cultivated areas. In 1882 the British agricultural expert Mackenzie Wallace described the 'white nitrous salts covering the soil and glistening in the sun like untrodden snow'. In the early twentieth century the first attempts were made to control the flow of the Nile by building a dam at Aswan on the upper Nile so as to be able to release water as required, thus avoiding flooding or water shortages downstream. It was the construction of the present high dam, which began in the 1950s, that was finally to undermine the long established Egyptian agricultural system. Although it solved one problem by regulating flood levels, it undermined the real secret of success by retaining the silt behind the dam. As a result the natural fertility of the Nile valley was destroyed and had to be replaced by expensive artificial fertilizers. It constituted a forcible entry into the modern agricultural system of high input farming but many of the peasant cultivators were unable to afford the expensive new artificial fertilizers.

Many of the earliest settled societies were unable to strike a balance between their need for food for the populace as well as for the rulers, bureaucrats, priests and soldiers and the ability of the environment to sustain intensive agriculture over a long period. Some overreached themselves in the end, although for a considerable period, often many centuries, they appeared to be highly successful. In Mesopotamia, the Indus valley, the jungles of Mesoamerica and other areas too, a fragile environment collapsed under pressure. The demands of an increasingly complex society began to overstretch the capacity of the agricultural base of the society to support the large superstructure that had been erected. In the end, the unwanted, and unexpected, side effects of what at first appeared to be solutions to environmental difficulties became problems themselves. The result was falling food production and increasing difficulty in supporting a large number of non-producers. Attempts to increase the proportion of the declining amount of crops going to the elite often produced internal revolt and the strain of provisioning a sufficiently large army often led to conquest by enemies. Only in a few cases, like the Maya, was there a dramatic collapse of an entire society or wholesale abandonment of land as no longer fit for agriculture. In the Mediterranean and China there was long-term degradation which seriously damaged the resource base of these societies. The struggle to provide enough food was to be one of the central features of nearly all the rest of human history. It remains acute for the majority of the people in the world.

6
THE LONG STRUGGLE

Agriculture did not solve the problem of producing enough food to meet the needs of the world's population. It had been adopted by human societies around the globe mainly because rising population meant that more intensive ways of obtaining food were necessary. Yet, until about the last two centuries in every part of the world nearly everyone lived on the edge of starvation. Throughout this period and all the changes of political systems, the rise and fall of empires, the emergence of new states and their decline, the underlying economic and social conditions remained broadly unchanged for thousands of years. Although areas less environmentally sensitive than Mesopotamia, in the Indus valley and the tropical jungles of Mesoamerica a complete collapse of society did not take place, there was still a high price to pay in terms of individual suffering, reduced human potential and at times wholesale loss of life. About 95 per cent cent of the people in the world were peasants; directly dependent on the land and living a life characterised by high infant mortality, low life expectancy, chronic undernourishment and with the ever present threat of famine and the outbreak of virulent epidemics. The food they ate was almost entirely vegetable in origin (especially in Asia, Africa and the Americas) and the dietary staples were the three major crops of the world – rice in Asia, maize in the Americas and wheat (supplemented by oats and rye) in Europe. Because of the overwhelming dependence of these societies on agriculture there were limits on the extent of other activities and the numbers of soldiers, priests and craftsmen that could be supported by the peasantry.

The human condition around the world varied from place to place and period to period depending not just on the factors affecting agricultural output but also on those affecting the level of population. Although the number of people in the world was far lower than at present, there was the persistent threat of overpopulation and starvation because of the inefficiency of the agricultural system. Agriculture allowed far more people to be supported than in gathering and hunting societies but reliance on a small number of crops grown in a specialised environment increased vulnerability to crop failure. Continuous cultivation of the same area lowered soil fertility and a vicious circle was established between the need to use as much land as possible to grow crops for direct human consumption, the limited amount of land available for animals and the lack of animal manures to maintain soil fertility. The limitations on agricultural output were exacerbated by problems in distributing food. The total amount that could be stored was limited and the losses were high because of inadequate facilities. A primitive transportation system meant that anything more than local distribution of food, except by water, was extremely difficult. The market for food was therefore limited and very often crop failure in one area could not be alleviated by moving in supplies from elsewhere because they were not available or, even if they were, they could not be transported. These problems were further accentuated by the religious and secular elite who enforced collection of food through taxes, tithes and other forms of direct appropriation, often leaving the peasantry with insufficient food for survival. Armies moving through the countryside looting the food they needed and destroying crops and animals made the situation worse.

Only very slowly did changes in agricultural systems leading to higher productivity, better storage and distribution facilities begin to alleviate these problems. For most societies until the nineteenth century population size and the amount of food available were often out of balance, both in the short term and the long term. In the short term, annual fluctuations in supply as a result of bad harvest or an outbreak of warfare could bring disaster. In the long term, population could increase to a level where it was almost impossible for a large part of the population to obtain an adequate diet. Adjusting either side of the equation was problematic – it was difficult to increase food production at a rapid rate and, although many of these early agricultural societies around the world used fairly crude methods for restricting the growth in numbers (the practice of infanticide or a tradition of late marriage for example), food supply and population size were only rarely in balance. Over the very long term it is clear that slow improvements to the agricultural system meant that more people could be fed. But overall population growth rates remained very low. Until about three hundred years ago the world's population never increased by more than about 0.1 per cent a year – a twentieth of the current rate. Within this gradual

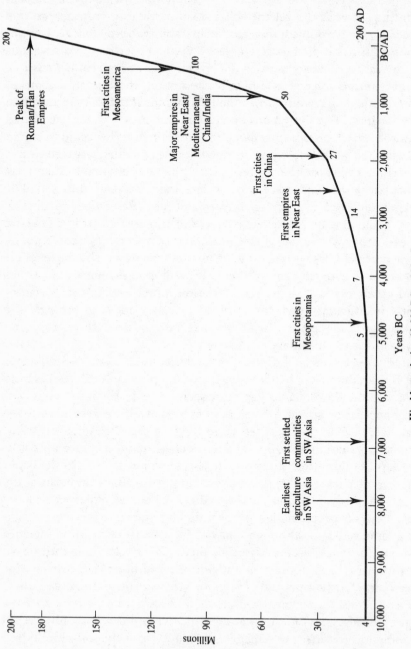

World population 10,000 BC – 200 AD

upward trend there was no steady growth in population or in food production. Instead there were bouts of rapid growth in numbers followed by sudden halts and declines caused by population levels outstripping food supplies or by the consequences of war and disease. More often than not, increasing population put ever greater pressure on a limited agricultural system, producing more poverty and malnutrition. The conflict was normally only resolved in a drastic fashion through mass starvation and death until the population was more in balance with the output from farming.

There are no reliable population statistics until the last two hundred years. Nevertheless, working from partial censuses, contemporary estimates and returns produced for other purposes such as taxation, demographers have been able to make estimates which, although not accurate in detail, give a broad picture of the number of people in the world, their distribution and the main periods of growth and decline. About the time agriculture was adopted in the three core areas the world's population was about 4 million (the same as one large city today). The spread of agriculture enabled more people to be fed and human numbers rose steadily, doubling every thousand years to reach about 50 million by 1000 BC (roughly equivalent to the current population of England and Wales). That figure doubled in only five hundred years to reach 100 million about 500 BC and numbers then grew to reach 200 million at the peak of the Han and Roman empires about 200 AD. With the decline of those empires a widespread increase in instability, warfare and destruction meant that there was little further growth anywhere in the world until about the year 1000. Then, in both China and Europe, numbers rose to reach a temporary peak of about 350 million people in the world by 1200. For a century population increased only slowly to some 400 million as the limits of food supply were reached. After 1300 starvation and plague sharply reduced numbers so that by 1400, when some recovery had taken place, there were still only about 350 million people in the world. Numbers rose sharply in the next two centuries to reach about 550 million by 1600. Then for the next century a deteriorating climate affected food production and restricted the growth in numbers so that the world's population in 1700 was just over 600 million. The eighteenth century saw the most rapid growth in history to that date, bringing the total to 900 million by 1800. The world's population first reached the one billion mark about 1825.

The distribution of people in the world also changed markedly over this long period. Before the spread of agriculture the world's population was fairly evenly distributed across the globe but the rise of settled communities reduced the share of Africa, the Americas and Oceania from about 40 per cent to less than 15 per cent of the total as the great empires of the Near East, Mediterranean, India and China became the main centres of human society. Within this general picture there have nearly always been more Chinese or Indians than Europeans. That pattern was established very early once the temporary importance, around 3000 BC, of the societies in the Near East, stemming from their early adoption of agriculture, had diminished. By the time of the Roman and Han empires there were about 35 million Europeans but 50 million Chinese and about the same number again of Indians. At the same time the total population of the Americas was about 5 million, that of Oceania about 1 million and Africa had about 20 million inhabitants, over half of whom lived in North Africa near the Mediterranean. These broad relationships still applied a millennium later between Europe (60

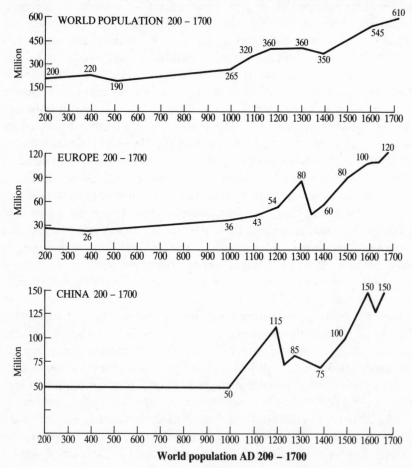

World population AD 200 – 1700

million), China (85 million), India (90 million), Africa (46 million), the Americas (14 million) and Oceania (2 million).

The examples of China and Europe show that although very different agricultural systems evolved both were restricted by environmental limitations and neither was able to sustain a long-term balance between population and food supplies. In China the development of agriculture and the emergence of a settled society took place in the north, where it was based on the dry farming of millet. Until the end of the Han empire in 220 AD the centre of the Chinese state remained in the north. It was in this period that one of the most distinctive features of Chinese society developed – the almost complete dichotomy between the ruling elite and the bulk of the population who were peasants living in small villages. Throughout Chinese history there have been periods of political unity followed by disunity but the way of life of the over-whelming majority of the people continued basically unchanged in the village world. The main task of the elite was to ensure that enough food was obtained from the peasants to maintain themselves and the army that was largely stationed in the north to provide protection against attacks from the nomads of central Asia. The collapse of the Han empire under the pressure of barbarian attacks pushed the centre of gravity of the Chinese state slightly south towards the Yangtse river, into an area which became one of the main grain producing areas. The later reunification of China, under the Sui dynasty after 589, made it necessary to transport the food surplus northwards to the military centre of the empire. The huge Grand Canal, which extended for almost 1,200 miles, was built in the early seventh century to move food supplies from the Yangtse valley to the north for the army and for the capital Peking, which alone required 400,000 tons of grain a year. By the eleventh century an army of 300,000 near Peking and over 750,000 on the frontier was being fed in this way. Not surprisingly it placed an enormous burden on the peasantry.

One of the most important changes in Chinese society took place with a wave of emigration to the south of the country after the fourth century, encouraged by a revolution in agricultural production. Rice had been domesticated and cultivated widely across south-east Asia about 3500 BC but it was grown as a dry crop like other grains such as millet or wheat. About 500 BC a new technique of wet-rice production in paddy fields developed in south-east Asia and spread slowly to reach China, Korea, Japan, India and Java in the next millennium. The inherently poor nutrient content of tropical soils was circumvented by growing the rice partially covered in water in special fields fed by complex water management techniques to produce large quantities of slowly moving water. This provided extra nutrients in two ways – it encouraged the growth of algae which were able to fix nitrogen from the atmosphere and secondly it allowed large amounts of organic matter – vegetable waste and both human and animal manures – to rot down in the water. The continual trampling involved in working in the fields made the soil impervious and therefore able to retain the nutrients. This system produced huge increases in crop yields but required enormous amounts of labour not only for cultivating the crop but, more importantly, for constructing and maintaining the fields and the water control systems. In the centuries after about 400 AD there was a steady wave of people moving south to open up and settle new lands using paddy field systems. The main rice growing provinces of the Yangtse delta, the Hsiang valley, Szechwan and Kwangtung were colonised, and steady if unspectacular improvements in techniques further increased production. The most important of these was the introduction, in the eleventh century, of new varieties of quicker growing rice from Indo-China that enabled two crops a year to be grown in the most favoured areas in the south and both a rice and a wheat crop further north.

The Chinese developed the most sophisticated agriculture in the world (based on techniques such as crop rotation that were still largely unused in Europe), producing very high yields from intensively farmed land. By about 1200 China was the largest, most literate and most advanced country in the world. The expansion of settlement into the new rice growing areas in the south allowed population to grow from about 50 million under the Han (a level that was maintained for several hundred years afterwards) to reach about 115 million in the early thirteenth century. However there were a number of structural problems that ensured that the balance between food supply and population was never satisfactory. Improvements in techniques or farming of new land brought only temporary increases in per capita food supply which were soon counterbalanced by increases in population.

The Chinese were unable to make the necessary structural changes in the agricultural system that might have increased food supply on a large scale. Yields were about as high as was possible before the introduction of modern artificial fertilisers. The most fertile areas were already densely populated and inputs could not be increased because there was not enough land to keep more animals which might have provided the extra manure. Social mores emphasised equal land division within the family, which meant a multitude of very small farms, each of which could only produce a very small surplus, if any. Output could only be increased by small improvements in productivity and by cultivating new land, although this was often of marginal quality and therefore produced lower yields. The Chinese agricultural system was certainly impressive in its total output and its very intensive production methods. However, the high level of population and the difficulty of making any significant qualitative changes meant that the mass of the population were dependent on a system that could produce only a low level of food for each individual. Disasters like the Mongol invasion which resulted in the deaths of about 35 million Chinese (most in the north of the country) or the massive epidemics in 1586–89 and 1639–44, which killed about a fifth of the people on each occasion, reduced the pressure of population for a while. But after about 1600 there is no evidence of any significant increases in yields and, although the area under cultivation rose, the amount of food available per person was about the same in 1850 as it had been three hundred years earlier. The result of this high intensity system (dependent on a large amount of labour to produce high levels of food from the land used) was that the overwhelming majority of the population lived permanently on the verge of starvation.

Chinese agriculture was able to maintain a large number of people on the brink of starvation. Medieval European agriculture was a low productivity system that kept a smaller number in the same condition. Europe too found it difficult to expand output on a sustainable basis. The overriding problem here was that soil fertility was steadily reduced through continual cropping, leaching out of nutrients in rain and low level soil erosion, and there was a lack of replacement nutrients. Fertility in the arable fields could only be maintained through use of animal manures, but the number of animals that could be fed throughout the year was very small because of the lack of fodder crops. Many animals had to be slaughtered in the autumn because of a shortage of winter feed. Keeping animals on pasture was difficult in the long term when the manure was removed to fertilise arable fields, because yields of hay and grass for the animals would then fall. A vicious circle was therefore established. As the number of animals that could be fed declined so did the manure available for arable fields and with it crop yields. Most manure was also stored in the open for long periods which severely lowered its nutrient value. Crops were reduced by the use of only a two-field rotation system under which fields alternated between being planted in the autumn with winter grain and being left fallow for a year. This resulted in an inadequate amount of time to restore nutrients and remove any diseases or pests in the soil that might reduce yields. A shortage of marls (or liming materials) also meant that it was difficult to reduce the acidity of soils and this kept yields low. The consequence was that in medieval Europe the agricultural system was only able to sustain a low level of productivity. In the short term it was sometimes possible to increase production. Extra inputs could be introduced by keeping more animals in new fields or new arable fields could be brought into use but these improvements could not be sustained in the long term because of the draining of nutrients from the pastures and fields. There was therefore a tendency for the fertility of the soil to fall back to a level where the risk of crop failure was high.

Changes to the European agricultural system came gradually. About 800, in north-eastern France a new three-field rotation was adopted. Under this system one field was planted in the autumn with winter wheat or rye and a second the following spring with oats, barley or perhaps peas whilst a third was left fallow. This not only increased fallow periods and the variety of crops grown but also helped to some extent to raise fertility levels and distributed work more evenly throughout the year. The three-field system spread across Europe – but only slowly. Its use was not widespread in England until after 1250 and even later in other areas. However the output of food was still constrained by the amount of inputs available. An important contribution to raising output was the invention of the heavy plough which was probably developed in the sixth century and its use spread across Europe during the next four hundred years. The earliest ploughs were simply an enlarged digging stick dragged by a single animal or a pair of oxen; they did not turn over the soil and left a wedge of undisturbed earth between each furrow. This plough was not well suited to the heavier soils of northern Europe, particularly in the lowlands. The heavy plough needed a team of eight oxen to pull it but it did enable a much larger area to be cultivated than before, though it could not solve the problem of low nutrient levels. Improvement in crops came very slowly with the increasing use of legumes capable of fixing nitrogen and therefore improving soil fertility and of fodder crops to provide winter feed for animals. It was not until about 1300, and then only in a small area of Europe (principally Flanders), that their use became at all widespread.

For thousands of years European agriculture remained at a low level of productivity and the majority of the people lived on the edge of

starvation. There is evidence that European societies were more successful than those elsewhere in the world in limiting their population.
This was achieved through a number of responses loosely linked to the
fortunes of the main economic activity – agriculture. The most important of these responses were late marriages or fewer marriages. There is
some evidence that the age of marriage and the number not marrying
rose when population was higher and so nearer the limits of food
production and fell when population pressure eased following famine or
disease. These methods could never be more than partially successful
and there were still many occasions when even at the relatively low
levels common in the medieval and early modern periods Europe was
'overpopulated' in relation to the supply of food.

In 1000, the population of Europe was about 36 million. In the next
three centuries, numbers more than doubled to reach 80 million in
1300. Many parts of Europe became severely overcrowded – the
population of northern Italy, Flanders, Brabant and the Paris area was
probably as high as in the early nineteenth century despite the lower
level of agricultural productivity. The supply of new land was virtually
exhausted in the late thirteenth century, and yields were also falling as
more land was put under crops as a short-term measure to try and
increase food production, thus reducing the number of animals kept
and therefore the amount of manure produced. The shortage of land,
combined with the rising population, was causing cereal prices to rise
and many people suffered from underemployment and must have lived
at a very low level of subsistence. The growing shortage of food was
exacerbated by the fact that the nobility and clergy were taking about
half of the peasants' output of food once tithes, rents, taxes and the time
they were forced to spend working on the lord's estate are taken into
account. Most of this wealth was spent on conspicuous consumption.
By 1300 European population was beyond the optimum that could be
supported by the technology and institutions of the time. At the
beginning of the fourteenth century there is clear evidence of falling
population brought about through permanent malnutrition and near
starvation in many areas of Europe from Tuscany and Provence to
Normandy and south-east England. The major famine of 1316–17
added to the number of casualties but the pressure of population on
resources was not removed until after the outbreak of the Black Death
in 1346 and the subsequent recurrences of the plague for the rest of the
century.

The period from the late fourteenth century until the mid-fifteenth
was one of comparative prosperity as population remained below the

peak of 1300 for about two hundred years. However by 1600 it was near 90 million, slightly higher than in 1300, even though there had been little improvement in agricultural productivity. The signs of 'over-population' and an imbalance between food supply and numbers appeared again. Settlements expanded into new areas but often the soils were poor and output low. In England agricultural prices were rising from about 1500 as shortages started to develop and real wages fell by a half in the period 1500–1620 causing immense distress to those already on the margins of society and unable to find any form of regular work. By the 1620s population growth slowed down as malnutrition and higher mortality caused by inadequate food supplies took their toll. The same symptoms can be found in France. By 1570 most usable agricultural land was in production and, although numbers were kept in check by the continual civil wars of the period, a crisis was reached early in the seventeenth century. Food prices continued to rise, land holdings got smaller and real wages fell drastically. Population rose on occasions to about 20 million but fell back rapidly since at that level it was out of equilibrium with the number that could be fed in the long term. A series of severe famines between 1690 and 1710 demonstrated that population was still higher than the agricultural system could regularly feed.

In all the agricultural societies around the world the outcome of the harvest was crucial. A bad harvest was a calamity but two in succession could bring disaster – not just for the poor who were the first casualties of reduced supplies and increased prices but also for the peasants and eventually even for the whole of society. The temptation, especially for the peasants, not surprisingly, was to consume what little food was available leaving inadequate quantities of seeds to plant for the next crop, thus increasing the chance of disaster the next year. The elite in each society were normally in a position to be able either to force the peasantry to hand over enough food or to buy it even at highly inflated prices. Starvation affected those unable to retain enough of their crop to live on until the next harvest and those, mainly in the towns, who could not pay high food prices. Under such circumstances large numbers, already badly nourished, easily succumbed to the outbreaks of disease that normally followed a period of bad harvests.

The most important influence on the outcome of the harvest and, because of the overwhelming importance of agriculture in the economy, the state of society, was the weather. Any one of a number of permutations – a wet, cool period that reduced the chances of seed germinating, a dry spell when the crops were growing or wet weather during harvesting – could threaten output by severely reducing the harvest. Nearly every government paid great attention to detailed accounts of the weather from around the country, the prospects for the harvest, the price of grain and bread as one of the main indicators of the level of social unrest. Crops were affected not only by annual variations in the weather but also by the long-term cycles in the earth's climate, which could cause widespread dislocation of agricultural systems. For example, colder periods shortened growing seasons, made some areas marginal for crop production and, in general, reduced yields. While they lasted there would be an increased risk of a poor harvest in any particular year and a succession of poor harvests resulted in the build up of internal strains within society. Warmer periods increased the areas where crops could be grown, improved food supply and reduced the pressure stemming from the number of people who had to be fed. Most of the available evidence about these long-term climatic cycles comes from Europe and the detailed effects of the changes were different in other parts of the world – for example, one of the coldest spells in Japan coincided with one of the warmest in Europe.

Since the end of the last ice age there have been alternating periods of warmer and colder weather in Europe. After a steady improvement from about 10,000 BC, which marked the end of the last ice age, the warmest period of all came in the two thousand years after 5000 BC when temperatures were between one and two degrees centigrade above twentieth century levels. Vegetation zones moved northwards and it is interesting that this period of climatic optimum coincided with the development and spread of agriculture across Europe. A general decline in temperatures then set in, reaching a low point between 900–300 BC, a time of very high rainfall too. An improvement was noticeable by around 100 BC when vines spread further north, but it petered out

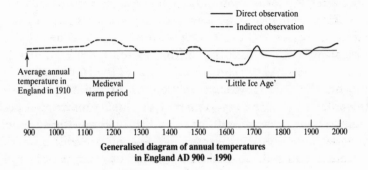

Generalised diagram of annual temperatures
in England AD 900 – 1990

around 400 AD with a cool spell that lasted for around four hundred years. Then a warm period that was shorter and less intense than the first peak (perhaps one degree centigrade warmer than today) reached its height about 1200. A steady decline followed, reaching a long low between 1430–1850, the 'Little Ice Age', when temperatures were between one and two degrees centigrade lower than at present. The main impact was felt in very severe winters, with summer temperatures not much different from current levels. These climatic changes have been established through a multitude of different techniques – pollen records from mud cores, isotope analysis of foraminifera in ocean cores, the recording of changes in lakes, glaciers and tree lines plus some historical records. Although the broad trends have been firmly established, it is only for the last two periods – the warm spell that ended around 1200 and the 'Little Ice Age' – that detailed analysis of the effects of climate is possible.

At the height of the warm period which lasted for about four hundred years before 1200 the tree line in central Europe was about 500 feet higher than today, vines grew in England as far north as the Severn and farming was possible on Dartmoor as high as 1,300 feet. Large parts of the uplands of southern Scotland were arable land and in 1280 the sheep farmers of Northumbria were complaining about the continual encroachment of arable fields on their upland pastures. One of the most important effects of the milder climate was on the Viking voyages and settlements. Iceland was colonised from Norway in 874 at the beginning of the warmer period and Greenland from 986. Both of these societies were on the climatic margins of Europe and their existence was largely dictated by the weather. The Greenland settlement flourished during the warm period with a population of about 3,000, almost 300 farms, sixteen churches and even a cathedral in the main village. But it remained a marginal and highly vulnerable society, dependent on the mild weather for its very existence.

The gradual deterioration in the climate after 1200 caused a steady decline in Greenland. The hay growing season gradually became shorter and shorter, yet the Viking settlers tried to retain their way of life based on cattle instead of shifting to the more readily available marine resources. As the climate deteriorated the Inuit moved further south and the Viking western settlement of Godthaab Fjord was destroyed shortly after 1350. The severer climate meant that pack ice remained in the seas around Greenland throughout the summer and contact with the rest of Europe was lost after 1408. The eastern settlement at Julianehaab died out, probaby under Inuit attack, about

1500. Iceland, too, became a much more marginal society under the impact of a worsening climate. Wheat growing died out (a one degree centigrade fall in annual temperatures in Iceland reduces the growing season by almost a third) and marine resources became overwhelmingly important in the economy. In the harsher climate the numbers that could be supported were much less and the population fell from about 77,000 at the height of the warm period around 1100 to 38,000 in the late eighteenth century.

The increasingly colder climate affected the rest of Europe too. The uplands of southern Scotland reverted to pasture and the growing of vines for wine-making died out in England about 1400. But the real impact of a much worse climate was felt after the middle of the sixteenth century – a series of severe winters and a period of much greater climatic instability began that was to last for almost three hundred years. After 1580 the glaciers in the Alps, Iceland and Russia advanced, in many places by over a mile, and did not begin to retreat until after 1850. Between 1564 and 1814 the Thames froze in the winter at least twenty times, as did the Rhone three times between 1590 and 1603 and even the Guadalquivir at Seville froze in the winter of 1602–3. At Marseilles the sea froze in 1595 and in 1684 there was pack ice off the coast of England. From the 1580s the Denmark Strait between Iceland and Greenland was regularly blocked by pack ice even in summer. Across Europe the lower temperatures reduced the growing season by about a month and lowered the height at which crops could be grown by about 600 feet, with consequent adjustments to the cultivation areas of nearly all crops. Outbreaks of even more severe weather within the overall pattern of a deteriorating climate could have devastating effects. For example, a series of cold mistral winds destroyed many of the olive groves of Provence between 1599 and 1603 and very heavy frosts around Valencia in the same period ruined many of the fruit trees.

The effects varied in different parts of Europe. There was no simple relationship between the temperature, the amount of rain and the size of the crop since the most important factor was how these influences were distributed through the seasons. The overall decline in temperature had its greatest impact in Scandinavia, where the reduced growing season made many areas extremely marginal for growing crops. Further south a very cold winter might have some beneficial effects by killing a higher than normal number of pests. But even here the consequences of a deteriorating climate can be detected. In England there was a shift towards spring rather than autumn sown crops in order to try and avoid damage from a harsh winter. In the Netherlands, buckwheat, which is hardy and has a short growing season, but which was hardly grown in Europe before 1550, became increasingly important in the next hundred years. Other evidence from the Netherlands suggests that a cold, late spring reduced grass growth so that pastures were late to develop, reducing dairy output, increasing prices and also leading to a slaughter of cattle the following year if the hay crop was not sufficient to provide enough feed till the new grass had grown. In other areas increased rain could be most damaging, especially in the winter, by reducing arable yields because of waterlogged soils. This long period of poor climate came at a time when European population was already at the limit that the agricultural system could support. The worsened growing conditions meant a significant reduction in food production leading to increased malnutrition, widespread famine and death. One consequence was a period of much greater internal instability within the European states, which was particularly acute in the early seventeenth century.

For the overwhelming majority of people food meant vegetables. Nearly all the available land was needed to feed humans rather than provide pasture and there was not enough surplus grain to feed many animals. Where animals were kept their output was low. A medieval cow in Europe produced about one-sixth of the milk and one-quarter of the meat of a modern animal. In China 98 per cent of the calorific value of the diet came from vegetables, primarily rice. In Europe most people survived on a monotonous diet of vegetable and grain gruels and bread; meat and fish were very rare items except for the upper classes. As late as 1870, 70 per cent of the French diet consisted of bread and potatoes and in 1900 only 20 per cent of the calories came from animal products. Throughout Europe the majority of people lived on a maximum of about 2,000 calories a day (about the level of modern India), slightly higher in more prosperous countries such as England and Holland, but everywhere there were gross inequalities within society that meant that many obtained far less than this. In the early nineteenth century, in Norway, France and Germany, the average food consumption was still below 2,000 calories a day – less than contemporary Latin America and North Africa. The poorer regions of Europe had a particularly meagre diet. In some areas of France in the eighteenth century, for example in the Auvergne and the foothills of the Pyrenees, large parts of the population were still dependent on chestnuts for two to three months a year together with slops of maize and buckwheat, with some milk from a cow fed on weeds from the side of the road, and their intake was probably as low as 1,800 calories a day. This compares badly with the bushmen of the Kalahari desert who live on about 2,100 calories a day obtained by about three days work a week.

There was no steady improvement in food supplies. For a century or more after the plagues of the fourteenth century people were reasonably well fed because of the reduction in numbers but standards fell dramatically between 1500 and 1800 – indeed the level of meat consumption in Germany did not return to medieval levels until the mid-nineteenth century. Supplies also fluctuated during the year. Everywhere in Europe (and the pattern would have been the same elsewhere) the best time of the year would be the harvest (assuming it was at a reasonable level), which would be a time for celebration and for eating more food than usual. Winter was a bad time but the worst period was the early spring – before the first crops were ready and when food supplies laid in from the previous year were at their lowest. These problems were exacerbated by any outbreak of animal disease (which could spread rapidly in what were often undernourished herds) such as the epidemic of rinderpest that spread from Russia into western Europe between 1709 and 1714 and which killed one-and-a-half million cattle. For human beings a permanent state of poor diet led to constant malnutrition, susceptibility to disease and a continuing high level of mortality. For example, in France in the late seventeenth century between a fifth and a quarter of the population died before their first birthday, half before they were twenty and only one in ten lived till they were sixty.

This endemic level of inadequate diet and malnutrition for most of the people in the world was frequently turned into disaster by the outbreak of famine, which usually stemmed from crop failure following bad weather. In China in two thousand years between 108 BC and 1910 there were 1,828 years (over 90 per cent of the total) with recorded famines involving at least one province in the country. In France between 970 and 1100 there were sixty years of famine (about 45 per cent of the total at a time of expanding agricultural output) and in Tuscany between 1351 and 1767 there were 111 years of famine but only sixteen with good harvests (less than 4 per cent of the total). In Ethiopia in the two hundred years after 1540 there were ten major famines affecting the whole country. In France the rate of general famine affecting the whole country was high between the tenth and eighteenth centuries. In that period by far the worst century was the eleventh, with twenty-six famines affecting the whole country, but the lack of any overall improvement in the situation is demonstrated by the fact that the eighteenth century had the second worst record with sixteen famines. The best, or least bad, century was the twelfth (when new land was being brought into production) with only two famines, followed by the fourteenth which had four, an improved performance largely due to the fact that the population was severely reduced by the plague after 1346. When food supplies did fail the scale of the subsequent tragedy could be immense. In 1696–97 in Finland between a quarter and a third of the population died as the result of famine. About the same proportion died in Bengal in 1769–70, when the total number of deaths was around 10 million, and Ethiopia suffered a similar loss of its population between 1888 and 1892.

The origins and effects of widespread famine can be illustrated by the events of 1315–17 when medieval Europe experienced its worst ever food shortages at a time when the population was at the very limit that the agricultural system could support. In 1314 the harvest was reasonable but the weather in 1315 was dreadful, being wet in every season. The spring sowing failed in most areas because of waterlogged fields, ploughs stuck in the mud and the hay crop was not properly ripe or dry when cut and stored. Crop yields were about half the normal level and what was available was of a low quality. By early 1316 food was already in short supply across the whole of Europe and seed for the next crop was being eaten. The winter and spring were again very wet and the rain continued through the summer producing another harvest at about half the average level. The resulting food shortage brought catastrophe to most of Europe. Wheat prices rose to three times their normal level and in some places of acute shortage they were over eight times higher. This meant that many of the poor could no longer buy food but people with money often could not buy simply because there was no food available – as even Edward II discovered for himself when the court arrived in St Albans in August 1316. The King of Bohemia lost thousands of sheep because he could not buy feed for them. All over Europe animals were killed in huge numbers as feed supplies ran out. The poor were dying in large numbers or turned to robbery in an attempt to get food; huge bands of starving peasants swarmed across the countryside. The food that was available was often of very low quality – bread would be mixed with pigeon and pig droppings, and animals that had died of disease were eaten causing outbreaks of disease in the human population. Some people were driven to even more desperate measures, as many reports of widespread cannibalism in an area stretching from England to Livonia on the Baltic coast bear witness. In Ireland in 1318 bodies were dug up from graves to provide food and in Silesia executed criminals

were eaten. There were still cases of people eating human flesh into
1319. Animal diseases, probably aided by the lack of feed, added to the
carnage, killing about 70 per cent of the sheep in some areas and in the
four years 1319–22 some two-thirds of Europe's population of oxen
died. Only slowly did better weather and improved harvests bring some
relief from the catastrophe.

The conditions that agricultural societies, utterly dependent on
fragile food supplies, faced during a time of harvest failure is illustrated
in graphic and harrowing detail by an account, contained in the parish
register of Orslosa in western Sweden, of the terrible famine at the end
of the sixteenth century:

'In 1596 at midsummer-tide the land was abundantly covered with
splendid grass and much corn, so that everybody thought that there
would be sufficient corn in the country. But . . . when the people
were at Skara market [June], there came so much rain and flood that
all the bridges floated away. And with that same flood . . . the water
went over the fields and pastures, so that the corn and the grass were
ruined, and thus there was little of both grain and hay. . . . In the
winter the cattle fell ill from the rotten hay and straw which was taken
out of the water. . . . It went the same way with the cows and the
calves, and the dogs which ate their dead bodies also died. The soil
was sick for three years, so that it could bear no harvest. After these
inflictions it happened that even those who had good farms turned
their young people away, and many even their own children, because
they were not able to watch the misery of them starving to death in
the homes of their fathers and mothers. Afterwards the parents left
their house and home going whither they were able, till they lay dead
of hunger and starvation. . . . People ground and chopped many
unsuitable things into bread; such as mash, chaff, bark, buds,
nettles, leaves, hay, straw, peatmoss, nut-shells, pea-stalks, etc. This
made people so weak and their bodies so swollen that innumerable
people died. Many widows, too, were found dead on the ground with
red hummock grass, seeds which grew in the fields, and other kinds
of grass in their mouths. . . . Children starved to death at their
mothers' breasts, for they had nothing to give them to suck. Many
people, men and women, young and old, were compelled in their
hunger to take to stealing. . . . At times these and other inflictions
came and also the bloody flux [dysentry] which put people in such a
plight that countless died of it.'

Europe emerged from the constant threat of famine very gradually. The 1594–1597 famine affected the whole of the continent after a succession of four bad harvests that again produced widespread cannibalism and the eating of cats and dogs. That period marked the last severe famine in southern England although the north of the country was still seriously affected in 1623 when, for example, one in eight of the population of Penrith died. France was still badly affected by famine throughout the seventeenth century and the first decade of the eighteenth. In 1693–1694 about 10 per cent of the population of northern France died: in the Auvergne it was twice this figure and the total number of deaths may have been near two million. In 1709–1710 a famine of similar proportions occurred and also affected Prussia on a large scale. The last severe crisis to affect the whole of Europe came in 1816–1817. Although partly the result of the dislocation caused by the Napoleonic wars, its main origins lay in appalling weather across the continent (it affected the United States too), probably as a result of the large amount of volcanic dust in the atmosphere following the eruption of the Tomboro volcano in Indonesia in 1815. Throughout the summer the weather was cool (July was the coldest on record) and rainfall was 50 per cent above average. In England two-thirds of the year's rain fell in the summer months of July, August and September. As a result the harvest was six weeks late and the wine harvest was the latest ever known – extending into November in some places. Crop failure was widespread, wheat prices doubled from an already high level and the real wages of peasants and workers fell drastically. The result was widespread food riots in England, France and Belgium in 1816 and across most of the continent the following year. Death rates rose, though they were not as high as in earlier famines, and the number of epidemics increased, especially in southern Europe.

The last major famine to strike Europe came about thirty years later in Ireland. The social and economic conditions and its fragile agricultural base were in many ways similar to those in the rest of Europe centuries earlier. The root cause of the famine was population pressure on the available land. The population of Ireland rose ten-fold from about 800,000 in 1500 to eight-and-a-half million in 1846 and inheritance practices had produced a large number of very small holdings averaging half an acre. There were also about 650,000 landless labourers living in permanent destitution and most of the rural population lived in squalid, one room cabins. The need to provide food from tiny plots of land encouraged adoption of the potato, universally regarded throughout Europe as the food of the poor. Half an acre of land solely growing potatoes could provide a family with a monotonous diet but one that supplied a minimum level of nutrition. By the early nineteenth century potatoes took up about 40 per cent of the total crop area in Ireland and constituted the sole food of nearly half the population. However the potato was a crop vulnerable to a number of diseases and not well adapted to growing in the wet climate of north-west Europe. Disease and poor weather brought about widespread crop failure in 1739–1741 and about 500,000 people died. By the 1830s poor harvests were almost becoming the norm, which meant that even in good years a high proportion of the population would be on the edge of starvation, particularly during the early summer before the new crop was ready.

Catastrophe was triggered by the arrival in June 1845 from America of potato blight, a type of fungal disease which causes a rapid deterioration in healthy plants and spreads quickly given the right weather conditions. It can wipe out a whole crop and cause tubers to rot in storage. By August the disease had spread throughout Europe and for the next two years virtually no potatoes were on sale anywhere. The failure of the 1845 crop in Ireland was only partial but that of 1846 was almost total. The human consequences of that failure in Ireland were largely the result of the policies adopted by the British government and their determination not to interfere with the workings of the free market in food. The Corn Laws were repealed to allow the import of grain (partly because the English harvest had been bad). Although a large quantity of grain was imported, the problem was that the impoverished Irish peasantry had little money with which to buy wheat or maize and often no utensils to cook it. At the same time a large part of the Irish grain harvest was exported, often under armed guard. At the height of the famine in the summer of 1846 the government closed all public relief works, such as road building, in order to stop the people becoming dependent on government welfare. The only works that were allowed had to be paid for by the local districts which, because of the famine, had little revenue to fund such projects. The provision of relief food was left to private enterprise or voluntary efforts. Later in the year some works were reinstated but only for about 500,000 people – when even in a good year about two or three million would have been destitute. Government food stocks were only sold at market prices so as not to undercut private traders. Not until the winter of 1847 were soup kitchens provided, although in parallel all relief works were stopped as were any government imports of food. The consequence was that, overall, about one million people died either directly from lack of food or from the subsequent outbreak of diseases that affected the under-nourished population. Another million people emigrated during the famine period and immediately afterwards, often in wretched conditions. By the end of the nineteenth century a further three million had left Ireland and the population of the island was four-and-a-half million, almost half what it had been in the mid-1840s.

The Irish famine illustrates two important aspects of the problem of food supplies. First, that it was still possible even in a supposedly advanced area of the world such as Europe in the nineteenth century for a million people to starve to death. Second, that famine is not just a simple matter of food shortage. There was plenty of food in Ireland – those who died could not afford to buy it and the authorities were not prepared to give it to them. The question of who is entitled to obtain food (either through purchase or gift) has formed a central part of contemporary analysis of recent famines in the Third World. In cases such as the recent famines in Ethiopia, the Horn of Africa and the Sahel there is normally plenty of food in the country and exports also continue. What happens is that certain groups of people are unable to obtain food, either because their own crops have failed or because they cannot afford to buy food at the high prices which are a consequence of the famine. For example, in Bengal in 1943 (when about three million starved to death) people died despite well-stocked food shops that were protected from looting by the police and the army. In Russia in 1911–1912 there was a major famine affecting sixty regions in the country, but amidst widespread starvation and death a fifth of its vast grain production was exported to the west (about a quarter of the world's trade in grain). In the Soviet Union, in the early 1930s, peasants died because the government appropriated the harvest to feed the cities and to provide exports to fund imports required for the industrialisation drive. But this is not just a contemporary phenomenon – similar examples can be found throughout history.

In its deepest sense the problem of famine stems from the change of attitude towards food that goes back to the emergence of agriculture. Gathering and hunting groups do not regard food as something to be traded but as available to all within the group. The problem of entitlement arose once ownership of land and food became the norm when settled, agricultural societies emerged. The dependence of these societies on a limited range of crops increased the risk of failure and when this happened the poorest members of society found themselves unable to obtain food. The problem of access is evident in the earliest accounts of famine in ancient societies although in some cases, and the later great medieval famine of 1315–1317 is probably an example of this, there was an absolute shortage of food.

The problem of access to food emerges plainly throughout Europe once contemporary accounts are available. The frequent response of those suffering from an inability to buy food at prices they could afford was to turn on the merchants, who were accused of withholding supplies from the market or moving them out of the region to areas where they could be sold at even higher prices. Fearing social unrest governments often intervened to try and provide food, particularly in the important towns. Occasionally they tried to buy food or force merchants to sell it but the normal response to shortage from ancient Greece and Rome through medieval to early modern Europe was to try and fix prices. It was rarely successful and often counter-productive by ensuring that food was withheld from the market. The scale and frequency of outbreaks of popular discontent is illustrated by the series of riots in various towns across France at the turn of the fourteenth and fifteenth centuries; there were violent protests against merchants moving food out of the area in Bayonne (1488), Montauban and Moissac (1493), Paris (1500), Agen (1514) and Lyons (1517). For at least another three centuries these events were constantly repeated across France (and other parts of Europe). The fears and perceptions of the people about the supply of food and those they believed were withholding it from the market were a central factor in influencing the actions of the crowds during a number of crucial episodes during the French Revolution. The same reactions to food shortage were still apparent as late as the agricultural crisis that affected Europe in 1816–17. For example, in 1816 at Dumfries in Scotland, a crowd seized oatmeal at the docks when it was being exported and took it to the town where they forced it to be sold to the public at what they thought were reasonable prices. A year later in Toulouse crowds stopped the export of grain and forced its sale in the town.

An existence under the constant threat of starvation and in the face of the daily reality of an inadequate diet and malnutrition has been the common lot of most of humanity since the development of agriculture. Only slowly, in a few areas of the world, did some societies (principally Europe and its colonies in North America and Australasia) emerge from this long struggle to survive. They were able to do so as a result of a combination of developments which made much larger quantities of food available to them. Over the centuries a number of small-scale improvements slowly raised agricultural output and productivity. Once records are available it is possible to trace a slow improvement in

European output and efficiency in the six hundred years after 1200: by 1800 yields were about two-and-a-half times higher. This was the result of a wide variety of changes. The range of fodder crops was increased, legumes were more widely used to improve fertility, better breeding of animals and more cross-breeding enhanced output, rotations became more complex and manuring more widespread as more animals could be fed during the winter months. Just as important though was the introduction of new crops and animals, which widened the agricultural base, provided greater stability against failure and improved food output. Some of these changes were the result of the slow diffusion of animals within a limited area – particularly from southern Europe to the northern parts. For example the Romans introduced the chicken from the Mediterranean region to north-west Europe and the white grape to the Moselle valley. Rabbits were introduced into Britain from southern Europe as a domesticated animal in the twelfth century and only subsequently escaped into the wild. Pheasants and fallow deer were also introduced about this time although the latter did not become a wild animal until the 1920s. But the major changes in the distribution of plants and animals in the world took place in two phases – in the Islamic world from the seventh to the tenth century and following the first European contacts with the Americas after 1492.

There was no contact between the agricultural systems of Europe and the Americas until the sixteenth century AD. The various empires that

The Worldwide Diffusion of Crops and Animals

Chief Centres for the Diffusion of Major Crops and Animals			
South East Asia	Europe	Americas	Africa
Sugar Cane	Wheat	Maize	Hard Wheat
Rice	Barley	Tobacco	Sorghum
Orange	Oats	Potato	Coffee
Lemon	Sheep	Tomato	
Lime	Cattle	Manioc	
Spinach	Horse	Cocoa	
Aubergine	Pig	Rubber	
Banana	Bee	Pineapple	
	Rabbit	Avocado	
		Peppers	
		Squash	
		Pumpkin	
		Sisal	

dominated Mesopotamia had numerous contacts with western India (and often controlled parts of the area) but very little with states further to the east. Even at the time when both the Roman and Han empires were at their height there was only a small amount of contact between them (little of it direct) and they continued to develop in their own way.

The rapid rise of Islam after the death of Muhammad in 632 and the conquest of most of the Near East, North Africa, Spain, Armenia, Georgia, Afghanistan and north-west India by the early eighth century did not result in a long lasting unified empire, but it did produce a vast area of considerable cultural uniformity which extended its influence further into south-east Asia and along the east coast of Africa through trading links. The creation of the Islamic empire with its trading network brought about a substantial diffusion of crops from south-east Asia and India westwards to the Near East, the Mediterranean region and eventually parts of southern Europe. India was a major centre for the transmission, especially after the conquest of Sind in 711, and Oman was also an important area where the sub-tropical crops of south-east Asia were gradually acclimatised to new growing conditions. From these centres the new crops spread into North Africa, with some reaching as far west as Spain and others penetrating west Africa, and progressing along the trade routes of the east coast of Africa to reach Zanzibar and later Madagascar.

Some of the crops such as the coconut palm could only grow in sub-tropical climates and therefore did not spread beyond the Gulf area and East Africa but most were gradually acclimatised to new growing conditions over a wide area. The most important of these crops for the future history of world agriculture was sugar cane. It was brought from India to Mesopotamia in the seventh century and then it spread westwards to the Levant, Egypt and the islands of the eastern Mediterranean, especially Cyprus, by the tenth century. Because of the large amount of labour required on the plantations, slavery became the basis of sugar cane cultivation in the areas dominated by Europeans from Cyprus to the islands of the Atlantic and the Americas. Almost as important as sugar cane was the slow spread of hard wheat from Ethiopia to the Mediterranean, where it became a staple part of the diet in North Africa (cous-cous) and in Italy (pasta) after the thirteenth century. Rice also spread from the Near East to large areas of Africa and reached the Po valley in northern Italy by the late fifteenth century. Citrus trees, the sour orange, lemon and lime, were brought by Islamic traders from south-east Asia (though they originated in eastern India) to the Mediterranean, where their cultivation spread quickly, reaching Seville in southern Spain by the tenth century. Sorghum, which had originally spread from Africa to India about 2000 BC moved westwards to North Africa and Spain. Vegetables such as spinach and aubergines were brought from Persia and India to North Africa and eventually came to Spain by the eleventh century.

The new crops diffused through the Islamic world and beyond did not transform agriculture or provide more than a few mainly supplementary crops. A much more radical change took place after the Spanish conquered the Caribbean islands and the Aztec and Inca empires in the early sixteenth century. The Europeans who went to settle the Americas took with them their own crops and animals (wheat, sugar cane, cattle, sheep and horses). In the process they significantly altered the environment (a story that will be examined in detail in later chapters). But equally important were the consequences of bringing back previously unknown American crops, which influenced the agriculture of not just Europe but also the Near East, India, Africa and China. The two most important introductions from the 'New World' were the dietary staples of Mesoamerica and Peru – maize and potatoes. Maize was a highly productive crop (the yield was about twice that of wheat) but it took a long time to spread, particularly in Europe, even after the development of new varieties, possibly because of the poor climate in the area during the 'Little Ice Age'. The central point for the dispersal of maize was the Mediterranean area, where it could be grown without difficulty. It proved particularly well suited to conditions in Egypt, where it became a staple crop by the seventeenth century. In Europe it did not reach the Balkans until the eighteenth century and its movement further north had to await both an improvement in the climate and the development of types able to thrive in cooler conditions and a shorter growing season. Maize was not common in India until the early nineteenth century but then spread rapidly. China however adopted maize very early in the sixteenth century and it was soon a primary food crop in the upland areas of the south west of the country but did not reach the north for another three centuries. The great attraction of maize was its high yield enabling more people to be fed from the same amount of land. In China, particularly, this was important at a time when rice growing had begun to reach its natural limits. In the seventeenth century rice constituted about 70 per cent of the national food output, but this had fallen to less than 40 per cent by the early twentieth century as crops originally of American origin became more important. Maize also arrived in West Africa from Brazil in the sixteenth century and rapidly replaced millet and sorghum to become a central part of the diet because of its higher yields.

Adoption of the potato as a major crop was as long drawn-out a process as the spread of maize. It reached Spain by 1570, England and Germany by the end of the sixteenth century and Scandinavia about a hundred years later, and was introduced into North America from Europe in 1718. It seems that most people did not take readily to eating potatoes and originally they were grown as a fodder crop rather than for human consumption. Only in Ireland and parts of the Balkans did the potato become a staple food in Europe before the nineteenth century. Its chief advantage – the ability to provide a large amount of food from a small area – was widely recognised but the potato was normally only adopted after the failure of other crops. The other major crop of the Americas to be widely adopted was a tropical plant – manioc. In the early seventeenth century it was brought from Brazil to the mainland of Africa, where its very high yields combined with drought and pest resistance were rapidly appreciated. Once the problems associated with processing it into an edible food by removing the poisons were understood, it formed a vital part of the diet in the tropical areas, becoming particularly important in the nineteenth century. In this period farmers also adopted it in the southern parts of India. Apart from the major crops of maize, potato and manioc, the Americas also provided important supplementary crops. Particularly important was the tomato, adopted initially in the Mediterranean area (and also in India and the Near East) and later further north as varieties capable of growing in a cooler climate and shorter season were developed. (Europe now produces about 40 per cent of the world's tomato crop.) A wide variety of beans (an important source of protein) were rapidly adopted as were flavourings and spices such as chillies, to such an extent that they are now seen as integral parts of the 'local' cuisine of many areas of the world and especially India.

One major beneficial effect of the spread of new crops was that the subsistence base of many societies, which was often narrow and therefore highly vulnerable, became wider and this reduced the risk of catastrophic crop failure and famine. Another important gain was nutritional. Not only was more variety available in the poor and very limited diets of the majority of people but many of the foods, particularly plants such as tomatoes and chillies, were rich in vitamins and could help to reduce the risk of some deficiency diseases. However in some areas over-reliance on maize (especially without adopting the American way of preparing and cooking it) produced the deficiency

disease-pellagra. Despite improvements in reliability, quality and variety associated with the introduction of new crops the basic problem
remained that of quantity. Some of the more productive crops,
especially maize and potatoes, improved food output but in nearly
every society these new crops did not solve the age-old problem of
keeping a balance between human numbers and the amount of food that
could be produced. In many cases the new higher yielding crops, rather
than providing more calories per head, had the effect of allowing the
population to grow more quickly until it reached a point at which it was
out of balance with food supplies, as happened among the potato
growing peasantry of Ireland before the disaster of the famine.

Only slowly, and in the relatively recent past, did a few societies
begin to escape from a situation where a large part of the population
lived on a poor diet barely adequate for minimum subsistence and
under the constant threat of starvation. The first to move along this
path was the Netherlands in the sixteenth and seventeenth centuries.
Here the population doubled from around one million in 1500 to two
million in 1650, which required a major adjustment in the agricultural
system. Food output was increased as new land was brought into
cultivation (some of it was completely new land created from drained
marshes or reclaimed from the sea) and more intensive farming systems
were introduced (using clover, legumes and fodder crops together with
increased amounts of manure from the extra animals that could be
kept). In this period Dutch agriculture was certainly the most productive in Europe with yields about two-thirds higher than in England.
However, much of the extra food required by the rising population was
imported from the semi-colonial grain growing areas around the Baltic
through the Dutch domination of the trade of the area. Without this
additional source of food it is doubtful whether the larger numbers
could have been fed.

England gradually adopted many of the improved agricultural
methods developed in the Netherlands so that by the middle of the
eighteenth century, output was rising faster than population growth.
But the gain proved only temporary as the country experienced an
unprecedented high growth in population between about 1780 and the
end of the nineteenth century, and again population threatened to
outstrip the capacity of even the improved English agricultural system.
Growth averaged about 1 per cent a year and the population of England
and Wales rose from 7½ million in 1780 to 14 million in 1831 and 32½
million in 1901. The response of English agriculture to this rise was
much the same as in the past – new land was brought into cultivation

(about a 50 per cent rise between 1700 and 1850), fallow land was reduced (equivalent to a further 40 per cent increase) and lower quality food was grown (the area under potatoes increased three-and-a-half fold in the first half of the nineteenth century). Agricultural productivity rose, partly through the further spread of some of the new ideas introduced in the eighteenth century but also through the introduction of more machinery, new fertilizers and new feeds such as oilcake (which was becoming common in the 1820s). Another bonus (a side effect of the large amount of cheap labour available in the countryside) was achieved by more weeding.

The rural population rose rapidly in this period (almost doubling) producing immense social pressure through rising rents and prices. Poverty was on the increase, especially in the east and south of the country where new machinery was introduced, and the number dependent on the potato rose to about two million. It was only the drift of a large part of the rural population into the new industrial towns in search of employment that avoided a major rural crisis in early nine-teenth century. Even so, by the 1840s, only minor improvements in subsistence levels had been achieved for most of the population. This period, marked by the triumph of the industrial over the agricultural interest with the repeal of the Corn Laws in 1846, saw the swing towards importing food. In the 1840s about 5 per cent of Britain's food was imported. By the end of the century the situation had been transformed: 80 per cent of the grain for human consumption, 40 per cent of the meat and 72 per cent of dairy products were imported. It was only this use of other countries to supply the food that Britain needed that was to provide a solution to the perennial problem of feeding a rapidly rising population and improving the amount of food available per head.

The experience of Europe in the early nineteenth century demon-strates that the process of escaping from the problems of the past was slow and sporadic. Rural problems were particularly acute in the period between 1815 and about 1850 and population growth had reached the maximum that could be sustained, with a rapidly increasing subdivi-sion of landholdings, rising rents and prices and therefore falling real wages together with the adoption of inferior foods such as the potato. In the early nineteenth century the response of the agricultural system was much the same too – an increase in the cultivated area even though this meant using more marginal land and reducing the amount of fallow land. Agricultural techniques had been improving fairly steadily for centuries but in this period these measures were only just sufficient to maintain food output per head. Some of the pressure was relieved by the steadily improving climate after 1850 and, in the case of England, through movement into the new industrial towns, whereas in other countries, such as Ireland and Norway, emigration to the United States or elsewhere was the only solution.

The real revolution in the European food situation came after about 1850 with large-scale importation of food from the rest of the world and the use of imported resources such as guano from South America and other fertilizers from colonial territories to improve domestic productivity. This solution was not possible for other societies such as China that lacked colonial territories to exploit and they, therefore, continued to suffer the traditional problems of malnutrition and starvation stemming from population pressure. One of the main reasons for Europe's success in breaking free from the long struggle to survive that had dominated the experience of nearly every society since the development of agriculture lay in its changing relationship with the rest of the world and, in particular, its ability to control an increasing share of the world's resources.

7
THE SPREAD OF EUROPEAN SETTLEMENT

The history of the spread of European settlement falls into two phases – internal expansion followed by external colonisation – which can be seen as part of a single process driven by the same sort of pressures. The combined impact of these two movements has in effect formed the modern world. They transformed Europe from being one of the more backward societies in the world, which was the case until at least the fifteenth century, into the most advanced, able and willing not merely to influence the pace and nature of development elsewhere, but also, though a variety of means, to impose radical changes on the rest of the world. These changes involved the way people thought about the world around them, the use of natural resources and the exploitation of much of the rest of the world for the benefit of Europeans. The effects are still being experienced worldwide. But the most striking and immediate effect of the spread of European settlement beyond the boundaries of Europe itself was its lethal impact on indigenous peoples and societies. The sequence of events set in train by the arrival of the Europeans, despite differences in the native cultures and the country of origin of the settlers, reveals a consistent pattern. If events are interpreted in terms of the spreading of European culture, the opening up of new territories and the building of global empires, then it may be seen as a story of success. If the focus is on what happened to the people, the land and the environment generally, then it is an altogether different story.

For most of history, Europe, apart from the Mediterranean area, was a backwater. The earliest gathering and hunting groups only settled the area intermittently and at the height of the last ice age, when the people living in south-west France were producing their great cave paintings, the local population was probably no more than 10,000, with perhaps 100,000 in the whole of Europe, about five per cent of the world's population. The development of agriculture took place outside Europe and only spread there thousands of years later. The first settled societies

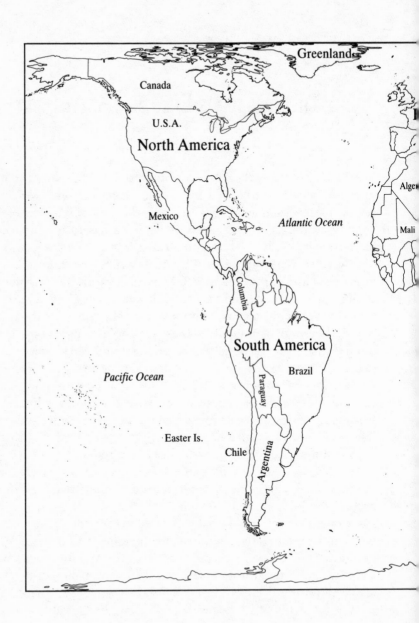

emerged in Mesopotamia and Egypt and it was only at a much later stage that complex, hierarchical societies emerged in Europe. Even then they remained concentrated around the Mediterranean – Minoan Crete, Mycenae, the city states of Greece and their colonies, the empires of Alexander and his successors, the Etruscans and the Carthaginians. Only with the rise of Rome did these more advanced societies begin to control northern and western Europe, away from the Mediterranean. Even with the development of agriculture the population of this peripheral area remained small – perhaps three million people in France, about half that number in Germany and only a few hundred thousand in Britain. At the height of the Roman empire, around 200 AD, the total population of Europe was about 28 million (compared with almost twice that figure in both China and India) but a quarter of that total lived in Italy, which was then still the centre of the empire.

The collapse of the Roman empire in the west and the loss of control over north and west Europe to Germanic invaders meant a continuation of the Mediterranean area (especially the eastern part) as the core of the late empire and the successor Byzantine state. The rise of Islam and the establishment of the Omayyad empire (stretching from western India to southern Spain) as the most sophisticated and advanced society in the western world reinforced this trend. Northern and western Europe remained a backward region of thinly spread peasant farmers living in tribal groups and forming part of small, primitive kingdoms. The empire of Charlemagne (at its height around 800) was short-lived and western Europe was again overrun by new waves of settlers and raiders – the Vikings and Hungarians. Only in a few places – the Ile-de-France, England, Flanders and the western parts of Germany – did more effective political entities slowly begin to emerge in the tenth and eleventh centuries.

Early medieval Europe was still a vast wilderness with a scattering of small, largely self-sufficient villages which had only very limited outside contacts. At most there were about 36 million people in the year 1000, perhaps 5 million of them in France and 4 million in Germany. England had about 1½ million people (equivalent to one large city today); its most densely inhabited county (Norfolk) had a population of about 100,000 while others such as Kent, Hampshire, Sussex and Wiltshire had 40,000 (the equivalent of a modern country town) and the western and northern parts of the country were even more thinly populated. It was in the three hundred years after 1000 that a huge extension of the settled area and a transformation of the European landscape took place. The driving force behind this expansion was a very rapid rise in population from the 36 million of 1000 to over 45 million in 1100, over 60 million in 1200, and about 80 million in 1300. This doubling in the population meant that a huge amount of new agricultural land was required in order to produce enough food. The problem of growing more food and bringing new areas into cultivation was eased in this period by the relatively warm climate that occurred between the ninth century and about 1200.

The natural ecosystem of most of northern and western Europe is temperate forest, with oak predominant and elm, beech and lime the other main trees. The spread of agriculture in the three millennia after 5000 BC saw the first clearing of the natural forests. In its early stages agriculture in Europe was based on a swidden system: people would make clearings and cultivate the ground for a few years and then allow it to revert to secondary growth and forest once the initial fertility had declined. Only as population slowly increased were permanent fields established. The swidden system survived in the less densely settled parts of Europe until comparatively recent times. As late as the eighteenth century many parts of Sweden and Finland were still farming by cutting down trees (although the stumps were left in the fields to save labour), growing crops for four to six years and then allowing the land to revert to scrub and eventually woodland. In this way the same ground only came into use about four times every century. But even in areas where permanent fields were established the overall population was still low and therefore the amount of forest clearance was limited and remained so until about the end of the tenth century. The process took place through clearing waste and woodland around existing villages to create new fields and through the establishment of new settlements, often no more than individual cottages or hamlets at first, within wooded areas. It was an insidious process, happening over many centuries, but its ultimate impact on the environment was considerable. Forests originally covered about 95 per cent of western and central Europe. By the end of the great period of medieval colonisation this had been reduced to about 20 per cent.

The timing of the clearance varied from area to area. Some of the earliest instances were in places such as Burgundy that were relatively remote from the ninth and tenth century invasions and began the process of population growth earlier than elsewhere. In Brabant the forest areas were settled by the Franks in the sixth and seventh centuries and later became centres of charcoal production – here as early as about 800 large parts of the great climax forests were being destroyed. Other regions, especially the core areas of the newly developing kingdoms, were also cleared at an early stage. The forest clearance of the Ile-de-France was largely completed by about 1080 and much of south-east England had been cleared by 1086 when the Domesday Book was compiled for the new Norman rulers. Other areas, too, such as Cambridgeshire had also been largely deforested. But the extent of this early clearance was far from total. The Weald and the Chilterns in the south east were still almost entirely woodland and some of the villages recorded in Domesday Book had enough woods around them to support the foraging of as many as 2,000 pigs. In the eleventh and twelfth centuries the main movement of settlement in Europe was into the lowland forests, aided by the ability of the new heavy plough to cultivate the heavier soils. In areas remote from the main centres of population newly founded monasteries, particularly Cistercian, carried out extensive clearance but in most places it was the slow creation of new fields around old villages and the making of new settlements in the woodland that created the new landscape. By about 1200 most of the best soils of western Europe had been cleared of forest and new settlements were increasingly forced into the more marginal areas of heavy clays or thin sandy soils on the higher ground and the heathlands. In France this movement involved the Argonne region, the higher lands of Lorraine (especially around the Moselle), the Vosges, central Beauce and the poor soils of upland Brittany. In England the chalk downs, which had been sparsely populated in 1086, were well settled by the middle of the thirteenth century.

In eastern Europe the major colonisation movement was that of the Germanic peoples eastwards into the lands occupied by the Slavs. It lasted from the tenth century until about 1300 and changed the ethnic map of Europe by producing not a clear frontier line but a complex mixture of peoples that has bedevilled the history of the area ever since. In the main, it was a movement of farmers clearing woodland and using the heavy plough into an area where the Slavs still practised swidden agriculture, with the emphasis on stock-rearing in conjunction with hunting and fishing. The first stages of the movement began between 919–932 when the Germans settled the area between the Elbe and the Saale rivers. It was then held up by the Hungarian invasions, although Vienna was founded in 1018. The major thrust eastwards did not start in earnest until the mid-twelfth century when Holstein, Mecklenburg and Brandenburg were settled. Once political control had been achieved through war the settlers moved in. They were organised by agents acting for the various princes or bishops who controlled the area.

The agents would divide up the land, provide the equipment for the settlers and develop villages and towns, often to standardised designs. The agents were paid by grants of land from the bishops and princes. Only in the south with the movement along the Danube were some of the settlements developed around mines rather than for agriculture. The movement eastwards continued into Livonia and Courland (1186), Riga (1201), East Prussia (1231) and by 1240 had advanced as far as the Oder river and Silesia and further south into the Erzgebirge and Sudeten mountains. Only in the late thirteenth century, by which time many of the best lands were occupied, did the thrust of the movement weaken. Throughout the area forests had been cleared and turned into fields as part of a sustained and deliberate policy of development. The attitude of the new arrivals was expressed by the abbot of Fellarich, one of the new German settlements, when he said: 'I believe that the forest which adjoins Fellarich covers the land to no purpose, and hold this to be an unbearable harm.' The newly settled area, particularly those parts with easy access along the rivers to the Baltic ports, were soon turned into a major grain producing region exporting to western Europe.

The great medieval internal colonisation of Europe came to a halt nearly everywhere around 1300. Population was at a peak and probably too high for the agricultural system to sustain in the long term. The climate was also deteriorating. Settlements in the thirteenth century had been increasingly pushed into marginal areas where the yields were lower, which worsened the imbalance between population and food supply. The decline in European population that began, at the latest, in the first years of the fourteenth century halted further colonisation. Indeed the catastrophic loss of population in the Black Death (in places as high as a third) and the periodic recurrences of the plague that continued for the rest of the fourteenth century produced a marked reduction in the settled area: many villages were abandoned and never subsequently reoccupied. In Spain the *reconquista*, which had been at its height in the twelfth century, as new villages of Christian peasants were established behind the military frontier as the Kingdoms of Castille, Aragon and Portugal moved south into the old Arab ter-ritories, came to a halt. It was not completed until the end of the fifteenth century.

A similar, but later, advance of settlement can be traced in Russia after the recovery of the Russian state from the Mongol invasions and its steady expansion from the fifteenth century onwards. As in western Europe there was a process of forest clearance as population rose and more land was needed for cultivation. There were periods of stagnation or even retreat as numbers stopped rising, or even fell, but, in general, the process was inexorable. At times it could have a dramatic and highly visible impact on the immediate environment of a district within the space of a few years. For example in one district along the Volga the area of cleared ploughland rose five-fold in the ten years between 1613 and 1622. By the late eighteenth century about three-quarters of the great forest steppe in the north had been cleared of trees and ploughed. In the south, which was settled later, the clearance also came slightly later – it was about one third complete by 1800 but over 80 per cent of the land had lost its forest cover a hundred years later.

Apart from the loss of its natural forests the European landscape has also been transformed by the draining of marshes and fens and the reclaiming of land from the sea. Some of the first drainage projects were undertaken by the Romans, both in Italy and in the provinces. For example in Britain they drained part of the Fens along with Otmoor near Oxford but many of the settlements in both areas were abandoned following the end of Roman rule. Resettlement of the Fen area began in the Anglo-Saxon period and the Domesday Book shows that by the end of the eleventh century there were about fifty villages on the higher land away from the coast, protected by a specially constructed seabank and an inland bank, both about fifty miles long. New Romney, the first settlement in the Romney Marshes on the south-east coast, is dated to 1000 but here the process of drainage seems to have gone ahead in slow stages. The same is true of later developments in the Fens. Here as the population continued to grow the number of settlements and the extent of the reclaimed area also expanded, particularly in the period from 1150 to 1300. The so-called 'Roman Bank', running for about sixty miles around the Wash, was constructed in this period but nearly all the reclaimed land and new settlements came not from some overall scheme but from the gradual and piecemeal work of the village communities, secular landowners and great abbeys of the area. By the fourteenth century this was one of the most prosperous areas of England: the reclaimed land provided high quality pasture for animals, peat for fuel (digging for peat formed the network of waterways known as the Norfolk Broads), and reeds for thatching houses. Other areas in Europe saw similar large-scale reclamation projects. In France the Poitevin marshes were drained after 1100 and those around Arles about fifty years later. In the Po valley work went on from the early twelfth century, when the monks of Chiaravalle abbey began a series of water control projects, to the fifteenth century. The outcome was a huge area of new land, 97 per cent of which was owned by large landlords (who financed much of the work) and where the labourers, employed part-time in the new rice fields, lived in conditions of extreme poverty even by the standards of the time.

A more extensive, difficult and long-lasting struggle to create new land took place in the Netherlands. Until the sixteenth century nearly all the effort went into reclaiming land from the sea, especially around the great river estuaries. Once the sea had been excluded from the area the land provided excellent, fertile, flat and stone-free soil. The process, which was started in Flanders and Zeeland around 900 and in Holland about three hundred years later, was a response to the steadily rising population and the requirement for more agricultural land. Hundreds of small islands in the river estuaries and just offshore were slowly made into larger units, not by working steadily outwards from the shoreline, but by extending existing islands and forming new ones in an unplanned process that created a new landscape. As new land was being formed, existing areas were being lost as the sea encroached. Indeed some of the reclamation began as a secondary consequence of building sea defence walls to protect existing low-lying land at a time when sea levels in the area were rising. Between 1250 and 1480 the modern Zuider Zee was created by flooding but the most catastrophic loss of land occurred in 1421. The 'Elizabethvloed' on 19 November, which killed ten of thousands of people, led to the permanent loss of over 40,000 acres of land and created the Biebosch marsh out of previously fertile polderland. In 1507 a large amount of fertile land at the mouth of the Ems also had to be abandoned.

During the sixteenth century the Dutch shifted attention from the coastline to inland and began the long process of internal drainage in the Netherlands which has continued to the present day. This was a technically more complex process than reclaiming land from the sea. It required large amounts of capital (provided by private consortia who owned the new land) to build windmills to carry out the considerable amount of pumping needed to lower the water table – the draining of Lake Beemster in 1612 used forty-three windmills to drain the thirteen feet deep, twenty-five square mile expanse of water and it produced 17,000 acres of fertile land. The peak of activity in the Netherlands was between 1615 and 1640 and overall a total of nearly 400,000 acres was reclaimed in the hundred years after 1550. Some of the major schemes took centuries to complete – for instance the draining of the Haarlemmermeer, begun in the seventeenth century, was not finished until 1852. In the twentieth century even larger projects have been undertaken by the state, including extensive works in the Wadden Sea and turning the Zuider Zee into an inland lake (the Ijsselmeer) in 1932 followed by steady reclamation of large sections. As a result of this sustained effort of modifying and controlling the environment about two million acres of land has been created in the Netherlands since the thirteenth century with the result that forty per cent of the country is now below sea level.

The sophisticated techniques developed by the Dutch in the sixteenth century were also applied in other countries, in particular England. In the Fens, in the early seventeenth century, large landowners were given extensive powers to reclaim land, override the rights of other, smaller landowners and suppress comon rights. The inhabitants were made responsible for the upkeep of the new works whilst the speculators took the profits. The result was large-scale development, mainly supervised by a Dutch engineer, Vermuyden. New canals were dug and the Great Ouse diverted for twenty-one miles (the longest artificial watercourse built since Roman times). The outcome of much of this effort was an ecological disaster. No allowance was made for the shrinkage of the peat once the water was removed. The consequence was that the ground level fell and the rivers were left above ground level. Around the Wash the coastline was also extended by about three miles, between 1620 and 1770, and major areas such as Canvey Island reclaimed. Other large scale schemes undertaken by Vermuyden, such as those along the Yorkshire and Lincolnshire border, failed and had to be abandoned. Elsewhere in Europe other schemes reclaimed the area around Narbonne and the Rhone estuary in southern France in the mid-sixteenth century. But many were unsuccessful – the Duke of Tuscany failed to drain the Maremma and in a large area of the Adige valley the amount of marsh actually extended after a botched attempt at drainage. Other large-scale drainage schemes had to wait until the twentieth century to be carried out successfully. They included the marshes in the plain of Salonica, the Ebro delta and Pontine marshes, all of which were drained in the 1920s.

Despite the rise in population and the large extension of the settled area, Europe in the thirteenth and fourteenth centuries remained a backward region, on the margins of the main developments of world history. China was the most populous and advanced country in the world and the Islamic states of the Mediterranean and Near East, about to be revived under the Ottoman empire, were culturally far in advance of a relatively impoverished Europe. The crusades were a short-lived enterprise and Christian control of parts of the Levant, in most places maintained for no more than a few decades, passed almost without disturbing the Islamic world. In 1241 the Mongols reached the river Oder and western Europe only avoided invasion after the Mongol victory at the battle of Wahlstatt because of the death of the Mongol leader Ogodai and the resulting internal confusion within the empire. Nevertheless a few decades later the Mongols ruled the most extensive empire the world had ever seen stretching from the Volga in the west to China in the east and taking in large parts of south-west Asia. The rise of the Ottoman Turks in the fourteenth century destroyed most of the last remnants of the Byzantine empire (which had already been undermined by the conquest of Constantinople by the western Christians during the Fourth Crusade in 1204), although Constantinople itself survived until 1453. But the Turks pushed further westwards and defeated the Christians at the battle of Nicopolis in 1396 to extend their control over most of the Balkans and later conquered Cyprus and other islands in the eastern Mediterranean. At the same time the Chinese were also exploring further westwards – the eunuch admiral Cheng Ho led seven armadas of sixty-two vessels and 37,000 soldiers, between 1405 and 1430, to twenty countries as far apart as Kamchatka in the north and Zanzibar off the east coast of Africa. If it had not been for the death of the Emperor and the subsequent faction fighting at court that brought about a new policy of shunning external contacts, the Chinese might well have gone on to 'discover' much of the world before Europe did so.

The remarkable transformation in the fortunes of Europe that was to lead not just to a reshaping of the political map of the world but to extensive control over the world's resources began in the fifteenth century. The great advantage for the countries of western Europe was that exploration westwards encountered no strongly organised states like those in the Mediterranean and further east which were able to challenge European power. Spain and Portugal, the first nations to explore the eastern Atlantic and launch the long period of European expansion overseas, established control over the Atlantic islands (the Canaries and the Azores) in the fifteenth century and the Portuguese continued their voyages down the west coast of Africa. Once they had rounded the Cape in 1488 they were able to make use of the already well-established trade routes of the Indian ocean to obtain goods for sale in Europe. The Portuguese, with a population of only about one-and-a-half million, had little military power and were not able to challenge seriously the existing states of India and south-east Asia. They were, however, able to capture a few key trading sites – Goa (1510), Malacca (1511) and Hormuz (1515) – their main aim being not conquest of territory but trade and exploitation of the wealth of the area. The Spanish, moving westwards into the Caribbean after Columbus's voyage in 1492, encountered only relatively primitive tribes on the various islands. When they reached the mainland they found more advanced states in the Aztec and Inca empires but, because of the slow development of complex societies in the Americas, technologically these indigenous empires were still at least three thousand years behind the Europeans. Conquest, also taking advantage of internal dissension within the empires, was therefore a relatively easy task even for the small number of Spaniards involved. The Portuguese found people at a level equivalent to those of the Caribbean islanders in Brazil after 1500 and soon established settlements along the coast.

The first phase of European expansion, from 1500 to about 1700, was largely confined to the Spanish and Portuguese conquests of central and south America, the settlement of north America, principally by the British and French, and the extension of trade along the African coast and into the Indian ocean and south-east Asia. The second phase, lasting from about 1750 to 1850, saw the British defeat the French for control over the Indian sub-continent, growing trade between Europe and China and the settlement of Australia and New Zealand. In the last phase after 1850 attention was concentrated on carving up Africa and in 1919, after the defeat of the Ottoman empire in the First World War, France and Britain established control over most of the Near East. The last European war of conquest came in 1935 when Italy defeated the long-lived empire of Ethiopia. Throughout this period there was a wave of European settlement spreading across the globe. The settlers of North America pushed westwards to the Pacific, the new colonies of Australia and New Zealand were founded and the colonial settlements along the coasts of South America pushed further inland. In parallel with these developments came the great expansion of Russia moving out from its narrow enclave in the north centered around Moscow. In 1552 and 1554 the Khanates of Kazan and Astrakhan on the Volga were conquered, opening up the regions to the south and east of Moscow to settlement. For the next three centuries Russians from the north and Ukrainians from the west moved into this wooded steppe area and by the early eighteenth century a quarter of the Russian population was living in the region. At the end of the eighteenth century the defeat of the Turks opened up the grass steppes around the Black Sea to settlement. In the first half of the nineteenth century about fifty million acres of new land were brought into cultivation by farmers in the Ukraine and Volga areas. But the Russians were also moving eastwards. In 1581 they crossed the Urals and parties of traders and developers rapidly moved across Siberia, covering over 3,000 miles in sixty years, founding Tomsk in 1604 and reaching the Pacific coast at Okhotsk in 1649. By 1707 Kamchatka was conquered and thirty years later settlements in Alaska were established. This process was nominally under state control but in practice, especially outside the towns, Russia was as much a frontier society as the United States.

Although the Spanish easily conquered the societies of the Caribbean together with the Aztec and Inca empires, the extension of European settlement was a slow process. In Africa new settlements were largely confined to coastal trading posts until well into the nineteenth century. In China influence was restricted to a few trading stations until the middle of the nineteenth century. Even in North America, European settlement was almost entirely in an area to the east of the Appalachians until about 1800. By that date only a small number of Europeans had settled abroad. The white population of North America was about 5 million, that of South America some 500,000 and Australia 10,000 (New Zealand had still not been settled). Few of these were free settlers. About two-thirds of the whites who went to America before the Revolution were indentured servants forced to work for their masters for a period of years before being granted their freedom – if they lived long enough, and most did not. Until the 1830s the majority of emigrants to Australia were convicts and only New Zealand was entirely settled by free people. The great wave of European emigration did not begin until the 1820s when the combined pressures of rapidly rising population in Europe, poor food supplies and a low standard of living (plus better transport) all encouraged emigration. Between 1820 and 1930 about fifty million people emigrated from Europe. Apart from the White Highlands of Kenya, and Costa Rica, few settled in the tropics; most went to the United States and the white colonies of Canada, Australia and New Zealand together with South America. The same upsurge can be seen in the movement of people from Russia to the sparsely populated and difficult lands of Siberia. In the early eighteenth century the total population of Siberia was about 250,000 (although European settlers already outnumbered the natives). A hundred years later there were 1½ million people living there, and the figure was 9 million by 1914. It is now over 30 million.

The expansion of Europe resulted in a complex clash of cultures. The long-established, advanced and culturally secure societies such as India and China survived best, although they eventually succumbed in differing degrees to European political, military and economic power. (Only Japan was able to maintain its independence politically and economically.) The people who suffered the most were the less developed societies, in particular the population of the Aztec and Inca empires, and the native peoples around the globe who were still gatherers and hunters or primitive agriculturalists. Many indigenous societies disintegrated under European pressure when they were not deliberately destroyed. The stark truth is that the native peoples lost their land, livelihood, independence, culture, health and in most cases their lives. Despite differences in approach the common themes running strongly through European attitudes to the process were a disregard for the native way of life and an overwhelming urge to exploit both the land and the people. In every continent people such as the native Indians of North and South America, the Aborigines of Australia and the islanders of the Pacific found that their societies collapsed under European influence. The story of the natives under the impact of Europe is one of soaring death rates brought about by disease, alcohol, and exploitation together with social disruption and the decline of native cultures, especially under the influence of the missionaries. The Europeans showed little or no interest in native beliefs or customs until anthropologists in the last hundred years tried to investigate the remains of the shattered societies.

Just how rapidly the vulnerable native societies in the Americas could collapse is demonstrated by events on Santo Domingo, one of the first islands to be discovered by Columbus. At the time of the Spanish conquest the population was about one million yet within forty years, after intense exploitation, slavery and many deaths through European diseases, there were only a few hundred natives left. The same happened on an even larger scale in Mexico after the Spanish conquest of the Aztecs in 1519. There the population fell from about 25 million in the early sixteenth century to some 6 million by 1550 and to 1 million about 1600. The complex culture which had evolved over thousands of years could not withstand such catastrophic losses. The people were unable to come to terms with this disaster and their way of life and beliefs disintegrated. Many of the surviving natives were enslaved even though native slavery was technically illegal in the Spanish empire after 1542. In the first half of the sixteenth century over 200,000 Indians were taken from Nicaragua alone as slaves. Slavery continued on the borders of the Spanish empire for centuries – the Araucanians in southern Chile were used as slaves until the 1680s and the Apache, Navaho and Shoshoni in the north until the nineteenth century. After the conquest of the Incas in Peru in the 1530s the native population fell to about a quarter of its pre-conquest level under the pressure of the forced extraction of food, slaughter of the flocks of llamas, new European diseases and labour exploitation by both the Spanish civil and religious powers. The natives were forced into two highly dangerous occupations. The first – cultivation of the coca plant took place in the lowlands where the natives from the Andes found it very difficult to live. About half of the workers died during their spell at the plantations, most from 'mal de los Andes', a wart-like disease spread by an insect, that destroyed the nose, lips and throat. The second area where the Spaniards exploited native labour was in the silver mine at Potosi, 12,000 feet up in the Andes. It was discovered in 1545 and forced labour was introduced in 1550, after the Spanish found that African slaves could not live at this height. By the early seventeenth century about 60,000 Indian labourers were employed at any one time in wretched conditions. They were forced to stay underground for a week at a stretch without coming up to the surface. Not surprisingly such treatment, together with the miserly rations they received and the use of highly toxic mercury in processing the metals, produced a very high death rate. In both Mexico and Peru the indigenous culture was destroyed, much of it simply to secure loot. Nearly all the great treasures of the Aztec and Inca states were melted down and shipped to Europe. Altogether between 1500 and 1650 Spain imported about 450,000 pounds weight of gold and thirty-five million pounds weight of silver from the Americas.

Like the Spaniards, most of the Portuguese regarded the Indians as inferior beasts to be exploited as much as possible. The missionaries wanted their souls (but also their bodies for work) and others just wanted their land and labour. Even when the number of European settlers had increased significantly and the number of Indians was reduced, the disregard of the natives' rights and welfare continued. The first settlers did not plan to work themselves and expected the Indians to do it for them. The Indian attitude, like so many gathering and hunting groups, was that they had no need to work because they already had the goods that they needed. The Portuguese rapidly captured and enslaved as many Indians as they could and when the supply proved to be inadequate moved in people from Africa as slaves. As one early commentator on the Portuguese immigrants in the mid-sixteenth century wrote:

'The first thing they try to obtain is slaves to work the farms. Anyone who succeeds in obtaining two pairs or half a dozen of them has the means to sustain his family in a respectable way, even though he may have no other earthly possessions. For one fishes for him, another hunts and the rest cultivate and till his fields.'

By 1610 in the province of Bahia there were 2,000 white settlers, 4,000 black slaves and 7,000 Indian slaves on the large-scale sugar plantations that were already well established. In 1600 when almost all the eastern seaboard of Brazil was under Portuguese control there were about 50,000 white immigrants but 100,000 slaves. Many of the coastal Indians died of disease or migrated to the interior so that by the 1630s when the Dutch captured north-east Brazil they found a largely deserted land – along 800 miles of coast where a century earlier there had been hundreds of thousands of Indians there were a mere 9,000 left.

As the Indians moved inland to avoid the white settlement, large slaving expeditions were set up to find the slaves the whites still wanted. There was a long tussle between the Jesuits, who set up 'missions' that were effectively sugar and cattle plantations where the Indians were forcibly converted, and the settlers over who should have control of the remaining Indians. The Jesuits organised some of these slaving expeditions (the rebuilding of the cathedral of Sao Luis in 1718 was financed by one of them), branded the natives on capture and forced them to work on their missions. In the seventeenth century white settlement was moving away from the coast into the dry *sertao* inhabited by the Tapuia Indians who were forcibly removed as large cattle ranches were set up. In the 1690s the discovery of gold in north-east Brazil brought on a gold rush in which the local Indians were enslaved and exploited by the prospectors. Even though slavery was abolished at the end of the nineteenth century in Brazil, the exploitation and destruction of the natives continued. Numbers fell rapidly – about half the tribes still in existence in 1900 are now extinct and the Indian population, which probably numbered about two-and-a-half million in 1500 before the arrival of the Portuguese, is now less than 200,000 and still declining. Since independence the Brazilian government has made only token gestures towards protecting the Indians. In 1967 the official government agency for protecting the Indians (SPI) had to be disbanded after an investigation showed that it had carried out deliberate genocide by introducing disease amongst the Indians and joined with speculators in large-scale robbery and murder. It was described by the Brazilian Attorney-General as 'a den of corruption and indiscriminate killings'.

Its successor FUNAI has done little to protect the Indians. The attitude of the Brazilian government is best summed up by an official spokesman who said:

'When we are certain that every corner of the Amazon is inhabited by genuine Brazilians and not by the Indians, only then will we be able to say that the Amazon is ours.'

The Indians of North America suffered as much as those further south. In 1500 the native population of the current area of the United States was about one million, with a wide variety of cultures and ways of life. Within four hundred years these had virtually been wiped out. The Indians were able to adapt to some of the things that the Europeans brought with them such as horses and metal tools. The plains Indians abandoned agriculture, domesticated the horse and used it to hunt buffalo. Others such as the Iroquois used European weapons to establish a large empire, covering present day New York, Pennsylvania and the upper Ohio valley. Many of the first European settlements such as Jamestown actually depended on the Indians for their very survival in their early stages but once they were firmly established the latent hostility of the settlers soon surfaced. Within a few years of the first settlements in New England, the Puritans, who believed God was on their side in killing the heathen Indians, were at war with the local tribes. Already in the seventeenth century the first 'reservations' were established to remove the Indians from land the Europeans wanted and all along the eastern seaboard Indian numbers were in decline. Of the early settlers only the Quakers in Pennsylvania treated the Indians with any degree of decency and humanity.

From very early in the European settlement of North America a pattern in the treatment of the Indians emerged. The first contacts were usually with European fur traders, who encouraged the Indians to trap animals and trade them for a variety of European goods. This phase of relative prosperity rarely lasted long and the Indians soon came under pressure from the advancing frontier of European settlement. In many cases the Europeans at first bought land from the Indians but, sooner rather than later, war broke out, which, even if they had a few initial successes, the Indians eventually lost and they were then forced to cede large amounts of land. Once they were in decline the Indians would be forced to give up more and more land until they were no longer able to support themselves on what remained of their ancestral territory. Then they migrated westwards (putting more pressure on other tribes) or were forced onto reservations where the poor land, combined with disease, alcohol and massive cultural disruption, led to very high death rates and often extinction of the tribe. For the first two hundred years of European settlement this encroachment was largely confined to the area east of the Appalachians. From the early nineteenth century the Indians had to face the full weight of American expansion. Although land sales were enforced (at nominal prices) this method proved inadequate in clearing the amount of land the whites wanted. In the southern United States, as the pressure to extend cotton cultivation increased, the Cherokees, who had adopted a settled and reasonably prosperous way of life with schools and even their own newspaper, remained a major obstacle to white exploitation of their land. A forced removal bill was passed through Congress; the Cherokees were paid half a million dollars in compensation and a total of 90,000 Indians were forced westwards by the army. About 30,000 died as a result of conditions on the march. The process continued with other tribes and in other parts of the country. For example, between 1829 and 1866, the Winnebagos were forcibly moved westwards six times and the population fell by a half. By 1844 there were less than 30,000 Indians in the whole of the eastern United States, most of them living in a remote area around Lake Superior.

In a series of brutal wars in the 1860s and 1870s the Indians on the Great Plains were brought under control and removed from all the best land. About twenty-five tribes were relocated to 'Indian Territory' (now Oklahoma), where rudimentary attempts were made to make them break with the past and lead settled lives but most of the government assistance was squandered by corrupt contractors. When Oklahoma was opened for white settlement in the early twentieth century the Indians were removed to even worse land. Between 1887 and 1934, the Indians lost two-thirds of their remaining land (86 million acres) and were left with the worst desert or semi-desert parts that the whites did not want. Conditions on the reservations were terrible and most Indians had to exist on meagre government grants at the bottom of the social and economic ladder and with their institutions and way of life rapidly disintegrating. Despite some improvements in the 1930s and after, the Indians remained the most depressed minority in the United States, suffering from discrimination, a very low standard of living and high infant mortality, and left largely dependent on federal government welfare.

The impact of the Europeans on the peoples of the Pacific was equally dramatic. Before the arrival of the Europeans the area was not quite the

Arcadia that some accounts, and European wishful thinking (particularly prevalent in the eighteenth century) about an idealised primitive existence, suggested. Warfare and cannibalism were, in fact, widespread but the area was relatively free of disease – it had no smallpox, measles, typhus, typhoid, leprosy, syphilis or tuberculosis – subsistence was obtained with little effort and the way of life was easy going. The European impact from the late eighteenth century meant the arrival of alcohol and a host of fatal diseases and the onset of massive cultural disruption. By 1900 the native population had collapsed to about a fifth of its level before the arrival of the Europeans. The population of Hawaii fell from about 300,000 at the end of the eighteenth century to 55,000 in 1875 and that of Rarotonga in the Cook Islands went from 7,000 in 1827 to 1,850 in 1867. In places the native society was effectively wiped out altogether. For instance, when the Russians arrived in the Aleutian Islands in the 1750s they forced the natives to work, hunting sea otters, so that the furs could be sent back to Europe and China. As a result, the animals were virtually extinct within thirty years and when the native population had collapsed to about five per cent of its original level, the survivors were resettled on the Pribilof Islands to continue working for the Russians.

The story of Tahiti is an illustration of what happened across the whole of the Pacific in the late eighteenth and nineteenth centuries. On his second visit to the island in 1773, Captain James Cook was already worried by the impact the Europeans were having on native peoples, as he wrote in his journal:

'We debauch their morals already prone to vice and we introduce among them wants and perhaps diseases which they never before knew . . . If any one denies the truth of this assertion let him tell what the natives of the whole extent of America have gained by the commerce they have had with Europeans.'

The violent crews of the whalers which called at the island (about 150 a year by the 1830s) introduced prostitution, venereal diseases and alcohol but the changes deliberately imposed by the first missionaries after 1797 had the effect of permanently undermining the islanders' way of life. The native religion was abolished and Tahitian music, tattooing and the wearing of floral garlands were banned. The natives were forced to wear European clothes and to work gathering coconut oil for export. Within a relatively short period the population was drastically reduced and the local culture was destroyed. In the 1770s, when the first

Europeans arrived, the population was about 40,000: it had dropped to 9,000 when the islands were annexed by France in the 1840s and eventually fell to less than 6,000. When the author of *Moby Dick*, Herman Melville, visited the islands in the 1840s whilst working on a whaler, he was shocked at the condition of the islanders, as was the painter Paul Gaugin when he arrived in the 1890s:

> 'The natives, having nothing, nothing at all to do, think of one thing only, drinking . . . Many things that are strange and picturesque existed here once, but there are no traces of them left today; everything has vanished. Day by day the race vanishes, decimated by the European diseases . . . there is so much prostitution.'

On one of his voyages to the Pacific Captain Cook also visited Australia where he came across the Aborigines still living in much the same way as when they first arrived on the continent 40,000 years earlier. He was impressed by the friendliness of the natives and their way of life, writing that, 'they may appear to some to be the most wretched people on earth but in reality they are far happier than we Europeans.' The botanist on the expedition, Joseph Banks, reached the same conclusion: 'Thus live these I had almost said, happy people, content with little, nay, almost nothing.' The British government, though, decided to turn the country into a penal colony and the first fleet of prisoners arrived in what is now Sydney Harbour in 1788. The Aborigines tried to live their lives in the face of a wild frontier society run by slave labour and violence and up against a continually expanding area of European settlement, but coexistence proved impossible. All land was declared a possession of the Crown but the natives could not understand the idea of land ownership, which was utterly alien to their traditions, and could not adjust to that or the equally strange new legal system introduced in the colony. The indigenous population were denied any claim to the land or to the same rights as Europeans. For example, in 1805, the colonial authorities decided that since the Aborigines could not understand European law there was no need to put them on trial and they could therefore be dealt with by immediate settler 'justice'. As the Europeans took more and more of the land, the Aborigines resisted but the conflict was hopelessly one-sided – some 2,000 Europeans were killed along the frontier but about 20,000 Aborigines died. Those who were not killed on the frontier or forced to retreat into the more inhospitable parts of the country were left as beggars and prostitutes, ruined by alcohol, on the edges of the towns.

By the 1840s in the Sydney area there were just a handful of survivors.

When a Pole, Count Strzelecki, visited the country in the 1830s, he left an account which contrasts vividly with Captain Cook's experience only sixty years before. This time the Aborigines were described as:

'Degraded, subdued, confused, awkward and distrustful, ill conceal-ing emotions of anger, scorn or revenge, emaciated and covered with filthy rags; these native lords of the soil, more like spectres of the past than living men, are dragging on a melancholy existence to a yet more melancholy doom.'

That doom came first on Tasmania. Sporadic warfare between the Europeans and the natives, who numbered about 5,000 at the end of the eighteenth century, began in 1804 and continued with a long series of atrocities committed by the whites. By 1830 only about 2,000 Abor-igines were left alive but the Governor of the island decided to remove them altogether from the settled central part of the island. A seven week drive across the island by a line of troops and settlers captured only a small number of Aborigines but by 1834 all of them had been expelled from Tasmania to Flinders Island in the Bass Strait. There, thoroughly disoriented, particularly by the attempts of evangelical Christians to make them wear European clothes and give up their native habits and traditions, they declined rapidly. By 1835 there were only 150 of them left alive and by 1843 just forty-three remained. The last lonely and neglected survivor of the Tasmanian Aborigines died in 1876. The Aborigines on the mainland declined too as their ancestral lands were expropriated by the white settlers and they were forced into ever less hospitable country, attacked by the whites or left on the fringes of white society. A few managed to preserve their way of life in the more remote areas but all of them suffered from extensive discrimination.

The last major area of the world to fall under European domination was Africa. Although the sheer scale of the continent and the problems of access made it difficult to wipe out whole peoples and cultures, the results of European intervention and eventual control were still drastic. The slave trade was the main form of contact between Europe and Africa for the first three hundred years after the Portuguese made their voyages along the coast, and economic exploitation was to remain at the core of the relationship. Unlike the native Americans and the inhabi-tants of the Pacific, the Africans were part of an area subject to many of the same diseases as Europeans and so did not suffer the rapid decline in numbers experienced by the other groups – indeed the Europeans suffered more, especially from tropical diseases. In the areas where the Europeans did choose to settle, a common feature was expropriation of native land. In Algeria 20,000 French settlers took 6 million acres of the best land and left 630,000 natives with 12 million acres of poor land. In Southern Rhodesia 50,000 whites owned 48 million acres and 1½ million blacks had 28 million acres. In South Africa the blacks (over three-quarters of the population) were left with just 12 per cent of the land and nearly half of that was in semi-arid areas. When South Africa took over the former German colony of south-west Africa in 1919 under a League of Nations mandate, 16 per cent of the population was white but they owned 60 per cent of the land including all the best farm land, the mineral deposits and the ports. As Leutwein, the first German Governor, wrote in July 1896, in a moment of candour: 'Colonization is always inhumane. It must ultimately amount to an encroachment on the rights of the original inhabitants in favour of the intruders.'

The Europeans also brought with them an innate sense of superiority, tinged with a strong degree of racism. Although some Europeans tried hard to improve life for the natives through medical and educational programmes, many undermined the local culture by forcing them to adopt European ways. Few seemed to be worried by the decline of native culture. The British Commissioner of Kenya wrote in 1904: 'There can be no doubt that the Masai and many other tribes must go under. It is a prospect which I view with equanimity and a clear conscience.' Beneath the surface, and often not even well disguised, was a contempt for the Africans, well expressed in a petition from the German settlers in south-west Africa to the Colonial Office in July 1900:

'From time immemorial our natives have grown used to laziness, brutality and stupidity. The dirtier they are, the more they feel at ease. Any white man who has lived among natives finds it almost impossible to regard them as human beings at all in any European sense.'

The history of German south-west Africa (now Namibia) gives a striking picture of the realities of European colonialism. It is an important example because it took place not in the sixteenth or seventeenth centuries but at a time when Europe prided itself on being the most advanced society in the world. South-west Africa was inhabited by three main tribal groups – the Ovambo in the north, the Herero (nomadic cattle raisers) and the Nama, who had been forced into the region by the expansion of white settlement in South Africa – and there was continual conflict between the different tribes. The area was allocated to Germany at the 1884–1885 Berlin Conference, which divided most of the remaining independent parts of Africa between the European powers. Within twenty years the Africans were dispossessed of all their land and turned into an underclass of labourers living in appalling conditions. German settlement remained small – 2,000 in 1896, 4,700 in 1903 and 14,000 in 1913 – compared with a native population estimated at 500,000 in the 1890s. German control was exercised through a steadily expanding area of direct military administration and indirect rule through the tribal chiefs. The German plan for the colony was to set up large-scale cattle ranches owned by the settlers and employing cheap African labour. This inevitably involved taking over tribal land, dispossessing the natives and disrupting African life. The outbreak of a rinderpest epidemic in 1897, which killed ninety per cent of the Herero's cattle, followed by a malaria epidemic brought about the disintegration of Herero society. During the next seven years the Germans showed no concern with preserving the native way of life even in the areas allowed to them and were in the first stages of establishing an apartheid society with the Africans confined to native reserves.

In 1904 the Herero and Nama, faced with a bleak future as labourers on land they once owned, rose in revolt. In response the German authorities embarked on a policy of suppressing and destroying the African inhabitants. At the end of a brutal military campaign the Herero were reduced from a population of about 80,000 to 16,000 after many were imprisoned in camps that were little better than death camps. The Nama revolt lasted till 1907 and by the end half the tribe were killed. A large part of the remaining Herero and Nama tribesmen were pursued into the desert where, as the official German report commented: 'The arid Omaheke [a desert in north-east Namibia] was to complete what the German army had begun: the extermination of the Herero nation.' All land still occupied by Africans was expropriated, they were banned from raising cattle and all tribal organisations were dissolved. The Africans were turned into a class of landless labourers needing an identity card and travel permit to move around the country and ninety per cent of males were forced to work for Europeans. In 1915 a survey showed that three-quarters of the Africans were either paid wages insufficient to buy a subsistence diet or instead given food that was similarly inadequate for their needs. The Africans were, therefore, reduced to scavenging to try and survive. With their culture and native way of life destroyed and continuing to suffer a low level of violence and killings from the white settlers, the Africans had been reduced to an underclass. There was no change for the better when the territory was administered by South Africa after 1919.

The expansion of Europe was a disaster for the native peoples of those areas of the world which could not survive as independent, or quasi-independent entities or restrict the amount of European contact. Some, such as the Tasmanian Aborigines, were exterminated, others suffered a huge fall in numbers through various different combinations of disease, warfare, alcohol and economic and social disruption. All saw their native culture and way of life undermined and often destroyed by Europeans determined to impose their own values. This saga of displacement and destruction was not confined to the early stages of European expansion and colonialism but continued throughout the nineteenth century and into the twentieth. In many areas of the world it is still continuing as newly independent states continue the assault on the few remaining native tribes in the world who still try to maintain their old way of life. The expansion of Brazilian settlement and economic exploitation into the Amazon has resulted in the extermination of some tribes and the few now remaining are on the verge of destruction. Indonesia's vast transmigration programme – the move of settlers from the densely populated central islands such as Java to the outlying islands – has meant tribespeople have been attacked and killed.

The spread of European settlement overseas opened up huge new areas of the world for exploitation, with a devastating impact on the flora and particularly the fauna of the world. It also meant a recasting of economic relations and increasing European domination and manipulation of other economies so that they grew the food and produced the goods that Europe required. As part of the same process European ideas have also come to dominate the world. What ideas about the relationship between humans and the rest of life on earth had Europe inherited and how did it develop, transform and add to them?

8
WAYS OF THOUGHT

Human actions have shaped the environment in which successive generations and different societies have lived. The driving force behind many of these actions has been simple – the need, as human numbers have steadily increased, to feed, clothe and house them. But the way in which human beings have thought about the world around them has been important in legitimising their treatment of it and in providing an explanation for their role within the overall structure. The way of thinking about the world that has become dominant in the last few centuries originated in Europe. Other traditions, particularly those of the eastern religions, have provided radically different interpretations, but they have been less influential.

One of the fundamental issues addressed by all traditions is the relationship between humans and the rest of nature. Are humans an integral part of nature or are they separate from it and in some way superior to it? The answer to this question is crucial in determining how different thinkers and religions decide which human actions can be regarded as legitimate or morally justified. From this flow other related questions about whether all the plants and animals in the world are there solely for the benefit of humans; about whether humans have a responsibility to guard and take care of the rest of nature (or God's creation). In the last two hundred years or so these religious and philosophical questions have been very largely overtaken by questions of economics – how should life be organised and scarce resources used and distributed. Although these may not seem at first glance to be philosophical questions, they have exercised an influence way beyond the sphere of economists and academics. They, too, have had a fundamental impact on the way humans view the world and justify their actions.

The origins of European thought about the relationship between humans and nature can be traced back, as in so many other areas, to the

influence of the philosophers of ancient Greece and Rome and the ideas
that the Christian church inherited from its Jewish origins. The strong
conviction running through both classical and Christian traditions has
been that human beings have been put in a position of dominance over
the rest of a subordinate nature. Although the idea that humans have a
responsibility to preserve a natural world of which they are merely
guardians can be traced through a succession of thinkers, it has
remained a minority tradition.

Many thinkers have looked at the world around them and seen that
what is now recognised by ecologists as competition and co-operation
between plants and animals in ecosystems, has produced an ordered
world in which every part seems to have a role and purpose within an
overall plan. This has led them to argue that such a plan can only have
been conceived by a God, or the gods, and they have gone on to
speculate about the position of humans within this plan. One of the first
to do so was Xenophon in his *Memorabilia*. He attributes to Socrates
the argument that everything about humans (such as the eyes and
hands) has a purpose and that the gods have also provided everything
carefully for the benefit of man. Euthydemus, one of the participants in
the fictional debate, responds by saying that, 'I begin to doubt whether
after all the gods are occupied in any other work than the service of
man.' But he is worried that, 'the lower animals also enjoy these
blessings' until Socrates reassures him that within the overall plan it is
clear that these animals are only produced and nourished for the sake of
humans. This argument, based on a perceived plan and design within
nature, makes frequent reappearances in western thought until the
nineteenth century when developments in scientific thought, notably
Darwin's ideas on the origin of species, operating through natural
selection and adaptation, served to undermine it. Over the centuries the
argument developed mainly in the sense that new thinkers proposed
new evidence from within nature to illustrate the diverse way in which
plants and animals were so well adapted to their particular roles. This
tended to reinforce the idea that, since everything had been so well
provided for humans, then they must indeed be the most important
creatures on earth and so entitled to use others as they saw fit. Another
early expression of this ultimately anthropocentric view of the world is
to be found in Aristotle. In the *Politics* he argues that plants are made
for animals and concludes with the statement that, 'Now if Nature
makes nothing incomplete, and nothing in vain, the inference must be
that she has made all animals for the sake of man.'

With the Stoics (especially Panaetius, who lived on Rhodes in the second century BC) and also Cicero, some more subtle arguments were added to this general approach, by emphasising both the aesthetic and utilitarian aspects. To them the world is seen as both beautiful and useful. Beauty is pleasant to look upon and therefore ought to be preserved, but human beings, by meeting their demands for food, resources and goods, improve upon nature. Cicero, for example, makes little distinction between the untouched, natural world and that modified by human action – the two are assumed to be identical. Although the Epicurean thinkers emphasised the harsher aspects of nature – wild beasts, natural disasters, crop failures – that went with the beauty, classical thought was generally characterised by an idea of humans as orderers of nature. Humans were placed on a higher plane than other animals: their ability to create their own world implied a superior position as a finisher of raw creation. The classical thinkers were well aware that human actions were changing the world around them (as Plato makes clear in the passage from the *Critias* about deforestation and soil erosion cited earlier p. 76) but apart from those who, like Xenophon and Hesiod, saw human history as a story of decline from a past golden age, they generally regarded human actions in modifying the environment as perfectly natural and beneficial.

The rise of Christianity and its adoption as the state religion of the late Roman empire in the fourth century introduced a new element – Jewish thought – which had until then been confined to a small and previously uninfluential people on the margins of what contemporaries regarded as the civilised world. The Christians incorporated into their sacred texts earlier Jewish religious books. Genesis, which became the first book of the Christian Bible, contains two different creation myths (neither, though, very different from many others in Near Eastern religions) but both give essentially the same view of the relationship between God, human beings and the natural world. In the first of these (Genesis Chapter 1) God creates humans as the climax of his previous five days work. With divine blessing they are granted dominion over the rest of creation:

'Be fruitful and multiply, and fill the earth and subdue it; and have dominion over the fish of the sea and over the birds of the air and over every living thing that moves upon the earth . . . Be fruitful and multiply and replenish the earth and subdue it.'

In the other myth (Genesis Chapter 2) man is created first and then the Garden of Eden with all the plants and animals and then finally woman.

But in this myth too the animals are still created for the benefit of humanity and it is Adam who gives them their names. Then God nearly destroys the world in a great flood but in a new contract with Noah and his family as the only human survivors, God once again, this time in even starker terms, gives them and their descendants dominion over the world:

> 'Every moving thing that lives shall be food for you; and as I gave you the green plants, I give you everything. . . . The fear of you and the dread of you shall be upon every beast of the earth, and upon every fowl of the air, upon all that moveth upon the earth, and upon all the fishes of the sea; into your hand are they delivered.'

This theme appears in many of the other Jewish sacred books incorporated into the Bible. Psalm 8 for example says, 'Thou hast given him [man] dominion over the works of thy hands', and Psalm 115 has the same message: 'The heavens are the Lord's heavens, but the earth he has given to the sons of men.'

The early and medieval Christian thinkers accepted, almost without demur, the view inherited from Jewish writing that God had given humans the right to exploit plants, animals and the whole world for their benefit. Nature is not seen as sacred and therefore it is open to exploitation by humans without any moral qualms – indeed humans have the right to use it in whatever way they think best. God is typically portrayed as above and separate from the world and what matters above all is the relationship of the individual with God and not with the natural world. Indeed in this way of thought human beings are not seen as part of the natural world since they are unique and have been placed on a pedestal by God above all other living things.

In medieval Europe this view, increasingly influenced after the twelfth and thirteenth centuries by classical writers, provided a widely accepted framework for understanding the world and the human position within it. Although different writers might emphasise different aspects, typically the world was seen as a planned and ordered creation, made by God in his goodness, that would survive until the day of judgement. The ordering of the natural world was evidence of the work of a benevolent creator. Humans enjoyed a wholly different status from other animals as the only creatures with a soul and a life after death. The sixth century writer Cosmas Indicopleustus proclaimed in his *Christian Topography*, that man was 'the king of all things on earth and reigns along with the Lord Christ in the heavens.' Thomas

Aquinas, incorporating much classical thought (especially Aristotle), encapsulated these views, and provided, as he did for much of medieval Christian thought, their most coherent and logical expression. He argued that there was a hierarchy of beings from the most insignificant up to God but, although there was a reason for the existence of each, the whole plan was known only to God. Humans took their unique place above the animals and their dominion over nature was part of the logical divine plan – rational creatures should rule over irrational ones (animals) and this was well illustrated by the human ability to domesticate animals. Similarly the work of human society in altering nature by extending cultivated areas and using the resources of the world was seen as part of the divine plan to tame the wild and as part of a continuous process of improvement on nature. The Reformation in the sixteenth century brought no fundamental change in this point of view, indeed by re-emphasising the importance of biblical texts it tended to reinforce it. Calvin, one of the leaders of the movement, stands firmly behind the view that it had taken God six days to make the world perfect for the arrival of humans and that God 'created all things for man's sake'. The unique position persistently attributed to humans in Jewish and, following from it, Christian theology produces a highly anthropocentric view of the world which was to have a profound and enduring impact on later European thought even when it was not specifically religious.

Within Judaism and Christianity there were exceptions: the special position of humans in the world was challenged by a few thinkers. In this minority tradition slightly different aspects of the Jewish creation myths were emphasised, particularly that of the Garden of Eden. Humans are depicted essentially as the stewards of God's creation with the task of caring for it on his behalf. This viewpoint is well illustrated by the Jewish thinker Maimonides, who wrote:

'It should not be believed that all beings exist for the sake of the existence of man. On the contrary, all other beings, too, have been intended for their own sakes, and not for the sake of something else.'

This same note of dissent from the widely accepted tradition can also be found in the ideas of Francis of Assisi. His views reflect much of mainstream Christian thought, in particular the idea that nature, its purpose and order, and the way each part of it was so well adapted to its way of life, demonstrated the work of a benevolent creator. For him the natural world could, therefore, be seen as being, like the Bible though at a lower level, an illustration of the nature of God. Francis saw all creatures as equal parts of this creation, each a part of God's plan but not put there for the utilitarian purposes of humans. This idea, which was revolutionary in its implications and, like much of his thought, widely detested within the Church, was never more than a minority viewpoint within the overall structure of Christian belief, although, against a background of growing public concern about the environment, it has been emphasised more strongly in the last few decades.

The increasingly rapid development of secular thinking in Europe from the sixteenth century produced little alteration in the assumptions and beliefs inherited from classical and medieval thought about the relationship between humans and the natural world. The basic anthropocentrism of Christianity continued, though in a slightly modified form. The world was still seen as part of an organised and rational divine plan. Writers used the increasing amount of biological knowledge to illustrate, with ever more examples, the wisdom of God in providing such a perfectly adapted world. This approach is perhaps best exemplified by the work of Ray, an English writer at the end of the seventeenth century encapsulated in the title of his book *The Wisdom of God Manifested in the Works of the Creation*. Humans were still regarded as placed in a special position by God, above other creatures and able to use them and the natural world for their own benefit. Interventions in, and modifications to, the natural world could readily be interpreted as taking part in God's plan to improve upon creation. This concept of a special role led some to adopt more extreme positions. For example Marsilio Ficino, an Italian Renaissance author, wrote that, 'Man not only makes use of the elements, but also adorns them . . . man who provides generally for all things, both living and lifeless, is a kind of God.' A similar viewpoint is found in the writings of Sir Matthew Hale, a seventeenth century English lawyer, who, in *The Primitive Origination of Mankind*, wrote that:

'this was the one End of the Creation of Man, namely To be Vicegerent [sic] of Almighty God, in the subordinate Regiment especially of the Animal and Vegetable Provinces.'

For these thinkers the unique position of humans and their right to exercise control over nature stemmed from their position as the highest link of what was widely seen at the time as a great chain of being, stretching from the most insignificant to the most important. The idea that humans needed to interfere with, or add the finishing touches to, nature in order to maintain civilisation was a widely held assumption, as was the idea that nature was at its best not in its primitive or brute state but when it was controlled and shaped by humans. From such views it was a small and logical step to welcome the way that increasing human knowledge brought the prospect of greater control over the natural world and to believe that this would be pleasing to God because humans were taking full advantage of the wonders of his creation.

One of the major themes of seventeenth century writings was the emphasis placed on human domination over nature and their role in completing God's work. Human actions directed towards this end were seen as being beneficial and harmless. At this time, a slowly developing scientific method and a growing body of scientific knowledge were working in the same direction. René Descartes in his *Discourse on Method* emphasised the importance of scientific method through the use of mathematics to measure and quantify, together with a process of analysis designed to reduce wholes to their constituent parts. The widespread adoption of this reductionist approach to scientific enquiry was to have a profound impact on the shaping of European thought generally. It inevitably led to a fragmented view of the world – to a focus on the individual parts of a system rather than on the organic whole, on studying the way in which the constituent elements operated separately rather than the ways in which they interacted, both by competition and co-operation. This tendency was reinforced by a mechanistic approach to natural phenomena, which can again be traced back to Descartes who wrote, 'I do not recognise any difference between the machines made by craftsmen and the various bodies that nature alone composes.' Animals were therefore mere machines and, although made by God, incapable of thought as such, only endowed with natural impulse. Whatever new intellectual methods Descartes wanted to pursue, God was still central to his view of the world, and humans still occupied a special place in that scheme, set apart through the possession of minds and souls which enabled them to dominate nature. His mechanistic view of the world seemed to be vindicated by the spectacular success of Newton in the late seventeenth century in applying physical laws, such as that governing the force of gravity, to explain the workings of the universe. A popular new image of the relationship between God, humans and nature was launched. For the next two hundred years or more there are frequent references to the idea of God as the great designer of a machine the workings of which humans could, through their god-given intellectual faculties, seek to understand. Writing two hundred years after Descartes, the American economist H. C. Carey could still declare in

1848 that, 'the earth is a great machine, given to man to be fashioned to his purpose.'

The idea that the application of science is a powerful aid to progress and a vital tool to enable humans to dominate the world is strongly expounded in the work of Francis Bacon. He started from the traditional view when he wrote that 'the world is made for man, not man for the world', and:

> 'Man, if we look to final causes, may be regarded as the centre of the world, insomuch that if man were taken away from the world, the rest would seem to be all astray, without aim or purpose.'

He went on to urge that the whole point of scientific endeavour was to restore the dominion over the world that had been lost with the fall of Adam and Eve in the Garden of Eden. As he wrote in the *Novum Organum*: 'Let the human race recover that right over Nature which belongs to it by divine bequest.' The way in which that right could be regained increasingly used the language of violence. A contemporary poet, Abraham Cowley, wrote of 'the husbandman's innocent wars, on beasts and birds', and words such as 'mastery', 'conquest' and 'dominion' were common in describing human efforts to control nature. Bacon in his correspondence with John Beale said that the purpose of studying the natural world was that, 'Nature being known, it may be master'd, managed, and used in the services of human life.' Descartes too saw the purpose of science and increasing human knowledge as being part of a wider struggle so that, 'we can . . . employ them in all those uses to which they are adapted, and thus render ourselves the masters and possessors of nature.'

During the second half of eighteenth century the idea of a perfectly designed world came under attack, notably in Voltaire's satirical attack on Leibnizian optimism in *Candide*. This vein in the work of philosophers was assisted by later developments in scientific thought. Charles Darwin's *Origin of Species*, published in 1859, opened up a debate about the origins of man, undermined the orthodox view of divine creation and put forward the idea of the natural selection of characteristics that helped survival in a highly competitive world. In the hands of philosophers such as Herbert Spencer, this theory about the origin of species was transmuted into a statement about the nature of society and the morality of human actions. Spencer in effect refurbished the old ideas about the special position of humans compared with the rest of the natural world in a Darwinian form. For Spencer all life was a struggle for 'the survival of the fittest'. Humans had to struggle against nature in order to survive and in doing so they demonstrated their fitness to be on the topmost rung of the ladder. Variations on the old theme appear in many other nineteenth century writings, evidence of the potent attraction of an idea which not only powerfully reinforced a sense of purpose and of superiority but also readily justified areas of traditional human interference with the natural world as well as new activities such as the vast increase in industrial output. The philosopher Immanuel Kant wrote that, 'As the single being upon earth that possesses understanding, he [man] is certainly titular lord of nature . . . he is born to be its ultimate end.' Given this position, Kant felt that the human relationship with nature could not be subject to any moral censure. Other familiar views also appear again in only slightly different guises in a number of modern thinkers. For example John Stuart Mill in his *Three Essays on Religion* wrote of nature that: 'Her powers are often towards man in the position of enemies, from whom he must wrest, by force and ingenuity, what little he can for his own use.' The founder of psychoanalysis, Sigmund Freud, said in *Civilisation and its Discontents* that the human ideal was 'combining with the rest of the human community and taking up the attack on nature, thus forcing it to obey human will, under the guidance of science'.

As well as the strong sense of continuity that emerges in European thinking about the relationship between humans and the natural world over many centuries it is also possible to trace the emergence of a powerful new element – the idea of *progress*. This idea is such a fundamental constituent of modern thought that it is very difficult to appreciate just how recent it is or how other societies viewed the world before the idea took hold. The ancient world had little concept of the idea of progress: history was usually seen as having no particular direction at all or, if it did have one, to be a story of a decline from a golden age. For writers such as Xenophon, Hesiod and Empedocles human society had been steadily decaying from an age of gold to one of silver to the age of iron in which they lived. Other societies, for example the Cherokee Indians, have had the same idea of a lost golden age as have Chinese thinkers such as the Taoist, Chuang Tsu. Both the early Christians and those of medieval Europe saw the history of the world as one of decline, of innocence lost in the Garden of Eden, never to be regained on earth. They also believed that a day of judgement would occur in the not very distant future that would mark, not just the final trial for both the living and the dead, but also the end of all earthly history. Many secular figures in the fifteenth and sixteenth centuries believed that, although they had rediscovered much of the culture of the ancient world, their own age was far inferior to the revered Greeks and Romans, not just in cultural terms, but also in civic virtue and valour. Within an intellectual framework of this sort it was almost impossible to interpret human history as one of uninterrupted progress.

It is not until the end of the seventeenth century that the continuing increase in scientific knowledge and the steady advance of technology (both areas in which Europe by then was demonstrably in advance of ancient societies) began to convince some thinkers that history might be a chronicle of progress rather than of decay. Gradually it came to be commonly accepted among European intellectuals that history was the story of a series of irreversible changes in only one direction – continual improvement. The eighteenth century was marked by a wave of optimism about the future and the inevitability of progress in every field. In 1793 the English writer William Godwin in his *Political Justice* wrote in glowing terms of the prospects:

'Three-fourths of the habitable globe, are now uncultivated. The improvements to be made in cultivation, and the augmentations the earth is capable of receiving in the article of productiveness, cannot, as yet, be reduced to any limits of calculation. Myriads of centuries of still increasing population may pass away, and the earth be yet found sufficient for the support of its inhabitants.'

In the same year the Marquis de Condorcet published his *Sketch for a Historical Picture of the Progress of the Human Mind*. The book was a statement of his belief in human potential and the unlimited scope for human progress:

'The perfectibility of man is truly indefinite; and that the progress of this perfectibility, from now onwards independent of any power that might wish to halt it, has no limit than the duration of the globe upon which nature has cast us . . . this progress . . . will never be reversed as long as the earth occupies its present place in the system of the universe.'

It is perhaps possible that if Condorcet had known that he was to die the next year in jail during the period of terror in the French Revolution he might have taken a less sanguine view of human nature and history.

Certainly the Reverend Thomas Malthus took a much darker view. His *Essay on the Principle of Population*, published soon afterwards in 1798, argued that there was a permanent cycle in history in which human numbers increased until they were too high for the available food supply, at which point famine and disease would reduce the population until it was again in balance with the amount of food that could be produced. Malthus could see no way out of this terrible cycle. During the nineteenth century this Malthusian view of history was largely ignored and the idea of progress became almost universally accepted as the natural, unspoken assumption. Such optimism was felt to be justified by the huge material progress made by Europe in the nineteenth century: its ability to feed an ever larger population, the growth of cities, new inventions and the development of industry. The acceptance of progress was at the heart of the thinking of European intellectuals such as Saint-Simon, Comte, Spencer and John Stuart Mill. Its strongest manifestation is in the thought of Marx and Engels with their idea of the inevitable progress of human societies through different economic stages and their related power structures. Human history was, they argued, the march of progress from tribal through feudal and capitalist societies until its climax in the inevitable victory of the proletariat and socialism. By the late nineteenth century the idea of progress had become a part of popular culture as well – something so ingrained in the unspoken assumptions of nearly all European thought that almost any change could be automatically equated with progress. Although battered by some of the events of the twentieth century, it remains a widely accepted assumption about the nature of human history.

Although the religious element had dwindled or disappeared from much of European thought by the end of the nineteenth century, many of the assumptions that lay at the centre of Christian thought for two thousand years, together with the earlier classical and Jewish influences, had been incorporated, almost unthinkingly, into the general pattern of assumptions that formed the foundations of the European view of the world. Humans were regarded as apart from, and superior to, a separate natural world which they were entitled to exploit as they saw fit. This exploitation was viewed as perfectly natural and a way of improving a rough, unfinished, natural environment. The consequences of human actions were beneficial and part of an unbroken story of progress that would inevitably continue into the future. It was this world view that formed the background to the most active period in the expansion of Europe and one which, given the apparent success of

Europe, appealed more and more to people who came into contact with Europeans and their higher material standards.

This anthropocentric view of the world was not held universally within Europe. The idea of humans having only a stewardship over the world remained a minority tradition within both Judaism and Christianity. And even this tradition in many ways involved a change of emphasis rather than a radically different approach, since it retained humans in a special position, in charge of the world and able to use it for their own purposes, although in a more moderate and restrained fashion. Other religious traditions in the world did not place humans in such a special and dominant position. Chinese Taoist thought emphasised the idea of a balance of forces, within both the individual and society. Both ought to try and live in a balanced and harmonious way with the natural world. The Indian tradition, as exemplified in writings such as the Upanishads and religions such as Jainism and Buddhism, is built on a radically different view of the world. All creatures, including humans, are seen as part of a suffering world, all needing release from a continuing cycle of existence in which, through karma and reincarnation, actions in one life affect the next. Overwhelming importance is attached to compassion for all creatures trapped in this cycle of existence. Humans are in a privileged position but not because they are rulers of the world on behalf of God. Rather they are the only creatures able to achieve enlightenment and therefore should make the best use of a rare opportunity to escape from the cycle of suffering. Although the variety of different strands of thought within all the major religious traditions, including Christianity, makes it dangerous to generalise, the world view of the 'eastern' religious tradition, developed centuries before the rise of Christianity, does emphasise a less aggressive approach by humans to the natural world. It does not conceive of humans as being placed above and beyond a natural world which is theirs to exploit. Humans are only a small part of a much greater whole and what sets them apart – greater intellectual and spiritual capabilities – should be directed to the goal of enlightenment and enable them to act wisely towards other creatures and not take life unnecessarily. Central to this way of thinking is not dominion over the world but the idea of suffering and the need for universal compassion.

The available evidence about the outlook and beliefs of gathering and hunting groups, suggests, not surprisingly given their close relationship with the natural world in the hunt for food, a variety of beliefs revolving around the interdependence of humans and plants and animals. In general they do not see, as modern societies do, a distinction between nature and society. Their world is simply composed of people, animals and inanimate things all of which are linked together in a single whole without distinct categories. Perhaps the most explicit statement we have of these beliefs comes from Chief Seattle of the Squamish tribe, who wrote to the president of the United States in 1854 to protest (without effect) on the way the white settlers were treating the Indians and the environment of North America:

> 'What is man without the beasts? If all the beasts were gone, men would die from great loneliness of spirit, for whatever happens to the beasts also happens to the man. . . . Teach your children what we have taught our children: that the earth is their mother. Whatever befalls the earth befalls the sons of the earth. If men spit upon the ground, they spit upon themselves. The earth does not belong to man, man belongs to the earth. Man did not weave the web of life, he is merely a strand in it. Whatever he does to the web, he does to himself.'

It is difficult to imagine a statement more at odds with the prevailing European view about the relationship between humans and the world around them.

While the influence of western religious and philosophical thinking clearly continues to colour the way in which Europeans, and increasingly the rest of humanity, view the world around them and reach decisions on what actions are permissible, it is apparent that during the last two hundred years the growth of the discipline of economics has introduced a powerful new element. Indeed in every part of the world contemporary arguments about the way society should be organised now revolve around the health and management of the national and international 'economy'. This 'social science', a relative newcomer among academic disciplines and one ridden with controversy among its practitioners, nevertheless has come to exercise a profound influence upon the way the world is seen and analysed. Economic thinking is now central to the way in which human societies treat the environment. Not only the professed economic system of a society, but the hidden assumptions of economics and the value systems that it enshrines, are central to understanding the modern view of the relationship between humans and the natural world. For all the apparent gulf between the market-dominated economies of the West and the centrally planned economies of the communist world, when it comes to attitudes to the natural world their outlook turns out to be remarkably similar.

It is easy to forget that economies and societies dominated by market mechanisms are a comparatively recent phenomenon. Not until the nineteenth century did societies emerge that were controlled by the free (or mainly free) operation of markets for land, labour and capital, with other considerations subordinated to this requirement. For thousands of years societies were organised in a very different way. Gathering and hunting groups generally had few possessions, the idea of land owner-ship was completely alien to them (which explains why they could not come to terms with the European system) and goods vital for the continuation of the group, particularly food, were regarded as freely available to all and to be shared if necessary. The first settled societies were dependent on the redistribution of food between members of the community, a task normally undertaken by the priests or secular rulers on behalf of all. The population of Rome, similarly, was fed through free distribution of grain by the state. In these ancient societies, and every society across the world until the last few centuries, most people lived in small units, essentially self-contained for most purposes, engaged in semi-subsistence farming and with much production only for personal use or barter within the community. In the absence of markets in which goods were traded the secular and religious elite retained or patronised artists and craftsmen to obtain their require-ments. These societies were overwhelmingly agricultural and trade was largely restricted to a few items closely connected with that sector of the economy together with a few luxury goods for the elite. In the 'feudal' societies of medieval Europe land was at first rarely traded; it was exchanged in return for military service or rent, in kind rather than money. Only very slowly over a period of centuries did a market in land develop. For centuries, although there was a market in labour it was far from free. It was largely organised in guilds (of both owners and workers) that regulated working hours, pay, apprenticeships and out-put. Merchants existed but they played a minor role and trade in goods operated in a different way from modern markets. Instead of prices fluctuating according to supply and demand, markets tended to operate with fixed relationships between different goods so that profit came not from price differentials but from turnover.

In Europe this situation began to change after about 1100, first in more developed areas such as northern Italy and Flanders, and then more widely across the continent. Trade expanded and the number of merchants grew, banking developed, the market in land steadily in-creased and labour became more of a commodity to be bought and sold. But even as trade grew it was still heavily regulated, often by the state for strategic reasons, and the labour market was still partially controlled, particularly in the limitations placed on the wages that could be paid and on freedom of movement. Social attitudes also placed constraints on economic behaviour, particularly profit-making. By the eighteenth century however a free market in land, labour and capital was emerging in Europe, particularly in the more developed countries such as Britain. The first writer to provide a systematic analysis and apologia for the revolution in behaviour and social organisation that was taking place was Adam Smith (now regarded as the founder of modern economics) in his *Inquiry into the Nature and Causes of the Wealth of Nations*, published in 1776 at a time when new methods of economic organisation were beginning to emerge in Britain. He argued that individuals acting in their own self-interest, whether as producers or consumers, in the pursuit of greater wealth, but regulated by competition between them, would produce the most beneficial outcome for the whole of society. His view was of a society engaged in a process of continual improvement to be brought about through investment, greater productivity and the accumulation of individual wealth. He shared the common eighteenth century belief in the inevitability of progress and assumed that the betterment of society was equivalent to the production of material wealth – an assumption that many might dispute since it leaves out a number of important values, but it is a belief that has been highly influential. Smith, together with other writers such as Ricardo and John Stuart Mill (now categorised as classical economists), placed the production of goods at the centre of economics. From the start, therefore, economists concentrated much of their effort on studying the organisation of production – how the various factors responsible for it (land, labour and capital) interacted.

There is little doubt that Smith's theory of competition and of a self-regulating market operating through prices set by a balance between supply and demand is, in practice, a highly effective way of matching production and demand. The assumptions of classical economics have, over the last two hundred years, been widely accepted in western, industrialised societies. There is, however, a fundamental flaw in classical economics (and the modern systems derived from it – Marxist, welfare, Keynesian and ultra liberal economics). They all ignore the problem of resource depletion and deal only with the secondary problem of the distribution of resources between different competing ends. The crucial defect is that the earth's resources are treated as capital – a set of assets to be turned into a source of profit. Trees, wildlife, minerals, water and soil are treated as commodities to be sold or developed. More important, their price is simply the cost of extracting them and turning them into marketable commodities. (Some such as air never even enter a market mechanism.) Yet this view overlooks the basic truth that the resources of the earth are not just *scarce*, they are *finite*. Since classical economics is unable to incorporate this fact into its analysis, the economic systems based upon it encourage both the producer and consumer to use up available resources at whatever rate current conditions dictate. It assumes, in defiance of all logic, that resources, in terms of materials and energy, are inexhaustible, that growth in the overall level of the economy can continue for ever and that substitution of one material or form of energy for another can continue indefinitely even though in reality the total supply is limited. In this system there is no way that current prices, and therefore levels of economic activity, can take account of the problems that will have to be faced in the future. Indeed, if the most rational action for humans is, as classical economics suggests, to pursue immediate self-interest, then there is no need to take account of posterity. But since in the real world resources are finite, consuming them now has a very real price – they are not available for future generations.

The development of Keynesian economics in the 1930s, which showed how demand in the economy might be regulated by government to maintain full employment, brought in its train new methods for measuring the level of economic activity in a country. Economists evolved Gross National Product (GNP) as a measure of the amount of production, consumption and investment. The success of an economy is now generally judged by the rate at which GNP is increasing. But the way that GNP is defined has a number of defects. It does not measure every sort of economic activity and the way it is calculated provides a distorted view of economic success. GNP only measures certain monetary flows within an economy and, therefore, cannot cover the 'black economy' of undeclared activities or non-monetary transactions such as barter, subsistence agriculture, housework and voluntary community work. GNP, measuring the size of an economy, includes many items that are not benefits to society as a whole. For example, the shorter the life of cars, and the more often they break down, the greater will be the amount of activity in an economy (more car sales and more repairs) which is reflected in GNP figures. This ignores the fact that individuals (unless employed in a car factory or garage) would be better off if they had more reliable, longer-lasting cars. GNP calculations also take no account of the social costs of some forms of production, such as higher levels of pollution or greater traffic congestion, and delays or social problems such as bad housing and crime levels. It is difficult to put a price on such items, and they are left out of most economic models and pricing mechanisms, reduced to a category of 'externalities'. In the long term the notion of GNP takes no account of the fundamental question as to whether its level at any one time, let alone continual growth in the future, is in fact desirable or sustainable.

In some ways the most radical dissent from classical and liberal economics came from Marx and Engels, in their theoretical works published in the mid-nineteenth century, and their followers, in particular Lenin and the revolutionaries who took power in the Soviet Union after 1917. However, Marx and Engels, in the way they treat resources and the environment, adopted many of the assumptions of classical economics (and previous western thought) and in many cases take such views to an extreme, unmatched elsewhere. Marx and Engels, like early classical economists, argued that the 'value' of any product came from the amount of human labour put into it. Such a view neglects the resources involved: it judges 'value' solely by the amount of human labour involved in extracting and processing them and does not take account of their finite nature.

In some of his early works such as the *Economic and Philosophical Manuscripts* written in the early 1840s, Marx adopts a more idealistic view of nature than in his later work (and this is consistent with parts of Engels' work which shows that he was aware of some of the environmental problems caused by human activities in the past). But even in these works Marx adopted the common European view that nature only had meaning in terms of human requirements, for example, when he wrote that, 'Nature taken abstractly, for itself, and fixedly isolated from man, is nothing for man.' In his later works Marx argues that the 'great civilising influence of capital' is that it rejects the 'deification of nature' so that 'nature becomes, for the first time, simply an object for mankind, purely a matter of utility.' Engels took the same view, arguing that humans will, in the future, be able to 'learn and hence control even the more remote natural consequences of at least our most ordinary productive activities.' Marx, Engels, and in turn Lenin, rejected any of the more libertarian socialist ideas that increased happiness might be obtained by reducing the amount of consumption in society and seeking a simpler, more harmonious life. Instead they saw their first aim as being to bring the proletariat up to the level of consumption achieved by the bourgeoisie in nineteenth-century Europe. Socialism was to be built on the productive capacity of an advanced industrial society organised through the factory system and with a large degree of state power to achieve these ends. The general optimism of Marxism, which specifically rejected the pessimism of writers like Malthus in favour of the limitless possibilities open to human society through greater production, is well summed up by Engels when he declared that, 'the productivity of the land can be infinitely increased by the application of capital, labour and science.'

Marxism in practice turned out to be even more committed to the overwhelming importance of production than even the western economies. Lenin, both in his theoretical writings and in practice in the Soviet Union after 1917, was obsessed with industrial production and retained a high regard for the ability of what he saw as monopoly capitalism to produce large quantities of goods. Once the Soviet Union was established the development of industry became a high priority, especially once 'socialism in one country' was accepted as the policy of the new state in the late 1920s. The environmental consequences of these policies were potentially highly damaging but this aspect was largely disregarded in the context of a materialist philosophy which saw the highest human achievement as the ability to alter the natural world as required and which focussed on a glowing vision of the future as evoked by the Soviet historian, M. N. Pokrovskiy in his *Brief History of Russia*, published in 1931:

'It is easy to foresee that in future, when science and technique have attained to a perfection which we are as yet unable to visualise, nature will become soft wax in his [man's] hands which he will be able to cast into whatever form he chooses.'

The strength of the Marxist view that the ability of humans to mould nature to their own ends was the highest task can be judged by the fact that Pokrovskiy's book was later condemned for giving the role of the environment too much importance in human history!

It has suited many practitioners and politicians to represent economics as a science and an objective tool for analysing human activity and managing economic affairs. Yet it never was and never can be value-free. Its very emergence as a separate discipline in the nineteenth century reflects the importance in the industrialised countries of Europe and North America of the expansion of production and consumption. These became the centre of attention and concern and other considerations, especially judgements about the quality of life, outside of material goods, were largely ignored. Although as a subject, economics itself has evolved a good deal, most of its analysis is essentially static. Its classic texts describe how economies do or should work but contain little or nothing about the long-term dynamics involved. They quantify the current level of production but say nothing about how sustainable this is in the long term and the rate at which non-renewable and scarce resources are being consumed. Most mainstream economic thinking throws little light on the immediate and future consequences of current production and consumption (apart from their influence on inflation and unemployment) and offers few solutions to questions about the levels of pollution and damage to the environment which are involved.

Only a small minority of economists have tried to deal with these deeper questions. E. F. Schumacher in his book *Small is Beautiful*, published in the early 1970s, argued for an approach to economics 'as if people mattered'. For him this meant concentrating on questions of the appropriate size and scale for both activities and technology and identifying the real needs of people rather than pursuing absolute levels of production, an approach he characterised as 'Buddhist Economics'. Although his writings became international bestsellers, his ideas have had little impact on policy makers or mainstream economics. Another trenchant analysis of the shortcomings of conventional economics was made by Hazel Henderson in her book *Creating Alternative Futures* published in 1978. Like Schumacher she criticised the fragmentation of economic thought, its failure to recognise the values that lie deeply embedded within it and its failure to take into account humanity's dependence on the natural world. The result, according to Henderson, is that:

'Economics has enthroned some of our most unattractive predispositions: material acquisitiveness, competition, gluttony, pride, selfishness, shortsightedness, and just plain greed.'

At the risk of grossly oversimplifying, it is possible to draw together the various elements that make up a 'European' view of the world. This view is composed of many different traditions – philosophical, religious and scientific – and they have been channelled in many different ways. Europeans came to see humans as being placed in a special position, above and beyond a separate 'natural world' which they could exploit with impunity. The influence of scientific thinking can be seen in the dominance of reductionist modes of thinking – the emphasis on observing and understanding parts of the system rather than looking at the whole. They became aware that their material position and level of knowledge were greater than that of their predecssors and called this 'progress'. Higher levels of material consumption and a greater ability to alter the natural world were regarded as major achievements. Progress was by definition beneficial and something all human societies should aim for in the future, and progress became associated, above all, with economic growth.

It would be naive to assume that this intellectual background provided the motivating force behind the rise of Europe and it is difficult to disentangle which was cause and which was effect. But the way Europeans thought about the world around them was important. It did help to provide an intellectual self-justification for what the Europeans did to the natural world, the way they reshaped other societies to their own ends and how they exploited the world's natural resources.

9
THE RAPE OF THE WORLD

Over the last 10,000 years human activities have brought about major changes in the ecosystems of the world. The universal expansion of settlement and the creation of fields and pastures for agriculture, the continual clearing of forests and other wild areas, and the draining of marshy areas, have steadily reduced the habitats of almost every kind of animal and plant. The deliberate hunting of animals for food, furs and other products (and in some cases for 'sport') and the collection of plants has drastically reduced numbers of many species. Humans have introduced new plants and animals into ecosystems often with unexpected and near catastrophic results. The scale of wildlife losses in earlier periods is difficult to assess. There is more evidence, though still very patchy, for the period after 1600 but it is not until the present century that detailed research has been undertaken, largely prompted by a growing awareness of the increasing scale of the losses. There is no doubt though that the pace of destruction has been increasing, particularly following the expansion of Europe after 1500.

A reduction in wildlife habitats and extinction of species on a local scale can be identified from the time of the first human settlements. In the Nile valley the extension of the cultivated area, the draining of marshland and the organised hunting of animals led to the elimination of many species originally native to the area. By the time of the Old Kingdom (2950–2350 BC) animals such as elephants, rhinoceroses and giraffes had disappeared from the valley. The spread of settlement around the Mediterranean produced the same results with the destruction concentrated on the vulnerable animals at the top of the food chain. By about 200 BC the lion and leopard were extinct in Greece and the coastal areas of Asia Minor, and wolves and jackals were confined to the remote mountainous areas. The trapping of beavers in northern Greece had also driven them to extinction. The Roman addiction to the deliberate killing of wild animals in games and other spectacles added to the slaughter. The scale of the continuing destruction to amuse the crowds across the Roman empire, year after year, for centuries, can be guessed at from the fact that 9,000 captured animals were killed during the 100 day celebration of the dedication of the Coliseum in Rome and 11,000 were slain to mark Trajan's conquest of the new province of Dacia. By the early centuries AD, the elephant, rhinoceros and zebra were extinct in north Africa, the hippopotamus in the lower Nile and the tiger in north Persia and Mesopotamia.

The great spectacles of the Roman empire ceased in western Europe after the fifth century but the destruction of wildlife continued in other ways. Early medieval Europe consisted mainly of large areas of virtually undisturbed natural ecosystems with a small population living within it in scattered settlements (the exact opposite of the later landscape). The expansion of the settled area gradually reduced the habitats on which the plants and animals depended for their survival. Whole species became extinct and others disappeared across large areas or were severely reduced in numbers. The aurochs (the wild ancestor of modern cattle) was a woodland animal that suffered particularly from deforestation. It was extinct in Britain about 2000 BC and slowly disappeared from the rest of the continent. The last known specimen died in the Jaktorowa forest in Poland in 1627. The European bison was still found in the early medieval period across a wide area of Belgium and Germany but by the eighteenth century it was only found in eastern Europe and the last wild animal died in the Bialowieza forest of Poland in 1920. The great auk, a flightless seabird, was once found in huge colonies along the Atlantic coasts of Scotland, the Western Isles, Orkney and Shetland and Iceland. It was a highly vulnerable prey – in one episode in 1540 two ships were filled with freshly killed auks in half an hour (producing five tons of salted birds) and the crew killed more birds to eat fresh. The eggs were also eaten by sailors and since the auk only laid one egg a year, its ability to breed was easily undermined. By the eighteenth century the bird was becoming rare around the British coast. The last pair were killed in Iceland in 1844.

Many more species which were once common in the whole of Europe have become extinct across large areas of the continent. Wolves were found in large numbers throughout western Europe until about 500 years ago. As late as 1420 and 1438 wolf packs were seen in the streets of Paris in daylight. In 1520 enough still survived for Francis I to organise official hunts and about a hundred years later in 1640 there are accounts of wolves coming down from the hills of the Jura to terrorise the inhabitants of Besançon. In Britain there were still enough wolves to warrant full scale hunts in Scotland during the sixteenth century. The last recorded sighting of a wolf came in 1486 in England, 1576 in Wales, in Scotland in 1743 and in Ireland during the early nineteenth century. The Brown Bear was also common across medieval western Europe (although it had died out in Britain by the tenth century). However, numbers declined steadily through hunting and destruction of its habitat and it now only survives in a few remote mountainous areas. The same pattern of events affected the beaver, which was also common in medieval Europe and was trapped for its fur. It died out in Britain as early as the thirteenth century and later across most of the rest of Europe.

Britain, as one of the first countries to become densely settled and industrialised, illustrates many of the forces that affected the whole of Europe. The crane became extinct in the sixteenth century. The sea eagle was still common as late as the 1870s but is now extinct. The conversion of grassland to arable farms, combined with extensive hunting, made the great bustard extinct by 1838. The osprey, which was so common in the eighteenth century that its occurrence was not a cause for any special comment, was, wrongly, believed to be a major predator on salmon. With the increase in salmon fishing in the nineteenth century it was ruthlessly hunted and driven to extinction. A few pairs returned in the twentieth century but it now only breeds under extensive protection. The game bird of the Scottish forests, the capercaillie, was once common across the whole of the country, but relentless clearance of the forest reduced its numbers. By the seventeenth century it was restricted to the area north of the river Tay and the last example was seen in Inverness-shire in 1762. It was reintroduced in 1837 but the continuing clearance of the forest again reduced its numbers to a critical level – it is now estimated that only about 2,000 still survive. The golden eagle was still found in Derbyshire in the early seventeenth century and the Cheviots in the nineteenth but has now been driven to remote areas of the Scottish highlands. The chough was common in inland areas of Scotland till the early nineteenth century but is now rare even along the coasts. The red kite was once one of the commonest birds of prey. In the sixteenth century it was still found in the centre of London scavenging on rubbish in the streets. Over the next centuries it was hunted and its habitats destroyed. By the early twentieth century it had been reduced to about five birds and even now has recovered to less than a hundred pairs confined to central Wales.

While some of this trail of destruction was the side effect of agriculture and some the deliberate result of hunting and commercial exploitation, it is also evident from contemporary texts that the idea of conservation and the preservation of wildlife was mainly noticeable by its absence until comparatively recent times. The general attitude towards the natural world was well summed up by the seventeenth century English clergyman, Edmund Hickeringill, who wrote that, 'So noisome and offensive are some animals to human kind, that it concerns all mankind to get quit of the annoyance, with as speedy a riddance and despatch as may be, by any lawful means.' In 1668 John Worlidge published his *Systema Agriculturae* which contained a calendar for the year with the following tasks affecting animals regarded as 'harmful' to agriculture:

'February: pick up all the snails you can find, and destroy frogs and their spawn
April: gather up worms and snails
June: destroy ants;
July: kill . . . wasps and flies'

Official policy followed the same trend. In 1533 the English Parliament passed an act (the Scottish parliament had passed a similar one in 1424) requiring all parishes to have nets to catch rooks, choughs and crows. This was extended in 1566 so that churchwardens were authorised to pay for the corpses of foxes, polecats, weasels, stoats, otters, hedgehogs, rats, mice, moles, hawks, buzzards, ospreys, jays, ravens and kingfishers. In every area of England large hunts were carried out to try to exterminate various animals. In 1732 at Prestbury in Cheshire 5,480 moles were destroyed, at Northill in Bedfordshire between 1764 and 1774, 14,000 sparrows were killed (and 3,500 eggs destroyed) and at Deeping St James in Lincolnshire in 1779, 4,152 sparrows were killed. On one estate in the Scottish county of Sutherland in the early nineteenth century, 550 kingfishers were killed in just three years. In the same county on just two estates 295 adult and sixty young golden eagles (plus an unknown number of eggs) were destroyed between 1819–1826 (in an attempt to preserve fish and game for sport). The deliberate slaughter continued into the twentieth century – during the First World War the British government ordered the destruction of sparrows in order to try and increase crop yields and special clubs were set up to carry out the task. Their success can be judged from the fact that the one at Tring in Herfordshire killed 39,000 in three years.

Hunting for 'sport' across Europe has been another destructive force although it is almost impossible to measure the scale of the killing, particularly of wild birds, carried out year after year, century after century. Some idea of its huge cumulative impact can be gleaned from a few isolated examples. At Wainfleet, in Essex, 31,200 ducks were killed in just one year in the mid-eighteenth century. At one village in Lincolnshire an average of 3,000 widlfowl were killed every year between 1833–1868. Trapping and shooting of migratory birds has continued in many parts of Europe until the present day. It is now estimated that one in six of the migrating birds in Europe is killed in this way, and in Italy about 200 million birds are still shot every year. Shooting birds for food has been continual and on a massive scale – 270,000 wild quail were on sale in 1898 in the markets of Paris alone. The range of birds eaten in the past was also much wider than today: it included curlews, plovers, blackbirds, larks, thrushes and even gannets (in the nineteenth century 1,300 a year were being killed on the Bass Rock alone). Eggs of wild birds were also a much sought after delicacy – by the 1870s the lapwing was almost extinct in the north of England because of the demand for its eggs. Other human demands could have an equally devastating effect. The great crested grebe was driven to the point of extinction in nineteenth-century Britain because of the market for its down to make ladies' muffs. In 1850 the large copper butterfly became extinct in England because people collected its caterpillars. The nineteenth century craze for birds in cages was also highly destructive. In 1860, 14,000 goldfinches a year were being captured just from the area around Worthing in Sussex and in the early twentieth century over 7,000 linnets a week were being sold in the London markets.

In every part of Europe both the variety and the extent of wildlife has been seriously reduced over the past centuries. The impact of European expansion on the rest of the world involved losses on an even bigger scale and in a shorter period. When the first Europeans reached the Americas, Australasia and the Pacific they were struck by the new and strange plants and animals they encountered. One European arriving in Australia in the 1830s noted some of the more striking differences:

'trees retained their leaves and shed their bark instead, the swans were black, the eagles white, the bees were stingless, some mammals had pockets, others laid eggs . . . even the blackberries were red.'

But above all the first explorers and settlers were stunned by the sheer profusion of wildlife in areas that had often seen little or no human settlement. Their accounts give some idea of the teeming mass of life that untouched ecosystems could support. In 1658 when the French explorer Pierre Radisson reached Lake Superior, he reported that there were 'stores of fishes, sturgeons of vast bigness, and pikes seven feet long. A month's subsistence for a regiment could have been taken in a few hours.' Thirty years later one of the first settlers in Florida reported that 'quantities of wild pigeons, parrots and other birds were so numerous that boatloads of birds' eggs were taken.' In 1709 when an English sailor, Woods Rogers, landed on Mas Afuera, one of the Juan Fernandez Islands off the coast of Chile, he wrote that the seals and sea lions were 'so thick on the shore, that we are forced to drive them away, before we could land, being so numerous, that it is scarce credible to those, who have not seen them.' At the end of the eighteenth century Captain Cook arrived in Australia and found that the sea was so full of fish that they broke the fishing nets and flocks of thousands of birds could easily be shot since they had no fear of humans. On the Great Barrier Reef the botanist of the expedition, Joseph Banks, wrote in his journal that the butterflies were so numerous that:

'the air for the space of 3 or 4 acres was crowded with them to a wonderful degree; the eye could not be turned in any direction without seeing millions, and yet every branch and twig was almost covered with those that sat still.'

A few years later Captain Thomas Melville was sailing into Sydney harbour when he saw more sperm whales in a day than he had seen in six years in the old whaling grounds off the coast of Brazil. He wrote that 'we sailed through different shoals of them from 12 o'clock in the day till sunset, all round the horizon, as far as I could see from the mast head.'

The profusion of wildlife appeared to these early explorers and settlers as a huge and readily available living food store. They proceeded to draw freely on this, without concern for the fate of any individual species, however strange or attractive or vulnerable it might be. This unrestrained killing fairly soon had a drastic effect in the case of islands where isolated populations had developed, often dominated by flightless birds because of the lack of predators (90 per cent of bird extinctions have occurred on islands). On Mauritius, for example, the introduction of the pig and rat, together with hunting by sailors looking for food, made the ground nesting dodo extinct by 1681. The example of Australia illustrates a number of major wildlife extinctions and substantial reductions in numbers since the start of European settlement. The introduction of rats killed seven of the twelve bird species on

Lord Howe Island off the east coast of Australia. The duck billed platypus was common in the Blue mountains in 1815 but had disappeared by 1850. An expedition to the Murray-Darling basin in 1856–1857 recorded thirty one species of native animal – twenty two of them are now extinct. The widespread hunting of wild animals for 'sport', particularly organised mass kangaroo hunts, was one of the prime causes of the destruction. In 1850 one hunter, Captain Foster Fyans, lamented that in Victoria:

'Emus and kangaroos on our arrival were plentiful in all parts . . . also bustards in large flocks of . . . 40 or perhaps more. The bustards now are scarce, and only met with in distant places. The kangaroo and emu are nearly extinct in the district; the country is almost void of game.'

By the end of the nineteenth century some of the rare marsupials such as the hare-wallaby and the banded hare-wallaby were already extinct and the last of the bilbies, which in the early nineteenth century had been the commonest form of native game, was shot in 1912.

The vogue for big-game hunting in the nineteenth and early twentieth centuries in Africa and India also had a major impact on animal numbers, especially carnivores such as lions and tigers at the top of the food chain. Some of the fashions of the period (many of which still continue), including crocodile skins for shoes and handbags, elephant tusks for their ivory and rhinoceros horn for its supposed aphrodisiac properties, added to the demand for large-scale slaughter of certain species. The demand for exotic feathers in hats in the nineteenth century meant that in 1869 Brazil alone exported 170,000 dead birds for their plumage and in 1913 the London salerooms were able to offer the feathers from 77,000 herons, 48,000 condors and 162,000 kingfishers. Plants were affected too. The collection and introduction of new species into Europe from all over the world (in the form of live specimens and not just seeds) was keenly pursued in the nineteenth century by plant hunters working for private collectors. These plant safaris probably did little damage except on a local scale but the rise of a mass market was a different matter. For example the craze for rare orchids in nineteenth century Europe meant that Brazil was exporting a minimum of 100,000 a year from the tropical forests.

The human impact on the wildlife of North America was even more devastating than in Australia. When the first Europeans reached the Great Plains of central North America they found huge bison herds roaming the area. The minimum size of the herds was about 40 million animals and they may have reached a total of 60 million. When the Indians obtained horses and rifles from the Europeans they started hunting the bison for food and hides but they only killed abut 300,000 a year, well below the natural replacement rate. The herds were therefore still around their original size when the Europeans began to exploit them in the 1830s. The bison were killed first for their meat – about 2 million a year – a rate which soon began to reduce the size of the herds. The slaughter was stepped up after 1871, when bison hides were first made into commercial leather, to about 3 million animals a year. This indiscriminate killing could not be maintained for very long. It lasted until the last decade of the nineteenth century when the herds were driven to the point of extinction. The bison now survives in a few carefully managed herds.

Probably the most terrible example of mass slaughter in the history of wildlife was not the bison but the passenger pigeon – a story that almost defies belief. The early Europeans in North America frequently commented on the huge numbers of blue, long-tailed, fast and graceful pigeons in the country. One of the first settlers in Virginia wrote that, 'There are wild pigeons in winter beyond number or imagination, myself have seen three or four hours together flocks in the air, so thick that even have they shadowed the sky from us.' Similar reports can be found from the Dutch on Manhattan Island in 1625, from Salem in Massachusetts in 1631 and some of the first explorers in Louisiana in 1698. As late as 1854 in Wayne County, New York, a local resident wrote that, 'There would be days and days when the air was alive with them, hardly a break occurring in the flocks for half a day at a time. Flocks stretched as far as a person could see, one tier above another.' On 8 April 1873 at Saginaw in Michigan there was a continuous stream of passenger pigeons overhead between 7.30 in the morning and 4 o'clock in the afternoon. Other reports describe flocks a mile wide flying overhead for four or five hours at a time during their migration in the early spring from the south to their breeding areas in New England, New York, Ohio and the southern Great Lakes area. The flocks were so thickly packed that a single shot could bring down thirty or forty birds and many were killed simply by hitting them with pieces of wood as they flew over hilltops. Their roosting sites were correspondingly enormous – some covered an area five miles by twelve with up to ninety nests in a single tree – branches broke and whole trees were toppled by the sheer weight of roosting birds, often standing on top of each other, and leaving a pile of droppings several inches deep under the trees. The

exact number of passenger pigeons in North America when the Europeans arrived is not known but the best guess is 5 billion – about a third
of all the birds in North America at the time and the same as the total
number of birds to be found today in the United States.

One reason why the passenger pigeon existed in such prodigious
numbers was the lack of natural predators apart from hawks and eagles.
It was, however, surprisingly vulnerable to human intervention. Each
female laid only one egg a year, which made it difficult to replace any
losses quickly. Only a flimsy nest was made and its habit of nesting in
vast colonies and migrating in huge flocks made it very easy to attack.
The birds fed mainly on acorns, chestnuts and beechnuts in the
extensive woodlands of North America and so when these were steadily
cut down their habitat and food supplies were reduced. Human intervention was at first relatively restrained, largely because of the limited
numbers living in North America. The Indians captured the pigeons in
large nets and by the 1630s the settlers of New England were doing the
same. The young squabs were regarded as a great delicacy and the
adults were sought after for their feathers as well as their meat. In the
first couple of centuries of European settlement it is doubtful whether
the number of pigeons declined very much given the relatively small
number of humans in the area. After 1830 the practice of releasing live
pigeons from traps for shooting practice began, but this in itself would
not have proved fatal to the existence of the species even though about
250,000 a year were being killed in this way in the 1870s.

The population had certainly been reduced by the middle of the
nineteenth century but was still several billion strong. The real
onslaught began with the onset of large-scale commercial hunting
carried out by well-organised trappers and shippers in order to supply
the developing cities on the east coast of the United States with a cheap
source of meat. It began once railways linking the Great Lakes area with
New York opened in the early 1850s. By 1855 300,000 pigeons a year
were being sent to New York alone. The worst of the mass slaughter
took place in the 1860s and 1870s. The scale of the operation can be
judged by figures that seem almost incredible but which were carefully
recorded as part of a perfectly legal and highly profitable commerce. On
just one day in 1860 (23 July) 235,200 birds were sent east from Grand
Rapids in Michigan. During 1874 Oceana County in Michigan sent
over 1,000,000 birds to the markets in the east and two years later was
sending 400,000 a week at the height of the season and a total of
1,600,000 in the year. In 1869, Van Buren County, also in Michigan,
sent 7,500,000 birds to the east. Even in 1880, when numbers had

already been severely reduced, 527,000 birds were shipped east from Michigan. Not surprisingly, even the vast flocks of pigeons could not withstand slaughter on this scale. Numbers fell rapidly and by the late 1880s large flocks, which had once been so common, had become a matter for comment and investigation, and most were no more than a few hundred strong. The last known specimens were seen in most states of the eastern United States, in the 1890s, and the passenger pigeon died out in the wild in Ohio about 1900. The last survivor of a species that had once numbered 5 billion died in captivity in 1914.

Europeans also made their mark on the ecosystems of the rest of the world by introducing new species as well as exterminating many of those they encountered and severely reducing the numbers of many more. People who went to settle in these new areas took with them domesticated animals and also, accidentally, many of the pests they had known in Europe. Ever since the continents had drifted apart tens of millions of years earlier the flora and fauna of the Americas and Australasia had developed in isolation from their counterparts in Eurasia. Now, after 1500, they were brought into contact, often with far-reaching results. The peoples of the Americas and Australia had virtually no animals suitable for domestication and the Europeans therefore took their own animals (pigs, cattle, sheep and horses) with them. When these escaped and went wild they spread rapidly into a large variety of habitats.

Pigs were introduced everywhere. Once in the wild, they multiplied rapidly in the forests where they could find plenty of food. Australia now has over twenty million wild pigs. Cattle were first carried to the Americas by Columbus in 1493 and within fifty years were found in huge herds as far apart as Florida, Mexico and Peru. They flourished on the pampas of South America – by 1700 there were as many as fifty million of them. By the middle of the nineteenth century they were so numerous that walls for fields were made from cattle skulls placed nine deep. In Australia the wild herds can be traced back to eight animals that escaped from a domesticated herd in 1788. Domesticated sheep did not flourish in the Americas until they were taken to Mexico in the 1540s. Within thirty years there were immense, migrating wild herds, 200,000 strong in the Michoacan area alone, and by 1614 there were 620,000 sheep in the area around Santiago in Chile. In Australia and New Zealand there were no hoofed animals before the arrival of the Europeans at the end of the eighteenth century, yet within a hundred years there were a hundred million sheep and eight million cattle in

Australia. In New Zealand there were nine million sheep within thirty years of its annexation by Britain and there are now some seventy million sheep and eight million cattle in the country. This massive increase in the number of grazing animals had major consequences for many of the native grasses of the area, especially kangaroo grass, which were not adapted to intensive grazing. They were replaced by European varieties. Horses were also taken to the Americas by Columbus in 1493 and they soon became wild. They migrated from Mexico to the Great Plains, where they were domesticated by the Indians, bringing a fundamental change in the way of life. From gatherers and agricultural- ists some of the Indian tribes became hunters of the great bison herds. Europeans, moving westwards over the Appalachians in the eighteenth century, regarded the huge herds of wild horses as a pest and shot them in large numbers. Horses also went wild in Australia and again quickly became a nuisance. The camel was introduced into the central deserts of Australia in the late nineteenth century as a pack animal but the experiment was not a success and camels were allowed to go wild. Now regarded as pests, there are more camels in Australia than in Arabia. The honeybee was introduced into North America (which had no bees at all so the Indians used maple syrup as a sweetener), where it became naturalised by about 1800. Europeans also took honeybees to Australia in 1822, where they soon outnumbered the native stingless bee, and to New Zealand in the early 1840s.

The greatest ecological disaster caused by the deliberate introduction of a new animal came in Australia after Thomas Austin, a farmer near Geelong in Victoria, established a few rabbits for game in 1859. Well known as rapid breeders, in Australia, with no natural predators, they excelled themselves and were soon devastating crops over a wide area. By 1880 they had reached New South Wales and were also affecting sheep farming in parts of South Australia. Large scale eradication campaigns were mounted but to little effect – in the mid-1880s 1.8 million rabbits were killed in Victoria and nearly 7 million in New South Wales without perceptibly slowing up their relentless spread. By the 1890s the rabbit population was advancing across the Nullarbor desert towards Western Australia and new countermeasures were tried. A 1,000 mile-long fence was built from the north to the south coast in 1902–7 in an attempt to exclude the rabbits but it was breached in the 1920s.

The rabbit population of Australia increased, in less than a century, from a handful to about 500 million by 1950, and they were causing huge crop losses over much of the country. Almost continual eradication campaigns had proved unsuccessful in stemming the rising flood of rabbits and in desperation in that year the disease myxomatosis was deliberately introduced from Brazil. Within a year an area the size of western Europe was affected and the death rate among the rabbit population was about 99.8 per cent. But bacteriological warfare against rabbits provided only a temporary respite: the tiny part of the population that was naturally immune to the disease was able to continue breeding and within seven years the death rate had fallen to less than 25 per cent. Despite subsequent periodic outbreaks of myxomatosis the rabbit population is once again growing rapidly. If Thomas Austin had known what had happened to the island of Porto Santo in the Madeiras in the fifteenth century, he might have thought again before introducing the rabbit into Australia. When the first Portuguese settlers arrived in the 1420s they found an island where the flora and fauna were completely unaffected by any previous human settlement. This soon changed when the rabbits they brought with them escaped and, benefitting from the absence of any natural predators, began to breed rapidly. Within a few years the land was devastated – large areas had lost all their plants and the bare soil was eroding away in prodigious quantities. The situation became so bad that the settlement had to be abandoned and all the people moved to Madeira. The island was only re-colonised with great difficulty thirty years later.

Accidental introduction of new animals, especially mice and rats which came unnoticed on many of the early ships, could be just as disruptive. Both the early settlements at Jamestown in Virginia in 1609 and at Sydney in Australia in 1790 were nearly wiped out because rats from the ships ate most of their precious stores of grain. During the 1570s, about fifty years after the Spanish conquest, Peru was already suffering from large scale plagues of rats. Much the same occurred in Australia after mice escaped from some of the early ships which visited the colony. There were no natural predators to restrain numbers and they multiplied rapidly. The scale of the problem can be judged from the fact that in just one area of South Australia thirty-two million mice were killed in only four months during 1917. Native animals could also be displaced by the introduction of European species. European starlings were first introduced to the United States in 1891 as ornamental birds in Central Park, New York. Some escaped and by 1926 flocks were reported from as far afield as Georgia, New England and Kentucky and after another thirty years the starling was established across the whole of the continental United States. Displaying its aggressive rather than any ornamental side it took over the ecological niches of a number of native birds and devastated the population of bluebirds and flickers.

The introduction of new animals could also affect plant life, often in dramatic and unexpected ways. Since goats were introduced to the island of St Helena in 1810, twenty-two of the thirty-three native plant species have become extinct because of their comprehensive grazing habits. In the 1830s when Charles Darwin visited the plains of Uruguay he found that hundreds of square miles of land were impenetrable because of the growth of the prickly cardoon, which had flourished thanks to the overgrazing of other edible plants by the huge herds of wild cattle and horses. The native plants of the Americas and Australasia have also been badly affected by the introduction of European species. European weeds such as ferns, thistles, plantain, nettles and sedge are now common in the United States, South America, Australia and New Zealand. In many cases they spread rapidly after initial introduction. Christmas Island in the Pacific was only settled in 1888 yet, by 1904, thirty species of European weed were flourishing on the island. In California there were only three non-native plant species in 1769 but within a century this had risen to ninety-one and European species constituted about half of the vegetation. By 1832, 137 European weeds were recorded in New York state and different ones had adapted to the different conditions in the southern states. On the pampas of South America in the eighteenth century the artichoke and giant Mediterranean thistle, which grew to about six feet high, went wild and created huge impenetrable areas. By 1877 there were 153 different types of European plant growing around Buenos Aires and fifty years later only a quarter of the plants on the pampas were of native origin. Even in Australia where, because of the harsh climatic conditions in the interior, the area open to colonisation by European plants was more limited, many native species were replaced. Within less than a hundred years of the first settlement there were 139 alien plant species in southeast Australia and the number is now over 800. In the more temperate climate of New Zealand, once the European bee had been introduced, new plants flourished so that over half of the plants now found in the country are of European origin. In some cases the introduction of new plants may have added to the variety of local flora but in many the consequences have been highly disruptive, often because the plant's natural enemies were left behind. A particularly telling example of this second category is the history of the prickly pear in Australia. Introduced in 1839 in order to provide hedges, it quickly went wild in Queensland and New South Wales creating barriers over six feet high.

By 1925 over sixty million acres of land were affected and in half of this area no other plants could grow. The prickly pear was eventually brought under control by importing south American caterpillars which feed on the plant.

The increased communications between different parts of the world also resulted in the spread of plant diseases and pests. These often proved to be more devastating in the new environment than in the old. For example, Asiatic chestnut blight, to which Asian species have developed considerable immunity, arrived in New York in 1900 and caused extensive destruction among native American species. It also arrived accidentally in Switzerland and Italy in 1938 and spread to many parts of Europe. The introduction of the potato to Colorado altered the habits of the Colorado beetle, which had until then fed on the wild sand-bur. The beetle rapidly became a major pest destroying potato crops across the United States as it spread to reach the east coast by 1874. Despite rigorous controls it reached France in 1920 and then spread to the rest of western Europe, reaching the Soviet Union in 1955. In the 1850s the American vine aphid (phylloxera), which normally lived on wild vines east of the Rocky mountains, was brought on board ships to Europe. It spread rapidly through the vineyards of Europe causing extensive destruction, even threatening the future of the wine industry. The outbreak was only brought under control by grafting European vines onto American rootstock which was resistant to the root phase of the aphid.

The effects of the expansion of Europe – its people, its plants and animals – were far-reaching and irreversible. The wildlife of the world was never the same again. Many species were driven to extinction or so reduced in numbers that they could barely survive in a few limited areas. Many animals and plants of European origin were spread around the world, disrupting natural ecosystems and again causing the extinction or decline of many native species. European domination of the world greatly increased the pressure on animals which could be killed for food or to provide furs, skins, oil and feathers to meet a wide range of utilitarian or luxury requirements, either for the settlers themselves or, more importantly, for the European market. In the face of some of the extreme examples it is difficult to answer questions such as why did the slaughter go on so indiscriminately and why wasn't it seen as ultimately counterproductive? The extinction of the passenger pigeon (and other animals around the world such as the great auk and the dodo) and the near extinction of the American bison illustrate what the American ecologist William Ophuls has dubbed 'the problem of the commons'.

No one 'owned' these animals and no one therefore had an interest in controlling the rate of killing and in ensuring a sustainable basis for continued exploitation. Because there was no ownership and because the cost of exploitation was very low (a horse and a rifle for the bison and a net for the passenger pigeon) many hunters were tempted into the market. In a highly competitive situation the most rational action for any individual hunter was to seek to maximise the immediate kill before a competitor did the same. The faster the overall population fell, the greater the temptation to kill as many as possible as quickly as possible. All the pressures, therefore, encouraged people to treat the animals as a short-term resource to be exploited as quickly as possible – indeed anybody who took the opposite view and tried to limit the numbers they killed would be far less successful economically and only increase the opportunities open to their competitors. This pattern of seeking to maximise the immediate short-term gain at the expense of any longer-term considerations is a central feature of the way in which modern societies have hunted and exploited animals. Little or no effort has been made to devise mechanisms that ensure that species are not over-exploited and driven to the point of extinction. The history of four major areas of exploitation – fishing, the fur trade, sealing and whaling – all illustrate the same dismal truth.

As only a small number of domesticated animals could be supported in medieval Europe, fish formed an important part of the diet. Later they provided not only variety but also, while stocks lasted, a cheap food. Until the sixteenth century fishing was largely confined to the coastal waters of Europe but even here the tell-tale signs of over-exploitation were already starting to appear. Stocks fell drastically and by 1500 fishing for herring in the Baltic had almost come to a halt. Within a few decades the same problem was affecting cod fishing off the coast of western Europe. By then, though, attention had turned to the Grand Banks off Newfoundland where the fish were so plentiful that they could be scooped out of the sea with buckets. Until the present century the stocks of fish in the vast oceans of the world seemed to be inexhaustible. It was not, however, until the development of mechanisation and factory fishing by fleets from the major fishing nations in the latter part of the nineteenth century, particularly in Britain and the rest of western Europe, that serious problems began to emerge. There was no attempt to limit catches and all the attention was devoted to increasing the effectiveness of exploitation. Fish numbers fell in area after area and as they did so the fleets turned to catching younger and immature fish, which only exacerbated the problem. The fall in numbers in the area around western Europe can be traced for particular species and different fishing grounds. It first occurred in 1890 for plaice in the North Sea, in 1905 for haddock and in 1920 for cod in the same area. In the 1920s stocks of hake off Ireland and the south-west approaches, plaice off the Kola peninsula, cod and haddock east of Iceland, plaice to the west of Iceland and haddock off the North Cape had all fallen drastically because of overfishing. In California the sardine industry showed the symptoms of rapid expansion and equally rapid decline. It began about 1900 but really took off after 1915 with the development of an export trade in cheap canned fish. By the mid-1930s about 600,000 tons of sardines were being caught every year. Within ten years the industry collapsed because of overfishing.

Responding to improved technology and higher demand, the global fish catch rose rapidly after 1945, almost quadrupling from seventeen-and-a-half million tons a year to reach sixty-five million tons in 1970. But this was only achieved by intensive short term exploitation of a number of different fisheries and the rate of expansion has fallen off sharply – since 1970 the global catch has only increased by 18 per cent. Many more areas have been virtually exhausted since 1945. By 1955 the once prolific cod and perch fisheries near Newfoundland were suffering the same fate as the North Sea. In the north-west Atlantic the haddock catch fell from 250,000 tons in 1965 to less than 20,000 tons ten years later. The total catch of all species in this area reached a peak in 1968 and despite the fact that more boats fished the area the total catch fell by a half in only five years. The North Sea industry, the scene of the longest and most intensive exploitation, was badly affected. The industry itself had been unable to devise controls and governments belatedly introduced severe restrictions and quotas but too late to save the fishing industry, which has contracted drastically. The restrictions also came too late to save the fish. The total stock of fish in the North Sea is estimated to have fallen from about four million tons in the mid-1960s to less than one million tons twenty years later. The number of young haddock and cod around Britain in the late 1980s was at five per cent of the level only ten years earlier. The Japanese catch of chub mackerel in the north west Pacific fell from over one-and-a-half million tons in 1978 to less than half that figure four years later. As the more accessible areas have been overfished to the point of exhaustion, the world's fleets have moved on to the last remaining unexploited areas such as the south Atlantic and Antarctic. Here the same symptoms, particularly the fall in the krill catch, are becoming apparent. The krill population grew rapidly because of the fall in the numbers of whales which fed on them. Extensive fishing did not start until after the early 1960s when just four tons a year were being caught. By 1982 this had risen to 520,000 tons a year but the symptoms of over-exploitation appeared and by the mid-1980s the catch had fallen to only 130,000 tons a year. The United Nations Food and Agriculture Organisation now estimates that eleven major oceanic fisheries have been overfished to the point of collapse.

A similar sequence of events (overfishing reducing once plentiful fish populations so drastically that it is no longer possible to exploit them economically) can be identified in some of the major lake and river fisheries which have also been affected by increasing levels of pollution. In the Caspian Sea the sturgeon catch is now only a quarter of the pre-1917 level and overall the fish catch has fallen by a half since the 1930s. The Great Lakes of North America tell the same story of an almost total disintegration of the fishing industry in the present century. In the eighteenth century sturgeon was so common in Lake Erie that they could be killed by hitting them with an axe handle. At the end of the nineteenth century the annual catch was over one million pounds weight a year. By 1964 it had fallen to less than 4,000 pounds. In the 1930s fourteen million pounds weight of cisco were caught every year but by the mid-1960s this had fallen to about 8,000 pounds a year. On Lake Michigan the annual catch of trout was about seven million pounds in 1943 but within a decade it had fallen to just 4,000 pounds a year. The development of salmon fishing as a 'sport' in the middle of the nineteenth century had a drastic affect on some rivers, particularly in Scotland. The salmon catch on the river Tweed at Berwick fell from 149,000 in 1842 to 40,000 a year by the late 1870s.

Trapping animals for their fur sustained one of the major trading activities in Europe until the nineteenth century. The fur trade in the earliest periods was a matter of exploiting European animals for the European market but when these supplies were virtually exhausted it became one of the driving forces behind the expansion of Europe, particularly the Russian drive eastwards into Siberia and the spread of European influence westwards across North America. The fur trade can be traced back to the Roman empire when merchants were obtaining furs from the nomadic tribes of Russia. But the real growth in the trade took place in early medieval Europe, when furs were sought after, not just for practical purposes such as keeping warm, but also as a status symbol, an indispensable part of the wardrobe of the upper classes. In England for example many regulations were made to try to restrict the wearing of furs to those of high status. In 1337 the English Parliament reserved the wearing of furs to royalty and members of the nobility with incomes over £100 a year. In 1363 another Act was passed, this time to limit the wearing of the highest value furs to the nobility and clergy. There were many other regulations too but the fact that they had to be repeated suggests that they were to a large extent ineffective.

To provide one pelt meant killing one wild animal – by means of traps to preserve the value of the skin. Most of the animals whose skins were in demand in medieval Europe were small – squirrels, martens, ermine, sable and foxes. The relative value varied from time to time depending on their rarity and also on changes in fashion. In the thirteenth and fourteenth centuries grey squirrel fur (not the red of the then common European animal) was highly fashionable. In the fifteenth century when squirrel fur became widely available the wealthy switched to wearing the rarer furs such as sable, fox and marten. Large numbers of furs were required to make even one garment, particularly from the small squirrel pelts – several hundred were needed to make the lining for a cloak and 1,400 for an average counterpane. When Henry VIII had a gown made from sable fur it took 350 pelts. A few surviving documents give an idea of how many furs were bought for the English royal household – between 1285–1288 Edward I bought 120,000 squirrel pelts alone every year and in the early 1390s Richard II bought 109,000 pelts a year.

At first much of the trade was local as each country had its own wild areas where the fur-bearing animals could be trapped. But soon a number of main trapping areas emerged. English merchants obtained many furs from Scotland and Ireland and in the fourteenth century Inverness became an international centre for the collection of marten and beaver skins, selling to traders from as far away as Germany. Other important sources were the south of Europe – especially southern Italy, Spain, Burgundy and Germany. The local trade in skins continued for centuries – in the nineteenth century the market at Dumfries in south-west Scotland was still dealing in 70,000 hare and 200,000 rabbit skins a year – but the focus of the trade increasingly shifted to the great, unpopulated northern forests as the wild areas of western Europe were steadily reduced and overtrapped.

From the ninth century the Viking traders (the 'Rus') at Kiev developed an extensive trapping network for furs, particularly sable, black fox, ermine, beaver and squirrel, using the nomadic tribes to do the collecting (just as the Europeans were to do later in north America). They mainly sent the furs southwards to the Byzantine empire but by the twelfth century, as western Europe became wealthier, the Baltic was becoming an important trading area under the German Hansa merchants (about three quarters of the Hansa trade was in furs). Of the three main Russian centres, Novgorod concentrated on the more down market but flourishing squirrel trade, which became the economic foundation of the state. The value of land was reckoned in thousands of pelts and rents were paid in furs. Moscow and Kazan specialised in sable, fox and marten for the luxury market. They obtained supplies through a network of traders and the payment of tribute by nomadic tribes. The size of the Russian medieval fur trade and the extent of the corresponding slaughter of animals was huge, as a few surviving documents reveal. In 1393 one ship left Novgorod for Flanders carrying 225,000 furs and at this time London alone was importing about 300,000 squirrel pelts a year while Venice bought 266,000 skins from the Hanseatic merchants in 1409. The best estimate is that at the height of the squirrel trade Novgorod was exporting about 400–500,000 skins a year. There are no reliable figures for the Moscow and Kazan trade but its scale can be judged from the fact that in the early sixteenth century it was selling 40,000 sables a year just to the traders of the Ottoman empire.

Hundreds of millions of animals were killed at an unsustainable rate both in Russia and western Europe. As early as 1240 in the Denpr basin around Kiev, the original centre of the trade, no fur-bearing animals were left and Novgorod merchants were already trading 1,000 miles away beyond the Urals in an attempt to find adequate supplies. From the early fifteenth century imports into London were waning and Russian prices started to rise as the animal population declined. By the 1460s London merchants were complaining about inadequate supplies and the volume of exports from Novgorod had fallen by about a half, though they were still at the substantial level of some 200,000 skins a year. Other areas of Europe were also nearly exhausted. In 1424 the Scottish kings were driven to banning the export of marten skins and by the sixteenth century the beaver was virtually extinct in southern Europe. The main source of beaver furs – Spain – had dried up and only lower quality skins such as rabbit were available. In the fifteenth century sables were common as far west as Finland but by the late seventeenth century they were confined to Siberia.

By the sixteenth century the only remaining untrapped area was Siberia and it was the continuing demand for furs from western Europe that drove the Russian merchants, using native and Russian trappers, into this largely unexplored area. As in the medieval period in western

Russia, furs rapidly became the main trade in Siberia and the main currency – the price of an iron kettle was the number of sable or ermine pelts that would fit into it – and by the mid-seventeenth century over a third of the income of the Russian state came from the fur trade. The early trappers could hardly believe their eyes. They describe vast numbers of animals and ermine so tame that they would come up to the houses and be caught by hand. As elsewhere the huge numbers encouraged large-scale killing and once an area was exhausted the trappers moved further east to find more animals. By the end of the eighteenth century the fur-bearing animals of even such a vast area as Siberia were virtually exhausted and the Russian traders were turning their attention to the sea otter of the northern Pacific islands. Between 1750 and 1790 about 250,000 otters were killed before the trade collapsed because of overhunting. By the nineteenth century the heyday of the Russian fur trade was almost over. The white fox was nearly extinct but about 20,000 sables, 25,000 ermines, 20,000 red foxes and 2,000 blue foxes were still being killed every year in Siberia.

The virtual extermination of fur-bearing animals in western Europe and the western parts of Russia by the early sixteenth century meant that from the start of settlement in, and trade with, North America the search for furs was one of the driving forces behind European expansion across the continent. At the first contact between the French and the Indians in 1534 the Europeans exchanged their goods for beaver skins and they soon established an organised trade in furs. For a long period the Europeans did not trap the animals themselves but used the Indians to do so and traded the goods the local inhabitants wanted in return for furs. The habits of the beaver made it very easy to trap. They settled in dense colonies and were also sedentary, making it possible for the trappers to concentrate on particular areas. But their low birth rate also made it very difficult for them to recover from overhunting. What the fur traders and trappers preferred to do was exploit an area until it was no longer economic to continue and then move on. For example, by 1600 the region around the St Lawrence river was exhausted as was upstate New York shortly afterwards – beaver were common on the Hudson river in 1610 but extinct by 1640.

By the mid-seventeenth century the trade was well organised in the interior of North America, mainly along the St Lawrence river, and controlled through a series of fortified trading posts. The rivalry between the French and the British Hudson's Bay Company was intense and ensured a high rate of exploitation. Europeans were also becoming fur trappers as well as traders. (The consequences for wildlife in the area where the trappers wintered could be dire. For example, during the winter of 1709–10 at Port Nelson eighty men consumed 90,000 partridges and 25,000 hares.) The scale of the fur trade at this time can be judged from a series of examples. In just one year (1742) Fort York traded 130,000 beavers and 9,000 martens and at one trading post in Canada in the 1760s the Hudson's Bay Company was taking nearly 100,000 beaver skins a year. In 1743 the French port of La Rochelle (one of the centres of the trade with Canada) imported 127,000 beaver skins, 30,000 martens, 12,000 otters, 110,000 racoons and 16,000 bears. Similar figures were common at other French and British ports. It is not surprising, with this level of exploitation repeated in a large number of ports year after year, that by the end of the eighteenth century the animals were driven to extinction in area after area and the North American fur trade was in decline. The number of furs trapped in the Red River area fell by two-thirds between 1804 and 1808 and beaver skin exports from Canada fell from 182,000 in 1793 to 92,000 in 1805.

The American trade was sustained in a last burst through the opening up of new areas for exploitation in the far west and the Pacific coast at the beginning of the nineteenth century. In 1805 when the first American explorers (Lewis and Clark) travelled through the area west of the Mississippi into the Rocky mountains and on to the Pacific they reported that the area was 'richer in beaver and otter than any country on earth'. Within less than forty years the area would be virtually cleared of both animals and the American fur trade would have nowhere else to go. In 1840, a traveller, Frederick Ruxton, noted the achievements of the trappers: 'Not a hole or corner but has been ransacked by these hardy men. From the Mississippi to the mouth of the Colorado of the West, from the frozen regions of the north to . . . Mexico, the beaver hunter has set his traps in every creek and stream.' Trading was organised in the traditional way with Indian tribes working for European traders in return for European goods and white fur trappers working either independently or for the main firms involved – the British Hudson's Bay Company or the American, Jacob Astor. Unrestrained competition between them rapidly depleted beaver stocks. In the early 1830s the number of animals killed was already in decline as the beaver neared the point of extinction. By 1831 the beaver was extinct on the northern Great Plains and the trapping effort had to move further west to the Pacific area. Across the whole area overtrapping had reached such a point that yields of furs were down to a quarter of the level expected from new areas. In 1833 the situation was so bad that the Hudson's Bay Company issued instructions to its trappers not to hunt in certain areas where the beaver was almost extinct – the instructions were ineffectual. The next year saw the almost complete collapse of the beaver trade in the far west of North America because of overtrapping. By the late 1830s only 2,000 beaver skins a year could be obtained from the whole of the Rocky Mountains area. Beavers were only saved from total extinction by a change in fashion. Beaver skins were mainly used to make hats but prices rose as the supply collapsed and a new craze for silk hats made demand plummet. By 1840 beaver trapping in North America was over. The trapers switched to other furs – 500,000 muskrat skins were sent to England in 1842 and 137,000 martens in the early 1850s – but they too were soon exhausted.

By the late nineteenth century the killing of fur-bearing animals, which had gone on across the world as an international trade for at least a thousand years, had reduced the population of many types drastically and over large areas once flourishing species were extinct. As supplies from Russia and North America collapsed and the rarity value of furs increased, the nature of the trade altered. The last, remaining, untouched areas were utilised and exotic new species were killed – the chinchilla and ocelot are now virtually extinct in Latin America because of overtrapping. In Australia the platypus, opossum and different types of wallaby were hunted for their fur. The state of Victoria alone was exporting 250,000 skins a year in the early twentieth century and in 1919–1921 Australia sold five-and-a-half million opossum furs and 200,000 koala skins. Once supplies from the wild were no longer available in sufficient quantities, the fur trade came to depend largely on farming rather than trapping: animals were specially bred on 'fur farms' – 80 per cent of the world's trade in furs now comes from such farms.

The demand for fur and specialist skins was one of the main driving forces behind the hunting of many types of seal. As early as 1610 the Dutch were killing seals along the African coast for their skins but the sealing industry did not develop on a major scale until the late eighteenth century when other species were in drastic decline. It was dominated by western Europe, Russia, Canada and the United States with the main markets in Europe, North America and China. The animals were usually clubbed to death when they were onshore to breed and defenceless. The industry showed the same characteristics as the fur trade – rapid exploitation of an area until the seals were either extinct or so reduced in number that it was no longer economic to hunt them, followed by a move to a new area. In its first phase, between the 1780s and the 1820s, the trade concentrated on killing the southern fur seal which was found in large numbers across the southern hemisphere. One of the first areas to be exploited – and exhausted – were the islands of the south Atlantic. In the 1790–1791 hunting season one American ship took 5,000 skins from the island of Tristan da Cunha and the Falkland Islands and Tierra del Fuego were exhausted at about the same time. In the first quarter of the nineteenth century South Georgia was a major centre of the trade and, in total, well over a million seals were killed there. The South Shetland Islands were exhausted by two years' hunting (one ship killed 9,000 in three weeks and two ships took 45,000 between them in one season). Hunting moved on into the southern Indian Ocean centred on Kerguelen Island. Seals were killed there from the early nineteenth century but by the mid-1820s were extinct. In the Pacific, sealing was centred on the islands off the coast of Chile, in particular Mas Afuera in the Juan Fernandez Islands. One account describes how a single ship killed 100,000 seals in one visit and there were at times fourteen ships operating round the island. In just seven years between 1797 and 1803 over 3 million seals were killed on this one island and the herd was on the point of extinction. When the first Europeans visited Australia and the adjacent region they found large, undisturbed seal colonies but within twenty years these too were destroyed. For example, an onslaught on the seal herd along the Bass Strait killed 100,000 animals in a single season (1805) and reduced the herd to such a level that it was no longer economic to hunt them. On Macquarie Island, first discovered in 1810, 180,000 seals were killed in three years and within a decade the herd on the island was extinct. By the 1820s the southern fur seal had been almost wiped out: it was no longer worthwhile hunting it anywhere in the Atlantic or Indian Oceans. Altogether it is estimated that about six million fur seals were killed in the early decades of the nineteenth century.

In the north Atlantic sealing concentrated on the harp seal which in the autumn and winter migrates south from the Davis Straits to Labrador, the St Lawrence estuary and Newfoundland, where the young are born on the pack ice at the end of February. For ten days the newly born seals have their coveted white fur and they were the focus of the slaughter, although adults were also killed for their coarser fur and for oil. The Newfoundland sealing industry began in the early nine-teenth century and by the 1830s about 80,000 seals a year were being killed. At the peak of the trade, in the 1850s, the figure reached about 600,000 seals a year. The introduction of large steamships, which were much more efficient at processing the seals, meant that a single vessel could deal with 20,000 seals a day. The huge herds could not survive slaughter on this scale for long and by the early twentieth century the industry was in decline. Altogether between 1800 and 1915 it is estimated that about 40 million seals were killed in the area and the herds were reduced to about a fifth of their original size. In the far north sealing (also for harp seals) based on Jan Mayen Island inside the Arctic Circle, was a very brief affair. It began in the early 1840s and at its peak about 400,000 animals a year were being killed. The herds were driven to the point of extinction and by the late 1850s the industry there had collapsed altogether.

Sealing in the north Pacific was based on the northern fur seal, which migrated every year from the Bering Sea to the coast of central California. It mainly stayed at sea apart from coming ashore to breed in the summer – about four-fifths of the animals bred on the Pribilof Islands in the Bering Sea. The first hunters to reach the islands were Russians, who originally concentrated on the more valuable sea otter. When these had been killed they switched to the fur seal, which they proceeded to slaughter in such vast numbers (in 1791 127,000 animals) that they were soon piling up far more bodies than they could sell. In 1803 there was a store of 800,000 skins on the islands, 700,000 of which went rotten and had to be destroyed. By the 1820s the seals were so reduced in numbers that kills were down to about 7,000 a year – by then a total of about two-and-a-half million had been killed on the Pribilof Islands. The Russians next turned their attention to seals on the mainland coast and by the time Alaska was sold to the Americans in 1867 about four million seals had been killed in the area. In the meantime the seal herds on the islands had recovered and in the first year of American control 250,000 seals were killed on just one of the Pribilof Islands. Numbers fell rapidly but the Americans continued to kill about 100,000 a year until the 1890s when takes fell to about 17,000 a year. By 1910 from several millions the herds on the Pribilofs had been reduced to a mere 130,000. As the demand for seal skins was still high, the hunters had turned to the more difficult task of hunting the animals at sea. Between 1870 and 1910 another four million seals were killed in this way.

The elephant seal, the largest of the seals, was hunted not for its fur or skin but for its oil. It was found in large herds, but only on a few islands in the seas around the Antarctic and off the west coast of north America. It became the prey of whalers anxious to supplement their catch when the number of whales was declining. About one million of these seals were killed in the south Atlantic in the nineteenth and early twentieth centuries and the population there was only saved from extinction when both Kerguelen and Macquarie Islands, where the last few animals survived, were turned into nature reserves. In total probably about a quarter-of-a-million elephant seals were killed along the coast of California. Off that coast large numbers of elephant seals were still found as late as 1846, but a scientific expedition sent out in 1884 to report on the state of the herds found none at all. In fact a small colony of about twenty had survived and since then the animal has been officially protected and stocks have recovered somewhat. Sealing still continues around the world but at a very much lower level than in the past because of the heavily reduced stocks, a greater degree of protection given to the animals and an increasing consumer boycott of furs and skins, in part prompted by the sight of young seals being clubbed to death. It is difficult to estimate the number of seals killed worldwide at the height of the trade between the late eighteenth century and the first decades of the twentieth century but the total was probably of the order of sixty million.

The killing of walruses on an extensive scale began much earlier than the sealing industry but also petered out much earlier – after some three centuries of exploitation numbers had been reduced drastically. They were killed for oil, skin and the ivory from their tusks. In 1456 walruses could still be found in the Thames and as late as the mid-nineteenth century they were still common in both the Hebrides and the Orkneys. Now the total stock around the whole of the north Atlantic is no more than 25,000. The trade followed the same pattern of peripatetic thoroughness in its approach to hunting. For example, in the seventeenth century the English Muscovy Company eliminated a herd of 20,000 walruses on Bear Island, south of Spitzbergen, inside ten years. At the same time the herds that inhabited the area around the mouth of the St Lawrence river were destroyed – about 250,000 animals. Hunting then moved on to Labrador and the Arctic area but by the 1860s nearly every walrus in this area too had been killed. The last significant herd in the north Atlantic area survived on Spitzbergen until the 1920s when they were also hunted to extinction. In the latter part of the nineteenth century walrus hunting was mainly concentrated on the herds in the north Pacific. Between 1868 and 1873 about 85,000 a year were being killed but this rate of exploitation was short-lived. By 1891 the walrus was also extinct on the Pribilof Islands. The total number of walruses killed is unknown but the best estimate for the slaughter in the nineteenth century suggests a figure of about four million.

Although the trapping of animals for fur and the slaughter of seals and walruses were conducted on a massive scale, the most prolonged attack by humans on any single species has been directed against the whale. Whales are some of the largest animals to have lived – a sperm whale can weigh about 100 tons and measure over 100 feet long. They have few predators apart from killer whales and humans, and natural populations would therefore have risen to high levels despite their position at the top of the food chain. Although whales are long-lived (many survive into their seventies)their reproduction rate is low – about one to two per cent a year, and they take a long time to recover from any attack. Sustained killing of whales, particularly if concentrated on the breeding grounds, could very easily drive a local population to extinction. Whales fall into three main types whose characteristics have helped determine the development of whaling. The right whale (of which there are three sub-types – southern, northern and bowhead or Greenland) is slow and easy to catch. The fin whales (or rorqual from their Norwegian name), which include the blue, fin, humpback, sei and minke whales, are much faster and more difficult to catch. The sperm whale is toothed and particularly prized for the spermaceti found in its head. Whales were hunted less for their meat (except in the long established coastal fishery of Japan where it was used to supplement the shortage of domesticated animals) than for their oil, normally boiled down from the blubber. Before the rise of the gas and petroleum industries in the nineteenth century whale oil provided one of the major sources of lighting available throughout the world (the sperm whale produced the highest quality candles from its spermaceti). Millions of candles were manufactured from all kinds of whale oil and London even had 5,000 street lamps lit by whale oil in the 1740s. As well as providing virtually the sole source of lubrication for industrial machinery, it was also used to clean coarse woollen cloth. An important supplementary part of the industry was the use of whalebone in corsets, umbrellas, whips, fishing rods and cutlery handles.

The history of whaling shows the same main characteristics as sealing and the fur trade. An area was exploited, driven by severe competition between the fleets of different nations and between individual whalers, to maximise immediate gains without any thought of conserving stocks, until either the whales were extinct or their pursuit was no longer worthwhile economically. The whaling fleets then moved on to exploit a new area. Until the eighteenth century the whalers concentrated almost entirely on killing the right whale (so-called because it was the 'right' whale to catch). Their slow swimming speed meant they could be caught, especially in their breeding grounds, with the primitive technology then available. They could be chased in rowing boats and when harpooned with barbed spears thrown from the boat their speed was not sufficient to overturn the boat and the whalers could attach more ropes and hang on, for days if necessary, until the animal died from exhaustion. When dead they floated and so could be towed ashore for processing. Right whales had a 12–18 inch layer of blubber (ten times that of a sperm whale), which produced a large quantity of oil and they also produced about a ton of whalebone per animal.

The European whaling industry has a long history – whales were hunted and exterminated in the Mediterranean before the fall of the Roman empire. From about 900 it was concentrated in the Bay of Biscay and dominated by ports along the northern Spanish coast. Even this relatively small-scale industry so reduced local whale stocks that by the fifteenth century the whaling ships were already exploiting new grounds off Newfoundland as the Biscay whales neared extinction. By the sixteenth century the Biscay industry had collapsed, and the right whale in the area was extinct. A new large-scale whaling industry developed, dominated by the Dutch, and with the Germans and English also playing a large role, concentrating on the island of Spitzbergen where right whales had their breeding grounds. From about 1600 they were slaughtered in large numbers, young ones and pregnant females included. Within twenty-five years the whale population had virtually disappeared and the hunters were forced to turn further afield towards Greenland and along the migration routes of the whales. Arctic whaling was a technically more difficult operation than killings in the bays around Spitzbergen, since the whales had to be processed at sea alongside the ships. By the end of the eighteenth century it employed about 10,000 men, involving several hundred vessels and the slaughter of about 2–3,000 right whales every season.

The American whaling industry began about 1650 and initially concentrated its efforts along the eastern coast of North America. Stocks there were exhausted by about 1700 and the whalers were forced to move further afield to Labrador and the Davis Straits. The number of vessels involved rose rapidly – the major whaling port of Nantucket in New England had twenty-five whalers in 1730 but over 130 by the end of the century. By the end of the eighteenth century stocks here, too, were in severe decline and immature juveniles were being killed, thereby ensuring that any recovery in numbers was almost impossible. By 1830 the Arctic whaling for right whales was on the point of collapse and it was forced into the most difficult areas such as Baffin Bay when the whales died out in the accessible regions and catches everywhere fell drastically.

The main change in the industry in the eighteenth century was the move to killing sperm whales, which began off the American coast in 1712. The sperm whale produced less oil than the right whales but its spermaceti could be stored without processing and this, together with the very high value of the end product, made long voyages economically feasible. The whalers were now able to extend the hunt into the southern Atlantic, concentrating first on the areas off the southern African coast (after 1763) and Brazil (after 1774) and eventually moving into the Pacific. Many of the first settlements in Australia and New Zealand (especially Hobart on Tasmania) were dependent on whaling and vessels from both Europe and the United States were soon hunting across the Pacific. At the peak of the trade, about 1840, the Americans alone had over 700 vessels operating in the Pacific and every whaling ground from 88°N to 55°S was fully occupied. The sperm whale hunting area stretched from California to Japan, from Peru to the Gilbert Islands and from Chile to Australia. On average each vessel killed about 100 whales a season, which would mean that the Americans alone must have been killing about 70,000 a year in the Pacific. With other nations operating on a similar scale, overhunting brought the industry to the point of collapse. In the 1850s the north-west coast of North America had supported about 600 whalers every year, but a decade later hunting ceased as the whales neared extinction. By 1880 the once thriving Pacific whaling industry was reduced to a few areas off the coasts of Peru and Australia. By the latter part of the nineteenth century both the right and sperm whale populations of the world had been hunted to the edge of extinction. By the late 1980s, after a century of relatively limited killing, the right whale, which once swam in the world's oceans in hundreds of thousands, only survived in small populations of about 1,000 in the southern hemisphere, 400 in the north Pacific and a few hundred in the Atlantic.

The whaling industry might have shared the same fate had it not been transformed in the late nineteenth century by a series of technical advances. The most important developments were the introduction of fast, steam-powered boats and the explosive harpoon (which detonated inside the whale). These inventions made it possible to chase and kill the fast swimming and deep diving rorqual whales, which until then had been almost immune to human attack. The invention of the factory ship, which processed the whales at sea and stored the oil on board in vast quantities, also extended the length of time the whalers could remain at sea. Although the market for the traditional uses of whale oil – lighting and lubrication – and that for whalebone in corsetry – were in decline due to the use of petroleum based products and changes in fashion, a new market developed – processing whale oil into soap and margarine. The attack on the rorquals using the new technology showed the same basic pattern as in the past. First the more readibly accessible areas were denuded of whales, then gradually the ships moved into more distant and difficult waters. The first whales to be killed were the largest, such as the blue and the humpbacked, since they offered the quickest returns. When they had been driven to the point of extinction smaller whales such as the sei and minke, which involved more effort for a lower amount of oil, were hunted.

The new technical advances were made, and energetically implemented, by the Norwegians in the 1870s. Within a decade they had eliminated the rorqual whales along their coastline before moving further afield towards Iceland and the Faroes. By the end of the century they were killing about 2,000 whales a year in the area. Shortly after 1900 the European whaling grounds were exhausted and the Norwegians, together with the British and other nations, were moving into the last untouched area – the south Atlantic. In these waters the initial catches were large but it rarely took much longer than a decade before new hunting grounds had to be found. The fleets were first based around south Georgia, where in 1906–11 the Norwegians killed some 6,000 humpback whales every season. By 1913 numbers had fallen so much that only 500 a year could be caught and by 1917 the humpbacks were exhausted and the whalers turned to other species. By the mid-1920s blue whales were scarce around south Georgia. The whaling fleets moved on to the south Shetland Islands, the Ross Sea and the Antarctic and the breeding grounds off southern Africa, Madagascar and Peru. New entrants into the international whaling industry such as Japan and Germany sent fleets to the southern oceans which increased the competition still further. By the 1930s there were about 200 whaling ships operating in the Antarctic area, killing up to 40,000 whales a year.

After a quarter of a century of sustained attack stocks of all species were in steep decline and the fleets were reduced to hunting at sea on the migration routes or the less productive killing of smaller whales. (Although the number of factory ships increased by almost 60 per cent in the 1930s the amount of oil recovered rose by only 11 per cent.) The period since the 1930s has seen a major threat to the very existence of the whales and an almost total collapse of the international industry. In 1931 the boats in the Antarctic alone were still catching two-and-a-half million tons of whales but by 1979 the total world catch was only 200,000 tons. The industry became steadily less profitable as it turned to hunting the smaller sei and minke whales. Whereas in 1933, 28,900 whales produced 2.6 million barrels of oil, in 1966 double that number (57,900) produced only 1.5 million barrels of oil. The statistics for each species of whale vividly illustrate the state of the whale population and of the industry. In the 1930s 170,000 blue whales were still being killed every year, thirty years later the annual catch was down to about 7,000 and by the 1970s it had fallen to just twenty three. Humpback whales followed the same pattern, falling from 27,000 a year in the 1930s to about 200 by the early 1980s. The sperm whale catch rose more than ten-fold from 20,000 a year in the 1930s to nearly 250,000 a year in the 1960s. Within twenty years it had dropped to less than 5,000 a year as the species was hunted to near extinction. To compensate for the fall in the stocks of these species the fleets turned to the fin whale; the catch doubled between the 1930s and the 1950s to reach 280,000 a year. But this rate was unsustainable and by the 1970s the numbers killed had fallen to 22,000 a year. The annual sei whale catch rose from about 10,000 in the 1940s to a peak of 250,000 in the 1960s but fell drastically in the 1970s. As whale stocks fell and smaller animals had to be hunted, and as competition for the remaining stocks became fiercer, the whaling industry encountered severe economic difficulties worldwide. By the early 1950s many whaling companies were bankrupt and some countries ceased whaling altogether – the British industry folded in the early 1960s.

Although it was clearly in the long-term interest of the international industry to devise a scheme to control catches so that whaling could continue, albeit on a reduced scale, this did not happen. Instead there was intensified competition for the falling stocks as the fleets sought, as they had done in the past, to maximise short-term gains. The result of this uncontrolled competition was a disaster not just for the whales but also for the whaling industry itself. The idea of establishing quotas to control the level of killing was first mooted in the early 1930s but nothing was done before the establishment of the International Whaling Commission (IWC) in 1946. As a grouping of whaling nations, its members favoured a continuation of the slaughter even when scientific evidence about the dangerous decline in whale numbers was incontrovertible. Quotas were set but they were so high that most countries could not catch enough whales to meet them, and they failed to restrict the killing. Of the total number of whales killed in the Antarctic in the first seventy years of this century more than half occurred in the twenty years after the IWC was established. No effective controls on the type of whales killed were imposed – in 1961 over 70 per cent of the blue whales killed in the Antartic were immature and this unrestrained slaughter, by stopping the whales breeding, guaranteed that numbers would continue to fall drastically. Although pressure was growing on the IWC to bring in more effective measures it did not move quickly enough or far enough. A three-quarters majority of members was required before a new policy could be adopted and even then individual states were not bound by its decisions. This meant that those nations which were determined to continue whaling, in particular Japan, Iceland, Norway and the Soviet Union, were in a strong position to delay or prevent control measures. In the mid-1970s quotas were set for particular species designed to provide long-term protection, but the data on numbers and reproduction rates on which the quotas were based was inadequate and too favourable to the whalers. Countries such as Japan were also using other nations outside the IWC to do the hunting for them, thus circumventing the restrictions. Finally, under continuing external pressure, the IWC agreed in 1982 to a four-year moratorium on commercial whaling to start in the 1985–1986 season.

However, the 1982 IWC decision allowed 'scientific whaling' to continue during the moratorium. The idea of 'scientific' whaling (involving the killing of whales supposedly as a small-scale operation for the purpose of providing information about numbers and reproduction rates) had begun in 1962. When the four-year ban on commercial whaling was introduced, the three nations still left with a whaling industry – Japan, Norway and Iceland – seized on 'scientific' whaling as a way of keeping their industries alive. The Japanese Joint Whaling Company was miraculously transformed into the Cetacean Research Institute and its whaling ships suddenly became research vessels. In 1988 as many as 10,000 whales a year were being killed for 'scientific' purposes, although the value of the 'research' was far from clear and many of the animals ended up as meat in Japanese restaurants. For the whaling countries the main aim of the 'research' was to demonstrate that commercial whaling could be restarted at the end of the moratorium. The 1990 IWC meeting did not agree to end the moratorium but the pressure to resume commercial whaling remains strong.

The history of whaling demonstrates the inability of those involved to conserve the whales. Instead all the economic pressure worked to maximise short-term gains with little or no concern for the future, even in the face of mounting evidence that the whales were being killed at an unsustainable rate. The same sorry saga happened in sealing, the fur industry and also in many of the world's fisheries – in most cases industries were extremely reluctant to react to the rapidly diminishing resources on which they depended. Indeed humans have for centuries acted as though supplies of animals were limitless or as if it didn't matter if they ran through the supply. The consequence has been a monument to human short-sightedness. Not only have the industries involved declined but there has been a catastrophic loss of wildlife around the world. Across large areas species have become extinct and overall their numbers have fallen dramatically. Human actions, whether deliberate through hunting or indirect through the process of expanding settlements and clearing wild areas, have drastically affected the ecosystems of the world. Many species have died out and will never be replaced, others will probably never recover from the depradation. It has left an impoverished world.

A reaction to this widespread slaughter developed at the end of the nineteenth century with the rise of movements aimed at conserving the world's remaining wildlife. One of the earliest was in the United States and led to the creation of special wilderness areas such as Yellowstone National Park where development and exploitation was prohibited. Other countries moved much more slowly – National Parks were established in Britain in the 1940s and even later in other areas and it was not until the 1980s that Britain designated a few hundred small sites as of special scientific interest. Some of the more outstanding habitats such as the Great Barrier Reef off Australia, the Galapagos Islands and the Serengeti park in Tanzania, have now been designated as reserves but most of the world's ecosystems remain unprotected. Even those that are protected still face problems. In Britain major developments inside the National Parks are not prohibited, sites of special scientific interest can be destroyed and in many Third World countries a shortage of resources means that effective management is impossible and killing of the animals by poachers has continued. In many instances the National Parks are little more than lines drawn on a map and have little impact on the ground.

Part of the growing movement to conserve wildlife and the natural world has been the increasing importance of citizens' organisations and lobbying groups trying to change national policies. In the United States bodies such as the Audubon Society and the Sierra Club and in Britain the Royal Society for the Protection of Birds and nature conservation trusts have attempted to preserve some individual species or have bought small areas in order to protect particularly important habitats. In the last twenty-five years or so global organisations such as the World

Wide Fund for Nature, Friends of the Earth and Greenpeace have raised large sums of money and campaigned to preserve the world's natural heritage (as well as on many other 'green' issues). These groups have played a major part in influencing public opinion and governments against activities such as whaling and sealing and towards conservation measures.

In the last two decades there has been a series of international conventions and treaties designed to safeguard important sites and restrict trade in endangered species. The convention on the world's cultural and natural heritage is intended to protect the most important sites in the world and offers governments small sums of money to take the necessary action. The convention on wetlands is intended to do the same for sites particularly important for waterbirds. CITES (the Convention on International Trade in Endangered Species), signed by over eighty countries since 1973, prohibits commercial trade in several hundred of the world's rarest species. The problem with these international agreements has been that although countries have been willing to sign them, they have been less willing or able to enforce them. Many have turned a blind eye to the continuing trade in items such as crocodile skins, rare furs, ivory and rhinoceros horn.

The growing movement for conservation has succeeded in raising public awareness and has, on a small scale, achieved a number of important goals. But it has been overwhelmed by the tidal wave of destruction that continues to sweep across the world. In the twentieth century the rate of species extinction has increased significantly. Between 1600 and 1900 an animal species was made extinct about once every four years. By the 1970s this had risen to a rate of about 1,000 a year. At present about 25,000 species of plants, 1,000 species of birds (10 per cent of the world's total) and over 700 species of animal (including particularly vulnerable ones such as tigers, jaguars, leopards, cougars, cheetahs, ocelots, twenty-three types of whale, four types of rhinoceros, ten bear and two panda species, the mountain gorilla and the African elephant) are on the verge of extinction. In the tropical forests about fifty species of plants and animals are being eliminated every day. At this rate it is estimated that in the 1990s about 1 million species (almost 20 per cent of the total in the world) will become extinct.

10
CREATING THE THIRD WORLD

The rise of Europe in the four hundred years after 1500, from being a backward area of the world to dominate the rest of the globe not only drastically affected a whole range of ecosystems but also reshaped the relationship between different regions. Before the sixteenth century different areas of the world had evolved to a large extent in isolation. Although societies encountered the same basic problem of finding a balance between population, food production and damage to the environment, their interaction was very limited. The Americas, Australia and most of the Pacific were isolated. Elsewhere trade links were tenuous and contact between Europe and the major states of India, south-east Asia and China was sporadic. In the period after 1500 European expansion triggered off a process of gradual integration of the different parts of the world into a single system and created a world economy. That system was dominated by European states and the areas where extensive white settlement took place – North America, Australia, New Zealand and South Africa. The tropical colonies and those without substantial European settlement remained in a subordinate position. (The Japanese were one of the few non-European peoples who succeeded in avoiding this trap, mainly because they did not come under external political or economic control.)

In the earliest phases of European expansion, from the sixteenth until about the middle of the nineteenth century, Europe itself was still overwhelmingly an agricultural economy. The colonies provided an opportunity to grow crops (mainly for the luxury market) that could not be grown at home either because the climate was unsuitable or because the necessary cheap labour was not available. The colonies also provided some raw materials, particularly precious metals such as gold and silver (especially from Mexico and Peru) together with timber, to supplement European supplies. Increasing political control and the industrialisation of Europe in the nineteenth century intensified this process. Agricultural production for Europe was expanded and new crops introduced to meet changing demands and new industrial processes. Europe's demand for raw materials increased and the colonies provided an ideal source of supply. Third World countries became major producers of crops and raw materials for Europe rather than manufacturers of industrial products – that role remained almost entirely restricted to the European countries. Even after they achieved political independence the Third World countries found it very difficult to escape from this economic system.

The creation of the Third World was a complex process that took many centuries, but important features can be identified in the very first decades of European expansion, even before the Portuguese sailed into the Indian Ocean and the Spanish conquered Mexico and Peru. During the fifteenth century the Spanish and Portuguese conquered the islands of the Atlantic – the Azores, the Madeiras, the Canary Islands and the Cape Verde Islands. The Madeiras were unoccupied before settlers arrived from Portugal in the 1420s. On the island of Madeira itself the landscape was transformed by fires deliberately started by the early settlers to clear land for agriculture. The forests which, before settlement, had covered the island were destroyed. The first settlers introduced pigs and cattle, which also caused irreparable damage to the ecosystem of the island. In the 1450s the Portuguese began sugar cane cultivation. The idea was to produce it in large quantities and cheaply so they adopted the plantation agriculture already used to grow the crop on Mediterranean islands such as Cyprus. The plantations required a large labour force to build terraces and artificial water courses on the hilly island and also to cultivate and process the crop. So the Portuguese brought in slaves (Berbers from North Africa and Guanches from the Canaries) to work on the plantations. During the second half of the fourteenth century Madeira changed from a largely self-sufficient farming community of perhaps 500 settlers into a colony devoted to a single crop (sugar) exported to Portugal. By 1500 the population had grown to about 20,000, including several thousand slaves. The Cape Verde Islands further south off the coast of west Africa, first visited by the Portuguese in 1456, provided a variation on the same theme. By the end of the century African slaves had been brought from the Guinea coast to work on the plantations growing cotton for the Portuguese home market.

The Spanish conquest of the Canary Islands was a more difficult operation, lasting from 1402 and the capture of Lanzarote, to 1496 and the final subjugation of Gran Canaria. The seven islands of the group had been inhabited for more than a thousand years by the Guanches, who came originally from north Africa and numbered about 80,000 at the time of the conquest. Once the Spanish gained control of the first islands they enslaved the Guanches and introduced their own crops, especially sugar, grown on plantations for export to the home country. The islands were rapidly cleared of forests – to provide fuel for the sugar boilers – and a thriving population of rabbits, another Spanish import, prevented natural regeneration. The slaves suffered from the introduction of European diseases and the terrible conditions on the plantations. Guanche numbers fell rapidly in the sixteenth century and by 1600 they were all dead – only a few half-breeds remained.

The aftermath of the Spanish conquest of the Canaries and the Portuguese occupation of the other islands in the Atlantic illustrate a number of the crucial features in the expansion of Europe that helped, over the succeeding centuries, to create the Third World. First, the newly conquered and settled territories were exploited for the benefit of the home economy – in the main they produced crops that could not be grown at home. Second, these crops for export took up much of the best land and largely displaced traditional subsistence agriculture, and the local inhabitants were reduced to cultivating a small range of crops grown on the poorest ground. Third, export crops were grown primarily on large scale plantations owned and controlled by Europeans rather than on small farms run by local peasants. Fourth, cultivation of the crops relied on European investment and management but also on large amounts of cheap labour. Fifth, Europeans formed a small percentage of the total population and they expected others to do the manual work which they regarded as degrading.

European expansion was from the start built upon slavery and forced labour. Slavery was not invented by Europeans in the fifteenth century – it had been common since the first settled societies. For societies short of energy large-scale use of human power was essential, and slavery was the foundation of most of the city states and empires of the ancient world and was also found in medieval Europe. Europe had long exported slaves to the Near East and in the fourteenth century a major part of the trade of Venice for example consisted of the transport of Slavs and Greeks as slaves to Tuscany and Catalonia. From the twelfth century slaves provided the labour force for the sugar plantations on Cyprus and Sicily as they did in the later European colonies. The Portuguese relied heavily on the use of slaves from the start of their expansion overseas. Between 1450 and 1500 they brought over 150,000 slaves into their overseas possessions. The Spanish hoped to use the natives they found in the Americas as slaves. They did so on Santo Domingo and a number of other Caribbean islands and also on the mainland in places such as the Potosi silver mines in Peru. During this early phase of the Spanish empire new settlers would be granted *encomiendas*, which entitled them to the labour of a defined number of natives – Cortes for example was granted the rights to 115,000 people in Mexico. However the rapid decline in the native population (mainly as a result of the introduction of European diseases) made it necessary to look elsewhere for a labour force. Both the Spanish and the Portuguese soon turned to importing slaves from Africa. At first the English, too, used native Americans as slaves in their early seventeenth century colonies, both on the mainland in New England and the Carolinas and on islands such as Barbados, where the first slaves were brought from Surinam in 1627. However by the seventeenth century the African slave trade was well established and the English colonists found it easier to obtain cheap labour from this source than from the local Indians. The number of imported slaves in the colonies in the Americas rose rapidly. By 1600 there were more Africans than Spaniards in the coastal settlements of Peru, while in eastern Brazil at the same period there were twice as many slaves as white settlers. By 1700, a fifth of the population of the English colony of Maryland consisted of slaves and they also made up the overwhelming majority of the population on the island colonies of the Caribbean.

Slavery soon followed European expansion into most areas of the world. The Portuguese brought slaves from Madagascar and Mindinao to their settlement on the Cape of Good Hope and by 1633, 15 per cent of the population of the home capital, Lisbon, were slaves. The Dutch dominated the slave trade in south-east Asia and by 1694 half the population of Colombo, capital of their colony of Ceylon, was made up of slaves. Virtually every European nation was involved in slavery. The Portuguese, Dutch and Spanish dominated its early phases but by the eighteenth century the British shipped about three-quarters of the Africans taken to the Americas. The slave trade was concentrated on Africa and in particular the west coast (Arab traders controlled the slave trade of the east coast). Even though slavery had been common in Africa for centuries the development of the European trade had a devastating social impact. Until about 1700 much of the trade was concentrated in the Angola region but after that Guinea and West Africa became increasingly important sources of supply. Africans were in charge of the first stages of the trade, including the capture, maintenance and overland transport of the captives, and new states such as Dahomey and Asante rose to prominence based on their role in the trade. Extensive warfare to capture slaves became common.

The immense human suffering brought about by the slave trade, in terms of social disruption, ruined lives and early death, is incalculable. Between 1500 and the early nineteenth century (when the British abolished their slave trade) some ten million Africans were enslaved by Europeans and taken to the Americas (the Arabs took about one million from east Africa in the same period). In the nineteenth century before the final abolition of slavery another two million Africans were taken to the Americas and over one million others were enslaved by the Arabs. The trade between Africa and America grew as the demands of colonial agriculture increased. In 1600 about 5,000 Africans were enslaved every year but a century later the figure had risen to about 30,000 a year. By 1800, at the peak of the trade, about 75,000 Africans a year were being enslaved. About half the slaves from Africa were taken to the Caribbean colonies, 40 per cent to Brazil and only a very small proportion to North America. Many died in the appalling conditions on the voyage across the Atlantic – probably about one in five. Many others died soon after their arrival in a strange country where they were forcibly separated from their families and social traditions and subject to harsh treatment, poor food and new diseases. The mainland colonies of North America were one of the few places where the slave population grew by natural increase. Elsewhere death rates were very high and large numbers had to be imported in order to keep up the size of the labour force. The practice of slavery continued as a vital part of many economies far into the nineteenth century. It was abolished in British territories in 1833, in the United States in 1863, in Cuba in 1886 and in Brazil in 1888.

Slavery was not the only form of forced labour in the European colonies. The majority of whites who went to North America before 1783 were indentured servants who, in return for the cost of the voyage and their upkeep, were forced to work for their employers for a fixed number of years. Their living conditions were often little better than those of the slaves and only a fifth of them survived until they became free. Many convicts were also sent out from Britain to the American colonies and it was when this convenient dumping ground was closed off after American independence that it was decided to establish penal colonies in the antipodes. Until well into the nineteenth century the majority of settlers in Australia were convicted criminals controlled by a harsh, semi-military discipline.

When slavery was abolished in the nineteenth century it was necessary to look elsewhere in order to secure a cheap labour force that could be kept under tight discipline and in generally poor conditions in order to provide the crops and resources the Europeans wanted from their colonies. The main sources for this later intake of indentured labour were India, China and the Pacific islands. Indian labour was particularly important for the sugar plantations of the West Indies, Mauritius, Natal and Fiji and later for other plantations in Malaya, East Africa, Ceylon and Burma. In the century after 1834 thirty million people left India to work abroad as indentured labourers. By 1861 Indians made up two-thirds of the population of Mauritius and there were 60,000 on Fiji in 1879. Indians now make up about half the population of Guyana and of Trinidad. Most of the thirty million Chinese labourers who were recruited for work abroad went to southeast Asia. But large numbers were also taken across the Pacific. Between 1849 and 1874, 90,000 went to Peru to replace the Hawaiians who had died there digging out the guano beds to provide fertilizer for Europe, and 46,000 of them went to Hawaii, together with 180,000 Japanese and 160,000 Filipinos, to work on the sugar and pineapple plantations. The sugar plantations of Queensland in Australia used islanders from the Pacific. Between 1863 and 1904 a total of 60,000 labourers were used (about 10,000 at any one time); death rates were high (over three times that of the whites) and a quarter of the islanders died in Queensland and never returned home. Nearly every European colony depended to some extent on imported cheap labour either as slaves or indentured labourers. As well as the human suffering involved it also bequeathed a difficult social legacy of ethnic tension for many of the countries left with minority populations or, in the case of Fiji, with Indians outnumbering the native islanders.

When the Europeans took control of other parts of the world they inherited well-adapted traditional agricultural systems. Although all agricultural techniques involve major disturbance to natural ecosystems, most of these traditional methods had, by a series of techniques, evolved over a long period of time, limited the damage to the local environment and produced an agriculture that was stable, resilient and diverse, capable of maintaining output over the long term. The exact techniques adopted and the crops grown varied from area to area but in general external inputs were kept to a minimum and the emphasis was placed on growing a wide variety of crops in a multitude of micro-environments (gardens, orchards, dry land and small-scale irrigation plots). Hand cultivation reduced soil disturbance and therefore erosion (as did careful terracing); crop diversity reduced the damage done by any single pest and recycling of materials maintained soil fertility. Because of the diversity of crops that were grown these systems tended towards a high degree of local self-sufficiency and only a minimal amount of contact with external markets. Once the territory came under European control, these long-established systems and the societies that had developed from them were disrupted as local communities were made part of a wider economic structure. Agriculture in the colonial era became more specialised, in general each colony would concentrate on growing a limited range of crops for export (in some cases just one). This led to ecological problems by reducing soil fertility through the continuing growth of a single crop and increased susceptibility to pests because of the lack of diversity.

The way in which the agricultural economies of the colonial world were transformed can best be understood by studying the process from a number of different perspectives. First, the colonies of Indonesia and Kenya illustrate two different methods of obtaining the same result – the creation of a dependent agriculture tied into a world market. Second, the history of the development of plantations across the world and the balance between production of cash crops from large estates and their production by peasant smallholders illustrates another facet of the way in which a major change in the colonial economy and society was brought about. Finally it is possible to trace how the cultivation and export of the major cash crops – sugar, tobacco, cotton, rice, tea, coffee, bananas, rubber, cocoa and palm oil – developed around the world.

The pre-colonial agriculture of Indonesia was of two basic types. On the central island of Java there was an intensive *sawah* system of rice cultivation in paddy fields whereas on the outlying islands, where population density was much lower, a swidden system of shifting cultivation on land cleared from the forest for a few years predominated. Both of these systems had developed over a long period and were very stable. The establishment of Dutch control over the islands in the early seventeenth century was followed by their domination of the economy and its gradual restructuring to suit Dutch needs rather than those of the local people. The Dutch did not do away with the existing landholding systems and agricultural methods as such: they imposed instead their own requirements – notably an agricultural surplus of certain crops for their own use and for sale in the world markets. The colonial period in Indonesia saw the development of a dual agricultural system. The Dutch regulated the prices of commodities, local wages and methods of production and as the production of cash crops expanded and land and labour were switched into growing crops such as sugar, coffee, indigo and tobacco, subsistence agriculture contracted. When prices for these cash crops fell, as they often did, the peasants tried to compensate for the fall in their income (which they needed to buy food they were no longer producing themselves) by intensifying the production of subsistence crops such as rice. Both the expansion of cash crops and the intensification of rice production were ecologically damaging.

From the early seventeenth century until the end of the eighteenth century the Dutch commercial system in Indonesia was controlled by the Dutch East India Company. As part of the tribute exacted from local rulers once Dutch control was achieved, the company was able to obtain a high level of production of pepper, spices and sugar for export through the imposition of production quotas and forced labour by the peasants on the estates of local lords. In the early nineteenth century control of the colony passed into the hands of the Dutch government and after 1830 they introduced a new system. All peasants were now required to pay land taxes but the government accepted payment in the form of either government-owned cash crops grown on the peasant's land or labour on government-owned estates. These changes had a profound effect on both the economy and society of Indonesia. Sugar, indigo and tobacco were annual crops and could be grown in rotation with rice whereas coffee, tea and pepper were perennials which required special plantations owned by Europeans. The Dutch were able to ensure direct control over the production of sugar through their monopoly on sugar mills and processing. Coffee and tea cultivation required full time labour living on the plantations and as these expanded (the area growing coffee tripled between 1833 and 1850) the number of peasant smallholdings was reduced. In 1870 an agrarian land law was enacted by the Dutch which gave them control over all unused land (which was then leased out to large companies to turn into plantations) and which also allowed the renting of smallholders' land by companies for commercial crop production. This latter provision enabled companies to rent *sawah* land to grow sugar and other crops and resulted in a peculiar mixed system that was neither a true plantation nor a smallholding, and where the peasants cultivating the sugar were neither slaves, as on islands such as Jamaica, nor landless labourers as in Puerto Rico but they were still tied to producing a crop for the Europeans.

The Indonesian agricultural economy was therefore divided in two.

A plantation sector growing crops such as coffee, tea and pepper for export was largely isolated from the rest of the economy. The peasants who owned some land ended up with a large part of it devoted to cash crop production, especially sugar, either in lieu of their land taxes or under leases to companies in order to obtain money to pay their taxes. The amount of land available for food crops for local consumption was substantially reduced. The consequence was an intensification of rice production from the *sawah*. This was the only alternative open to the peasants since there was no unused land to bring into cultivation – that was controlled by the state and steadily leased to companies for plantation agriculture to grow export crops. Pressures to produce more rice on the *sawah* became ever more intense throughout the nineteenth century as the Javanese population rose from 7 million in 1830 to over 28 million by 1900. Even though new crops such as maize and soya beans were introduced during the nineteenth century, the Indonesian peasants were unable to break out of the steadily intensifying system.

On the outer islands of Indonesia a different process was at work. There the main cash crop, tobacco, was not integrated into the swidden system but grown on separate plantations, operated by a labour force brought in from outside. As the plantations grew in size they reduced the amount of land available for peasant agriculture. The main change, though, came with the introduction of rubber, which could be grown as a cash crop by smallholders. The cultivation of rubber trees meant that the smallholders abandoned the shifting, subsistence agriculture of the swidden system and bought imported rice with the money they made from selling rubber. These changes left them vulnerable to fluctuations in rubber and rice prices, enmeshed in a money economy over which they had little or no control. By 1945 when Indonesia became independent the agricultural system had developed over at least two centuries into a form that was very difficult, if not impossible, to change. It was linked to the international economy through the production of cash crops and the rest of the agricultural system had been moulded by this overriding requirement.

The reshaping of the Kenyan economy by the British in the early decades of the twentieth century was a more radical and more concentrated process than in Indonesia but the end result – European control and the increasing dependence of the economy on cash crops – was the same. The economy and society of Kenya were totally transformed between the establishment of formal British control in 1895 and the 1920s. In this period it was not African interests that determined the direction of Kenya's economic development; the key factor was the

British requirement that the colony should contribute to the overall development of the empire and produce commodities that Britain required. The approach was deliberate and the objective explicit: as the government commission on the development of East Africa wrote in 1925:

'Britain possesses a rich potential heritage in tropical Africa. From it, with wise capital expenditure, she can expect to receive in ever-increasing quantities supplies of those raw materials and foodstuffs for which she is at present so dependent on foreign countries.'

Although the number of white settlers was small in the early years of the colony (less than 2,000 by 1906) the British authorities allocated them the best land (where most of the Africans lived) on long leases. By 1910 over 600,000 acres a year were being granted to the whites. Both the settled Africans (the Kikuyu) and the pastoral tribes (Nandi and Masai) were removed from the land allocated to the whites even though as late as 1930 two-thirds of it was still not in use for agriculture.

From the start of British control the pattern of development was seen in terms of large plantations run by Europeans using cheap local labour. The main crops selected were coffee, sisal and maize. Until the latter part of the nineteenth century the main centre for coffee growing within the British empire had been Ceylon. However the spread of coffee leaf disease after 1874 severely reduced the crop (from 100 million pounds to just 18,000 by 1913) and Britain became dependent on Brazil. In order to reduce this dependence, cultivation was strongly encouraged in Kenya after 1907. By 1922 over 700 estates were growing coffee. Rubber plantations were tried but those in Malaya did better and Kenya turned to growing sisal (in order to break American control over the crop) and maize for local demand in East Africa. Recruitment of a labour force posed problems. The whites rejected the import of cheap Indian labour to work on the sisal plantations on racial grounds and expected the British government to make arrangements to ensure they had access to native labour on suitable terms. They complained to the government when they felt that too much land was left in the hands of the Africans because they argued it would undermine 'the foundation on which the whole of this enterprise and hope is based, namely, cheap labour'. A variety of measures were adopted to make sure that the Africans needed to work to earn money and did not remain as subsistence farmers. Both a hut and a poll tax, which had to be paid in cash, were introduced and the size of the 'native reserves' was reduced.

Import duties were imposed to raise the cost of goods to the Africans and only agricultural implements intended for the European farmers were exempted. Taxes rose sharply after 1920 and all Africans were required to carry passes which could only be obtained if they had a job. The colonial authorities also introduced their own forced labour schemes. Little or no help was given to native agriculture, which was confined to the less productive land on the overcrowded reserves. The number of Africans fell from about four million in 1902 to two-and-a-half million in 1921 and by the end of the 1920s the average per capita income of the whites was two hundred times that of the Africans. By 1930 the transformation of a traditional African economy into one controlled by the whites and integrated into the international economy was largely complete: agricultural products from white run plantations rose from a mere 5 per cent of Kenyan exports in 1913 to 76 per cent 1932 (coffee alone made up 40 per cent of the total).

Although the economies of virtually every European colony and many of the nominally independent countries (especially in Latin America) were drastically altered to provide the products that Europe (and increasingly the United States) required, the pace and nature of change varied from area to area. It depended on the nature and timing of European control and also on the characteristics of the crops that were grown. Until the nineteenth century the development of large-scale plantations growing a single crop was mainly confined to the Americas, where a plentiful supply of land was available, slaves could be transported from Africa and the climate was, apart from some tropical areas, tolerable for Europeans. While producing and trading in many goods for the European market, the territories of south-east Asia remained under local rulers until the nineteenth century, when more direct European control was imposed and plantation agriculture was introduced. Africa, with its generally difficult climate for Europeans and lack of good harbours, was not brought under effective European control until well into the nineteenth century. In all three continents methods of production were largely determined by who had access to land and capital and the type of crop (including how it had to be processed). Plantations were European owned, financed and managed – increasingly run by commercial companies. Smallholders were usually in a minority, although they became very important in the production of rubber in south-east Asia and remained so for many crops in west Africa. The nature of the crops also influenced the way in which they were grown. The main tropical tree crops – rubber, coconut, oil-palm, sisal, cacao and coffee – all involved a considerable time lag between planting and full production. This meant that matching supply and demand was problematic and prices could fluctuate a great deal. Normally only large companies were able to finance the risks involved in these industries. Annual crops such as sugar, cotton, jute and tobacco made it easier to adjust to changing levels of demand. However, they required intensive labour over a short period, unlike tea and rubber where the demand for labour was high but evenly spread over the year.

Plantation agriculture developed in the Americas in the earliest period of European settlement. At this time the estates were usually family owned and by later standards not particularly large. They were however characteristically devoted to the production of a single crop such as sugar, cotton or tobacco, all of which were highly labour intensive, particularly in the processing stages (sugar mills and cotton gins). The slaves who provided this large labour force were employed at other times of the year in hand cultivation of the fields so that ploughs and draught animals were rare on plantations, even in the United States. Many of the plantations were also self-sufficient, growing most of their food. The end of slavery in the nineteenth century led to the decline of the plantations and the rise of sharecropping, particularly in the southern United States, although on some West Indian islands with little land available the ex-slaves remained as landless labourers still working on the estates. In neither case were their conditions much better than under slavery. Latin America also saw the rise of the *hacienda* with large landowners controlling most of the agricultural land and worked by the peasants, who were little better than serfs (they even suffered from heritable debt) scratching a minimum of subsistence from their own small plot of land. Increasingly by the late nineteenth century in Latin America plantations were owned by large companies or, in the case of sugar production, by the mills themselves.

In Asia until the nineteenth century there were few plantations and most of the crops for export to Europe were grown by peasants. Then the opening of the Suez Canal and the development of the steamship (both of which significantly reduced sailing times to Europe), together with the invention of new industrial processes increased demand for rubber and vegetable oils. To meet this, new plantations were established, generally on a larger scale than in the Americas, owned by companies and run by managers. They also depended on imported labour – Tamils for Ceylon's tea plantations and Malaya's rubber estates, Biharis for Assam, India's main tea growing area and Chinese for Sumatra's rubber plantations. The only crop in which smallholders played a significant part was rubber, although even here the trees and the crop, if not the land itself, were often owned by large companies or merchants, giving the small-scale peasant producers very little real independence. Plantations in Africa were a very late development, confined to a few areas such as East Africa and associated with crops such as sisal and coffee together with palm oil and cocoa production in West Africa. Production by peasant smallholders for the international market remained important in West Africa although in some colonies such as the Ivory Coast the government used forced labour to ensure the Africans worked on the plantations. Nevertheless some plantations were huge – the Firestone Rubber Company owned one rubber plantation covering 127,000 acres in Liberia.

The first of the crops grown for Europe that transformed the environment, economies and societies of the rest of the world was sugar cane. Medieval Europe relied on honey as a sweetener as the only product readily available. The first European colonies on the Atlantic islands were used for sugar production and it was soon taken up by the Spanish American colonies and especially by the Portuguese colony of Brazil. Within a decade of the first settlers arriving sugar was exported to Portugal. By the late sixteenth century Brazil was the main sugar producing area in the world. The temporary conquest of Brazil by the Dutch in the early seventeenth century helped to spread sugar cane cultivation into the West Indian islands controlled by the Dutch, French and English. Production costs were usually higher than in Brazil but a protected home market enabled the plantations to flourish. The English islands of Jamaica and Barbados were particularly import-ant sources and large estates with their slave labour force proliferated. By 1680 half of Barbados was owned by just six per cent of the landowners and the top nineteen planters each owned over 200 slaves. On Jamaica in 1713 there were, on average, eight black slaves for every white inhabitant. Intensive sugar cultivation soon exhausted the soil on both Barbados and Jamaica (on Jamaica a sugar plantation could only be sustained for a few decades) and in the eighteenth century the larger French island of St Domingue, which still had empty land available, became one of the biggest sugar producers in the world. In the nineteenth century the Spanish islands of Cuba and Puerto Rico, where slavery still flourished and the soil was not exhausted, became the centres of production. In 1800 there were only 44,000 slaves on Cuba but between 1810 and 1870 about another half-a-million were brought from Africa to expand the industry. Although family estates on the islands collapsed after the abolition of slavery, large-scale production of sugar was sustained by the mills, which bought up the land and employed the ex-slaves as sharecroppers and labourers. The mills in turn were bought up by large companies and their number fell from over a thousand in 1877 to 185 in 1927 as the industry became concentrated in very few hands.

The second export crop to become important in the Americas was tobacco as the new habits of smoking and snuff-taking spread in Europe. Originally a Spanish monopoly, it was introduced into the faltering English colony of Virginia where it rapidly revitalised the economy in the decades after the first settlement. It did not need the capital investment, processing and storage facilities required for sugar cultivation. At first it was grown on smallholdings but later on large plantations worked by gangs of slaves. During the seventeenth century tobacco became the mainstay of the economy of Virginia and later the adjacent colony of Maryland, so much so that it was even used as the local currency. The scale of this growth can be judged from the fact that imports from the American colonies into London rose from 20,000 pounds in 1619 to 22 million pounds by the end of the century. The problem with growing tobacco was that it exhausted the soil very quickly (normally within three or four years) and so the frontier of cultivation moved steadily westwards across Virginia, Maryland and the other tobacco growing states.

By the end of the eighteenth century slavery in the United States appeared to be in decline – tobacco was no longer such a central crop in the economy and other plantation crops such as indigo and rice in South Carolina remained relatively small-scale and specialised. Slavery was revitalised, and vastly expanded, by the growth of cotton production. The major impetus was the rising demand from the expanding British cotton industry in the early stages of the industrial revolution – by the mid-1830s half of Britain's exports were cotton goods and raw cotton made up a fifth of all its imports. At the end of the eighteenth century half of Britain's imports of raw cotton came from its colonies in the West Indies and a quarter from Turkey. The invention of the cotton gin by Eli Whitney in 1793, which speeded up processing, and the development of new, easily processed varieties such as sea island cotton, transformed American production. By 1807 the United States was supplying 60 per cent of Britain's cotton and by 1820 it had become the largest producer in the world. US exports of cotton rose rapidly from 3,000 bales in 1790 to 178,000 by 1810 and to four-and-a-half million bales by 1860. (Between 1815 and 1860 cotton constituted half of all US exports). Most of the cotton was grown on plantations rather than on smallholdings. Like sugar and tobacco, continuous cotton cultivation rapidly exhausts the soil and in the first half of the nineteenth century the frontier of cotton-growing spread steadily westwards from the eastern seaboard states of Virginia, the Carolinas and Georgia into Alabama, Mississippi, Louisiana and Texas. Over 800,000 slaves were forcibly moved to these new territories between 1790 and 1860 and this westward expansion of slavery was one of the main causes of the increasing divisions within the United States that were to lead to civil war in 1861. Even after the abolition of slavery cotton cultivation continued to expand, from 4 million acres in the 1830s to about 30 million at the end of the century (it is about 9 million acres now). The fall in production in the twentieth century came from a combination of lower demand and prices, soil exhaustion and the spread of the devastating pest the boll weevil from Texas after 1894.

The development of plantations and the domination of the economies of south-east Asia by the production of cash crops began in the nineteenth century. Here three major crops were involved – tea, rice and rubber. Until the early nineteenth century the cultivation of tea was restricted to China and Japan. As tea drinking grew in popularity in Britain during the eighteenth century, the value of annual imports rose two hundred fold. Once the East India Company's monopoly on the tea trade was abolished in 1833 cultivation spread quickly into Assam and later into Ceylon and southern India. (By 1888 Britain was importing more tea from India than China.) Tea plantations were established on the hills of Assam by clearing the forests and by 1900 there were 764 estates covering about 350,000 acres. Tea cultivation moved into south India and Ceylon after coffee blight devastated crops in the 1870s – tea plantations on the island increased from about 1,000 acres in 1875 to nearly 370,000 acres by 1900. Harvesting the crop is highly labour intensive, needing about forty people per acre per day. In every area the tea companies which owned the plantations brought in large numbers of labourers – 400,000 into Assam alone by 1900. Many Tamils were taken to Ceylon, where they now form the main minority population and the resulting frictions within society led to civil war in the 1980s. Most of these labourers lived in wretched conditions in company barracks. Pay was kept low because labour costs constituted about two-thirds of production costs and the companies were determined to keep prices as low as possible to maintain tea as a popular drink in Britain.

Rice had been the staple food of south-east Asia for centuries before European control was established. It was grown by peasants mainly for their own use or sale in local markets. The first country to be transformed by rice production for export was Burma, the lower part of which was annexed by the British in 1852. Britain was cut off from its usual rice supplies from South Carolina by the American civil war in the early 1860s and the opening of the Suez Canal in 1869 also made it easier to transport Asian rice to Europe. The area under rice in Burma increased twenty-fold between 1855 and 1920 and by the latter date half of its rice production was being exported. These changes had devastating social consequences for the Burmese peasants. Landlords (half of whom were absentees) or those who owned rice mills had access to finance and were able to build up plantations and employ peasants at low wages. Those peasants who tried to compete with these large producers went into debt to moneylenders, who ended up owning over a third of the land. In this way Burma's peasants were being turned into landless labourers or poverty-stricken sharecroppers permanently in debt. The French also brought major changes to southern Indo-China, which they occupied in 1861. Here the area under rice increased five-fold between 1880 and 1940 while exports rose six-fold in the same period. Production was concentrated in the Mekong delta, where the French divided up the land and sold it in large blocks. The resulting large estates were generally worked by sharecropping tenants, kept in a position of quasi-serfs and tied to the land in a state of permanent debt. The situation in the colonies of Burma and Indo-China can be compared with the circumstances in Thailand, which remained nominally independent throughout the period. Here too the increasing demand for rice saw a six-fold increase in the area under cultivation between 1850 and 1940, with exports rising from about 50,000 tons in the late 1850s to 1½ million tons by 1940 causing problems in adequately feeding the local population. But with no colonial power to back the creation of large estates, small peasant producers remained the backbone of the cultivation system.

The rubber trade was very small in the early nineteenth century – Britain imported just over 300 tons in 1840. That year the accidental discovery of the vulcanisation process, which made rubber lighter, more flexible and less affected by heat and cold, greatly stimulated demand as did its use in new products such as bicycle and car tyres. (By 1900 Britain was importing 20,000 tons a year). For most of the nineteenth century rubber was gathered in the Amazon region from wild trees. The economy of this part of Brazil was transformed by the resulting boom in rubber – exports rose from 31 tons in 1827 to over 27,000 tons by 1900 and in the early twentieth century the town at the centre of the trade, Manaus (over 2,000 miles up the Amazon), had eight daily newspapers, an opera house, telephones, and electric trams (one of the first cities in the world to operate them). The British were however determined to set up their own source of supply within the empire. Seeds of the rubber tree were taken from Brazil in 1877 and used to start the first experimental plantations in Malaya. By 1895 it was clear that rubber could be grown in south-east Asia and the Dutch also started developing plantations on Sumatra after 1906. From a low base (fewer than 5,000 acres of rubber trees in the whole of the area in 1900) south-east Asia rapidly came to dominate the world market. The area growing rubber in Malaya rose from only about 300 acres in 1897 to 3.3 million acres in 1940 and by 1919 half the world's rubber was being grown in the country. Initially production was concentrated on large estates and when the local peasants proved to be uninterested in taking up cultivation the British moved in large numbers of Tamil labourers from India to do the work. From the 1920s more indigenous small-holders did take up rubber cultivation but they were tied to the large companies and traders.

The rapid growth of rubber cultivation in south-east Asia dealt a fatal blow to the future of Brazil's trade. In 1910 there were still over 150,000 tappers but collecting it from trees spread out in the jungle was a far less efficient method of production than working on the neat rows of the Malayan estates and Brazilian output was already only a third of that of its rival. Demand for Brazilian rubber fell and output dropped to less than 10,000 tons in 1930. In the meantime Brazil (and other countries in south America) had attempted to copy Malaya and set up rubber plantations but these proved a failure. Rubber trees flourished in the wild but when they were planted close together leaf blight disease spread rapidly and destroyed them whereas the trees in south-east Asia were immune. Brazil now imports more rubber than it produces. Another attempt to provide an alternative source of supply was more productive. This was initiated by the Americans, who were determined to break the almost total British and Dutch control over the rubber trade. In the 1920s the US tyre company Firestone, with the full support of the US government, turned to the American semi-colony of Liberia for the land to grow their own rubber. The Liberian government granted them a concession of 1 million acres of land at a price of 0.04 cents an acre. By the late 1920s Firestone already had over 80,000 acres of rubber plantations in the country and a large force of labourers working on them in very poor conditions. The domination of the Liberian economy by US companies such as Firestone was such that in 1943 the American dollar became the currency of the country.

Plantations and cash crops for export were a comparatively late development in Africa. Two of the most important crops – coffee and cocoa – were originally grown elsewhere to supply the European market. Although coffee is indigenous to Africa it was never really grown there in any quantity and it was the Dutch who began its extensive cultivation in south-east Asia for the European market. It was first grown in Ceylon in the late seventeenth century, where it became the major cash crop, and on Java after 1712. It rapidly rose to be the main export of the Dutch East Indies (by 1850 there were over 300 million coffee trees in the area) but production fell after the outbreak of coffee blight disease in the 1870s. This setback established Brazil as the major supplier in the world. Coffee was introduced into Brazil by the Portuguese at the end of the eighteenth century. Cultivation began near Rio de Janeiro in 1774 and moved steadily westwards as the soil was exhausted and as railways were built during the nineteenth century. Coffee was grown on large plantations dependent on slave labour in order to keep production costs as low as possible and cope with steadily falling prices. After the abolition of slavery in the 1880s the industry survived by employing many of the large flood of European immigrants into Brazil as cheap labour in squalid conditions. By the late nineteenth century Brazil produced about three-quarters of the world's coffee and the economy was therefore heavily dependent on the price of coffee on the world market. In the late nineteenth century the British sought to secure their own supplies at the expense of Brazil by setting up plantations in their East African colonies. Coffee cultivation began in Malawi in 1878, in Kenya in 1895 and in Uganda in 1900 on European owned estates using African labour (often provided as forced labour by the authorities). Only after 1950 did the number of smallholders growing coffee expand rapidly but they remained dependent on large marketing companies and subject to severe fluctuations in prices.

Cocoa was first grown as a crop to meet European demand by the Portuguese on their Atlantic islands and later South America became the main producer in the world until the 1880s. It was introduced into West Africa in the late 1870s unofficially but the British colonial authorities recognised that it could provide useful export revenue for what had until then been relatively unproductive colonies. From the 1880s cocoa production received strong official backing plus support from major British companies such as Cadbury who wanted to secure their own reliable supplies. European controlled plantations, often financed by chocolate manufacturers, were established and by 1911 Ghana was the world's largest producer. The French colony of the Ivory Coast also began cocoa production as a local African initiative but there too it was rapidly taken over by European owned plantations, which continued to spread across West Africa. These plantations employed natives as seasonal labourers or in some areas as share-croppers.

The development of two other major plantation and cash crops began in the wake of technical advances made at the end of the nineteenth century. The growth of palm oil production in West Africa from its initial, limited role as a lubricant and as a constituent in soap was encouraged by its new use as the major ingredient in the manufacture of margarine. By 1900 West African exports to the UK of palm oil had already risen to 50,000 tons a year – fifty times higher than in 1800 – but the main period for development of large-scale European owned planta-tions took place in the 1920s and after. Bananas were brought from the Canary Islands to the Americas by the Spanish in 1516 but remained a purely local food crop until it became possible to transport them in refrigerated ships to Europe and North America. By the 1890s bananas were grown extensively along the Atlantic coasts of central America, often using imported Indian labour. The crop needed investment in refrigeration and plantations and required cropping throughout the year to provide a regular flow to the consuming countries. Only a few large companies could provide the necessary finance and one in par-ticular – the United Fruit Company (UFC) – which set up its first plantation in 1889, soon dominated the trade. The UFC bought land and railways in the producing countries and controlled the production, transportation, shipping and marketing of the bananas. Contractors were brought in to supply the necessary labourers, who were housed in company barracks, paid a small wage and given notes to exchange for goods (at inflated prices) in UFC owned plantation stores. In the 1930s soil exhaustion and an outbreak of both Panama and sigatoka disease badly damaged the plantations and new ones were established along the Pacific coasts of the Central American republics. The economies of many of these states became highly dependent on this one export and the UFC wielded enormous influence in the region. After 1945 Ecuador became one of the major producers in the world, relying on production from smallholdings rather than plantations, but the large companies still dominated the sale and marketing of bananas.

By the early twentieth century, Europe, and increasingly the United States, had brought about a major transformation in the economies and societies of what is now known as the Third World. Countries which had been largely self-sufficient in food and which grew crops mainly for local markets had become part of a world economy dominated by Europe, its white colonies and the United States. In area after area the same sort of sequence of events had occurred. Through a powerful mixture of political control, economic pressure, investment and market forces, 'development' of these economies took the form of growing crops for other countries. The crops were either to provide luxury items in the diet of people living in Europe and North America (sugar, coffee, tea, cocoa, bananas) or to sustain manufacturing industry (cotton, rubber, palm oil) in countries where development meant something very different – the building of a thriving and varied industrial base with rising levels of consumption for the population. In this process the dependent and colonial economies were restructured to specialise in a few commodities or in some cases a single crop. A diverse agriculture was increasingly displaced over large areas by a monoculture, with harmful environmental effects, particularly in terms of damage to the soil and loss of biodiversity. The production of export crops in the Third World rose at an annual rate of three-and-a-half per cent in the first half of the twentieth century, whilst food production for home consumption grew more slowly than the rise in population. As a result these countries had to import much of the food they needed at high prices. The perverse effects of this cash crop-oriented agriculture for the population at large can be seen in many countries. Sugar cultivation was the biggest single element in the Cuban economy – by the 1950s it took up 60 per cent of all the cropland on the island and constituted three-quarters of the country's exports. As a result half of its food had to be imported. On Fiji by the early 1980s sugar made up over 80 per cent of exports and employed a fifth of the population. On Tahiti, by the 1950s, three-quarters of all agricultural land was being used to grow crops for export and in Gambia the figure was only a little lower. In the Philippines over 50 per cent of farm acreage is used to produce crops for export.

The achievement of political independence by the African and Asian colonies in the 1950s and 1960s did not transform their economic position. The experience of the Latin American countries, which had been independent since the 1820s, had already demonstrated how difficult this could be to achieve. By the mid-twentieth century the agricultural, trading and land-owning patterns were well established and there were strong forces, both internal and external, opposing change. Once an economy had been set in a certain mould by a colonial government, and when the western countries retained overwhelming economic and financial power and the terms of trade were in their favour, it was very difficult to change course. Given the difficulty of diversifying their economies many of the countries simply tried to increase their export earnings by producing more of the commodities introduced by the colonial powers. For example, the Ivory Coast had produced 75,000 tons of cocoa and 147,000 tons of coffee a year just before independence but by the mid-1970s these figures had risen to 228,000 tons and 305,000 tons respectively, resulting in an economy even more dependent on these two crops. Many other countries still depend for their foreign exchange earnings on a single crop – coffee, for example, constitutes 93 per cent of Burundi's exports. Attempts at co-operation by the producing countries to stabilise agricultural prices have usually failed, and fluctuating commodity prices continue to undermine vulnerable economies. Even where the major corporations that formerly owned large plantations have been dispossessed of their land or nationalised, Third World countries do not control trade in the commodities they produce because multinational companies still dominate processing and manufacturing. One of the major tea companies, Brooke Bond, now owns only one per cent of the tea plantations on Sri Lanka but still controls one-third of the country's tea exports and a similar degree of concentrated control is found in tropical fruit production, which is dominated by firms such as United Brands and Del Monte.

Despite major problems of hunger and malnutrition the Third World continues to export more food than it imports. Twenty per cent of the world's food trade flows from the Third World to the industrialised countries and only twelve per cent in the opposite direction. This balance does not just apply to tropical crops. Within a year of the opening of the Suez Canal, India became a wheat exporter to supply the British market. Even in the acute famine of 1876–1877 wheat was still exported to Britain and by the 1880s India was providing ten per cent of the world's grain exports. Latin America has increasingly provided large quantities of beef for the American market at the expense of home consumption. Between 1960 and 1972 Guatemalan beef production doubled but home consumption per head fell by a fifth. In the same period beef exports from Costa Rica quadrupled but there was a forty per cent fall in domestic per capita consumption. The average American cat now eats more beef than an inhabitant of Costa Rica.

The Europeans saw the rest of the world not just as potential suppliers of cheap food and industrial crops but also as a source of timber, minerals and other raw materials. Timber was one of the most important products sent to Europe from the early colonies; indeed the colony of British Honduras only existed as a result of a settlement by traders seeking mahogany for the European market. The scale of the operations, particularly in the nineteenth century, can be judged by British activities in India and Burma. By the early nineteenth century British merchants had almost completely destroyed the teak forests of India's Malabar coast and needed to find new sources of supply. The unexploited forests of Burma provided a strong motive for the initial British conquest in 1826 and the first area opened up (the province of Tenasserim) was stripped of teak within twenty years. The annexation of Lower Burma in 1852 allowed the massive forests of the Irrawaddy delta to be cut down to supply Europe with hardwood. By the end of the century about 10 million acres of forest had been cleared. In the western Himalayas, after British control of the Gorakhpur district was established in 1801, over one million trees were felled in the next twenty years. In other parts of the region commercial felling began with local Indian rulers selling rights to European merchants and by the 1850s severe depletion was already apparent across the whole area. In that decade the demand for railway sleepers rose rapidly as railways were built across India to move crops to the ports for export to Europe. As timber prices rose, felling moved further inland into the mountainous areas and by the 1870s half a million trees a year were being cut down just to provide sleepers.

Even very specialised trades could be highly destructive. In the early nineteenth century sandalwood was a prized commodity not just in Europe but also in China. It was obtained mainly from the islands of the Pacific but the trade lasted less than a quarter of a century until all the existing trees had been cut down. The European and American traders systematically exploited an island until it was exhausted and then moved on to another. The sandalwood trees on Fiji were destroyed between 1804 and 1809, those on the Marquesas Islands lasted for three years after 1814 and those on the Hawaian Islands for slightly longer — 1811 until 1825. Then the industry collapsed.

The establishment of American control over the Philippines after the Spanish-American war of 1898 provides a good example of the development of modern logging. Within two years a Bureau of Forestry was set up and commerical logging began in 1904. At that time about eighty per cent of the virgin forests were still in existence. Half had been destroyed by the early 1950s and by the 1980s less than a third remained. The newly independent countries treated timber as simply another crop and sought to increase production and maximise revenue as the industrialised countries' demand for tropical hardwoods increased (sixteenfold since 1950). The mounting scale of destruction is illustrated by the fact that Indonesian exports of timber rose nearly two hundred-fold in the twenty years after 1960. Similarly the Ivory Coast exported 42,000 tonnes of timber in 1913, 402,000 tonnes in 1958 and nearly 1.5 million tonnes by the mid-1970s. Rainforests covered 30 million acres of this former French colony in 1956, but only 10 million acres by the late 1970s when over one million acres a year were being cleared. Most developed countries tax processed timber imports which means that Third World countries are pushed into selling logs and they then import value-added products such as paper and board.

Mineral exploitation has also been an important factor in the creation of the Third World. The first European colonial venture in Mexico and Peru was, in its early years, largely driven by the search for gold and silver. Gold was also important in the first European trade links with West Africa. It was the final division of Africa among the European powers in the 1880s that marked the beginning of large-scale exploitation of mineral resources on the continent as Europe industrialised and cheap sources of supply were needed. Some areas were virtually controlled by mining companies. King Leopold of the Belgians actually sold Katanga with its rich copper deposits to a mining company in return for the company financing the conquest of what became in the early twentieth century part of the Belgian Congo. Two-thirds of all European investment in Africa until the 1930s went into mining enterprises, and mineral exports rose seven-fold between 1897 and 1935 to make up half of the continent's total exports, mainly copper from the Congo and Northern Rhodesia together with gold and diamonds from South Africa. Europeans were prepared to invest in order to bring the minerals to Europe but not to set up processing plants in the colonies. Railways were built to transport the minerals to the coast but the railways did little to develop the local economy – copper from Katanga in the Congo went via the Benguela railway to Angola for export. Europeans provided the skilled workers and Africans the unskilled workforce. The introduction of poll and hut taxes, which had to be paid in cash, forced African workers into the labour market to work in the mines as well as on plantations. The native mineworkers were housed in squalid barracks, separated from their families and often working hundreds of miles from their homes – by the 1950s two-thirds of the workers in the South African mines came from outside the country.

In the same way that cash crop agriculture became the major sector in many colonial economies, and remained a vital source of earnings after independence, mining became a central part of the economy of others and that too did not change after political independence was achieved. For instance mining still provides over 90 per cent of the exports of both Zambia and Mauretania. The Third World's share of global ore production rose dramatically in the twentieth century. Between 1913 and 1970 the proportion of the world's iron ore mined there rose from 3 per cent to 39 per cent and over the same period the rise in bauxite production was even more dramatic – from less than half a per cent to nearly 60 per cent. The overwhelming majority of all ores are used elsewhere – the Third World processes only 10 per cent of the copper ore, 4 per cent of the nickel ore and 17 per cent of the iron ore it produces. As before independence they are, for the most part, exporters of raw materials. Mining is largely in the hands of multinational corporations and the governments of the countries concerned are usually unable to exercise much control over this sector of their economy which remains largely autonomous. After 1945 Liberia awarded concessions to multinational companies to allow them to exploit the large iron ore reserves in the country. Four huge open cast strip mines (very damaging to the environment by stripping away vast quantities of top soil and rock and creating huge pits and canyons) were built together with railways to transport the ore to the coast but little local labour was employed in these highly capital intensive projects. Although the Liberian economy appeared on paper to grow with this new activity and exports rose, there were few benefits in other sectors of the economy. The same effects occurred in Mauretania with the exploitation of the large iron ore deposits in the country after 1959. The Mauretanian government had only a five per cent stake in the company set up to mine the ore. The company proceeded to build its own 400 mile-long railway to the port of Nouadhibou and even ran its own army to protect the mines. On paper the Mauretanian economy was two-and-a-half times larger after seven years of mining but few benefits had percolated through into other sectors from the largely autonomous mining company, which employed little local labour and imported most of its other requirements. Even a policy of nationalisation fails to change this state of affairs. The multinational companies are still employed on 'managements contracts' and through internal pricing arrangements are able to move their profits out of the country. The companies also exclude many Third World countries from the most profitable parts of the industry by refusing to build smelters and processing plants, as both Ghana and Guinea found even when cheap energy supplies were available. Alumina is worth six times as much as raw bauxite and the final product (aluminium) is worth twenty five times as much as the bauxite but these high value operations are almost exclusively confined to the industrialised world.

European demand for resources was not confined to metal ores. In the late nineteenth century the use of fertilizers to increase agricultural output rose dramatically. The United States had its own internal sources of supply but Europe turned to Morocco and Tunisia and also the large guano deposits off the Pacific coast of South America. The latter were originally part of Bolivia but Chile's victory in the war of 1881 (fought over the deposits) gave it control of the coast and the offshore guano islands and turned Bolivia into a landlocked country. The guano was worked in dreadful conditions by Chinese labourers; Chile was soon exporting over one million tons a year and the tax on the exports made up over eighty per cent of the government's revenue. The British empire was dependent on external supplies until the discovery in the early twentieth century of huge phosphate deposits in the Pacific on Nauru and Ocean Island. This opened up the prospect of an easily accessible and cheap source of fertilizer with which to increase agricultural output from Australia and New Zealand, for the benefit not just of their economies but also that of Britain, which relied heavily on imported food from the empire. The story of these two islands illustrates in dramatic form many of the consequences of the developed world's demand for resources and the far-reaching impact it could have both on the environment and the people of the Third World.

Ocean Island was small (three miles long and two-and-a-half miles wide), covered in lush, tropical vegetation and inhabited by about 2,000 Banabans following a typically Polynesian way of life. Nauru was slightly bigger (eight-and-a-half square miles) with about 1,400 people. Ocean Island was formally annexed by Britain in 1901 whereas Nauru was a German possession until 1914. The islands consisted almost entirely of solid phosphate deposits, perhaps the richest in the world. In 1900 the British owned Pacific Islands Company bought the rights to all minerals on Ocean Island in return for a payment of £50 a year (in practice made in over-priced company trade goods) in a 'treaty' of dubious legality – made with the local chief even though it was well understood that he did not have authority to lease land belonging to other individuals. The company began to export large quantities of phosphates – shipments from Ocean Island amounted to 100,000 tons a year by 1905. Mining rights on Nauru were obtained from the German authorities and, after the necessary works were completed by Chinese labourers, mining began there in 1907. On both islands the company did not employ the islanders but brought in about 1,000 outsiders to work as labourers, about eighty Europeans to supervise operations and a detachment of Fijian police to keep order. In 1919 the company was bought out and the British, Australian and New Zealand governments established the jointly owned British Phosphate Commission to take over the work and provide them with phosphate at cost price (and therefore well below the world market price).

By the early 1920s mining was producing about 600,000 tons of phosphates a year and it was evident to the native inhabitants what was happening to their islands as a result. The operations involved clearing away the vegetation and stripping out the top fifty feet or so of land, leaving an uninhabitable wasteland of jagged pinnacles on which nothing would grow. It was obvious that if the mining continued the islands would be ruined. Seeking to safeguard their future, the Banabans refused to sell or lease any more land to the Commission. But the pressure from Australia and New Zealand for cheap phosphate was growing. In 1927 the British government authorised deep mining over the whole of Nauru and the next year took powers to confiscate all land from the Banabans that they refused to make available for mining. By the 1930s phosphate output had reached about one million tons a year. On the outbreak of war with Japan the Europeans and most of the Chinese labourers were evacuated but the islanders were left behind. The Japanese occupied both islands and transported the natives to the Caroline Islands. Before the war the British authorities had considered removing the Banabans from Ocean Island in order to further extend mining operations and the Japanese action provided a convenient opportunity. The Banabans were not allowed to return and were resettled on Rambi Island (part of Fiji). 1,500 labourers were brought in to reopen the phosphate works and in 1947 deep mining over the whole of Ocean Island was authorised. The Nauru islanders were allowed home after the war, but in a second class capacity. Like the 1,300 Chinese labourers brought to the island, the natives were excluded from the company facilities (shops and recreation), which were restricted to the elite white workers. Throughout the 1950s about one million tons of phosphate a year were being extracted from the islands, rising to nearly three million tons a year by the mid-1960s. It was clear that at this rate the deposits would soon be exhausted. The last shipment from Ocean Island was made in 1980 and the Nauru deposits were then only expected to last until the 1990s. In eighty years of mining twenty million tons of phosphate were extracted from Ocean Island, and Nauru had provided almost three times that figure, giving a total of about eighty million tons from the two tiny Pacific islands.

The imminent exhaustion of the deposits on the ravaged islands raised in an acute form the question of how to treat their owners. In the case of Nauru (administered by the Australians under a United Nations mandate) the government wanted to resettle the islanders on the mainland and abandon the island when mining ceased. The islanders rejected this idea in 1965 when, for the first time, they were given the right to apportion the royalties they received on each ton of phosphate as they wanted rather than as the Australian government decided on their behalf. After a long struggle Nauru was granted independence in 1968 and management of the phosphate operation was transferred to them in 1970. The islanders now live along a narrow coastal fringe, the only part of the island not devastated by mining. Their traditional way of life has gone and their only means of subsistence comes from royalties and profits from the phosphates. These have been sufficient to provide almost a parody of western style development. The islanders do not need to work and their material standard of living is high. There is one road on the island, which goes nowhere, but there is one of the highest rates of car ownership in the world. The population depends on imported western food and many have started to develop the health problems normally found in people who live in the industrialised world.

The Nauru islanders faced enormous problems but the treatment of the dispossessed Banabans, who did not have the United Nations to protect their interests, was far worse. In 1911 the British government suggested that a trust fund should be set up for the Banabans, to be financed from the phosphate earnings. The British Phosphate Company proposed a munificent total annual payment of £250 at a time when it was making a profit of £20 million a year and paying dividends of 40–50 per cent every year to its shareholders. Eventually the British government persuaded the company to pay royalties of 6 pence a ton, supposedly to be held as a fund for the Banabans when the phosphates ran out. The government's action was less philanthropic than it seemed. They incorporated Ocean Island into the Gilbert and Ellice Islands colony, even though there were no natural links between the two and allocated most of the phosphate royalties to pay for the administration of the colony that had previously run at a loss. The Banabans were not told that 85 per cent of their royalties were being spent in this way. Indeed they were not told how much they were earning or what was done with any of the money and only very small sums were handed over because the government thought that they were 'feckless'. Some of the money was used to buy Rambi island on their behalf (the proceeds going to the colonial administration of Fiji), although they were not consulted about the purchase. After 1946 they were left on Rambi, an island with a totally different climate from their home. Eventually the British offered the islanders £500,000 as a final settlement for the effects of all the mining. The islanders rejected the offer and took the British government through the British courts in the 1970s in the longest civil case ever heard. They failed in the main part of the case because the court held that the 1900 agreement giving the company the right to mine the island in return for £50 a year was a legally binding contract. The court did find that the British government had breached its obligation to care for the islanders but refused to make any award of compensation. Eventually the phosphate commissioners offered a sum that just covered the costs the islanders had incurred in bringing the protracted legal case. By 1980 Ocean Island had been destroyed by the mining and the deposits exhausted. The islanders had lost their home and had received pitifully small compensation for their loss. That was the real price of the cheap fertilizers for Australian and New Zealand agriculture and cheap food imports for Britain.

The fate of the Banabans was symbolic of much that had happened to the Third World. The creation of a world economy from several smaller-scale, self-sufficient, regional economies should have produced, according to the liberal, free market economists such as Adam Smith and Ricardo, a world-wide division and specialisation of labour, allowing each country and area to concentrate on growing or making the commodities it was best suited to produce. As a result of this specialisation every area should, in theory, have benefited from the most efficient allocation of resources. The theory, however, ignores the political constraints involved, in particular on the selection of commodities that were produced – European control enabled the colonial powers to ensure that the commodities they required were produced and allowed them to enforce a highly asymmetrical series of exchanges of products between the home country and the colonies. The words of Cecil Rhodes, one of the driving forces behind the last period of British expansion in Africa, reveal how different it all was in practice:

'We must find new lands from which we can easily obtain raw materials and at the same time exploit the cheap slave labour that is available from the natives of the colonies. The colonies would also provide a dumping ground for the surplus goods produced in our factories.'

The way in which one part of the world – the West (Europe, North America and the white colonies) – became 'developed' and the way another part – given the collective title the Third World – became 'underdeveloped' are not separate phenomena; they are inextricably linked. In the world market that was created by Europe, one region was able to extract a large surplus of products and natural resources from the dependent area. The dominant economies of the West were characterised by the production of capital intensive goods and relatively high wages and profits whilst the subordinate economies concentrated on producing crops, raw materials and minerals that were of low capital intensity and linked to low wages and low profits. Although development took place in the subordinate colonial economies, it was almost entirely geared to the needs of the home economies. Railways and distribution networks were built but they were largely confined to links between the inland regions and the ports and were designed to facilitate exports. There were few, if any, links between rural areas, or often even between adjacent countries where they were under different political control.

The achievement of political independence in the Third World did not bring economic independence. Economies remained tied into the global system created by the industrialised world and their structure, which had been largely determined by the colonial authorities, proved very difficult to change. A few countries managed to avoid this trap – those that retained their political and economic independence such as Japan, together with those that escaped European colonialism such as South Korea and Taiwan, 'those that had small populations and vast resources required by the developed world such as the oil-rich states of the Near East', and the trade-based economies of Hong Kong and Singapore. After independence the model of development adopted by many countries in the Third World was, not surprisingly, given their limited room for manoeuvre, based on accepted western models emphasising industrialisation, free markets and international competition. Only a few countries such as India and Brazil were able to make even modest steps in this direction and even here inequalities in the distribution of the benefits have been particularly marked. For most countries in the Third World, particularly in Africa, but also the poorer countries of Latin America and Asia, the only available option was to increase production of a few cash crops or minerals in an attempt to raise income and exports. The problem with this approach was that increased production tended to lead to lower prices, lower income, increased dependence on a few commodities and greater vulnerability. Borrowing money from the West in order to finance development projects (often of dubious value or relevance to local conditions) led to even greater difficulties, as countries such as Egypt and Venezuela had already demonstrated in the late nineteenth century (long before the great debt crisis of the 1980s) when they defaulted on their loans and were either occupied by foreign powers or had their revenues taken over in order to fund the debt. The people in the Third World who benefited most from this form of development were the elite, closely tied to the industrialised world, rather than the bulk of the population.

The consequences of this unbalanced development had profound effects for both the industrialised world and the Third World. Political and economic control of a large part of the world's resources enabled the industrialised world to live beyond the constraints of its immediate resource base. Raw materials were readily available for industrial development, food could be imported to support a rapidly rising population and a vast increase in consumption formed the basis for the highest material standard of living ever achieved in the world. Much of the price of that achievement was paid by the population of the Third World in the form of exploitation, poverty and human suffering.

11

THE CHANGING FACE OF DEATH

Disease has had a profound effect on human history in three main ways. First, there have been highly lethal outbreaks of epidemics and plagues such as the Black Death, which killed between a quarter and a third of the people in Europe in the mid-fourteenth century. Second, there have been persistent, seriously debilitating but localised sources of infection such as trypanosomiasis (sleeping sickness) and onchocerciasis (river blindness), which have ruled out certain areas for human settlement. Third, throughout history human populations have suffered from a low-level of disease and poor health. Much of the suffering has been caused by inadequate diet and the most vulnerable have been the poor and those living on the margins of subsistence (often a majority of the population). A poor diet makes it much more difficult for the individual to combat disease.

The changing relationship between humans and the environment has been crucial in determining the impact of disease on human society. In the last ten thousand years there have been a number of alterations in the pattern of human diseases brought about by the same factors that have had such a fundamental influence on other areas of human history. Gathering and hunting groups had a very different pattern of disease from settled societies and the transition from small, mobile groups to large, sedentary communities affected the number and type of diseases to which humans were subject. The domestication of animals was also very important in altering the nature of human disease. Increasing contacts between societies that had developed in isolation in different parts of the world – first those between Europe and the Near East and between Europe and the Far East and then the shattering impact of the expansion of Europe to the Americas and the Pacific – substantially changed the spread of diseases in the world. In the last two centuries there has been another major change with the decline of infectious diseases and the increasing importance, mainly in the industrialised world, of 'diseases of civilisation', linked to new ways of life and alterations in diet.

The available information about the state of health of the earliest gathering and hunting groups is sketchy in the extreme. Nevertheless it is clear from studies of contemporary groups and archaeological work that although there were major differences between groups their practice of using a wide range of foods had two beneficial effects. First, malnutrition was rare and their food consumption was at least as high, if not higher, than the earliest agricultural groups. Second, deficiency diseases would have been more or less unknown. There is some evidence for intestinal parasites such as worms among modern gathering and hunting groups and these may have been common in prehistoric groups in some areas, in particular Africa. The spread of humans out of Africa into temperate areas is likely to have reduced this problem and in the case of some prehistoric groups, such as Indian tribes in Nevada, there is no evidence at all of intestinal infections. Death in childbirth and infant mortality are likely to have been fairly high, but probably no higher than in agricultural societies or even in early modern Europe, where, for example, in seventeenth century France about a quarter of all children died before their first birthday. Life expectancy was not high but studies of modern groups such as the bushmen of south-west Africa have found that about one in ten of the total population is aged over sixty, a rate similar to that in early agricultural societies.

The adoption of agriculture and the transition to settled societies exposed humans to a range of diseases they had never encountered before. The result was a major deterioration in health. The development of settled societies meant that a growing number of people came to be living in close proximity to, or at least in intermittent contact with each other and this fact had far-reaching consequences for the state of their immediate environment and their health. The major change was increased exposure to infectious disease, outbreaks of which form a permanent backdrop to the evolution of complex societies in most parts of the world. It is remarkable how many of these diseases are linked to changes in human subsistence. The domestication of animals, which involved close contacts between humans and animals (with animals often living in the same buildings as humans), exposed people to a range of diseases which already affected animals. Some of these were able to adapt to humans as new hosts and flourish in their new environment, others slightly changed their characteristics and became specifically human diseases. Many of the common human diseases are close relatives of animal diseases. Smallpox, for example, is very similar to cowpox and measles is related to rinderpest (another cattle disease) and canine distemper. Tuberculosis also originated in cattle as did diphtheria. Influenza is common to humans and hogs and the common cold certainly came from the horse. Leprosy came from water buffalo. After living for some ten thousand years in close proximity to animals, humans now share sixty-five diseases with dogs, fifty with cattle, forty-six with sheep and goats and forty-two with pigs. These diseases established themselves at different times in different areas and then slowly spread by human contact into new areas. The rate and timing of this transmission had major repercussions. In particular the lack of domesticated animals in the Americas meant that diseases did not spread from animals to humans as they did on other continents and infections such as measles and smallpox were unknown until introduced, with catastrophic consequences, by Europeans in the sixteenth century into populations with little immunity.

The rise of settled societies also exposed humans to a whole range of new infectious diseases simply because of the greater concentration of population. A large number of people living in cities of several thousand or even in villages of a few hundred posed a major problem of waste disposal. Few of the early societies solved the problem of keeping human excrement out of their drinking water and most used one water course for both purposes. This mixture of water and human waste provided a perfect habitat for intestinal parasites such as worms and made diseases such as cholera and dysentry endemic. The steady rise in human numbers and the increasing density of settlement (not just in one location but within areas that were in fairly constant contact such as the cities of Mesopotamia) provided a set of conditions within which a number of new diseases could become established. Infectious diseases such as measles, mumps and smallpox, which do not depend on transmission through water (as with cholera) or another species (as with malaria), require a minimum number of human hosts in order to survive. Recent studies have shown that measles dies out on islands where there are less than about 500,000 people but this level would have been exceeded in the first settled areas.

Agriculture greatly increased the opportunities for the spread of new diseases. In particular the development of irrigation led to the spread of schistosomiasis, a blood fluke which causes extreme debilitation and listlessness. The blood fluke has an elaborate life cycle that involves humans and water snails as hosts at different stages. Irrigation ditches turned out to be prime breeding grounds for the snail and people working in them were, therefore, exposed to infection. The disease was widespread in early societies such as Mesopotamia and Egypt that depended on large scale irrigation, and over a hundred million people suffer from the disease today. In West Africa forest clearance caused by the spread of swidden or 'slash and burn' agriculture created new environments for the mosquito that carries malaria and attacks humans. As a result malaria, which had been largely unknown in the area before the development of agriculture, became firmly established. In China the spread of settlement southwards from the Yellow river valley into the rice growing areas of the Yangtse also exposed the population to new diseases, in particular malaria and schistosomiasis (and probably also dengue fever). In India the spread of agriculture from its first location in the Indus valley into the valley of the Ganges with its high rainfall and high temperatures similarly exposed the settlers to a range of new diseases, especially malaria.

The growth of settled societies established a disease pattern that was to persist for thousands of years. Towns and cities, because of their lack of sanitation and the crowding together of large numbers of people, were extremely unhealthy places where diseases flourished. Until well into the nineteenth century in Europe and North America (and until the present day in much of the rest of the world) cities required a constant influx of people in order to sustain their numbers because of the very high death rates among their inhabitants. At first many of the new infections would have caused a large number of deaths because of the lack of any acquired resistance in the human population. But over time a degree of immunity to diseases would have developed and fewer people would have died from them. The history of ancient societies is one of a continuous low level of disease, punctuated by virulent outbreaks killing large numbers of men, women and children in a short period. Because of the lack of any reliable records it is difficult to establish exactly what diseases caused these very high death tolls. Most of the surviving records tend to refer in an indiscriminate way to 'plagues' although strictly that term should be reserved for the bubonic plague, which did not affect Europe and the Near East before the sixth century AD. The description of symptoms in the records is often vague and difficult to identify because many diseases have become less virulent over time as immunity has increased. Tuberculosis can be clearly identified as early as 3000 BC but most of the major outbreaks of disease which caused very high death rates are likely to have been more virulent forms of existing childhood diseases such as measles.

The lack of contact between the societies of the Mediterranean and the Near East on the one hand and India and China on the other (and of all four areas with the Americas) meant that the diseases that had established themselves in each area were in many cases unknown elsewhere. When contact was established, diseases spread with a terrible impact on people who had acquired no natural immunity or resistance to the infection. The early signs of this spread of disease from one area to another can be found in the wake of increasing trading contacts between the Mediterranean area and the states of India and south-east Asia in the first centuries of the Roman empire. A sharp fall in the population of the Roman empire began with the great 'plague' of 165 AD, when the death toll was around a quarter of the population (with further outbreaks in 251 and on a number of other occasions over the next five centuries). The disease was not bubonic plague but probably smallpox, which was new to the Mediterranean area and therefore in its virulent form had a very high mortality rate. China experienced similarly devastating outbreaks of disease in 161–162 and 310–312 AD, when death tolls reached 40 per cent in many areas. This infection, too, was almost certainly smallpox in its virulent form, which probably originated in India before spreading to the Mediterranean and China. Likewise bubonic plague was first experienced in India and the first known outbreak in the Mediterranean area was in 542, when the disease arrived by ship from north-east India spread by fleas on black rats. The population was extremely vulnerable and the death toll was high across the whole of the Mediterranean. The disease arrived in China in 610, again by boat from India, through the port of Canton, and killed about a quarter of the entire population. Leprosy became established in Europe in the sixth century as a result of contacts with India and south-east Asia and spread to become one of the major diseases affecting the population – there were 19,000 lazarets to accommodate and isolate infected people by the thirteenth century. The disease died out in Europe after the fourteenth century although the reasons why remain obscure. In the centuries after the outbreak of these various diseases the population gradually built up immunity, and death rates fell as the diseases became endemic, but less virulent in their impact.

The way in which better communications spread disease across Eurasia is illustrated by the history of bubonic plague in the fourteenth century. The establishment of the Mongol empire, which at its height between 1200 and 1350 stretched from European Russia and the Near East to China, opened up trade across the steppes and deserts of central Asia. In the process the burrowing rodents of the area, which were infected with bubonic plague and carried infected fleas, spread into China. An outbreak of plague started there in 1331 and the disease spread along the caravan routes to reach the Crimea in 1346 and then the Mediterranean. It was spread further afield by ships carrying black rats and infected fleas throughout Europe, where it was known as the Black Death. The disease was characterised by swelling of the lymphatic glands (or bubo) with secondary swellings in other parts of the body causing extreme pain followed by fever, vomiting, delirium and death within three or four days. Death rates were very high – in its pneumonic form, which was spread direct from person to person, it was a hundred per cent fatal, but overall about ninety per cent of those infected died. (Even in the twentieth century after the invention of antibiotics death rates were over sixty per cent of those infected.) In total about a third of the population of Europe died in the initial outbreak, although rates varied greatly from place to place. It would strike a city, ravage the population, causing immense suffering and social dislocation, and then die out. Many tried to flee (as did the ten wealthy young men and women from Florence who tell the stories in Boccacio's *Decameron*), thereby helping to spread the disease across the countryside, but most stayed in their homes. As with other diseases, medical treatment was largely ineffective and public health measures were mainly restricted to disposing of the bodies and boarding up infected houses together with their inhabitants.

After the first devastating outbreak in 1346–1349 bubonic plague reappeared at frequent intervals for centuries. Between 1347 and 1536 there was a major outbreak somewhere in Europe on average every eleven years and in the period 1536–1670 the rate only dropped to once every fifteen years. In the seventeenth century about two million people died of the plague in France, including 750,000 (about five per cent of the population) in just one outbreak in 1628–32 (in Lyon alone 35,000 people died). The Great Plague in London during 1665 was brought from Amsterdam and began in the western parts of the town before spreading to the central area. By September about 6,000 people a week were dying of the disease. The Court moved out to Oxford and Samuel Pepys, who worked in the Admiralty, left for the safer areas of Greenwich and Woolwich. In his diary he describes the impact of the plague during a short visit to the city on 14 September when he noticed that it had spread close to his home and was horrified to see:

'dead corps's of the plague, carried to be buried close to me at noonday through the City in Fanchurch street – to see a person sick of the sores carried close by me by Grace church in a hackney-coach – my finding the Angell tavern at the lower end of Tower hill shut up . . . to hear that poor Payne my water[man] hath buried a child and is dying himself – to hear that a labourer I sent but the other day to Dagenhams to know how they did there is dead of the plague; and that one of my own watermen, that carried me daily, fell sick as soon as he had landed me on Friday morning last . . . is now dead of the plague . . . to hear that Mr Lewes has another daughter sick – and lastly, that both my servants . . . have lost their fathers . . . of the plague this week – doth put me into great apprehensions of melancholy, and with good reason.'

The plague began to die out in north-west Europe in the late seventeenth century – the last outbreak in western Europe was in Marseilles in 1720–1721, but it remained endemic in eastern Europe and the Near East.

Until the end of the fifteenth century the Americas remained isolated from Eurasia and Africa and the disease pattern of the people before the European conquest is far from clear. Crowded and insanitary urban areas are likely to have produced intestinal parasites and diseases such as dysentery in the same way as the cities of Eurasia. It is certain however that the major diseases of Eurasia that had become endemic over the centuries had not spread to the New World. The Spanish conquistadors brought with them a wide range of European diseases. The first to strike was smallpox, which reached Hispaniola in 1518 and Mexico in 1520, carried by the relief expedition sent to help Cortes in the siege of the Aztec capital, Tenochtitlan. It arrived in Peru and the Inca empire in 1525–6. Everywhere the results in a population with no natural immunity were catastrophic: many millions died. Smallpox was followed by an outbreak of measles in 1530–1531, typhus in 1546 and influenza in 1558–9. These diseases killed many millions more of a population already devastated by the initial outbreak of smallpox. The horrendous scale of the disaster is evident, although the exact number of deaths can never be established because of the differing estimates of the population before the Spanish conquest. The most reliable figures suggest that in the valley of Mexico, the centre of the Aztec state, the population fell from about twenty-five million just before the conquest to six million by the mid-sixteenth century and to about one million in 1600. The effect of these European diseases (together with the brutality of the military conquest and its aftermath) was to destroy the once flourishing and powerful Aztec society and its culture. This dramatic collapse was repeated on a similar scale throughout the Americas from Peru to the Indians of North America as European diseases spread rapidly through the continent. The devastated population of the Americas was also affected by the arrival of more diseases new to them, this time from Africa as trade routes opened up (partly to bring in slaves). The tropical areas of Central and South America had been reasonably healthy until the introduction of malaria, probably in the late sixteenth or early seventeenth century and of yellow fever in 1648. Both diseases became endemic and undermined the health of the indigenous inhabitants of the tropical areas (and of the Europeans who tried to settle there too).

The transmission of disease between Europe and the Americas was almost certainly not entirely one way. In the 1490s Europe was ravaged by syphilis. Its effects were first widely noticed in the French army that invaded Italy in 1494 and from there it spread rapidly across the continent. It reached India in 1498 with the sailors on Vasco da Gama's voyage and by 1505 had travelled on to China and Japan. It was later taken by European sailors to the Pacific. The origin of syphilis is a matter of great controversy. Some experts have suggested that it was a new form of the disease yaws that was already endemic in Europe but which was now spread by venereal means. However in the fifteenth century people were convinced that syphilis originated in the Americas and had been brought back by European sailors on the first expeditions. Certainly the place and the date of its first recorded appearance in Europe – Barcelona in 1493 (a year after the first voyage to the Americas by Christopher Columbus) – lends weight to the contemporary theory of American origins. Although the effects of the disease on infected individuals were terrible, its demographic impact was comparatively limited and by 1600 it was already in decline in its most virulent form.

The worst effects of the spread of new diseases around the world diminished as new generations developed immunity and death rates fell from catastrophic levels to ones typical of endemic, low-level infection. In these conditions the rate of infection and death could vary enormously, depending mainly upon a number of environmental factors. In England between 1659 and 1840 it has been estimated that if the summer was one degree centigrade cooler than average, annual mortality fell by about four per cent: people suffered from a lower rate of intestinal infections because many of the bacteria involved bred less readily. However, poor diet, overcrowding in cities, pollution of drinking water and non-existent or bad sanitation were the main influences on disease rates. Typhus was brought back to western Europe by Spanish soldiers from Cyprus in 1490. Transmitted by lice, it was essentially a disease of overcrowding and poverty. It produced a steady death toll but not the major demographic catastrophe of a disease such as the plague. The environmental conditions in armies with their overcrowding and primitive sanitation, made them not just one of the main sufferers from disease but also one of the mechanisms for spreading it as they moved across the countryside. Until the present century armies nearly always lost more soliders to disease than they did as casualties to the enemy. In the Crimean war (1854–1856) ten times as many British soldiers died from dysentery than at the hands of the Russians. A similar situation applied in the American civil war, and in the Boer war at the end of the century disease killed five times more British soldiers than the Boers did. It was not until the Russo-Japanese war (1904–1905) that Japanese sanitation measures managed to reduce casualties from disease to a level only a quarter of that inflicted by the Russians. The role of the louse in spreading typhus was first identified around 1910 and the setting up of delousing stations during the trench warfare of the First World War prevented a massive outbreak of typhus amongst all the armies. In that war (as in the Second World War) the main epidemic disease the British army suffered from was syphilis.

New infections could still be spread around the world as late as the early nineteenth century by improved communications, growing urbanisation and poor sanitation. Cholera, which is transmitted through the pollution of drinking water with human wastes, was endemic in Bengal and it had often spread to affect adjacent areas. But in 1817 British troops carried it from Calcutta to the north of India and it also spread to south-east Asia and in 1821 from Muscat to East Africa. In 1826 it infected the Russian army and by 1831 had reached the Baltic. From there it spread to the towns of western Europe and by the early 1830s the United States and Mexico. Death rates were high (thirteen per cent in Cairo in 1831) and the disease caused panic in Europe, where primitive water supply and sanitation systems enabled the disease to spread rapidly, especially in the poorest areas. It was only countered by the steady improvements in sanitation made during the nineteenth century.

The most remarkable transformation in the pattern of human disease since the rise of settled societies has occurred in the last two centuries. For most of human history the majority of children died within a few years of birth (often only a third of babies survived until adulthood). Now in developed countries only about one in twenty babies fails to reach maturity and many of those who die do so because of inherited or incurable disabilities. Life expectancy at birth has increased dramatically from about thirty to forty years in the early eighteenth century to well into the seventies today. Death rates have fallen steadily since the early eighteenth century. As late as the 1840s in England and Wales annual death rates were about 20 per 1,000 of the population – current rates are between a quarter and a third of this figure. A similar pattern (though the exact timing differs from country to country) can be found throughout the industrialised world.

The main reason that people have been living longer is that fewer are killed by the infectious diseases that were a scourge of human history for several thousand years. How to explain this decline is the subject of considerable debate about the relative importance to be attached to different factors. Some diseases appear to have evolved over time into less virulent forms; this is certainly the case with scarlet fever in the nineteenth and twentieth centuries. But in most cases diseases have not changed and therefore explanations have to be sought elsewhere. Another factor is advances in medical knowledge and techniques, particularly the ability to promote immunity by inoculation. Inoculation against smallpox may have been used as early as the eleventh century in China and a few centuries later in Turkey. The practice was not adopted in western Europe until the early eighteenth century (1721 in England) and it was not until the much safer method of vaccination with cowpox was introduced in the 1790s that the technique spread at all widely in Europe (it was not made compulsory in Britain until 1852). Its adoption was followed by a decline in deaths from smallpox but this improvement contributed only about one-and-a-half per cent of the fall in death rates from all causes. The development of vaccines against other diseases came very late in the nineteenth century (the 1890s for cholera, typhoid and diptheria) and not until the 1920s was an even partially effective vaccine against tuberculosis developed. Again death rates from these diseases had already declined sharply long before vaccination was introduced. In the case of tuberculosis, effective medical treatment was only available after 1947 with the use of streptomycin. But by then the death rate from the disease was already only one-eighth of the level a century earlier and the best estimates suggest that improved medical treatment was responsible for only three per cent of the overall reduction in deaths from tuberculosis. The development of new drugs, such as the sulphonamides in the late 1930s and antibiotics after the Second World War, has similarly had only a marginal effect in reducing death rates from infectious disease. A detailed American study suggests that overall since 1900 medical intervention has contributed little to the decline in mortality – probably as little as three-and-a-half per cent of the total.

The major influences in reducing the impact of infectious diseases were better diet and environmental improvements. Poor diet increased vulnerability to disease and in the nineteenth century the quantity and variety of food available in Europe began to increase significantly. This increase was particularly important in reducing child mortality rates. Public health measures were also crucial in containing the spread of infection. The construction of effective sewers and the treatment of drinking water drastically reduced the impact of water borne intestinal diseases such as cholera. Overall about a fifth of the reduction in mortality in the nineteenth century is estimated to have come from water supply and sewage system improvements. Better housing, which reduced overcrowding, damp, and poor ventilation, further improved resistance to disease. In many cases it was a combination of measures, only some of which were medical improvements or steps specifically designed to reduce the rate of infection, which brought about significant reductions in diseases. In the case of tuberculosis, general public health improvements and better living conditions together with later measures such as sanatoria to isolate infected patients, prevention of spitting in public places and the slaughter of infected cattle, helped to bring about a drastic reduction in death rates during the nineteenth-century. The death rate from TB – a major killer – fell by half between 1838 and 1882, before the bacillus which caused the disease had even been identified. About a fifth of the overall fall in mortality rates in nineteenth-century Britain was accounted for by the reduction in tuberculosis deaths. The gradual adoption of other public hygiene measures such as the pasteurisation of milk (begun in Chicago in 1908) and the introduction of new techniques such as canning and refrigeration also reduced infection rates from contaminated food. The importance of these environmental changes in reducing mortality can be illustrated by the fact that the death rate for children infected with measles had dropped to one in a thousand even before the introduction of immunization.

In all parts of the world, poverty and poor living conditions remain one of the major causes of disease. The disease pattern that affected the whole world for thousands of years is still found in many parts of the Third World. Although the death rate from infectious diseases has fallen, chronic malnutrition or starvation make large numbers of people particularly vulnerable to infection, and bad sanitation together with a lack of clean water lead to widespread intestinal infections, particularly among infants. In the Third World about four-and-a-half million children under the age of five (80 per cent of them aged less than two) die of intestinal disease every year. Overall, infant mortality in the Third World is about twenty times higher than in the developed countries. But even in the developed world wealth is still a major determinant of health. Infant mortality in a relatively deprived area such as Northern Ireland is three times higher than in Iceland and twice the rate in Sweden. Infant mortality rates have been declining steadily in the developed world over the last century but at roughly the same rate for all social classes. In Britain the children of unskilled manual workers still have a mortality rate five times higher than the children of professional families. In nearly every case the incidence of disease is linked to economic and social conditions and falls with higher social class.

Although immunization programmes have reduced deaths from some diseases, in particular smallpox, other programmes such as malaria eradication have been much less successful, and infectious diseases still remain a significant threat despite major international efforts. Many diseases have been controlled rather than eliminated. For example an outbreak of plague in Manchuria in 1894 was quickly carried by rats on board ships to every part of the world. Only good public health measures ensured that there was not a major outbreak of bubonic plague. (The 1894 outbreak brought infected animals to the Americas and by 1940 thirty-four species of burrowing rodents and thirty-five species of flea on the continent carried the disease.) The evolution of a particularly virulent influenza strain in 1918, which swept across the world over the next three years, resulted in between fifteen and twenty million deaths with a particularly high fatality rate in Europe, where many people had been weakened by a poor diet because of the food shortages during the First World War. In modern societies large scale breakdowns caused by natural disasters such as earthquakes can still lead very quickly to the outbreak of infections. New infectious diseases still pose a major threat and illustrate the limitations of medical science in dealing with them. Aids was first recognised as a disease in the early 1980s and may be another example of a disease crossing from an animal population (monkeys according to some experts) to infect humans. With no vaccine available infection rates are rising rapidly particularly in Africa where it is almost impossible to estimate the true extent of the disease, and in the United States where about one-and-a-half million people are infected.

The general decline of infectious diseases in the industrialised world in the last two hundred years has been paralleled by the rise of new diseases that have radically altered the way of death for this section of humanity. High infant mortality and early death from infectious diseases have been replaced by cancer and cardio-vascular disease, which together now account for two-thirds of deaths in industrialised countries. The reasons for the greatly increased incidence of both diseases is still the subject of much debate. Part of the explanation for increasing death rates from these types of disease must be the fact that far fewer people die from infectious diseases and therefore they become more susceptible, with age, to degenerative diseases. However the main reasons have to be sought in the various changes in the way of life in the developed countries and in particular alterations in diet.

Some of the dietary changes in the last two centuries have been beneficial. One of the problems associated with the development of agriculture has been the reliance of a large section of the population on a limited range of foods which, in some cases, have not contained the full range of nutrients required by humans, leading to deficiency diseases. These have particularly affected the poor who have been unable to obtain a wide range of foods. Pellagra, which is caused by a lack of vitamin B_2, is the result of too great a dependence on maize. Once common among poor farmers in the southern states of the United States and deprived black mine workers in South Africa (who ate almost nothing but mealy-meal made from maize), it was eliminated as wealth increased and a more varied diet was available. Rickets (caused by vitamin D deficiency) is virtually unknown in skeletons from prehistoric gathering and hunting groups but it affected about seven per cent of the population in mid-nineteenth century London. The incidence of the disease declined as diet became more varied. The increased availability of healthy food has also made people bigger. Although it is difficult to generalise, the average height of the population of medieval Europe was much nearer five feet than six feet (hence the low ceilings of many buildings of that period). Contemporary British children are about twenty per cent taller than those of mid-eighteenth century London and European adult males are on average now about three inches taller than a hundred years ago.

However, there is an increasing amount of evidence to suggest that many dietary changes have been harmful. The novel features of the modern western diet are a reduction in fibre intake, a rise in sugar consumption, much higher levels of fat intake and a higher proportion of processed foods. White bread is just one example of processing which reduces the amount of fibre and nutrients in food. The removal of bran and germ from flour to produce white bread was probably first adopted in the fourteenth century, but white bread remained a luxury item because the frequent shortage of grain meant that it was essential to maximise bread production by using all of the flour. (At times of acute grain shortage the authorities often banned the making of white bread.) Before 1750 only about one in twenty of the population of France ate white bread. Improved grain supplies in the nineteenth century meant that after about 1850 the majority of people in the industrialised world began to eat white bread and by the twentieth century it dominated the market. This reduction of fibre in the diet has been associated with a number of complaints common in western societies such as constipation and intestinal disease. The rise in sugar consumption has had even more deleterious effects on health. Until the sixteenth century foods were sweetened by using honey (or maple syrup in North America) and consumption was at a very low level. The development of sugar plantations across the world increased production and consumption. By 1750 sugar intake in Europe and North America had risen from negligible levels to about four pounds a head, a year. It is now about 120 pounds per head every year. The most immediate effect was a rapid rise in dental caries. Prehistoric skeletons suggest that this disease affected less than three per cent of teeth and in many other societies with low sugar consumption tooth decay is almost unknown. Increased sugar consumption also led to increases in obesity and diabetes. The link between sugar consumption, obesity and diabetes was first apparent among the eighteenth-century English aristocracy, who had very high sugar intakes.

Fat intake has been increasing throughout history. The first fundamental change followed the domestication of sheep, goats and cattle, which introduced dairy products into the human diet for the first time. The small number of animals that could be maintained, because of poor grazing and lack of fodder in the earliest agricultural societies, limited intake as did primitive distribution systems for what, in most cases, were products with a very short life. Technological changes in the late nineteenth century – pasteurisation of milk, canning and refrigeration together with faster distribution through the railways – brought dairy products to the mass of the population living in cities and substantially increased consumption. Higher levels of fat in the diet (from dairy products and other sources such as meat) are related to an increased risk of heart disease. The technological changes at the end of the nineteenth century were also part of a new phenomenon – the rise of a food industry concentrating heavily on making and marketing processed foods rather than distributing fresh food. This trend has had a marked effect on health. The consumption of processed food in the United States per head of the population has tripled this century and three-quarters of all American food now consumed has been processed in some way. In parallel the consumption of fresh fruit and vegetables has fallen by a third since 1910. Processing food not only removes many of the nutrients and important trace minerals but also introduces additives such as antioxidants, emulsifiers, thickeners, dyes, sweeteners and bleaching agents. The average Briton now consumes three pounds of these chemical additives every year.

All of these changes in the diet have contributed significantly to increases in heart disease, many cancers such as those of the stomach, bowel and colon and other diseases such as gallstones. Changes in the quantity as well as the quality of food consumed have increased the rate of obesity – on average middle-aged males in Britain are now twenty pounds overweight and in the United States the figure is even higher. Medical studies have shown that those whose weight is more than twenty-five per cent above average have a death rate twice that of those of average weight. Heart disease, one of the primary consequences of these dietary changes, was almost unknown a hundred years ago except among the rich, who already had a diet high in fat and sugar and lacking in fibre and fresh fruit and vegetables. It now kills forty per cent of men and twenty per cent of women in the industrialised countries. Heart diseases are rare among non-westernised people until they, too, change their way of life and adopt elements of a western diet. Before 1940 Africans in Kenya and Uganda did not have rising blood pressure with increasing age, and coronary artery disease was not diagnosed at all in Uganda until 1956, and not until 1968 in Kenya and Tanzania.

European cancer rates are ten times higher than those in West Africa. Apart from diet, a number of factors increase the risk of contracting the disease, in particular environmental factors and the use of addictive drugs such as tobacco. The large increase in the use of tobacco since the seventeenth century in the form of snuff, cigarettes and cigars (particularly marked in the present century) is directly related to increased cancer rates. Smoking increases the risk of contracting cancer by about a third and is also associated with other complaints such as heart disease and bronchitis. Lung cancer rates in the industrialised world rose by eighty per cent in the twenty years after 1960, largely as a result of increased smoking. The greater consumption of tobacco is now having a similar effect in the Third World. Another important factor is the rise in the production of a wide range of highly toxic chemicals which exposes people either directly, or indirectly through pollution, to hazardous and carcinogenic compounds. Areas around toxic waste dumps or near nuclear sites have been found to have higher-than-average cancer rates and the impact of environmental factors can also be seen in the rise of childhood cancers where smoking and diet play only a small role. The incidence of cancer in the industrialised world has also been increasing steadily – one in three Americans contracts cancer (compared with one in twenty-seven in 1900) and one in four dies of the disease. Male deaths from cancer in the western world rose by fifty-five per cent between 1960 and 1980 and female deaths by forty per cent.

The relationship between humans and disease has followed the same sequence as many other aspects of the interaction between humans and the environment. The first great transition in human history – the emergence of agriculture and settled societies – also marked a profound change in the impact of disease on humans. It exposed people to a wide range of new infectious diseases, many transmitted from the animals that they domesticated, and these diseases played a major role in human history for thousands of years. The gradual emergence of a single world, particularly after the expansion of Europe, enabled a much greater variety of crops to be grown in many parts of the world but it also spread new diseases, often with a shattering impact on societies that had previously been isolated. The rise of industrialised societies also marked a major change in disease patterns in this part of the world. Infectious diseases declined in importance but people began increasingly to succumb to non-communicable diseases directly linked to the new ways of life in the industrialised world.

12
THE WEIGHT OF NUMBERS

One of the greatest changes in human history has been the unprecedented, rapid increase in population, partly caused by the fall in the number of deaths from infectious diseases during the course of the last two centuries. The most graphic way to convey the accelerating rate of growth is to consider the varying lengths of time it has taken to increase the world's population by one billion. The total number of people in the world first reached one billion in about 1825, and it had taken about two million years to reach this level. The next billion was added in only a hundred years. A further billion (taking the total to 3 billion) took about thirty-five years from 1925 to 1960. The next billion was added in only fifteen years (by 1975) while the increase from 4 billion to 5 billion took about twelve years and was completed in the late 1980s.

Within this overall increase the pattern of growth varied widely from continent to continent, and there were also considerable variations between countries at different periods. In Europe the story is of a period of dramatic growth in the late eighteenth and nineteenth centuries giving way to a period of much slower growth. The population of Europe had grown slowly, with fluctuations mainly due to outbreaks of disease and famine, to reach about 140 million by the middle of the eighteenth century. In the course of the next hundred years the increase in numbers was the most rapid ever experienced – they rose by 80 per cent to 250 million in 1845 – and then grew even faster to add another 80 per cent in the space of only seventy years – to reach a total of 450 million by 1914 (the figure would have been even higher but for the 40 million Europeans who emigrated during this period). Most of this growth was concentrated in north and west Europe, and later in the east, rather than in the Mediterranean region. England, the Benelux countries and Germany became the most densely settled areas of Europe. After about 1900 growth slackened – European population grew by just over 60 per cent in the next eighty years compared with a

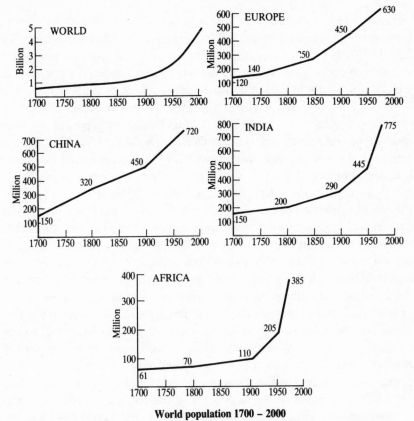

World population 1700 – 2000

world average of over 140 per cent. What happened in England and Wales (where there are one of the most reliable series of population estimates for this period) illustrates the general trend. The population was just over 6 million in 1750. It then increased by 50 per cent in fifty years, reaching 9.2 million in 1800, and doubled in the next fifty years to a total of 18 million in 1850. At this stage, growth slowed down, but still rose by 75 per cent to a figure of 33 million by 1900. But there were exceptions among European countries. The population of Ireland fell drastically in the second half of the nineteenth century because of the effects of famine and emigration, while in France the population rose more slowly than during the medieval period, only increasing from about 24 million in 1750 to 40 million in 1900.

The period of rapid growth in population after the mid-eighteenth century was largely the result of a decline in mortality levels. The subsequent slackening in growth was the result not of an increase in mortality but of a fall in birth rates, altering a pattern that had been established for hundreds of generations. People had much smaller families than in the past. Just how significant this transition to a lower birth rate has been can be judged from the fact that it is estimated that had the birth rate in England and Wales remained at late eighteenth and nineteenth century levels during the twentieth century, the population would now be about 140 million instead of about 50 million.

In Asia and Africa the story of population growth starts off in the same way but has a very different ending. Numbers grew at very high rates in the eighteenth and nineteenth centuries but, unlike Europe, the period that has seen the highest rates of growth has been the twentieth century. The population of Asia was about 415 million in 1700. Since then each century has seen ever higher levels of growth – 50 per cent in the eighteenth century (625 million in 1800), 55 per cent in the nineteenth (970 million in 1900) and a huge leap to over 130 per cent to reach 2.3 billion in the mid-1970s. China's experience illustrates this pattern in detail: there were 150 million Chinese in 1700 and there were nearly 1 billion by the late 1980s. India's growth rate has been only slightly less – the population has increased from about 145 million in 1650 to over 750 million by the late 1970s. The major exception to this trend has been Japan. There population reached about 30 million in 1700 but did not grow at all before 1850 because numbers had already reached the limits that the agricultural system could support – population was controlled through the widespread practice of infanticide. In the course of the next century the population rose by about 150 per cent to a total of 84 million but growth then began to slow down appreciably (partly because of a very high abortion rate) and the total is now about 120 million. Africa has seen one of the highest rates of population growth in the modern period. From a total of about 60 million in 1700 it increased to 70 million in 1800 and 110 million in 1900. In the twentieth century the population has almost quadrupled to reach over 400 million.

In the Third World growth rates in the twentieth century have been on average over two per cent a year – far higher than in nineteenth century Europe when the maximum recorded was about one-and-a-half per cent a year during the first three decades of the century in England and Wales. Fertility has been much higher than in Europe because of the young age and high rate of marriage. Mortality rates have also fallen rapidly – for example, by a half in Egypt between 1946 and 1971, a change that took from 1800 to 1920 in Sweden. Unlike Europe there has been little opportunity for the increasing population of the Third World to emigrate on a large scale except to the towns, which has created more problems.

In the Americas and Oceania the picture is much more complex and reflects a different series of developments. Numbers have risen very sharply, largely as the result of immigration from Europe, especially in the nineteenth century and then by natural increase. The population of the United States for example was only 6 million in 1800, but was 76 million a century later and is now about 220 million. Oceania grew from just over 2 million in the mid-nineteenth century to 23 million in the mid-1970s.

This unprecedented rise in human numbers has had profound consequences for the environment. All these people needed housing and therefore the number and size of human settlements across the globe has increased significantly in the last two centuries. At the same time they have consumed more of the earth's resources in terms of energy and minerals. In doing so they have inevitably increased the amount of pollution in the world. These themes form the basis of the succeeding four chapters. But first and foremost the rapidly increasing numbers of people had to be fed, and it is the way in which this has been done, and the consequences for the environment, that is considered in the rest of this chapter.

In the period up until about 1800 (see Chapter 6) the traditional limits on food supply were set by the amount of suitable land available for cultivation, the level of agricultural productivity and technology, the amount of trade and commerce, wider social and political factors (such as the amount of production taken up by the non-productive parts of society and access to extraneous sources of supply) and the climate. In the last two hundred years there have been revolutionary changes in all but the last of these areas (and even climatic factors have been partially offset by the development of new varieties of crops). The fact that the earth now supports five times as many people as it did only two hundred years ago seems, at first glance, to be a triumph of human ingenuity in getting round the limitations on food supply that had prevailed for thousands of years and restricted the growth in human numbers to very low rates. However, many problems have remained unresolved, many have worsened and the impact on the environment of these changes has been profound.

In medieval and early modern Europe and China the response to rising population was to bring more marginal land into production, even if yields from the new areas (with their more difficult soils and climate) were lower than those from long-established agricultural regions. This is what happened again from the mid-eighteenth century.

However Europe had the great advantage of exercising political and therefore economic control over large parts of the world. The major European states had established colonies, or created informal empires in areas such as Latin America after independence, and they dominated world trade. Europe thus gained access to the new lands of the Americas, Australia and New Zealand to provide additional food for its growing population. The people of Asia and Africa were not in a position to take advantage of overseas food production; they had to depend on their own resources whilst increasing amounts of land in their countries were devoted to growing crops for the industrialised world. Between 1860 and 1920 across the world about one billion acres of new land was converted to agricultural use (about 40 per cent of it in the United States mainly in the corn belt, 20 per cent on the black earth soils of Russia and another 20 per cent in Asia). In the sixty years after 1920 about another one billion acres was brought into production, much of it in Latin America and with the smallest increase in Asia. The arable area in Europe itself actually fell in this period. Overall in the hundred years after 1860 the area under crops in the United States increased two-and-a-half-fold, in the Soviet Union it quadrupled, in Canada it increased eight-fold and in Australia, it was twenty-seven times larger at the end of the period than at the beginning. In Brazil the increase was also very rapid – six-fold in the forty years after 1930.

This extra land could not have provided food for Europe (and to a lesser extent the rest of the world) without a combination of developments which made a vast increase in the international food trade possible. Behind this upsurge in trade were two technological revolutions. The first affected transport – the use of cheap and fast steamships on the oceans and railways opened up the interiors of the previously unsettled continents and improved distribution within the industrialised countries. The second involved the development of chilling and refrigeration to enable perishable products to be transported around the world. Low-cost shipping increased the bulk transport of grain to Europe during the nineteenth century from overseas territories where cheap land kept production prices low enough to compete with, and in many cases undercut, the home-grown product. The building of railways opened up new areas of supply – in the United States the first transcontinental railway was completed in 1869 and in the next twenty years American wheat exports increased seven-fold. In South America British investment in railways opened up the great grasslands to produce beef and hides for Europe. Other products too were brought into this developing international trade. The first Spanish oranges were shipped to England in 1860 and a decade later to Germany and the United States. In the 1880s Spanish orange exports quadrupled as new markets were opened up. About the same time the first ships with chilled compartments brought meat from overseas to Europe – from New York to England in 1875 and from Buenos Aires to France two years later. Refrigerated ships that could store frozen meat were sailing by the late 1870s and brought meat from Australia to England in 1879 and from New Zealand three years later. By the 1890s butter and cheese from New Zealand were also being imported. In 1901 the first refrigerated banana boat brought fruit from Jamaica to England. The result of these technological changes was a vast increase in the amount of food traded in the world. In the 1850s total exports of food were no more than 4 million tons; by the 1880s they had increased to 18 million tons and at the outbreak of the First World War they had reached 40 million tons. They stayed at about this level until the late 1950s when they expanded again to reach 200 million tons by 1980 (a fifty-fold growth in the space of 130 years). The nineteenth century marked the end of several thousand years of largely self-sufficient agriculture (supplemented by small-scale or specialised trading in foodstuffs) and the transition to an era where much of the food consumed in the industrialised countries was imported. The nature of trade also changed significantly. Before the mid-nineteenth century nearly all Europe's food imports were luxury goods – sugar, coffee, tea and cocoa – whereas the new imports that developed in the nineteenth century were primarily bulk items that formed the basis of the diet – grains, meat and dairy products. European countries, especially Britain, became dependent on imported food in the late nineteenth century. In the years immediately before the outbreak of war in 1914 Britain imported 80 per cent of its wheat consumption, 65 per cent of its fruit and 40 per cent of its meat.

In parallel with the increase in acreage and trade in food the agriculture of the industrialised world – Europe, North America and Australasia – was transformed by increases in productivity. Until the mid-nineteenth century there had been only a slow improvement in agricultural techniques in Europe, associated with better equipment, improved rotations, new fodder crops and more drainage of land, and only a slow spread of these changes across the continent. But they were sufficient for crop yields to double between the thirteenth and nineteenth centuries (as they did for rice in China between 1450 and 1800). The first part of the century saw two useful improvements. The seed drill, which had been known in China for 1,500 years, was widely adopted and reduced losses from seeds that previously had been simply broadcast on the soil. Tiled underdrainage was introduced from the 1840s as were better animal feeds such as oil cake.

The period after 1850 witnessed two major revolutions – the mechanisation of agriculture and the adoption of high input farming. The use of more machinery was in part stimulated by the problem of labour shortages, which were particularly acute in the newly settled countries. Mechanical reapers for example were introduced in the 1860s in the United States but not until much later in Europe where labour was still plentiful. They were still pulled by teams of up to twenty horses because the large-scale application of steam power on farms was uneconomic. The real leap foward in the mechanisation revolution had to await the development of the internal combustion engine and the tractor. In the United States tractors were adopted very quickly (there were 250,000 tractors on American farms in 1920 and 2.3 million in 1945) but their use only became widespread in Europe after the Second World War (between 1950 and 1968 the number of tractors on West German farms rose seven-fold). The combine harvester was introduced in the US in 1920 but not until the 1950s in Europe – in 1944 Denmark had none but it had over 40,000 by the end of the 1960s. The first electric milking machines were introduced in 1895 and 70 per cent of farms in New Zealand used them by 1920. But again Europe only adopted them after 1945 – in western Europe in 1950 only 3 per cent of cows were machine milked, by the 1980s only 3 per cent were hand milked. Greater mechanisation made it possible to increase farm size, reduce the number of farms and also cut the number of people working in agriculture. In the United States the number of farms fell from 7 million in the 1930s to below 3 million in the 1980s and over half of all sales of agricultural produce came from just 5 per cent of the total number of farms. In Belgium the average size of farms doubled between 1950 and 1980. The paradox of modern agriculture in the industrialised world, which also marks a radical departure from previous practice, is that as output has soared the number of people working in agriculture has plummeted, with major implications for society and the countryside. The agricultural workforce has declined from over 11 million in the United States in 1910 to just over 3 million in 1970 and from 1 million in Belgium in 1856 to less than 200,000 a century later. In West Germany the agricultural labour force fell by a half between 1950 and 1965. Increasingly farms are owned not by families but by large firms or even investment trusts able to take advantage of numerous tax concessions.

Until the nineteenth century farms were dependent almost entirely upon manures and composts produced on the farm itself in order to maintain soil fertility and therefore mixed farming (combining arable and animals) was the norm. Then European countries, and later the United States, were able to use their increasing control over the world's resources to import new fertilisers. The first guano was brought to Europe from South America in the 1820s and the trade became increasingly important throughout the century. Later phosphates mined in various sites around the world – North Africa and some Pacific islands – widened the range of fertilisers available. New industrial processes also produced new artificial fertilisers – superphosphates in the 1840s and nitrogenous fertilisers in the 1920s – and increased the trend towards treating agriculture as a business, with close attention to inputs and outputs rather than the relationship with the land and the animals. Between 1950 and 1980 food output in the industrialised world doubled – but much of this increase came from extra inputs that treated the soil less as a living organism and more as a medium to hold crops in position whilst various chemicals were poured on to them. Fertiliser use in the United States trebled between 1950 and 1972 and rose five-fold in western Europe in the same period. In Canada it increased ten-fold and in the USSR fourteen-fold. The overall scale of the change can be judged from the British figures for the use of nitrogen fertilisers – 50,000 tons a year in the late 1920s and over 1 million tons fifty years later. In parallel, since 1945 there has been a shift towards increasing dependence on a single crop (and often only a few varieties of that crop) over a wide area and a decline in mixed farming. Monocrops are more susceptible to diseases and pests and this has resulted in the increasing use of chemical herbicides and pesticides on farms – the amount sprayed on to crops in the developed world rose fifteen-fold in the twenty-five years after 1953.

Traditional methods of raising domesticated animals were extensive and so numbers and output were limited by the availability of grass and winter fodder such as hay and root crops. Improvements were largely confined to selective breeding in order to improve some aspects of the animal, such as the increasing use of Merino sheep for their high quality wool. But during the twentieth century animal rearing systems have become more intensive. Instead of feeding outdoors on natural foods such as grass, animals have been brought indoors into highly artificial environments and fed on artificial feeds. Chickens are kept in overcrowded battery cages, cattle in small stalls and pigs are chained to walls in sties small enough to ensure that they can not move. Animals, which are herbivores, are fed on a diet which may include a high percentage of dead animals, recycled manure, growth hormones and also antibiotics to control the diseases that would otherwise be rife in such conditions. Even fish are now kept in artificial habitats on 'farms' (a quarter of the UK's fish now comes from this source), and again problems of health and nutrition have arisen. For example, salmon, deprived of their natural diet, have to be given a dye in their food to ensure that their flesh turns pink, and in crowded conditions diseases spread rapidly. Keeping animals in highly artificial habitats and intensive production units did not begin in the twentieth century – only the scale of this operation was new. In sixteenth-century England, one observer reported that many pigs were kept 'in so close a room that they cannot turn themselves round about whereby they are forced always to lie on their bellies'. For centuries poultry and game birds were reared in the dark, blinded, or in the case of geese had their feet nailed to the floor, or if they were chickens had their feet cut off, because it was believed that it made their meat more tender. In France geese were force-fed to produce pâté de foie gras. In 1686 a leading landowner interested in new farming techniques, Sir Robert Southwell, reported that he had seen a 'new invention of an ox-house, where the cattle are . . . to eat and drink in the same crib and not stir until they be fitted for the slaughter'.

Much of the large increase in agricultural output in the industrialised world in the last fifty years has come about as a consequence of government intervention. They have adopted policies towards agriculture designed to increase national self-sufficiency, boost farm incomes, support rural areas and buy votes. This intervention has usually taken the form either of deficiency payments (as a way of keeping production artificially high and giving the farmer an income greater than the market price would dictate) or through the creation of an artificial market as in the European Community where internal prices are usually higher than the world price. In addition, other forms of subsidy may be given to what had become by the middle of the twentieth century powerful vested interests. Because of these artificial conditions farmers in the United States and the European Community in particular have produced huge surpluses. Farming is now one of the most highly subsidised of all industries – in Britain subsidies amount to 40 per cent of the output of the industry and the consumer has to pay an extra £2 billion a year because prices are kept above world levels.

In parallel with these changes in agriculture in the industrialised world there has been a major change in the way food has reached the public with the rise of a food-processing industry and large-scale food retailers. Before the nineteenth century food processing was confined to a few products such as bread, pies and jam and carried out by small-scale firms. Most produce was eaten fresh but even here the range available, especially to those who lived in towns, was limited. One of the major developments in the nineteenth century was the rise of the dairy industry in the wake of a number of technical improvements, in particular, better transportation, pasteurisation and new methods of cooling milk and butter to ensure that such perishable products could be sold at a considerable distance from the farm. In 1861 just 4 per cent of the milk sold in London came by rail but thirty years later it had risen to 83 per cent. By 1914 much of the milk sold in New York came from over 300 miles away and in the 1930s most of the milk supply for Berlin travelled more than 400 miles. The consumption of milk and milk products increased enormously and a large number of farms changed over to raising dairy cattle (milk now constitutes over a fifth of the total agricultural output in both the United States and the European Community). Cheese was made in small quantities on farms until the nineteenth century when the first factories were established – in the 1840s in Ohio and the 1870s in Europe. The first butter factories started operation in the United States in 1861 and once a mechanical separator had been developed in 1879 large-scale production was possible and a new dairy industry was created.

Industrial scale production of food spread into other areas such as bread, while new processes such as canning and later refrigeration widened still further the range of products available and made it possible to supply fruit and vegetables out of their natural season and country of origin. Completely artificial products such as margarine were also developed and formed the basis for new industries. Increasingly food processing companies took control of production, buying the output of whole farms or even owning large plantations, as in the case of Del Monte, which specialised in canning fruit. Looking for new growth areas the industry began to refine and alter its products so as to add value, in terms of profits rather than nutritional content. Natural products were processed to an ever greater extent (often removing much of the nutritional content): most of the costs (and profits) now come from processing rather than growing food – the average American farmer receives just 4 per cent of the price of chicken in the shops, 17 per cent of a can of peaches and 12 per cent of a can of corn.

The rise of processing also increased the opportunities for adulterating food and passing off inferior products as high grade food. Again this was not a new phenomenon. In the fifteenth century a proclamation by the City of London condemned pastry cooks who 'have baked in pasties . . . garbage not befitting and sometimes stinking, in deceit of the people, and have also baked beef in pasties and called it venison'. Bread was regularly contaminated with alum, bone ash or lime in order to whiten it and vinegar often consisted of dilute sulphuric acid coloured with wood chips. In the 1850s the British medical journal *The Lancet* carried out a detailed survey of food on sale in London. They found that all the bread tested was adulterated as was half of the oatmeal and all but the very highest quality teas, all the butter had been watered down and half of the jams contaminated. Some of the most flagrant abuses were eliminated by legislation in the late nineteenth century and later, often in the wake of major public scandals such as the publication in 1906 of Upton Sinclair's novel *The Jungle*, which exposed the terrible conditions in the stockyards and slaughterhouses of Chicago and brought about new laws within six months.

The processing of food now involves more sophisticated methods of manipulation and adulteration. In the United States three-quarters of all food sold is processed in some way and much of it consists of highly artificial products such as 'cream' containing no dairy products, 'orange' drinks that contain no orange, or sausages with little meat (and most of that ground up parts of the animal that would normally be inedible). This processed food contains many additives, some designed to ensure longer life for products that have to be transported through long distribution chains and be kept in shops for long periods before sale, some to make poor quality food palatable and others just to increase the water content and hence profits. Many of the products contain large amounts of sugar or salt and additives such as artificial colourings, flavourings, preservatives and emulsifiers (to provide an artificial texture). Recent studies have shown that nearly 90 per cent of all additives are essentially cosmetic; they are there to provide artificial taste and appearance. Many of these additives have deleterious side effects when consumed in any quantity.

The agricultural history of the Third World in the last century has been very different from that of the developed countries. Unlike Europe and the United States, they had only limited access to the products of the new lands in North America and Australasia; most of the newly cultivated land in Latin America was used to provide food for export, and the amount of new land available in Asia was very limited since production was already at an intense level and had expanded onto most of the productive land. These Third World countries faced two problems. Because of European political control, increasing amounts of land were devoted to growing cash crops for export. In addition, land was very unequally distributed – in Latin America two-thirds of the land is now owned by just one-and-a-half per cent of the total number of landowners, a third of the population own just one per cent of the land and many are landless labourers; in Africa three-quarters of the agricultural population own just 4 per cent of the land. Apart from the appalling social problems caused by this highly unequal distribution, food output is also significantly reduced because the large landholdings tend to be less productive and concentrate most on export crops. The consequence of these problems and the rapidly rising population has been that the amount of arable land per head of the population has been falling in the Third World – since the 1870s in China for instance, since the turn of the century in India, South Korea, the Philippines and Vietnam and since 1920 in Java. This meant that cultivation had to become more intensive in order to produce enough food. This has been done by intensifying existing methods such as paddy field production but also, since the Second World War, through the so-called 'Green Revolution' – the introduction of high-yielding varieties of wheat and rice. First developed in research institutes, in Mexico in the case of wheat, and in the Philippines in the case of rice, these new types of plant did increase crop yields. The new wheat strains were first grown in Mexico in the 1940s and over the next twenty years agricultural production rose at an average of 5 per cent a year, largely attributable to cultivation of the new varieties. They were introduced into India and Pakistan in 1965 and here wheat yields doubled in less than a decade. The new rice varieties came late in the 1960s and had the same effect.

At the time the 'Green Revolution' was hailed as the solution to the problem of growing enough food to support the expanding population of the Third World. It has since become apparent that this is not the case. The impact of these high-yielding varieties on the overwhelming majority of people in the Third World has, in practice, been disastrous. The problem with the new types of wheat and rice is that, in order to produce high yields, they require large amounts of fertiliser and also, because they lack natural immunity to pests, large quantities of pesticides. (The use of chemical fertilisers in Asia has risen thirty-eight-fold since 1950 compared with a world average of a six-fold increase during this period.) The financial cost of growing the new varieties was therefore much higher than for the types of plant that had been grown for generations. This meant that only those farmers who could afford the higher inputs could hope to achieve the higher yields and the 'Green Revolution' therefore accentuated existing social differences and accelerated trends towards greater mechanisation and larger holdings. Small peasant farmers (the majority) did not have enough land and capital to make it worthwhile adopting the new types, and the large landowners, who had the necessary resources, were able to become richer, expand their holdings, buy up peasant land and turn the peasants into landless labourers. In Mexico, 80 per cent of the extra production from the new types of wheat came from just 3 per cent of the total number of farms, the average numbers of days worked every year by the landless labourers fell from 194 to 100 and their real income fell by a fifth. Those farmers who successfully adopted the new methods became more dependent on imports of fertilisers, pesticides and farm machinery and also on world markets for the export of produce. Local autonomy and self-sufficiency were reduced even further.

The combined effect of the 'Green Revolution', the extension of the cultivated area and use of more artificial inputs was to increase food production in the Third World – by between 30–55 per cent, depending on the region, between 1960 and the mid-1970s alone. The problem is that the gains have been unevenly spread and inadequate to cope with a rapidly increasing population. After 1945 the situation deteriorated sharply – by the 1980s over fifty countries that had been self-sufficient in the 1930s had become net importers of food. In the thirty years after the Second World War, in thirty-four countries, affecting a quarter of the population in the Third World, food output did not keep pace with population. The worst affected area was Africa, where across the continent the food supply per head began to fall in the early 1960s. By the late 1980s Africa as a whole was importing as much food as it exported. The large-scale production of cash crops for export to the industrialised world only exacerbated this situation by taking up land that could be used to grow food for the local population and by using fertilizers that could be used to increase crop yields of food for local consumption. In Kenya only 3 per cent of the fertiliser used in the country is for smallholders' crops and in Brazil and Ecuador two-thirds of the fertiliser is applied to just three cash crops.

The result of all these changes in food production, trade and population growth has been to create an unbalanced world agricultural system. It reflects the distribution of political and economic power between the industrialised countries and the Third World that emerged in the period following the great expansion of Europe after 1500. The agriculture of the industrialised world is not necessarily more 'efficient' than that of the Third World – what it is able to do is purchase more inputs and therefore ensure higher output. In energy terms it is actually *less* efficient. Overall there is enough food in the world to feed everybody at an adequate level – the problem is its unequal distribution. Put simply, the people of the industrialised countries eat half the world's food although they only constitute a quarter of the world's population. More food is sent from the Third World to the industrialised countries than in the opposite direction (most Third World countries are net exporters of food); a large proportion of this trade has been to provide more variety in the diet of those who are already well fed, for example by making available tropical and out-of-season fruits and other luxuries such as coffee, tea and cocoa. The industrialised countries have also made very inefficient use of the food they have available. A quarter of the world's total production of grain is fed to animals in the industrialised world to be turned into meat even though it could be used much more efficiently as grain to provide food for humans. It has also been estimated that a quarter of all the food produced in the United States goes to waste at some point in the production, distribution and consumption chain. Even in the industrialised world there are marked inequalities in food consumption. Although the average American eats half as much again as the average inhabitant of the Third World, this disguises very real differences within American society – about 15 million people do not earn enough to consume a well-balanced diet and another 15 million are constantly hungry (a total of over 10 per cent of the population).

The situation in the Third World is far worse. Although the percentage of the population in the Third World living on an inadequate diet declined between 1950 and 1980, the number of people affected remained the same because of the rise in population. The most reliable estimates suggest that about half the world's population, or two-and-a-half billion people, are undernourished, with the most severe problems found in the Andean republics, parts of Africa and in south Asia. This general lack of food is reflected in the fact that four out of five Indian children have been diagnosed as having reduced growth because of their inadequate diet. The scale of severe food shortage, rather than general inadequacy, is immense. Outside China (where the extent of the problem is not publicised) at least 800 million people get less than 90 per cent of the food required for an active working life and about a further 400 million do not eat enough food to avoid stunted growth and serious health risks. About 40 million people die every year from hunger and related diseases – equivalent to 300 Jumbo jet crashes every day – with half of the passengers being children.

Although in Europe the spectre of famine that had haunted the continent for thousands of years disappeared in the eighteenth and nineteenth centuries as production increased and more food was imported from abroad, it remains ever present in the Third World. As in medieval and early modern Europe, the people most affected are the poor, who are unable to afford to buy food at the highly inflated prices that prevail during a shortage. In none of the twentieth century famines has there been an absolute shortage of food; the problem has been unequal access due to poverty, a problem that resort to food aid has not solved. In Bengal in 1943–1944 about three million people died after rice prices quadrupled in two years. Worst affected were the rural areas, where wages had not kept pace with wartime inflation, and some towns where workers were unemployed because of the dislocation caused by the war. People without money were unable to buy food and the British imperial authorities took little action (apart from moving food to Calcutta because they feared mass civil unrest). One of the worst famines of modern times therefore took place when the amount of food per head in Bengal was actually 7 per cent higher than in 1941 and food stocks were at record levels. In Ethiopia, in 1972–1974, about 200,000 people died in the provinces of Wollo and Tigre even though the country's food production only fell by just over 5 per cent – during this period food was still being exported from the affected provinces and from the country as a whole. In Bangladesh in 1974 when rice prices doubled in three months after severe flooding, those who were out of work because of the disruption caused by the floods could not afford to buy food. As a result one-and-a-half million people died of starvation. But there was no absolute shortage of food – production of rice in Bangladesh, both in total and per head terms, was the highest ever in 1974 – once again it was a problem of who had the resources to buy food at the higher prices.

The huge increase in the amount of land under cultivation (at least two billion acres in the last 130 years), the extension of pasture land into new areas and the intensification of agriculture have all led to a massive loss of natural ecosystems in the last two centuries. They have been destroyed through deforestation, the ploughing up of grasslands, the extension of the cultivated area on to marginal land and steep slopes with a consequential increase in soil erosion, degradation of land and in many areas the extension of deserts. The associated environmental damage has now reached the point where more arable land is being lost to cultivation than is brought into production.

Britain provides one example of the speed and extent of the loss of natural habitats in the industrialised world. Since 1945, 95 per cent of its lowland meadows, 60 per cent of its lowland heaths, half its ancient lowland woodlands, lowland bogs and wetlands, a third of its upland heaths and a quarter of all its hedgerows (amounting to 140,000 miles) have been destroyed. Across the world, the drainage of wetlands to provide agricultural land has also led to a steady loss of natural ecosystems – in the last century the United States has lost over half its wetlands. The biggest loss has been in the Florida everglades after drainage started in 1883, partly to provide land for urban development (the population of the area has risen from 11,000 to four million) but mainly for sugar cane cultivation. Rivers were dredged and new canals dug and the natural drainage of the area was destroyed. The water table fell by over two feet, sea water flowed in from the ocean, the main lake was affected by eutrophication (excessive plant growth resulting in the death of animal life through lack of oxygen), peat dried out and the land level fell by one foot a year. Most of the wildlife, including 90 per cent of the two-and-a-half million wading birds, died out. In Brittany 40 per cent of the wetlands were drained in just twenty years after 1965.

Much of the destruction has been concentrated, just as it was in the past across Europe, the Near East and China, on the easiest way of obtaining new agricultural land – clearing the natural forests. In China, an area where the weight of numbers has been particularly marked for centuries, it is estimated that natural forests originally covered about three-quarters of the land. The slow extension of cultivation, together with cutting to provide firewood, steadily reduced this area until by the early nineteenth century large areas of the country had been completely deforested. By the early twentieth century forests were restricted to the inaccessible and mountainous areas and now cover not much more than 5 per cent of the country (about 50 million acres were deforested between 1950 and 1980). Much the same process occurred in India and in some areas the results were catastrophic. What is now the Thar desert in Rajasthan and Punjab, an area extending over about 100,000 square miles, was still impenetrable jungle 2,000 years ago. European settlement of the new lands of the Americas and Australasia also triggered off destruction of forests on a vast scale. For example, on Haiti (which means 'green island' in the local language) less than 10 per cent of the original forests remains. In 1790, when settlements were still largely confined to the eastern seaboard, forests covered about one million square miles of the United States. By 1850, as the frontier of settlement moved further westwards, about 40 per cent of these ancient forests had been destroyed and thirty years later three-quarters had been cleared. The rate of destruction slowed as the settlers moved out on to the treeless Great Plains but by 1930 only 13 per cent of America's original forests were still in existence and in the next sixty years half of these were destroyed too. Since the first settlements in Australia at the end of the eighteenth century about half of the original forests have been destroyed (including over three-quarters of the rain forest). When New Zealand officially became part of the British empire in 1840, over half the country was forested. By the 1870s, once the best agricultural land had been settled, sheep pastures were extended by clearing the forests, particularly on North Island. By the 1980s half of the country's virgin natural forests had been destroyed.

The extension of European control into the Third World and the subsequent cultivation of cash crops for export also had a drastic effect on the forests. In the Philippines, at the time of the Spanish conquest in the mid-sixteenth century, about 90 per cent of the country was covered in forest. The development of sugar plantations resulted in extensive deforestation in order to provide land and also fuel for sugar processing. By 1870 the island of Cebu was already severely deforested and by the end of the nineteenth century about a fifth of the forests had been destroyed. Sugar plantations had the same effect in Brazil, as the frontier of cultivation moved steadily inland to find new soil to replace exhausted areas and as the sugar industry's demand for fuel increased. The development of coffee plantations from the late eighteenth century wreaked further damage because these were normally planted on deforested slopes, leading to very high rates of soil erosion. In western India the area under cotton cultivation increased four-fold between 1870 and 1920 as the British introduced production for export. This increased output was obtained on new land, the result of large-scale forest clearance, and by the late nineteenth century the peasants in the area were already having to rely on cow dung as fuel because of the shortage of wood. In Algeria, after the French conquest and expropriation of land for European settlement, the local inhabitants had to move into new areas and clear the forests to provide enough land to grow food – between 1890 and 1940 about 1.2 million acres of forest were destroyed. The emergence of tobacco as a major cash crop in many Third World countries has also had a devastating impact on the forests because of the large amount of fuel required to cure the tobacco leaf. It is now estimated that 12 per cent of all timber cut down is used in the tobacco industry.

The scale of forest destruction has been growing since the Second World War as population in the Third World has risen sharply and the demand for more land has similarly increased. It is the tropical forests of South America, west Africa and south-east Asia that have borne the brunt of the destruction – overall since 1950 about half of the world's tropical forests have been destroyed and three-quarters of that clearance has been to provide land for agriculture. By the 1980s the best estimates suggest that about 28 million acres a year were being cleared. About two-thirds of the total loss was in Africa, in particular countries such as the Ivory Coast, Nigeria, Liberia, Guinea and Ghana, although by the late 1970s destruction in the Amazon area was growing rapidly. (These figures are probably an underestimate of the scale of destruction since they do not include land that has been severely degraded and which, whilst retaining some forest cover, will probably remain as scrub and never regenerate into true forest.) In the tropical forests of central and South America much of the clearance has been to provide pastureland where large landowners can raise cattle to provide beef for the United States (the US buys three-quarters of all central American beef exports). In Costa Rica cattle ranches took up only about 12 per cent of the land in 1950 but forty years later the area devoted to ranching had almost tripled and amounted to two-thirds of the available farmland.

Because of the fragile nature of the ecosystem, destruction of the tropical forests only offers a short-term solution to the problem of finding more land for agriculture. Most of the nutrients are held not in the soil but in the trees and plants and when these are burnt during clearance the nutrients are destroyed. The underlying soils are poor and provide few nutrients for crops or grass. Tropical soils are quickly degraded and erode easily once they are exposed to the wind and rain. The land is often cleared by small farmers, who are encouraged to settle in the forest regions to reduce the pressure for land reform in the well settled areas. They grow corn for a couple of seasons until the soil is exhausted and are then bought out by large landowners who convert the land to pasture for cattle. The soil is so poor that even grassland is only usable for about five years before it too has to be abandoned – nearly all the ranches established in the Amazon area before 1978 had been abandoned by the mid-1980s. It is a striking example of how quickly a highly productive natural ecosystem can be transformed into an unproductive, artificial one.

Large-scale clearance of forests, particularly in tropical areas, can also alter the climate of an area, leading in turn to further environmental degradation. When vegetation cover is removed, solar energy, instead of being partly absorbed by the trees, is reflected from the bare ground, increasing temperatures, drying the soil, creating dust in the atmosphere and helping to stop rain clouds forming. Estimates suggest that about 100,000 square miles of forest needs to be cleared before these effects are noticable on a significant scale. In the last century about four times this area of forest has been cleared in west Africa. The consequences are now becoming apparent. Since 1968 there have been twenty-three years of constant aridity across sub-Saharan Africa (with some of the effects extending as far east as Ethiopia). In 1989 Gambia experienced its twenty-first consecutive year of below-average rainfall and in general rainfall has been a third less than it was a hundred years ago. As a result, crop cultivation in west Africa has become more difficult, soil quality has deteriorated and deserts have increased in size.

In every part of the world modern agriculture has led to severe soil erosion in the wake of deforestation, ploughing up of grasslands and the cultivation of steep slopes. These actions have been exacerbated by the introduction of extensive monocropping and overgrazing. Depending on the geography of the affected area, soil erosion has led to duststorms, flooding, loss of fertility and even the abandonment of cultivation. It is now estimated that about 15 billion tons of topsoil are being lost every year just in the United States, Soviet Union, China and India, which account for only half the world's cropland. India alone is losing about 6 billion tons a year and over 300,000 square miles of the country is affected by soil erosion. In other parts of the world the problem is even worse. Haiti has no quality topsoil left, in the Philippines a third of the agricultural land suffers from serious soil erosion, and in Turkey about three-quarters of the land is affected, half of it seriously.

This is a problem that has been experienced by many societies in the past, often with devastating results. The Mediterranean landscape is the outcome of a process of soil erosion that has continued for thousands of years. Even in western Europe, with its richer soils and higher rainfall, problems have been encountered. The extension of the agricultural area as population rose between the eleventh and thirteenth centuries increased soil erosion in north-east France and parts of Germany. The soils of the lands brought into production in this period were poor and the general lack of manures (because of the difficulty of feeding animals over the winter) meant that the earth rapidly became exhausted and damaged and, since ploughed fields were often left bare, high erosion rates were common. Erosion was also apparent later as population increased and more land was cultivated – severe upland erosion was apparent in the Massif Central by the seventeenth century. Modern agricultural techniques and the intensification of production after 1945 have produced similar problems, made worse by the widespread elimination of natural inhibitors of erosion such as hedgerows and trees. In England, soil erosion rates from agricultural land are eight times higher than on grassland and seventeen times greater than in woodlands.

The experience of the United States provides a particularly clear illustration of the growing problem of soil erosion on agricultural land. The agricultural practices adopted by the early settlers – when the amount to land available seemed to be almost unlimited – paid scant attention of the need to preserve soil quality. Cultivation was extensive, since it was relatively easy to abandon exhausted land and bring new areas into production. Because of soil exhaustion, by the mid-nineteenth century, wheat yields in upstate New York were half those obtained a century earlier. The most extensive problems occurred in the southern states and were particularly associated with the cultivation of tobacco and cotton. Tobacco requires eleven times the nitrogen and thirty-six times the phosphorous of a food crop and therefore exhausts the nutrients in the soil very quickly. Farmers growing tobacco found that the second crop on newly cleared ground was the best. After another one or two seasons its cultivation had to be abandoned in favour of maize or wheat, but even these crops could not be grown for long in the severely depleted soil. Land was abandoned and the ruined soil was easily eroded away by wind and rain. Settlers moved steadily westwards from the Tidewater to the Piedmont region, clearing away the forests and exposing the soil to the greatly increased risk of erosion. By 1685 (within less than a century of the first settlement) Virginia was already suffering severe flooding brought about by deforestation and in the next century Georgia was badly affected by erosion, with gullies over 150 feet deep in places. By 1780 the Chesapeake area was experiencing severe soil erosion caused by exhaustion following tobacco cultivation and water run-off rates were twenty times higher than natural levels. Continued cotton cultivation had the same effect and soil exhaustion was one of the main forces behind the constant westward extension of the frontier as farmers sought out new land. By 1817 in North Carolina the amount of abandoned land was equal in area to that under cultivation. Across the southern states of the United States area after area was ruined in the space of a few years and then abandoned but the same destructive practices continued in the newly cultivated areas.

Until the latter half of the nineteenth century the Great Plains area was avoided by settlers because the ploughs available at the time were not capable of breaking up the tough, compacted grass. The development of the heavy steel plough, pulled by teams of between six and twelve oxen, enabled settlements to spread into this virgin agricultural territory that had previously supported large herds of bison and their Indian (and later white) hunters and also large herds of cattle. The Great Plains were ploughed up to grow wheat even though the area was extremely marginal for cereal cultivation – the climate was semi-arid with rainfall of only about twenty inches a year and the thin topsoil was only held together by the grass. Despite the experience of previous centuries, the US Bureau of Soils claimed in 1909 (in defiance of all ecological principles) that, 'the soil is the one indestructible, immutable asset that the nation possesses. It is the one resource that cannot be exhausted; that cannot be used up.' Even as they made that claim the early stages of one of the world's greatest ecological disasters were being enacted on the Great Plains. The last large Indian territory, Oklahoma, was opened for white settlement in 1889 and in the next forty years about 40 million acres of virgin land were ploughed up and cultivated with new forms of drought-resistant wheat. After 1919, when Russian wheat exports were no longer available on the world market, American production was further expanded – output rose to two-and-a-half times the 1914 level, and in all 5 million acres of new land were brought into production between 1925 and 1930. The same policy of expansion of settlement and over-exploitation of the land that had characterised American history had been applied again but in this particularly vulnerable area it produced an ecological disaster – the 'dust bowl'.

In the early 1930s one of the periodic droughts that regularly affect the Great Plains occurred. The loose, fragile and dry soil, which had lost its protective grass cover, was blown away by the high winds and created huge dust storms across the region. The destruction was centered on an area of west Kansas, south-east Colorado, north-west Oklahoma, north Texas, north-east New Mexico and parts of Nebraska and the Dakotas. The first major storm in May 1934 picked up about 350 million tons of top soil and deposited it over the eastern United States (an estimated 12 million tons fell on Chicago alone) and dust was even detected on ships 300 miles out into the Atlantic. Frequent storms followed – between January and May 1935 Amarillo in Texas experienced seven of them which caused zero visibility in the town. In March 1935, 5 million acres of wheat were destroyed by dust storms and by 1938, 10 million acres of land had lost the top five inches of soil and another 13½ million acres the top two-and-a-half inches. Both the farmers and the people of a wide area of the United States suffered from the effects. The number affected by respiratory diseases rose by 25 per cent and infant mortality increased by a third. By 1938, when 850 million tons of soil were still being lost every year, 3½ million people had abandoned farms in the area. Oklahoma lost almost a fifth of its population and in some counties almost half the people left. Better conservation practices improved the situation in the 1940s but another of the periodic droughts occurred between 1952–7 when wind erosion affected twice the area damaged in the 1930s. Drought and high winds in the 1970s had the same effect and another 10 million acres suffered from severe erosion.

The creation of the 'dust bowl' acted as a catalyst in forcing the American government to carry out a full survey of the extent of soil erosion in the country. The results, published in 1938, revealed an alarming situation. Even in a prime agricultural area such as Illinois a third of the land was found to be damaged by erosion. In total an area as large as the state of South Carolina had been eroded away, an area the size of Oklahoma and Alabama combined had been seriously damaged by erosion, and the amount of sand and gravel washed down by the rivers would have covered an area as big as Maryland. The situation deteriorated still further in the next forty years. By the 1970s a third of the topsoil of the United States had been lost and nearly 200 million acres of cropland had been ruined or made highly marginal for cultivation. Another 166,000 square miles were judged to be suffering from unacceptable rates of erosion and 700,000 acres of productive land were being lost every year. Topsoil was carried away by water and wind eight times faster than it was being formed – a loss of 5 billion tons a year, a rate six times higher than in the late nineteenth century. This widespread devastation was the result of agricultural practices such as extensive and continuing monocropping on marginal land, lack of understanding of the processes that create soil and reliance on chemical fertilisers that do not contribute to the maintenance of a healthy soil.

In the Soviet Union the settlement and cultivation of the rich 'black earth' soils soon gave rise to erosion rates well above natural levels. As early as 1578, huge soil erosion gullies were present around the major settlements and by the nineteenth century about 5 per cent of the land had been permanently damaged, with some soil erosion gullies growing at nearly 200 yards a year. The first Five Year Plan of 1929 proclaimed that, 'We must discover and conquer the country in which we live . . . Our steppe will truly become ours only when we come with columns of tractors and ploughs to break the thousand-year old virgin soil.' The results were predictable – dust storms increased steadily; in the Ukraine they occurred, on average, every other year after 1930 and some cities suffered as many as seventeen storms a year. The greatest catastrophe in Soviet agriculture, though, occurred in the 1950s with the 'virgin land' programme – the drive to open up the marginal grasslands of areas such as Khazakstan to cultivation – in total about 100 million acres were ploughed up between 1954 and 1960. Yields peaked in 1956 and then fell steadily: practices such as deep ploughing and leaving the soil bare during fallow periods led to severe erosion triggered by a major drought in 1963. Even before 1963 land was being lost to erosion at a rate of over 31/2 million acres a year but between 1962 and 1965 a total of over 40 million acres was badly damaged so that within a decade of the start of the programme almost half the land had been severely affected by erosion. Severe wind erosion caused the abandonment of over 1 million acres of farmland in the region every year from the mid-1960s.

In Australia, the first proclamation restricting tree-felling because of the link with unacceptably high rates of soil erosion was issued in 1803, fifteen years after the first settlement. Most of Australia consists of desert or highly marginal land (70 per cent is semi-arid or worse) and the soils are very easily eroded, particularly if ploughed or overgrazed. By 1878 extensive soil erosion was affecting parts of Victoria, by the 1920s Sydney was experiencing heavy dust storms and by 1942 half of the state of New South Wales was affected to some degree by soil erosion. By 1984 it was estimated that half of the country's agricultural land was affected by soil degradation. In China, because of the extensive deforestation, by the end of the nineteenth century soil erosion affected large areas of the country. The situation worsened considerably in the twentieth century. Between 1957 and 1977 about 25 million acres of agricultural land were lost to soil erosion and official estimates, which may well understate the extent of the problem, suggest that a seventh of China's vast land surface is now affected by soil erosion. The dust caused by spring ploughing in China can be detected in Hawaii.

Extensive soil erosion causes a variety of secondary effects over a wide area depending on local factors. Large amounts of top soil are carried away by rivers and the increased deposition causes river beds to rise (increasing the risk of flooding), silts up dams and extends low-lying deltas at river mouths. In the Himalayas about 40 per cent of the forests were destroyed in the thirty years after 1955 to provide fuel and increase the amount of agricultural land as the population of countries such as Nepal rose sharply. The rate of erosion in the deforested areas was twenty times higher than in the forested parts and the results were felt over the whole region. The beds of the great rivers that flow out from the Himalayas rose at over six inches a year, causing extensive flooding and a rapid expansion of the already large deltas. In Bangladesh particularly, this has created large areas of very vulnerable land where large numbers of poor people settle but where they are subject to regular flooding, loss of life and loss of livelihood. Almost an eighth of the world's population now lives in the area affected by the flooding caused by deforestation and soil erosion in the Himalayan region.

Another contributory factor in increasing rates of deforestation and soil erosion has been overgrazing by the pastoral groups who live in the marginal areas of Africa, the Near East and central Asia in particular. They need to travel with their animal herds over considerable distances in a carefully integrated cycle of activities during the year in order to maintain their way of life and avoid overstressing the environment. In the nineteenth century the Sahel (now one of the areas most severely affected by environmental degradation) was well wooded (apart from around the main settlements): the land was exploited by farmers, using shifting cultivation with long fallow periods to allow the soil to recover, and by pastoralists, who had a well-established way of life which did not overtax the local environment. In the twentieth century these pastoral groups (about 30–40 million people across the world) have come under pressure from two sources – the expansion of the area under cultivation and the need to support increased numbers. The rapid increase in population in the Third World, combined with the extension of the area under cash crops for export, has forced farmers into ever more marginal areas in order to grow food. They have encroached on lands traditionally used by pastoral groups and forced them to spread onto even more marginal territory or to increase the intensity with which they exploit their remaining land. Additional pressure has been generated by a rise in the number of pastoralists and by an increase in the number of animals they have tried to sustain – in the Sahel area of west Africa for example the number of animals has doubled since 1940; in Rajasthan the area available for grazing fell by 15 per cent in the 1950s while the number of animals rose by 53 per cent. In some places aid programmes designed supposedly to help the pastoralists have made the situation worse. Attempts to restrict their movements by building deep boreholes to provide water and transform the pastoralists into sedentary herders has only concentrated the destructive effects of grazing, and the introduction of large herds of one species (mainly cattle for export) in place of the traditional small mixed herds has also put stress on fragile ecosystems.

The most extreme form of soil loss is desertification – the permanent loss of land to deserts. The twentieth century has seen the steady advance of deserts into once productive areas. Desertification now affects the south western parts of the United States, northern Mexico, north Africa, the Sahel, large parts of southern Africa (particularly South Africa where because of apartheid three-quarters of the population live on only 14 per cent of the land, most of it of very poor quality) and parts of Australia. Between 1925 and 1975 the Sahara desert grew by about 250,000 square miles along its southern edge – in parts of the Sudan the desert boundary moved south by about 120 miles between 1958 and 1975 – and it was also moving further north and encroaching on about 250,000 acres a year. In Chile the Atacama desert is advancing by almost two miles a year. The livelihood of 650 million people who now live in the arid and semi-arid areas of the world is threatened by this encroachment of deserts.

The intensification of food production has led to a vast increase in the amount of irrigated land in the world. In 1800 about 20 million acres were irrigated, whereas a century later the figure was about 100 million acres, by 1950 it was almost 300 million and by 1980 as much as 500 million acres. In total about 15 per cent of the world's arable land is irrigated, with the highest proportion in Asia. Irrigation does allow crops to be grown where otherwise it would not be possible and it does give very high yields (in south Asia only a third of the rice-growing area is irrigated yet it provides 60 per cent of the total crop) but there are significant drawbacks. It uses large quantities of what is a scarce resource – water. Irrigation now accounts for almost three-quarters of the world's water use and most of it is used very inefficiently. In India and China almost two-thirds of the water is lost through evaporation and seepage out of irrigation canals and in the United States half the water used is lost. In some places such as Saudi Arabia, where groundwater is already in short supply, irrigation depends on the use of aquifers (underground areas of rock that naturally store large volumes of water) which are being drawn down faster than they can be replenished. Another problem is securing a supply unpolluted by industrial wastes. In Japan, by the early 1970s, 3 per cent of the total agricultural land had been contaminated through the use of irrigation water containing large quantities of toxic heavy metals from industrial discharges. The process of irrigation itself may badly degrade the land through waterlogging and salinisation, as the first societies in Sumer found out to their cost over four thousand years ago. In the first stages yields are reduced and eventually cultivation may become impossible. These harmful effects can occur very quickly in unsuitable conditions – within a decade 12 per cent of the irrigated land in the Jordan valley was affected. Such effects are now found in half of all irrigated land in Syria and Iraq, nearly 80 per cent in the Punjab and a quarter of the irrigated land in the United States. Between 1960 and the late 1980s the Soviet Union lost more previously productive land to waterlogging and salinisation than the cultivated area of Ireland and Belgium combined. Overall, more than seventy million acres of irrigated land has been ruined and the adversely affected area is increasing by about three-and-a-half million acres a year. Across the world irrigated land is now being abandoned as fast as new schemes are introduced.

By far the most dramatic consequences of irrigation have occurred in the Aral Sea in the Soviet Union. This large inland sea in the southern republic of Kazakhstan was unusual: although two rivers flowed into it, none flowed out and the lake was maintained in size by high evaporation rates. Small-scale irrigation schemes in adjacent areas began in the 1960s and as water was diverted from the rivers flowing into the Aral Sea its area was reduced by 10 per cent. An ambitious plan, devised in the early 1970s to use these rivers to irrigate over eighteen million acres to grow cotton and rice in highly unsuitable climates and soils, entailed a major diversion of water away from the Aral Sea. Predictably the Aral Sea rapidly shrank in size – by the late 1980s two-thirds of the sea had dried up, exposing the seabed across an area of over 12,000 square miles (at present rates the Aral Sea will cease to exist by the end of the century). As the lake shrank, major climatic changes across the region became apparent as temperatures rose and humidity and rainfall decreased. The changes had a devastating impact on local agriculture, industry and the health of the population. Thirty-four out of the thirty-eight species of fish died out, the fishing industry collapsed and large numbers of villages were abandoned. The salinity of the Aral Sea tripled, the water table in the area fell rapidly, the sewage system collapsed (typhoid rates rose twenty-nine-fold) and 90 per cent of the children were diagnosed as being permanently ill. In 1990 an outbreak of plague led to the area being quarantined. The Aral Sea and the surrounding area is now the scene of one of the greatest of all ecological catastrophes.

Modern agriculture, like its predecessors, has produced a mixture of achievements, problems and environmental disasters. More people than ever before have been fed but food production is distributed in a very unequal way. Most of the population of the industrialised world has a rich and varied diet whereas most people in the much more populous Third World have one that is inadequate or seriously deficient. Large amounts of the world's grain output go to feed animals in the industrialised world. The need to bring more land into food production has involved damaging vulnerable new ecosystems or putting more pressure on those already modified. Deforestation, soil erosion, desertification and salinisation have all increased substantially. Such problems have been exacerbated by the highly unequal distribution of land, particularly in the Third World, which condemns many people to trying to scrape a living from a small amount of poor land or reduced to the state of landless labourers. The problem that has affected all agricultural societies throughout history – ensuring an adequate supply of food for all – has not been solved on a global scale. Another related problem has become worse. Agriculture has always meant disrupting natural ecosystems, but the growing weight of numbers has in many areas turned it into a positively destructive force, threatening ever more marginal and delicate ecosystems with increasingly damaging environmental effects.

13
THE SECOND GREAT TRANSITION

The sources of energy available to human societies have played a major part in determining the activities that they can undertake and the way in which they are organised. For all but the last two hundred years the sources of energy were few and the total amount of energy they could generate was small. The second great transition in human history, comparable in its importance with the adoption of agriculture and the rise of settled societies, involved the exploitation of the earth's vast (but limited) stocks of fossil fuels, a move that made possible an era of abundant energy for part of the world's population. All the forms of energy used until this transition were renewable, although trees, one of the most important sources, (which can be coppiced or replanted or allowed to regenerate naturally) were normally treated as non-renewable. The last two hundred years have, however, been characterised by a massive and continuing increase in energy consumption from non-renewable resources.

The basic human energy requirements fall into two categories. The first is for sources of lighting and heating (needed for cooking and in most climates to keep warm). The second is for power to carry out a range of tasks – in agriculture, construction, industry and also to provide mobility. Obtaining energy always involves a cost: this may be quite low in the case of gathering wood or very high as with the exploitation of offshore oil, which requires a vast energy input to build rigs and drilling platforms, construct pipelines and ferry workers to and from the site before any oil is obtained. For most of human history the use of energy has been constrained by problems of mobility – wood and coal are bulky to move in any quantity (except by water) and water (and to some extent wind) power can only be provided at certain sites. It was not until the development of electricity in the late nineteenth century that a flexible, easily distributed form of energy, capable of providing heating, lighting and power was available.

Until the development of gas and electric light in the nineteenth century all human societies had only a few options open to them to provide lighting and many activities were restricted to the hours of daylight. Lighting came from essentially natural sources – fires, vegetable oil lamps, rushlights and candles made from animal fat (especially whale oil). For heating and cooking the main energy sources available were wood, plant residues such as straw, and dried animal dung. Wood was overwhelmingly the most important fuel and growing demand for it led to the steady clearing of the forests in every part of the world, with only a limited amount of coppicing and replanting taking place in order to maintain supplies. But until about five hundred years ago supplies of wood seem to have been plentiful and there is little evidence of anything more than local shortages. Animal dung was usually a fuel of the last resort since, if it was used, the level of manuring on the land fell and crop yields therefore dropped.

Until the great transition in energy about two hundred years ago all societies suffered from a severe shortage of power that limited the activities which they could undertake. The main source was people. For thousands of years it was vast amounts of human toil and effort, with its costs in terms of early death, injury and suffering, that was the foundation of every society. Human power output is lower than that of the commonly used animals but humans ate less food and therefore were a more economic source of energy. They provided the main energy input into farming in every society until the mechanisation of agriculture, carrying out a multitude of tasks, such as clearing land, sowing, weeding, digging and constructing terraces and irrigation channels, with little assistance from animal power and with no more than primitive tools. As late as 1806 one French agricultural writer could still advocate abandoning the plough and returning to digging fields by hand which, he argued, although slower, was cheaper and more thorough. Humans also provided power for tasks such as grinding corn at mills and in industry – the Great Crane in the market place at Bruges, regarded as the technological marvel of the fifteenth century, was powered by a human treadmill. The highest lock on the Grand Canal in China was worked by teams of several hundred men using capstans and ropes. In the nineteenth century prisons in Britain operated a treadmill which could be hired by local industrialists. Human power was also the main form of energy in the house until the invention of a range of labour-saving household appliances, mainly in the twentieth century. As late as the first decade of this century two-and-a-half million people (84 per cent of them women) were employed as domestic servants in Britain and they constituted the largest single occupational category.

Although much labour throughout history has been provided co-operatively, much has only been made available under compulsion. One of the major problems societies faced was mobilising enough labour to undertake the projects the ruling elite wished to see completed. There were two main solutions. One was to impose forced labour on the majority of their own population, the other was to use slaves (often from prisoners of war or conquered peoples) to undertake the work. Most of the great monuments of the ancient world, from the temple mounds and palaces of Mesopotamia to the pyramids of Egypt, the Great Wall of China and the large ceremonial sites of the Americas such as Teotihuacan and the Mayan cities in the jungle, were built using their own population as forced labour. During the Fourth Dynasty in Egypt (2575–2465 BC) the building of tombs in the provinces and simple memorials for the bulk of the population, which had been common in earlier periods, virtually ceased. Instead efforts were concentrated on constructing huge pyramids for kings, officials and their important kinsmen. The vast amounts of labour involved were controlled centrally by the state authorities and there is no evidence that this labour was willingly given by the bulk of the population. Indeed within a few decades Egyptian society began to break down under the strain of this forced mobilization. In China the building of the Great Wall involved about 1 million workers, of whom half died during the work. The construction of the Grand Canal, to bring food to the capital Peking and the armies in the north, used about five-and-a-half million workers guarded by 50,000 police and again about half the workers died on the project.

Some form of forced labour was common throughout European history too. In the medieval period agricultural workers were required to work a certain number of days a year on their landlord's estate in return for the land they cultivated themselves. Only in this way could the landlord obtain a sufficient amount of labour to cultivate his land – serfdom developed later (and lasted longer) in eastern Europe and Russia and performed the same essential function. As late as the eighteenth century the corvée (or forced labour from local communities) to build and maintain roads still functioned in France. The totalitarian states of the twentieth century, from the Soviet Union's gulags to China and Nazi Germany, resorted to forced labour for many of their major construction projects. In addition to forced labour from their own citizens many societies relied upon slaves to provide an unpaid energy source that only required feeding. Slavery was common in the first settled societies and remained so across the world until the last century. The great states of the ancient world – the near eastern empires, the city states of Greece and also Rome – depended on slaves for much of the domestic work, agricultural labour and other jobs such as unloading ships, portering and working machinery. (About a fifth of the population of Rome in the first centuries AD consisted of slaves.) The rise of Europe expanded the use of slave labour, principally on overseas plantations to provide luxury foods for the home market (although they were also used in industry and as domestic servants).

Human power, harnessed in a number of different ways, has also provided transport. On land porters provided one of the commonest methods of carrying loads for thousands of years, and still do in many parts of the Third World. In the Inca empire the main method of communication, in the absence of domesticated animals, was a highly efficient network involving teams of runners to convey messages along the roads built by the state. At sea many ships relied on human rather than wind power, or in some cases a combination of the two. The great Greek fighting ship, the trireme, was human powered and in the Mediterranean galleys remained important as warships until the battle of Lepanto in 1576, when the Spanish and imperial forces defeated the Ottoman Turks. Galleys, both commercial and military, were powered by slave or penal labour in many societies from the Roman empire to nineteenth-century France. In Brazil, a shortage of animal power and a surplus of cheap slave labour led to slaves rather than oxen or horses being used to draw carts. In nearly every society people have transported other people and this form of transport has often been a powerful status symbol. The methods employed have included seats and baskets on the back of a porter (still found in many parts of the world), palanquins carried by four or six people, which were common in the east from the earliest near eastern empires until the nineteenth century, the sedan chair carried by two people, which was widely used in the cities of seventeenth and eighteenth century Europe, and the rickshaw and its modern variant still found in many eastern cities – the bicycle rickshaw.

Apart from people, the other readily available power source for most societies was animals. Even in the industrialised world the use of animals remained vital until well into the twentieth century. The main constraint on using animal power is the problem of growing enough feed. A horse needs about four or five acres of land to obtain sufficient food, although an ox, the other main source of animal power, can be fed from a smaller area. Because of low agricultural productivity most societies have required nearly all the available land to feed the human population and the number of animals that they could support was, therefore, normally extremely limited (which increased the importance of human power). Animals were probably first used to carry loads. Some of the earliest domesticated animals such as asses and onagers remained important in this role for thousands of years. Camels also proved highly effective pack animals, capable of carrying large loads in cold deserts where they performed a crucial role along the major trading routes between the Near East and China. Dromedaries were used in the hot deserts, particularly in the Sahara after the seventh century AD with the development of extensive trading routes between north and west Africa. Mules were also important, particularly in the Mediterranean area (Spain had twice as many mules as horses in the nineteenth century) and in Latin America after the Spanish conquest, because of the lack of native draught and pack animals. There were probably about two million mules in South America in the eighteenth century (twice as many as in Spain), including half a million in Peru alone. Virtually all these pack animals have been replaced in the industrialised countries but they remain a vitally important method of transporting loads in the Third World.

Wheeled vehicles were first used in Mesopotamia about 3500 BC (and slightly later in the Indus valley and Egypt). They were drawn by oxen or onagers. In Europe and the Near East the ox was the primary draught animal until the eighteenth century, when there were still about 24 million oxen, compared with 14 million horses, engaged in agricultural work in Europe; oxen are still used for ploughing in many parts of Europe. In India in the early twentieth century there were five-and-a-half million ox-carts and these remain an important form of transportation in the Third World. The horse was probably domesticated about 3000 BC, but for about four thousand years its use was limited mainly to carrying individual riders or packs because of the problems involved in harnessing it to pull loads. Until about 800 AD, a yoke harness designed for oxen was used but this tended to throttle the horse as it pulled and therefore severely restricted its ability as a draught animal. The invention and spread of the modern harness in Europe transformed the role of the horse and enabled its full potential (to pull loads faster and for longer periods than oxen) to be applied to agricultural work. In northern and western Europe horses needed to be shod in order to counter the effects of damp and the first clear evidence of the use of horseshoes is not found until about 900 AD. However, even after the introduction of the new harness and the horseshoe, it was a long time before horses replaced oxen: they cost far more to maintain, primarily because they needed more feed (in total the extra costs were about three to seven times greater depending on their role) and they had little value when they were too old to work, unlike oxen which were sold for meat. In western Europe the horse was not commonly found as a plough animal until about 1100 and in England the ox remained the dominant draught animal for many centuries after this. Only slowly did the number of horses engaged in agricultural work in Europe increase. By the nineteenth century they were the main power source for all agricultural work and remained so until the middle of the twentieth century when they were displaced by tractors. The agricultural horse population probably reached its peak in England about 1920 while France had as many agricultural horses in the mid-1930s as in the late nineteenth century. As late as 1939 Germany still had over three million horses on its farms.

Another area where animals were important was in warfare. Some of the earliest wheeled vehicles were chariots (drawn by onagers) and the horse was later adopted for this role. The development of cavalry and mounted warfare depended on the invention of the stirrup (probably in about the seventh century AD). Horses then formed a central part of all armies, both as cavalry and draught animals, until well into the twentieth century. Here, too, numbers were limited by the scarcity of feed. The specialised breeding of warhorses can be identified in England as early as 1130 but by the fourteenth century armies could still not support more than about 3–5,000 horses. The hey-day of the cavalry was in the eighteenth and nineteenth centuries (when more fodder was available) but they were to prove ineffectual in the increasingly technological warfare of the twentieth century. Nevertheless armies continued to rely on horses as the main means of transporting supplies. During the First World War, for example, the British army used 1,200,000 horses, and in the Second World War the German army had mechanised Panzer divisions but it also required the logistic support of 2,700,000 horses (twice as many as it used between 1914 and 1918).

In every part of the world, for thousands of years, animals were used to provide the means to operate machinery, in particular, mills for grinding grain. In the late eighteenth century the development of new industrial technologies, particularly in Britain, is generally heralded as the start of the 'industrial revolution'. What is perhaps surprising is that, at least in its early stages, it led to the increased use of animal and, in particular, horse power – hence the modern use of the term to measure power generation. Most of the early machines used in industry were small-scale and needed only a low power input – about two or three horse power for a fulling mill and about one horse power for every one hundred spindles in the earliest textile machines. Joseph Arkwright, whose name is particularly associated with the development of new textile machines, used nine horses at his first factory in Nottingham to power 1,000 spindles. Horses were also used extensively in mine drainage and the brewing industry. They were cheap to buy and flexible (although they required stabling) and manufacturers continued to use them for low power outputs up to around ten horse power. After about 1800 horses were gradually replaced by steam power, although the rate of change was variable, and they remained important in the provincial brewing industry in particular for decades.

As a means of transport the horse was vital until displaced by widespread use of the internal combustion engine. Most individual travel depended on horses and they provided the power for stage coaches and also for barges on the canals that were built on an increasing scale in the eighteenth and early nineteenth centuries. The development of railways in the nineteenth century did not bring about the demise of horse-drawn travel (apart from the stage coach). By generating more traffic, railways actually increased the demand for horses and their numbers reached a peak in both Europe and North America at the end of the nineteenth century. This trend can be seen very clearly in Britain, which had constructed one of the densest railway networks in the world. In 1810 there were about 15,000 privately owned carriages. The number increased to 40,000 by 1840 and to about 120,000 in 1870. (The number of carriages per head of the population tripled between 1840 and 1900). The number of horses kept in towns for both private and business traffic rose from about 350,000 in 1830 to 1,200,000 in 1900. Public transport in towns remained primarily horse drawn until the end of the nineteenth century. In 1902 London had 3,700 horse drawn omnibuses (each one drawn by two horses and needing about ten horses a day to maintain the service), 7,500 hansom cabs and 3,900 hackney coaches. Railway companies used horse-drawn vehicles to distribute goods from their depots – in London the railway companies owned 6,000 horses and coal merchants were using another 8,000. As late as 1913, 88 per cent of London's goods traffic was still horse drawn.

At the start of the twentieth century Britain had a horse population of about three-and-a-half million (about twenty-five times the current level), France had roughly the same number and the United States had somewhere between 20–30 million (over three million of these were in cities, including nearly 200,000 in New York alone). In Britain the number of horses reached a peak in the late nineteenth century when it was probably near the maximum that could be supported. In 1900 Britain's horses were consuming about four million tons of oats and hay every year (taking up the production from about fifteen million acres of land) – without cheap imports of grain Britain could not have supported such large numbers and provided enough food for the human population. Even so the logistical problems involved in moving such a large amount of grain around the country and within towns was enormous. The United States came up against the same constraints. In 1900 horse feed took up about ninety million acres of cropland (a quarter of the total) and was near the maximum that the agricultural system could support. With the introduction of the internal combustion engine the number of horses fell rapidly. In Britain for instance horse-drawn buses had virtually disappeared before the First World War and after the early 1920s, with the exception of the agricultural sector, the number of horses fell by a half in a decade.

Until the last two thousand years humans and animals were the only sources of power for machinery. The first significant use of water power to drive machinery occurred about 100 BC in Egypt with the development of an automatic irrigation wheel and a grain mill. These early mills were powered by horizontal wheels but, once the necessary cams and gears had been invented, vertical wheels, which gave much more power, were universally adopted. The spread of water power, which for many centuries was restricted almost entirely to grinding grain, was slow, at a time when human labour (much of it from slaves) was plentiful. But over a period of several centuries mills were gradually built across western Europe. The first firm evidence of the scale of construction comes from the Domesday Book, compiled in England in 1086. It records the existence of 5,624 water mills in the country serving about 3,000 settlements. In some areas they were very concentrated – the river Wylye in Wiltshire had thirty mills within ten miles. The same pattern of concentrated development was also found in France. In the early fourteenth century there were sixty-eight mills in less than a mile of the Seine near Paris and on the Grand Pont in the centre of the city there were thirteen mills under the arches of the bridge, where the river flowed faster. Elsewhere there was a steady upward trend in the number of mills, as seen along the river Robec near Rouen: in the tenth century it had just two mills but by the thirteenth this had risen to twelve.

Water power saved labour and time but its use posed a number of problems. Water flow in the rivers was very variable during the year and in the winter rivers froze in some places so that for considerable periods the mills were not operational. Other problems arose from competition between mills for the available water. At Toulouse, on the Garonne, floating mills under the bridges were demolished at the end of the twelfth century and a series of dams built to regulate the water flow to the mills. But this caused endless legal disputes about the heights of the various dams – if those downstream were built higher so as to increase their water flow, they diminished it for those further upstream. Despite all these difficulties widespread use of water mills for an increasing number of purposes produced an 'industrial revolution' from the eleventh century onwards. (Although the term 'Industrial Revolution' is normally reserved for the eighteenth century and later, viewed in the global context of ten thousand years of settled societies, there is really a single, protracted process of growing industrialisation, with occasional bursts of more intensive development, as in twelfth century Europe and a slightly earlier period in China.) The first use of water power for fulling cloth probably dates to 1086 in Normandy, for tanning leather to 1138 in Paris and for making paper to 1238 at Valencia. Other uses involved driving iron forges, sawing wood, operating bellows and grindstones and making mash for beer. In the course of the thirteenth century the widespread adoption of water power for fulling cloth transformed the woollen industry, greatly increased production and, in England, led to a major relocation of the industry to the north-west of the country where plentiful water power was available. By the sixteenth century water power was being used to polish precious stones and to mill coins.

Most of the early water mills were built on rivers, but Europe also made some use of tidal mills, although these remained limited in their scope and application, because they could only work for part of the day. The first tidal mill was built at the head of the Adriatic near Venice in 1044, and in the following centuries their use spread across Europe, especially in areas where rivers were not powerful enough to drive mills. They continued to be built until well into the nineteenth century – in the counties of Devon and Cornwall there were three tidal mills in the thirteenth century, eleven in the seventeenth and twenty-five in the nineteenth. Because of their limited availability most tidal mills were used to grind grain rather than for industrial purposes. Similar advances in the use of water power can be traced in China. In the thirteenth century China was the most industrialised country in the world and had developed an impressive technology to utilise water power, which included highly sophisticated hemp spinning machines which were in advance of anything produced in Europe before the eighteenth century.

Despite its limitations, water provided the chief source of power for machines throughout the world for centuries. The so-called 'industrial revolution' that developed in Britain in the late eighteenth century and then spread to Europe and North America did not immediately replace water with steam power; indeed, initially, it extended the use of water power. Many of the first factories and mills were water powered and many industries, particularly the textile industries of Yorkshire and Lancashire, were located along the banks of fast-flowing rivers. In the early nineteenth century water power was still used to pump water from the Thames to provide the major part of London's water supply. In 1900 Nuremburg still had 180 operational water mills. In the United States many industrial processes depended on water power until the 1880s and steam power was normally only used when it was essential to locate a factory away from streams and rivers. The scale of industrialisation that could be supported by water power can be judged from the situation in the north-east of the United States. The great textile centres of Lowell, Lawrence and Manchester along the Merrimack river in New Hampshire and Massachusetts had over 900 mills and factories powered by the river. The giant Mastodon Mill on the Mohawk river took water in 102 inch diameter pipes to turbines that generated 1,200 horse power and drove two miles of shafting, turning ten miles of belts, 70,000 spindles and 1,500 looms, which produced 60,000 yards of cotton a day. In Japan, too, the first textile mills were water powered and steam did not become at all important until the 1890s.

The main supplement to water power in both Europe and China was provided by the wind. Windmills, which were first developed in Tibet and China as prayer wheels, spread only very slowly and were not common in China as a source of industrial power until the late thirteenth century and they were not used for pumping water for another three hundred years. Their invention and development in Europe was a completely separate phenomenon; the European version involved a significant improvement over the eastern type of windmill – its ability to turn the sails into the wind obviously made for much greater efficiency. The first windmills in northern Europe were built in England in the twelfth century but, within a hundred years, the idea had spread across most of the continent (there were 120 around Ypres in the thirteenth century), they reached Poland and Russia in the fourteenth century and were adopted slightly later in the Mediterranean region. A vital source of power in areas where the rivers were too sluggish, their power output was as unreliable as water-powered mills, depending as they did on the vagaries of the wind, but at least they had the advantage of not freezing up in winter. They were first used for grinding grain but from the fifteenth century were used to pump water and, in the Netherlands, played a crucial role in draining land to extend the cultivated area. By the sixteenth century the Netherlands had over 8,000 windmills used to power saws, lift equipment from mines and in fulling cloth, dressing leather, making gunpowder, rolling copper plates and throwing silk.

In a great variety of different combinations humans, animals, water and wind provided the bulk of the world's power until well into the nineteenth century. The world's main source of fuel throughout this period was wood and apart from animal dung there was no real substitute. Wood had many advantages – it was easy to collect, readily available, burned well when dried and, in many cases, it was free. The problem was that wood was in great demand. Although some requirements could be met by methods short of felling whole forests (such as coppicing), most could not and little attention seems to have been paid to treating wood as a renewable source while supplies seemed virtually inexhaustible. Forests were destroyed not just to provide more land for agriculture but also for wood for fuel and timber. It was used in housebuilding and construction work of all kinds (including fortifications and bridges), in industry to make casks, vats and machinery, in shipbuilding, and, in the form of charcoal, as the primary fuel for industries such as iron smelting, brewing, glass making and brick production. A moderate sized house in medieval England required a dozen oaks to be cut down and in the fourteenth century work on Windsor Castle resulted in the felling of over 4,000 oaks in ten years.

Once industrial uses became important there was a big step up in demand for wood and charcoal. Charcoal production involved large amounts of labour and large quantities of wood. In 1475 the iron industry in the Oberpfalz district of the Rhineland created employment for 750 miners, 3,000 people to transport the wood and iron, and over 5,000 woodcutters and charcoal burners to produce about 10,000 tons of charcoal a year. In the United States in the nineteenth century an average blast furnace accounted for the destruction of about 250 acres of woodland every year and the Hopewell furnace in Pennsylvania was using up as much as 750 acres a year. The production of potash was just as destructive. One works near Archangel in Russia exported 1,000 tons every year and, for each ton produced, 1,000 tons of wood were consumed. By 1662 Russian potash production was using up a total of three million tons of wood a year. The process of evaporating water to produce salt also used prodigious quantities of fuel. In the Kama region of Russia, where there were over 1,200 salt works in the early eighteenth century, all the local forests had been felled and wood had to be transported from over 200 miles away to fuel the boilers.

Over the centuries this relentless destruction of the forests, with very little, if any, replanting, slowly exhausted the resources of both China and western Europe. The early industrialisation of China had produced acute wood and charcoal shortages in the north of the country by the thirteenth century. The first signs of a shortage of timber in western Europe can be identified in the shipbuilding industry in the fifteenth century. Venice, one of the great medieval maritime powers, exhausted local timber supplies and came to rely on imports from its colonies along the Dalmatian coast, while imposing draconian laws in an unsuccessful attempt to protect the last of its domestic oak forests on the Italian mainland. By 1590 the Venetians had to import completed hulls for their ships and could do no more than fit them out in the Arsenal. In rival Genoa, the price of oak for shipbuilding rose eleven-fold in the hundred years after 1460 (far faster than the rate of inflation). Portugal, the first European nation to explore the coast of Africa and the Indian Ocean, suffered from a timber shortage from the start of the voyages of exploration. By the sixteenth century nearly all Portuguese ships had to be built in the colonies, either in Goa, using the teak forests of the Indian west coast, or in Bahia, using Brazilian hardwoods. Spain faced similarly acute shortages of wood. When Philip II in the 1580s built the Armada to sail against Holland and England, he had to buy trees from Poland. In England the problem was first noticed during the wars against the French in the 1620s. By the middle of the century the shortage of home-grown timber was becoming acute, particularly for certain specialised requirements such as masts – a first rate, 120 gun ship needed a mainmast 120 feet long and over forty inches in diameter. Previously the navy had been able to rely on suitable trees from the oak forests of England, especially those of Sussex, whose timber was particularly prized. By the late seventeenth and early eighteenth centuries, the supply crisis was so acute that the Admiralty belatedly produced some officially-sponsored replanting schemes, even though these forests could not produce any new supplies for over a century.

In order to obtain the necessary timber England had to start importing supplies. At first the main sources were Scandinavia and Russia. The first recorded imports from Norway were in 1230 but it was not until the sixteenth and seventeenth centuries that large-scale importing of firs and oaks from the Baltic ports got underway. By the seventeenth century the areas around the chief ports of Norway, Sweden, Russia and Denmark had already been stripped of timber and supplies had to be brought down by river from further afield. In 1756 the British bought the right to export 600,000 trees a year from Russia in order to supply the Royal Navy. Agents acting for the British would buy up estates, put a stop to farming and set the serfs to work felling trees until there were none left and the estate would then be sold. Another important source of British naval timber were the new colonies in North America. The first pine masts were felled in New England in 1652 and in the late seventeenth century the economy of New Hampshire was almost totally dependent on the timber trade. In 1696 for the first time warships for the Royal Navy were built in North America because of the shortage of European timber and during the eighteenth century about a third of Britain's warships came from this source. By 1700 most of the timber within twenty miles of the main rivers of New Hampshire had been felled and within another fifty years most of the eastern sides of the mountains had been cleared of timber. By 1772 the newer colony of Maine had overtaken New Hampshire as the main source of supply. But by 1775 even North America had been stripped of the very tall pines needed for mainmasts and the Royal Navy had to resort to inferior composite masts made in Riga. During the American war of independence the Royal Navy suffered from an acute shortage of timber when it was cut off from its main sources of supply and throughout the Napoleonic wars it again had to rely almost entirely upon imported supplies, mainly from Canada. The ships of the Royal Navy that enforced the 'Pax Britannica' of the nineteenth century were not built from British oaks. Until the replacement of wooden ships by ironclads in the period after the mid-1860s, the Royal Navy had to import what it regarded as inferior timber from all over the world to construct its warships.

A shortage of timber for naval construction was only one symptom of a major problem affecting the whole of Europe. There was a serious and widespread shortage of wood, which meant that Europe faced an energy crisis. Much of its early industry depended on wood and charcoal. Local sources were becoming exhausted and the poor state of inland transport made it impractical to move supplies very far. The effects of the shortage were manifested across the continent in different ways. In

1560 iron foundries in Slovakia, for example, were forced to cut back production. In 1595 the bakers of Montpellier in the south of France had to cut down bushes to heat their ovens as there were no trees left around the town. In 1715 in Burgundy it was reported that wood was so scarce and the price so high that the poor had to make do without fires. A decade later at Wieliczka in Poland the salt evaporation works had to close because all the local wood was exhausted.

The crisis, and its consequences, can be traced in detail in Britain, which was one of the first countries to experience a severe energy shortage and therefore one of the first to make the transition to new forms of energy. Contemporaries were well aware of the problems. As one commentator, Edmund Howes, wrote in the early seventeenth century:

'within man's memory, it was held impossible to have any want of wood in England. But contrary to former imaginations such hath been the great expence of timber for navigation, with infinite increase of building of houses, with the great expence of wood to make household furniture, caskes, and other vessels not to be numbered, and of carts, wagons and coaches, besides the extreme waste of wood in making iron, burning of brick and tile, that at this present, through the great consuming of wood as aforesaid, and the neglect of planting of woods, there is so great a scarcity of wood through the whole kingdom.'

The scale of the problem first became apparent in the second half of the sixteenth century. Because of a shortage of domestic fuel about two-thirds of England's salt had to be imported from France, which could rely on the sun for the evaporation process. Government measures, which included a prohibition on cutting large trees and an enquiry in 1548–1549 into the large-scale cutting of timber by the iron industry in the Weald of Kent and Sussex, had no effect. The destruction of the forests reached unprecedented levels at this time – a survey in 1560 showed Duffield forest had 59,000 large and 33,000 small oaks yet within less than thirty years the numbers had fallen to about 3,000 of each type. One consequence of the timber shortage was a steep rise in charcoal prices. They increased by 65 per cent between 1560 and 1630 and by another 150 per cent in the next forty years. By the early seventeenth century the shortage of charcoal meant that armaments production had to be cut back and in 1632 England had to import iron guns from Sweden even though they were thought to be of inferior quality. The shortages got worse in the late seventeenth and early eighteenth centuries – by 1717 a newly constructed iron furnace in Wales could not begin production for four years until it had accumulated stocks of charcoal and even then it only had enough fuel to operate for thirty-six weeks before it was forced to close. In most areas of the country blast furnaces were only able to operate in short bursts of activity every few years.

The response to this increasingly severe energy shortage was a change to what was widely regarded as an inferior fuel – coal. As wood prices rose, first the poor, and later even the rich, were forced to use coal. As Stow's Annals for 1631 commented:

> 'there is so great a scarcity of wood throughout the whole kingdom . . . the inhabitants in general are constrained to make their fires of sea-coal or pit coal, even in the chambers of honorable personages.'

In 1550 English coal production was about 210,000 tons but by 1630 it had risen to 1.5 million tons. Coal from Newcastle had been brought to London by sea for centuries but the trade increased from 35,000 tons in 1550 to 560,000 tons by 1700 and it amounted to 850,000 tons a century later. Although given the choice, people preferred to use wood for household heating and cooking, they could burn coal on existing fires and stoves. This was also the case for some industries such as smithing, brewing and soap-boiling, which could operate with any form of heat. However in many industries the impurities in coal posed major technical problems that ruled out its use for a considerable period until new processes were developed. These developments enabled coal to be used for glass production after 1610 and for making bricks a decade later. By the 1640s coke was used to dry malt for brewing and by the 1680s to smelt lead, copper and tin. The last major industrial process to be adapted to coke was the production of pig iron. This was first achieved by Abraham Darby in 1709 although it was not until the invention of the puddling process by Henry Cort in 1784 that coke could be used to make wrought iron. Until well into the eighteenth century charcoal remained a vitally important fuel for many industrial processes.

The growing use of coal in place of increasingly scarce and expensive wood in western Europe, and particularly in Britain, from the seventeenth century onwards was of far greater significance than the simple substitution of one energy source for another. All previous human societies had depended upon renewable sources of energy – humans, animals, water, wind and wood. The fact that they had generally tended to 'mine' forests without sufficient replanting or other conservation techniques meant that this energy crisis was self-inflicted – the result of a short-sighted approach repeated over the centuries. Only when the shortage became acute did societies begin to exploit coal on a large scale instead of the more readily available and more flexible fuel and make the transition to definitely non-renewable sources of energy. The first major exploitation of the world's fossil fuel reserves, created from the great tropical forests that existed over two hundred million years earlier, began in the seventeenth century. Much of the historical treatment of this period, particularly the more popular accounts, concentrates on the idea of an 'Industrial Revolution'. Attention has therefore been focussed on changes in industrial technology and the adoption of new industrial processes. These were important in expanding production, utilising new materials and developing new industries, but the more fundamental change that occurred was the shift in energy sources. Although other sources of energy were important in the early stages of the process, ultimately the move to an industrialised society depended on the consumption of *non-renewable* energy resources.

All of the main coalfields of Europe were being worked by the thirteenth and fourteenth centuries, albeit on a small scale, and the coal came from open-cast working or from shallow pits no more than fifty feet deep (although mines did extend under the sea in the north east of England as early as the sixteenth century). The large-scale development of deep mines came later, after the increasing cost of wood and charcoal offset the extra costs involved and when the development of efficient pumping machinery at the end of the seventeenth century made it possible to remove water from deep shafts and galleries. These pumps were some of the first machines to utilise steam power derived from coal. Coal-powered industries developed only very slowly even when the main technological problems involved in using the new fuel had been solved. Much of the early industrialisation of the textile industry in Britain was based on the continued exploitation of water power because it was cheaper and more flexible than the use of coal and steam-powered machinery. Whereas wood and water power were available over wide areas, substantial coalfields were found only in a few areas such as Yorkshire, South Wales, the Ruhr, north-east France, Kempen in Belgium and Limburg in the Netherlands, and the cost of transporting coal meant that many of the new industries had to be located near coalfields. Nations such as Italy, Austria and the

Scandinavian countries, which had few coal reserves, were some of the last to industrialise.

Nevertheless the nineteenth century witnessed an enormous rise in coal production. In 1800 world output was about 15 million tons, by 1860 it had risen to 132 million tons and at the end of the century had reached just over 700 million tons (a forty-six fold increase). It was the labour of the hundreds of thousands of coalminers, often working in extremely difficult and dangerous conditions and without machinery (another example of the importance of human power), that supplied the energy that was the prerequisite for the large-scale industrialisation of Europe. In Britain, the most heavily industrialised country in the world for most of the century, production soared from 10 million tons in 1800 to 60 million tons in 1850 and 225 million tons in 1990. Per capita consumption increased four-and-a-half-fold. In the space of the two years at the end of the century (1899–1900) the world used more coal than in the whole of the eighteenth century. From a negligible contribution, coal came rapidly to account for about 95 per cent of the world's greatly expanded energy consumption. The new rates of energy use simply could not have been sustained with wood – in 1900 the world's coal consumption was equivalent to destroying and transporting a forest three times the size of Britain every year. There were not enough forests in the world to sustain production on this scale for very long, and the problems which would have been involved in transporting such large quantities of wood around the world were probably insurmountable.

Industrialisation in the United States in the nineteenth century followed a very different pattern of energy consumption from that in Europe, reflecting the fact that in a recently settled area large supplies of wood were still available. The transition to fossil fuels in the United States was a drawn-out process and the pace of change varied greatly from region to region depending on the availability of wood and cheap transport. But in general early industrialisation depended on wood and water power rather than coal. In 1850 wood still accounted for 90 per cent of the United States' fuel supplies and half of the nation's iron was still produced using charcoal. Steam power was not widely adopted in industry before the 1880s and areas such as transport and iron production, together with virtually all stoves and boilers, were designed to use wood. Steamboats on the great rivers such as the Mississippi were wood-fired as were most railway locomotives (unlike Britain where they were coal-fired from the start because of the shortage of wood). As late as 1870 wood still constituted three-quarters of the fuel supply for industry and transport. Not until the mid-1880s did coal become the principal source of energy in the United States – when its readily available wood supplies were largely exhausted. As in Britain, the increased use of coal, when it came, was dramatic – consumption rose thirty-fold between 1850 and 1900. By 1910 coal provided about three-quarters of the nation's energy. The experience of the United States showed, once again, that coal was not utilised until other more easily available and more flexible energy sources were on the point of exhaustion. The same pattern can be found in the later industrialisation of Japan. Water power sustained the initial rise of the textile industry and steam power was not adopted until the 1890s. In the late nineteenth century the main use of coal was to provide heat in the salt industry and as late as 1914 as much coal was used to fuel ships as to power the whole of industry. Nevertheless, as industrialisation spread, Japanese coal production did rise substantially, from less than a million tons in 1880 to over thirty-four million tons by the late 1920s.

The worldwide transition to fossil fuels can also be illustrated by the transformation of the shipping industry in the nineteenth century. Until then all ships had been powered by renewable resources (human or wind power). Improvements in technology such as the adoption of iron hulls in 1853, and steel hulls a decade later, enabled sailing ships of up to 2,000 tons to compete effectively with the more expensive steam-powered vessels which had begun to come into service in the 1840s. The development of the steel boiler working at higher steam pressures transformed the potential of the steamship so that by the late 1860s it could bring three times as much cargo from China to Europe in half the time taken by a sailing ship. The tonnage of steam-powered shipping in the world rose from just 32,000 tons in 1831 to over three million tons by the mid-1870s. Although the sailing ship remained important in Asia until the end of the nineteenth century, the steamship took over the world's main merchant and military fleets. By the end of the century the amount of shipping in the world had not only substantially increased but a fundamental change from renewable energy sources to fossil fuels had taken place. Nearly every ship was powered by coal and Britain had built a chain of coaling stations around the globe to sustain the worldwide deployment of the Royal Navy.

An important by-product of the rise of coal consumption was the use of waste gases to provide the first non-natural source of lighting. Town gas was first used to light a factory in Salford in 1807 (and only six years later a cotton mill in Rhode Island). The main advantage for the factory owners was that artificial lighting enabled far longer hours to be worked. Although the installation costs were high (laying gas mains and installing new street lights), gas was far cheaper and available in far greater quantities than whale oil, which had provided the main source of what street lighting there was until then. By 1814–1816 the first districts in London were lit by gas supplied from a central plant through underground mains and by 1823 gas lighting systems had been built in fifty-two towns. By the late 1820s the idea had been adopted in Boston, New York (which depended on imported British coal) and Berlin. The use of coal gas to light streets and houses (of those able to afford the installation costs) and eventually for cooking gradually spread throughout the industrialised world in the nineteenth century.

The peak of the world's dependence on coal came in the early twentieth century. Although world production has continued to increase throughout the century (doubling between the 1930s and 1970s) coal's share of world energy consumption has fallen from over 90 per cent to about 30 per cent. It is now the second most important energy source after oil. In industrialised countries two-thirds of coal production is used by power stations to produce electricity but in the developing world coal remains an important industrial and domestic fuel, particularly in India and China (the latter is now the world's largest producer). The decline in the importance of coal occurred first in the United States in the early years of the twentieth century; there the discovery of large oil reserves encouraged a very rapid switch. In Europe the change came much later. In the 1920s coal continued to supply 95 per cent of the continent's energy and as late as 1950 the proportion was still over 80 per cent. By 1970 though the proportion had fallen to less than 30 per cent as cheap imported oil replaced coal. This trend is well illustrated by developments in European railways. In the 1950s most networks still depended on coal-fired steam engines but by the late 1960s these had been replaced by diesel-powered locomotives and electrified systems.

One of the most significant energy developments over the last century has been the growth in the use of fuels to provide a highly convenient form of secondary energy – electricity. The first electricity generators were made in London in 1834 but it took decades of technical development before they could be applied commercially. The first large-scale lighting application was at the Gare du Nord in Paris in 1875 and factories and shops rapidly followed suit across the industrialised world as new developments, such as the carbon filament lamp (first used in England in the House of Commons in 1881) and the longer lasting tungsten filament introduced after 1911, made electric power and lighting more attractive. Although the first hydroelectric power station was built at Niagara Falls in 1886, the overwhelming majority of electricity has been generated from fossil fuel-fired generators – at first coal and then oil and natural gas. The twentieth century has seen the development of ever bigger power stations (the average output in the 1920s was about 30,000 kilowatts rising to 600,000 kilowatts in the 1970s) and the construction of both national and international high power transmission lines and grids (first pioneered by the Germans in 1885).

The rise of a highly convenient form of energy which, once the expensive infrastructure had been built, could be used in factories and homes for lighting, heating and power marked a fundamental shift in the ease with which energy could be obtained and led to a massive increase in energy consumption. Electricity did not just replace steam-powered machinery in industry, it made possible far greater automation of production processes, as through the use of machine tools and robots. It also provided the energy for completely new industries such as aluminium production. The increasing use of aluminium – the American aluminium industry alone quadrupled its output in the thirty years after the Second World War – has greatly increased the consumption of electricity. It takes six-and-a-half times more energy to produce a ton of aluminium than it does to make a ton of steel. At the same time there has also been a vast growth in the domestic consumption of electricity; nearly every household in the industrialised world is now connected to a mains supply to provide lighting, heating, cooking and power for a vast array of household goods such as refrigerators, freezers, televisions, washing machines and dishwashers. Rising electricity consumption has been one of the main causes of increased energy consumption in the world – overall it has increased twice as fast as overall energy consumption. In Europe, for example, electricity consumption rose twenty-six-fold between 1920 and 1970.

Oil had been obtained for centuries from places where it seeped onto the surface and was used mainly in the form of bitumen for caulking ships and even for medicinal purposes. It was not until the mid-nineteenth century that efforts to extract it and exploit the product on a commercial scale began: the world's first commercial oil came from the Drake well in Pennsylvania in 1859. The pressure to obtain large quantities of this new energy source and to overcome the technical problems in extracting, refining, storing and transporting it came from two sources. First, lubricants such as whale and vegetable oils were proving inadequate for the demands of new industrial machinery. Second, whale oil was in short supply, which was making it increasingly difficult and costly to provide both domestic and industrial lighting in areas which did not have town gas supplies. In the late nineteenth century 85 per cent of crude oil was refined into kerosene to provide illuminating oil and most of the rest went to make industrial lubricants. This situation was only transformed in the early twentieth century with the development of oil-burning furnaces – by 1909 fuel oil made up about half the output of what was becoming an increasingly important industry. Demand was given a further boost by the development of the internal combustion engine and the enormous growth in the number of vehicles. By 1930 gasoline had become the main refined product produced by the oil industry. From the late 1930s another new product – aviation fuel – became increasingly important (its consumption rose forty-fold in the United States in just twenty years after 1935). Plentiful supplies of oil and technological developments led to the production of artificial materials such as nylon, rayon and a whole range of plastics.

The twentieth century has seen the development of more oilfields right across the world, from the Near East to Nigeria and Venezuela. The level of technology used by the industry has become ever more complex as new and much more difficult fields have been exploited such as those in Alaska and offshore fields in the Gulf of Mexico, the North Sea and elsewhere. The United States has been one of the major producers in the world since the 1860s although after the Second World War continued large increases in consumption resulted in rising oil imports as well. In 1900 Russia was the largest producer in the world (mainly from the fields around Baku) and the Soviet Union still retains that place. The most important development in the twentieth century was the rise of production in the Near East after the Second World War. In 1938 the area produced just 16 million tons but by 1970 this had risen to 700 million tons – a forty-three-fold rise.

Just as coal proved to be the means to support an otherwise impracticable expansion of industry in the nineteenth century, the availability of cheap oil as an energy source has been the principal sustainer of continued economic growth in the twentieth century. The world's consumption of oil has increased astronomically in the last hundred years. In 1890 it was about 10 million tons. This rose nearly ten-fold to reach 95 million tons by 1920, trebled to 294 million tons by 1940 and then doubled every decade to reach nearly 2,500 million tons a year by the 1970s – overall more than a two hundred-fold increase. In 1900 oil provided only 4 per cent of the world's energy supplies but almost 50 per cent by the 1970s. These worldwide figures disguise the even bigger increases that occurred in the industrialised countries, in particular the United States. American oil consumption increased at an average rate of 9 per cent a year from 1890 to 1922, doubled in the course of the 1920s and then continued to grow at nearly 5 per cent a year. Overall per capita consumption of oil in the US rose thirty-five-fold in the first half of the twentieth century. The changeover to oil as the principal energy source occurred much later in Europe. In 1950 oil supplied only 14 per cent of the continent's energy but 60 per cent twenty years later. Nearly all of Europe's oil supplies had to be imported – imports rose from 11 million tons in 1938 to 605 million tons in 1970 (a fifty-five-fold increase).

A major by-product of the exploitation of the world's oilfields has been the increasing importance of natural gas an energy source in the industrialised world. Although it was used locally near American oilfields from early in the twentieth century, its widespread use had to await improvements in pipeline technology which allowed it to be pumped over long distances under high pressure. This was achieved in the United States in the 1930s but it was not until the 1960s that its use became widespread in western Europe. A large field off the coast of the Netherlands now supplies about a third of the country's energy and the development of major fields in the southern North Sea brought about the replacement of town gas in Britain in the 1970s. Nearly all the world's natural gas consumption is concentrated in the industrialised world and the Soviet Union is now the largest producer from extensive fields in Siberia (a large part of the output is pumped to western Europe). In 1900 natural gas provided just one-and-a-half per cent of the world's energy supplies but by the 1980s it was the third most important source (after oil and coal), making up just under 20 per cent of the total.

The history of energy in the nineteenth and twentieth centuries has, therefore, been dominated by ever-increasing consumption of the non-renewable fossil fuels – coal, oil and natural gas. Only two other technologies have contributed any real alternatives – hydroelectric and nuclear power. The use of hydroelectric power grew significantly in the first part of the twentieth century (forty-three-fold in the United States) and in 1929 it provided 40 per cent of the world's electricity. But it has become steadily less important in overall terms and now provides only a very small part of the world's energy (less than 2 per cent). Nuclear power began on a commercial basis in the 1950s as a spin-off from military programmes. It has been dogged by safety problems,

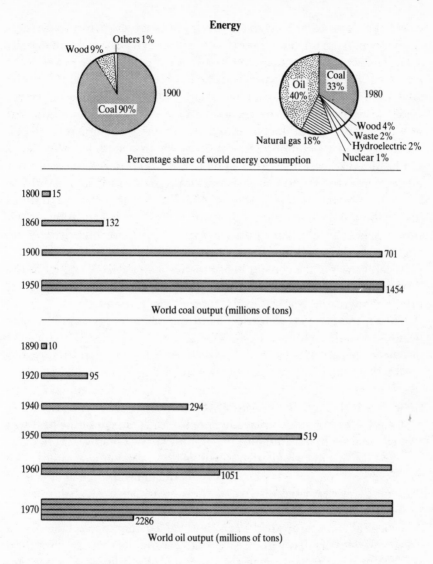

Energy

Others 1%

Wood 9%

Coal 90%

1900

Oil 40%

Coal 33%

1980

Natural gas 18%

Wood 4%
Waste 2%
Hydroelectric 2%
Nuclear 1%

Percentage share of world energy consumption

1800 ▧ 15

1860 ▨ 132

1900 ▨ 701

1950 ▨ 1454

World coal output (millions of tons)

1890 ▧ 10

1920 ▨ 95

1940 ▨ 294

1950 ▨ 519

1960 ▨ 1051

1970 ▨ 2286

World oil output (millions of tons)

poor designs and a consistent failure to produce electricity cheaper than other sources. About 400 stations are now operating in the world and in France, motivated by a lack of oil, it supplies about 60 per cent of electricity production, but overall it provides less than 1 per cent of the world's energy.

By the late twentieth century the world's consumption of energy reflected an entirely different pattern from that which had prevailed until the end of the eighteenth century. Until then renewable resources – human, animal, wind and water – had provided nearly all of the world's energy needs. Now, just over 90 per cent comes from fossil fuels (40 per cent from oil, 33 per cent from coal and 18 per cent from natural gas). The remainder comes from wood (4 per cent), waste materials (2 per cent), hydroelectric (2 per cent) and nuclear (1 per cent). Until the exploitation of fossil fuels human societies faced an energy shortage; since the eighteenth century the industrialised world has found ways of producing and consuming an abundance of energy. Since 1860 (when the increase in consumption was already well underway) world energy use has increased seventy-fold. The major fossil fuels have seen even bigger rises – the world's annual consumption of coal is now about 100 times greater than it was in 1800 and for oil it is now about 250 times higher than in the late nineteenth century. For most of the time energy supplies have been cheap – until the early 1970s crude oil prices on the open market were a few dollars a barrel, reflecting the economic (and political) power of the consuming countries, and until the late 1980s the Soviet Union also supplied its satellites in eastern Europe with oil at prices below world market levels, for political reasons.

During the last two centuries, as in the past, energy supplies have been used as though they are inexhaustible. The industrialised world has encouraged consumption not conservation. Cheap energy has meant that much of the energy consumed has been wasted through various forms of inefficiency compounded by poor decision taking. In the nineteenth century, as before, fuel efficiency was very low. Most coal was burnt in open fireplaces where over 90 per cent of the heat was wasted (mainly by escaping up the chimney). Wood stoves were more efficient, with only about two-thirds of the heat being wasted. The earliest steam engines were hopelessly inefficient – about 98 per cent of the energy was wasted. By 1910 the performance of steam-driven turbines had been steadily improved so that they were about 20 per cent efficient and this figure had been doubled by the 1950s. One of the greatest wastes of energy in the twentieth century has occurred through the loss of natural gas during the pumping of crude oil. For decades natural gas was wasted: it was used as a means of driving the oil to the surface and it was then flared off. In 1913 it was estimated that one Oklahoma oilfield was wasting natural gas worth more than the oil it was producing. In the late 1920s and early 1930s the US Bureau of Mines estimated that 1.25 billion cubic feet of natural gas were wasted every day in the United States – equivalent, over ten years, to 250 million tons of coal (about a quarter of the world's annual consumption). In the 1950s about half of the natural gas produced in the word's oilfields was wasted by burning it at the wellhead and it is still a common practice.

Although electricity provides a highly convenient form of energy it is a highly inefficient way of producing energy. Electricity generating stations have to be built and operated and transmission lines have to be constructed to bring electricity to industrial and domestic customers. At each stage energy is consumed and it is also lost through various inefficiencies in generating and transmitting the electricity. Power stations were only about 9 per cent efficient in the 1920s and even now they are still only about 25 per cent efficient. The overall scale of the wastage of energy involved in electricity generation can be judged from the fact that over a fifth of Britain's energy consumption is spent simply in making electricity. Homes are poorly insulated and domestic appliances such as refrigerators and light bulbs use more electricity than necessary. These problems have been compounded by government decisions, often made under the strong influence of electricity supply organisations and the industries involved in building power stations, which emphasise the increased supply of electricity rather than its more efficient use. The sharp rises in the price of crude oil in 1973–1974 and 1979–1980 did lead to programmes designed to save energy in most of the industrialised world but, once inflation brought about a decline in the price in real terms, these programmes were often quietly abandoned and the emphasis placed once again on making more energy available rather than using it efficiently. Car engines, for example, are larger than they need to be, leading to very high fuel consumption figures (less than 20 miles per gallon on many American cars).

If individual items of energy producing and using equipment are not always efficient, is modern industrialised society energy efficient as a whole? In the past it was possible to make some fairly crude calculations about energy use – for example, people could set the cost of feeding animals against the savings in time and effort to be gained from using them for agricultural tasks – but now it is possible to do sophisticated calculations about energy use. But even when the facts are known societies have found it very difficult to make the necessary adjustments to achieve more efficient use of energy. An example of poor use is found in modern industrialised agriculture. The most energy efficient agriculture in the world is the production of rice in paddy fields in China and south east Asia, where the output of energy is about fifty times greater than the input. Other so-called primitive agricultural systems are also highly energy efficient, producing about twenty times as much energy as they use. At best, modern industrialised cereal farming produces only about twice as much energy as it consumes in the form of fertilisers, pesticides and machinery. Modern agriculture is, moreover, becoming steadily less energy efficient. In the twenty years after 1952 energy inputs into industrialised agriculture rose by 70 per cent but food production only increased by 30 per cent. In the United States the production of corn shows an even worse situation. There energy inputs rose 400 per cent between 1945 and 1970 but this only increased yields by 138 per cent. Overall the energy efficiency of American corn production has fallen by half since 1915. Modern animal rearing systems are even less efficient once account is taken of the energy involved in producing artificial feeds and in building, heating and lighting large sheds to accommodate the animals. Meat production in the industrialised world now consumes between two and three times the energy that it produces. The process of catching and producing frozen fish is probably the most inefficient form of energy use in the sphere of food production – it consumes about twenty times more energy than it makes available for human consumption. If modern agriculture comes out badly when looked at from this angle, modern food retailing makes things worse. The processing and distribution of food before it is eaten takes about three times as much energy as producing the food itself. Once this is taken into account, then all food production in the industrialised world uses more energy than it creates.

The consumption of the world's limited stocks of fossil fuels has been primarily the responsibility of the industrialised countries, and in particular the United States. The people of the United States make up only 5 per cent of the world's population but they are responsible for 30 per cent of the world's energy consumption (in the 1940s it was even higher – nearly 50 per cent). The majority of the world's population in the Third World consume only 10 per cent of the world's energy. The average American now uses three-and-a-half times as much energy as his predecessor in 1900, twice as much as the average European and thirty times more than the average Indian. Throughout the twentieth century the gap in energy consumption between the industrialised world and the rest of the world's population has been growing steadily greater.

The energy problems of the Third World are closer to the conditions experienced in the whole of the world before the nineteenth century. Energy is still in short supply and human and animal power are still very important. Half the world's population (over two-and-a-half billion people) still depend on wood, charcoal and animal or crop residues for their fuel supplies. The rapidly rising population in the Third World in the last 150 years has placed a major strain on these sources, particularly wood. It is now estimated that about 100 million people in the world are unable to obtain enough fuel for even their minimum cooking and heating requirements and that well over one billion are depleting their locally available stocks of wood faster than the replanting rate. By the year 2000 about three billion people are likely to fall into this category. Shortages of wood also bring about a vicious circle in which dried animal dung is used for heating and cooking rather than as a manure, thus reducing soil fertility, crop yields and the ability to sustain the number of farm animals, and, thereby, exacerbating many of the other problems that people living in the Third World face.

The industrialised world has come to rely on continuing supplies of cheap fossil fuels to sustain industrial production and a high per capita level of energy consumption. In the last few decades the countries of the Third World have begun to move in a similar direction – constructing power stations, building electricity distribution networks, and increasing their oil imports at about three-and-a-half per cent a year. Their increasing dependence on this energy source has crucial social and economic implications. Very few Third World countries produce their own oil and so most of it has to be imported. This can only be paid for from exports – half of the Third World's export earnings are now going to pay for oil imports. Increases in the oil price affect these countries even harder than they do the developed world and place real restrictions on their plans for economic development.

The last ten thousand years of human history have witnessed an enormous change in the pattern of energy consumption, from the minimal demands of gathering and hunting groups to modern American levels. In order to obtain that energy, the trend has been to move towards increasingly sophisticated and technologically complex methods, from gathering wood and using humans and animals to simple water and wind powered machines, to deep coal mines, deep oil wells (especially those offshore), electricity generation and nuclear power. Throughout this period there has been a remarkable continuity of attitude towards consumption, emphasising short-term considerations and treating all sources of energy as though they were inexhaustible. Estimates of the point at which the world's fossil fuel reserves will be exhausted are difficult because of the problem of estimating the size of undiscovered reserves and future consumption rates. However most estimates agree that there is enough coal to last for several hundred years (even at increased consumption rates) while reserves of oil and natural gas may last for less than a century, perhaps only a few decades. Long before these reserves are exhausted severe problems will be encountered as supplies become more difficult to obtain from more remote fields that pose acute technical problems in their exploitation and as prices rise in consequence. By the late twentieth century concern about future energy supplies was reflected in greater interest in renewable energy supplies – hence the development of modern methods for harnessing solar, wind and water power (including waves and tides), and for using plant and animal wastes, and moves towards more efficient power generation in combined heat and power plants. But, despite some interesting experiments, the contribution of 'alternative energy' to world energy consumption remains miniscule. The industrialised world remains dependent on non-renewable sources, apparently entrenched in the habits and expectations of many thousands of years of treating wood and later fossil fuels as though they were inexhaustible.

14
The Rise of the City

One of the greatest changes in the way people live has been due to the rise of the city in the last two hundred years. Cities developed at an early stage in the growth of settled societies and have generally been regarded as one of the distinguishing characteristics of a civilised society. However for thousands of years they played a very small part in the lives of most people. Until 1800 only a tiny minority – no more than two-and-a-half per cent of the world's population – lived in cities. (There is no simple definition of what constitutes a city – many ancient and medieval cities would be no more than small towns in the modern world). With the use of fossil fuel energy sources and increasing industrialisation, truly urbanised societies began to emerge in Europe and North America. In 1900 about one in ten of the world's people lived in cities and during the twentieth century cities continued to increase in number, size and economic importance in the industrialised world. There was also a relatively sudden rise in their importance in the Third World so that by the 1980s almost half the world's population lived in urban areas. The scale of these changes can be illustrated best from the figures for the actual number of people living in cities rather than the percentages. In 1800 about 25 million people lived in cities, by the 1980s the figure had risen to about two-and-a-half billion. They live in what is probably the most extreme example of an artificial environment and one that has given rise to its own range of environmental problems.

The adoption of agriculture had as an inevitable consequence the emergence of a settled way of life. The earliest agricultural groups lived in villages of at most a few hundred people. Within a few thousand years of this crucial step being taken, cities such as Uruk, Ur and Lagash in Mesopotamia, and Mohenjo-Daro in the Indus valley, each containing several thousand people had developed. Early cities themselves were essentially ceremonial centres dominated by their cult functions but also with an important administrative function. Some of the cities (such as Teotihuacan, Monte Alban and the Mayan cities in Mesoamerica) were laid out according to complex designs reflecting religious symbols of divine order or oriented towards significant astronomical positions. The role played by the temples (and later the secular rulers) and their administrators in redistributing food and controlling much of the labour of the peasants, who made up the overwhelming majority of the population, was also important in the growth of the city. These ceremonial centres are found in virtually every early settled society in Mesopotamia, Egypt, the Indus valley, China, Mesoamerica, Peru and even as late as 1000 AD in south-west Nigeria as the first cities developed among the Yoruba. The nature and therefore the size of the population of cities did vary from area to area. The elite (both religious and political) of a society normally resided in cities but in some cases the peasants also lived there. In Egypt the ceremonial centres were mainly populated by priests, rulers, administrators and craftsmen, with the peasants living in villages in the rural areas. Some later 'cities' seem to have retained this structure – for example Sparta, which remained a dispersed series of settlements around a central religious and administrative area. On the other hand in Mesopotamia and many of the cities of Mesoamerica such as Teotihuacan and those of the Maya most of the population seems eventually to have moved from the rural areas into the cities and to have cultivated the surrounding areas during the day and returned to their homes in the cities at night.

The rise of empires and the steady increase in population and small-scale trade led to the development of what can be called 'pre-industrial' cities. During a long period (stretching over perhaps four thousand years) most cities were on the scale of small modern towns and villages, and many of the inhabitants were still engaged in agriculture in the surrounding areas. The largest centres of population were the great imperial capitals such as Rome, Peking, Pataliputra (capital of the Maurya empire in India) and even the centres of essentially seaborne trading empires such as Athens, Venice and Genoa. These cities depended on their flourishing empires for the import of food (Athens and Rome survived by importing grain from the Mediterranean and Black Sea areas). As the administratives centres of large empires they contained the elite and wealthy members of that society and attracted a large class of administrators and priests. The population of the capital city was swelled by their slaves and servants and a miscellany of craftsmen, traders, shopkeepers and employees of other 'service industries' and small manufacturing enterprises. Despite their parasitic nature, many grew to considerable size – Rome probably reached about

400,000 people at its height, and those in the east such as some Chinese cities and Edo (modern Tokyo), the effective capital of Japan in the Tokugawa period from the early seventeenth century, were probably twice as big as Rome. Lacking a firm economic base and dependent as they were on the fortunes of the great empires, these imperial capital cities often declined as quickly as they grew. Vijayanagar, the capital of the main Hindu empire in India in the thirteenth and fourteenth centuries, was virtually deserted after the Mughal conquest. The population of Rome fell drastically as the empire collapsed in the west and the focus of the imperial system shifted to the old Greek colony of Byzantium, renamed Constantinople. That city grew and flourished as the centre of a great empire but declined with it until the Ottoman conquest in 1453 when it once again became the capital of a major empire.

Other towns had a variety of origins. Some grew up at important strategic or economic locations – a river crossing or a fortified site. Others depended on their right to hold a market to meet the demands of the small amount of local trade that went on. Some stemmed from deliberate acts of creation: for example the Greeks founded new colonies such as Naples and Marseilles to absorb surplus population; Roman settlements were established at key geographical sites such as London, Paris, Seville and Cologne; and similarly Marakanda (modern Samarkand) was established as the Persian empire pushed into central Asia.

Pre-industrial cities typically had a number of characteristics that mark them out as different from modern industrial cities. In nearly every case they were surrounded by walls, which performed not just a defensive function but also demarcated the area of the city (which often had separate legal arrangements from the surrounding area). This allowed the city authorities to regulate trade and enabled taxes to be enforced as traders moved through a limited number of gates. Within the walls, the towns often retained a semi-rural appearance with many fields and orchards. Most of the inhabitants lived in narrow streets that were little better than alleys, suitable for pedestrians and pack animals but not for carts, which were confined to the main thoroughfares. The centre of the city contained the public buildings and houses of the wealthy citizens, whilst the poor lived on the fringes of the city – the opposite of most modern cities. Residential areas, and places of work, were also often carefully segregated within the city by type of craft, race or religion – Teotihuacan in Mesoamerica contained numerous compounds for different craftsmen and traders from other areas, and medieval European cities normally had Jewish ghettos.

The development of pre-industrial cities can be traced across the world. In India, after the collapse of the Indus valley cities about 1900 BC, new cities such as Taxila and Pataliputra arose in the north from the eighth century BC but only much later were cities built in the south of the sub-continent. In south-east Asia cities began to emerge in the first century AD, mainly under the influence of Indian traders as they developed trading networks across the region. In China capital cities and ceremonial centres were common shortly after the emergence of a settled society in the north but large cities such as Nanking date to the rise of the Han empire after the second century BC. A major urban revolution in China, partly linked to increasing industrialisation, occurred between the eleventh and thirteenth centuries. In this period perhaps about one in ten of the Chinese people were living in cities and in some of the more economically developed areas the proportion would have been much higher. Some of the biggest cities probably had a population of several hundred thousand. After 1300, as the Chinese economy stagnated and failed to sustain the growth in industrial production, the process of urbanisation seems to have slowed down and probably in many areas it went into reverse. The earliest cities in Japan such as Nara and Kyoto (the imperial capital) were artificial capital cities constructed on a strict rectangular plan adopted from the Chinese. From the thirteenth century the first small trading cities and settlements around castles began to emerge, in much the same way as they had in north-west Europe a few centuries earlier. Under the Tokugawa after 1615, with military conflict within society controlled, many of the castle sites grew into local trading centres and other trading and commercial cities, of which Osaka was the largest, flourished. But more important was the administrative capital of the country, Edo. This was essentially an artificial capital created by Tokugawa Ieyasu in 1590. Under the *sankin-kotai* system, as a measure of political control, every local lord was forced to reside there for at least part of the year. These local lords brought with them their families and large numbers of retainers and employees, who made up about half the population of the city, the other half being traders and craftsmen serving the elite. By 1800 Edo was probably the most populous city in the world, containing not far short of one million people.

In Europe, the Mediterranean area was the centre for all the most developed societies and empires until at least the eleventh and twelfth centuries. Even after the fall of the Roman empire in the west in the fifth century, the Mediterranean remained economically the most advanced area of Europe and the size of its cities reflected this fact. Constantinople, the capital of the empire in the east, contained at least 200,000 people and possibly as many as 400,000 at its peak. Cordoba, the capital of the Islamic empire in the western Mediterranean, probably had over 100,000 people and other important cities such as Seville and Palermo were only slightly smaller. The pattern of settlement in the north and west of Europe was very different. Under the Roman empire there had been only a few towns in the area, many linked to military settlements and most containing no more than a few hundred people. After the collapse of the empire nearly all of these Roman foundations decayed drastically. For five or six centuries there was little trade and industry in north-west Europe and the scale of its agricultural surplus was generally insufficient to support more than a very small urban population. In 1000 there were perhaps 100 towns or cities in the whole of Europe and half of them were concentrated in what was still the most developed part – Italy. In England, in 1086, just 67,000 people lived in towns (10,000 of them in London) out of the total population of slightly less than two million.

As trade and industry became more important in the economy between 1000–1300, towns in Europe away from the Mediterranean became more numerous and larger. By 1300 there were between 3,000–4,000 towns and cities in Europe but only nine of them had a population greater than 25,000. Of these Florence, Paris and Venice were the most populous with perhaps 100,000 people. London and Ghent, the next largest, contained about 50,000 people. Only in northern Italy and the Low Countries (the major centres of industry and commerce) was there a dramatic increase in the urban population – in Tuscany by 1300 about a quarter of the population lived in towns with more than 3,000 inhabitants. Most towns were very small; even the flourishing Hanseatic port of Hamburg only had a population of 7,000, and the majority of towns in northern Europe had less than 2,000 people. Towns of this size were really little more than large villages – most of the population continued to work in the adjoining fields and only a weekly market and the presence of a few craftsmen marked them out as separate economic entities within an overwhelmingly agricultural society. These European towns or cities were, however, generally self-governing and independent of the jurisdiction of the local landowner, in marked contrast with the towns and cities of China which were unable to establish such legal and economic independence.

Between 1300 and 1800 (and the onset of industrialisation) the relatively sharp increase in the urban population in Europe that had occurred in the previous three centuries was not maintained, partly because of the overall decline in the population and its slow rate of recovery after the Black Death. (Between 1350 and 1550 the number of market towns in England fell by two-thirds.) Some cities, such as Florence and Venice, declined as their political and economic influence waned and Valladolid suffered a rapid decline when the Spanish capital moved to Madrid. Around the Mediterranean area, where economic development was slower than in the north, many of the cities remained as centres of elite residence and consumption, depending on the agricultural surplus of the surrounding areas rather than contributing any significant economic activity of their own. Naples, capital of the Kingdom of the Two Sicilies, with a population of over 400,000 in the 1770s, was a prime example of a city in this category. A few new cities were founded, but most of them depended on their role as capitals or court cities in much the same way as similar cities thousands of years earlier. St Petersburg was an artificial construct by Peter the Great, and the growth of the Prussian monarchy transformed the small city of Berlin (which as late as 1700 consisted of no more than 30,000 people still living within the medieval walls) into a capital city with over 170,000 inhabitants a century later. (The urge to create artificial capital cities also produced Washington and in the present century New Delhi, Canberra and Brasilia).

The first European area to become urbanised was the province of Holland in the sixteenth century: the process began as wealth was created from its extensive trading system. In the early sixteenth century about a fifth of Holland's population lived in towns with more than 10,000 people. In the course of the next century the urban population rose by almost 500 per cent so that by 1622 as many as half the people lived in such towns. The fastest growing cities in northern Europe at this period were Paris and London. In the sixteenth century Paris was possibly the largest city in Europe. In 1550 it had a population of about 400,000 (four times its size two hundred years earlier) and it reached 500,000 in 1700. London increased from about 60,000 people in the 1520s to 250,000 in the early seventeenth century and to 400,000 by 1650. By 1700 it was more populous than Paris and the biggest city in Europe. It was the centre for the court, government and law and as a consequence drew in merchants, traders, shopkeepers and craftsmen to cater for the needs of the wealthiest part of society. It also drew in many of the poor from the rural areas where overpopulation and therefore lack of land and work were major problems. They hoped to find employment but many finished up in badly paid casual work or as beggars. By the eighteenth century London contained about one in ten of the people of England.

Cities formed an integral part of European colonies from their foundation: they were either based on existing centres such as Mexico City (the Aztec capital Tenochtitlan) and Cuzco (the old Inca capital) or new settlements, as in areas like North America which lacked towns altogether before European settlers arrived. But these colonial towns and cities were essentially centres for trade with Europe and at first they were neither numerous nor large. In 1790 the United States had only five places with a population greater than 10,000, of which New York was the largest at 40,000. In total, probably no more than 200,000 Americans lived in cities. Australia was remarkable in that most of the population lived in towns and cities from the start of European settlement in the late eighteenth century – within a century a third of the population could be classified as urban, a figure higher than anywhere else in the world apart from Britain at that time.

In 1800 the world's population was still overwhelmingly rural – only about two-and-a-half per cent lived in cities. Some of these cities were populous by pre-industrial standards – both London and Edo contained almost one million people and Canton and Peking in China had perhaps 800,000 inhabitants. Europe had the highest percentage of people living in towns or cities of varying sizes but even here about 90 per cent of the population still lived in the countryside. Even in Britain and Holland only one in five people lived in cities. After 1800 Europe and North America witnessed a revolution in the way people lived. The proportion of the population living in cities rose rapidly and the city itself changed in a number of ways. The results of this change were first apparent in Britain – in 1851 Britain was the most urbanised country in the world but more than sixty per cent of its population still lived in the countryside. (Apart from Britain, only in Belgium did more than twenty per cent of the people live in towns in 1850 and only in France, Saxony, Prussia and the United States was more than ten per cent of the population urbanised.) By 1900 about three-quarters of the British people lived in cities and one in five of the population lived in London. Discussion in terms of percentages alone can give a misleading impression. Britain was experiencing an overall rise in population and the rural population continued to increase as well until the 1850s when it went into absolute decline. The total numbers living in British cities rose from about two million in 1800 to almost 30 million in 1900.

By 1900 about one in ten of the world's population lived in cities (four times higher than a century earlier) and two-thirds of them were in Europe, North America and Australasia. Europe had seen its urban population increase six-fold in the course of the nineteenth century. The change that first affected Britain, and was felt by the rest of Europe and North America at a slightly later stage came against a background of a rapid rise in population, growth of industry, trade and finance and the exploitation of fossil fuel reserves. For the first time, cities, although still reliant on the countryside for their food supplies, ceased to be parasitic on the national economy and began to make a major contribution, primarily through increased industrial output. New factories and industries were set up and they attracted the rural poor who were seeking work and then became self-sustaining through natural population increase and the development of new industries and jobs as industrial output grew. In 1750 London was the only city in England with a population of more than 50,000 – a century later there were twenty-nine such towns, nearly all of them dependent on manufacturing. These included the cotton towns of Lancashire, the woollen towns of Yorkshire and the mining and metal industry centres in areas such as Sheffield, the Black Country and South Wales. Manchester for example grew from 27,000 inhabitants in 1770 to 180,000 in 1830. Birmingham showed an equally rapid growth. Other towns were dominated by single industries such as Swindon and Crewe and their railway works. Others were artificial constructs to house the workers in new factories, for example Port Sunlight and the Lever Brothers plant. In old established towns, manufacturing also became more important – for example London developed extensive sweated workshops particularly in the clothing trade. However, London continued to be Britain's dominant commercial and financial centre.

In Europe and the United States the same pattern occurred later in the nineteenth century. New industrial towns developed across the continent of Europe, but particularly near the coalfields which provided the primary energy source for industrialisation – Belgium, the Ruhr and northern France. For the first time manufacturing became of overwhelming economic importance in towns – for example it provided over 80 per cent of the employment in Bochum in the Ruhr by 1882. Many of the new towns were dominated by single industries, as in the case of Leverkusen and the Bayer chemical plants. Berlin grew from 170,000 in 1800 to over one-and-a-half million in 1900 as the capital of the newly united Germany became the hub of the railway system and a centre of the increasingly important electrical industry in the late nineteenth century. But Germany remained much more balanced in its urban growth than Britain, with the importance of Berlin offset by the great manufacturing centres in the Ruhr and by important ports such as

Hamburg. In the United States in 1830 there were still only twenty-three towns with more than 10,000 people and only two big cities – New York (200,000) and Philadelphia (160,000). But as immigration from Europe grew and industrial cities such as Pittsburgh developed, the urban population doubled every decade to reach 6 million by 1860 with over nine cities having more than 100,000 people (New York had reached 800,000). By 1910 there were fifty cities with over 100,000 people.

Before 1800 most cities in the world were small in area – they were places which people could walk across to conduct their business. Rome in the second century AD was still largely contained within the Aurelian wall which enclosed an area of about five square miles. Roman colonial cities were much smaller – London covered 330 acres and Bath only 23 acres. The area of medieval London was about 700 acres. Cities in the nineteenth century began to sprawl. At ever greater distances from the centre suburbs grew up, mainly relying on new transportation systems to bring the ever greater urban population into their workplaces. Such developments significantly changed the nature of cities. Until the widespread growth of suburbs, the centres of towns had been the place where the wealthy lived. Industrialisation and the massive influx of mainly poor people seeking work led to very high population densities, particularly in mid-nineteenth century England. Huge slums developed in the centres of cities, such as the Covent Garden and Holborn areas of London, and many of the wealthy, together with the growing number of people working in offices and other service industries, moved out into the more salubrious suburbs and surrounding countryside.

Cities spread out across what had once been countryside, destroying the market gardens and fields, incorporating the villages (such as Hampstead and Highgate near London). Large new estates were built of terraced houses, apartments or, in the wealthier suburbs, villas with gardens and plenty of space. Most growth was unplanned, the result of speculative development, often following the building of new transport systems, as the ability to travel back into town to work became a major consideration. The result was the development of suburbs – places where people lived but did not work.

Some of the first suburbs grew up following the construction of bridges and ferries – for example Southwark in medieval London and Brooklyn in New York. But the most profound changes in nineteenth-century cities came with the development of public transport. The first horse-drawn omnibus started in France but it was New York in 1829 that witnessed the first extensive system along Broadway and by 1853 there were nearly 700 vehicles operating. Horse-drawn public transport had some effect on living patterns but the development of railways brought about major changes. In London the steady building of railway lines from the 1840s led to the growth of new, largely residential suburbs such as Camberwell, Hornsey, Kilburn, Fulham and Ealing. Residents of some of the first suburbs in the United States were transported by a horse-drawn street railway introduced in New York in 1832 (which eventually had 150 miles of track) and adopted in eight other cities by 1860. In New York in the second half of the nineteenth century these streetcars acted as feeders to a more ambitious system of elevated railways from 1869, which enabled people to live still further away from the centre and travel more quickly. In other cities such as Chicago cable cars were important – the city had eighty-six miles of track and 1,500 cars in the 1890s. That decade also witnessed the end of horse-drawn railways in the United States and their replacement by electrified trolleys – in 1890 there 5,700 miles of horse-drawn track in the country and 1,260 miles electrified, but ten years later only 250 miles were still horse-drawn and 22,000 were electrified. The other major urban transportation development in the late nineteenth and early twentieth centuries was the development of the underground railway. The first was built in London in 1863 and over the next forty years the network grew in size. Only after electrification was it possible to exploit the full potential of the system to move large numbers of people into and around cities. Other cities began to build an underground railway much later than London – Boston in 1897 (there were 50 million passengers in the first year on a tiny network), Paris in 1900, Berlin in 1902 and New York in 1904 (within ten years over one million people a day were being carried on its one route).

Suburban development was a common phenomenon around the cities of the industrialised world. The exact pattern depended not only on the timing of the construction and the extent of the transportation system but also on other factors. In the United States, where land was generally cheap, the density of settlement was far lower than in Europe and the cities spread over far greater areas. In 1850 the edge of the city of Boston in Massachusetts was two miles from the business centre. By 1900, with the development of mass transportation systems, the city extended ten miles from the centre. In New York, where cheap housing spread out along the developing subway lines, instead of the 200,000 people living in the boroughs of Brooklyn, the Bronx and Queen's in

1890, there were 2.7 million by 1940. In London during the nineteenth century the population grew from 1 million to 4½ million and another 2 million people lived in the adjacent areas of what came to be called 'Greater London'. In Berlin the suburbs grew faster than the centre after the 1870s and what had originally been separate towns such as Charlottenburg and Spandau were incorporated into the city. The only major city which did not experience such rapid territorial expansion was Paris, where a poor suburban railway system kept the city more concentrated during the nineteenth century – the population density in the centre of the city was about three times greater than in London.

One of the consequences of the development of suburbs was the transformation of the city centre. The heart of most major cities became a hub of financial and commercial activity (with only limited industrial work). As a result population fell – that of the City of London began to decline from the 1850s and within a few decades went from about 130,000 to almost none as offices took over. In New York, in 1905, over half the population lived within four miles of the centre of the city but twenty years later less than a third did so and the area of densest settlement was a region eight to twelve miles from the centre. The peak population of Manhattan was 2.3 million in 1910; by 1980 it had fallen by half. The continuing importance of public transport in establishing this new working and living pattern is shown by the fact that in the 1920s, despite the increasing dispersal of the population away from the centre, 86 per cent of the people of New York still lived within the area served by subways and the elevated railways.

During the twentieth century cities have continued to grow, with transportation again acting as one of the key factors determining the course of events. In London the extension of the Metropolitan railway into the countryside north of the capital led to the development of a whole series of suburbs dubbed 'Metroland'. In Berlin a poorly integrated public transport system slowed up the growth of suburbs whereas in Paris major investment in suburban railways in the 1920s led to the development of cheap, often self-built housing in areas without proper facilities and over one million commuters a day travelling into the city from the surrounding districts. The most significant development, though, was the rise of the private motor car. The new-found ability to drive independently to work affected settlement patterns in the United States as early as the 1920s, and in Europe from the early 1950s. Increasing car ownership strengthened the tendency of cities to sprawl over ever bigger areas and for commuting distance to work to rise still further. The urbanised area of New York in the 1980s covered about 2,200 square miles – five times the area in 1920 although the population had only doubled. Cities such as Los Angeles, built around a road network, exemplify this trend on an even bigger scale. Another phenomenon of the period after 1920 was the tendency for industry, particularly light industry, to move out to the periphery of the major cities. The first signs of this move were apparent in Berlin as early as the 1890s, when the electrical industry moved out along some of the major waterways, but it was very noticeable later in Britain and the United States. Around London, major roads such as the A4 and A40 to the west, and areas such as Enfield and Edmonton to the north, became the focus for new industries such as medical products and radio and electronics. By the middle of the century industry had moved further out in the United States, attracted to new peripheral motorways around cities such as Boston, New York and Washington, a trend also seen around London after the construction of the M25 motorway in the 1980s. As population moved out of city centres, major new shopping facilities were built on the edges of the built-up area, largely dependent on the ability of people to travel by car, a phenomenon that started in Kansas City as early as 1922.

The growth of the city was, for the most part, unplanned, or at best loosely organised, with the authorities struggling to provide or maintain services. There were a series of attempts to influence the environment of the city or control overall numbers, for example, through slum clearance schemes, or redevelopment programmes (such as Haussmann's work in mid-nineteenth-century Paris, or the building of new towns and garden suburbs and the creation of new estates, but the forces driving urban expansion have proved very difficult to restrain or control. A formal 'Green Belt' was established around London in 1937 in an attempt to restrict the growth of the capital and preserve open countryside. Although the designated area has largely been kept free of suburban development, the consequence was that urban growth simply leapt over the belt and continued even further from the centre of the city. The area of the south-east of England that is socially and economically effectively part of 'London' is now even larger and commuting times and distances have become that much greater. The relatively feeble planning controls in Britain have only managed to avoid some of the worst excesses of urbanisation and in the United States controls have been even weaker and less effective.

The highly planned economy of the Soviet Union also proved unable to assert control over the same sort of problems in Moscow. The capital city's population grew from 275,000 in 1811 to over one million a century later when it had become an industrial city and a focus for the railway system in much the same way as Berlin. Some of the pressure for the continued outward growth of cities in the Soviet Union was contained by the construction of new towns – over 800 since 1926. (In the 1920s only one in five of the population lived in cities, now the figure is about two out of three.) Nevertheless Moscow's population doubled between 1926 and 1939 to four million, producing serious over-crowding in the centre (295,000 people per square mile) because the in-adequate transportation system limited the growth of suburbs (less than a third of the population lived outside the city centre in 1939). By the mid-1950s overcrowding was even worse than in the 1920s and new apartment block construction in the suburbs was not started till the end of the decade together with better transport. In 1935 the Soviet government decided that the population of Moscow should not be allowed to increase beyond five million (a rise of about 20 per cent). However, even with the draconian state controls under Stalin, includ-ing an internal passport system to limit movement, the authorities were unable to enforce the decision. In 1971 they decided on a maximum population of seven-and-a-half million (the then current level) with a contraction to six-and-a-half million by 2000. The current population is just over ten million and Moscow experiences the same problems as urban populations elsewhere in the world – lengthy commuting times, sprawling satellite towns and poor quality living conditions.

Urbanisation in Japan followed much the same pattern as in Europe and North America but it began later. Although Edo was one of the largest cities in the world in the mid-nineteenth century and other new cities such as Yokahama (founded in 1858 as a fishing port) were growing, Japan remained a predominantly rural country. As late as 1920 over 80 per cent of the population still lived in the countryside and not till 1955 did a majority of the population live in cities. In 1884 there were only nineteen cities with populations greater than 50,000, by 1972 there were 614 such cities. The greatest expansion occurred around Tokyo (as Edo was renamed after the Meiji restoration in 1868). Suburbs did not develop on an extensive scale until after the introduc-tion of the electric tram in 1903, and the process was reinforced by construction of an underground railway following the great fire of 1923 which destroyed much of the city. The population of the suburbs rose from just over one million in 1920 to nearly three million in 1930 as these new railways were built. By 1945 Tokyo covered an area twice as big as in 1923, by 1960 the 'green belt' had disappeared and by 1970 weakly regulated development had produced an urban area fifty miles wide.

Concentrated industrialisation in the nineteenth century, based on the exploitation of deposits of coal and other raw materials, brought about the formation of the first conurbations – large, formless, urban masses caused by the expansion and joining up of a number of smaller settlements without a single urban focus. In Britain this was first noticeable in the Black Country and the Five Towns of the Potteries by the middle of the nineteenth century. One of the most extreme examples of this form of development came in the Ruhr after the start of the deep mining of coal and the development of a railway network in the 1840s and 1850s. A mass of immigrants formed the labour force and the villages of the area grew in an unplanned fashion until, eventually, they joined together in an industrial and urban sprawl. By 1871 the population had risen to 900,000, by 1910 to three-and-a-half million and to four-and-a-half million by 1939. By the 1980s the Ruhr was an agglomeration of eleven cities and four districts, with a population of about five-and-a-half million. The individual cities retained much of

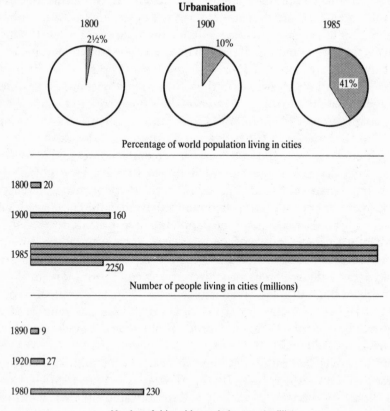

Urbanisation

1800   1900   1985

2½%   10%   41%

Percentage of world population living in cities

1800 20
1900 160
1985 2250

Number of people living in cities (millions)

1890 9
1920 27
1980 230

Number of cities with population over 1 million

their administrative independence and although a federal structure was tried for a period after 1920 it proved almost impossible to devise effective planning across such a complex area.

A similar phenomenon developed in the Netherlands in the mid-twentieth century with the creation of what is known as the *Randstad* or 'ring city'. This was brought about not by the concentration of raw materials but instead by the acute shortage of land in the Netherlands, which constrained urban growth in some areas and meant that the chief cities of the country gradually expanded until they joined together to form an almost continuous urban unit with many different functions. The *Randstad* comprises the cities of Dordrecht, Rotterdam (port/ industrial), the Hague (government), Delft, Leiden, Haarlem, Amsterdam (finance and culture) and Utrecht. This urban complex now contains a third of the population of the Netherlands living on just five per cent of the land area of the country. Urban growth in other countries has produced a similar situation. In Japan there is now an almost continuous urbanised zone between Tokyo and Kobe. In the United States there is a string of cities linking Boston and Washington DC and containing over fifty million people (about a quarter of the population) in just one-and-a-half per cent of the area of the country.

The twentieth century has also witnessed the growth of the large metropolis – a huge city, normally only one in each country, concentrating in most cases on tertiary activities rather than manufacturing, and with as many links with other major cities in the world as with the rest of the country. Worldwide the number of large cities has increased and they have themselves grown even bigger. In 1890 there were only nine cities in the world with more than one million people – London (4.2 million), New York urban area (2.7 million), Paris (2.4 million) followed by Berlin, Tokyo, Vienna, Chicago, Philadelphia and St Petersburg. By 1920 twenty-seven cities had more than one million people and five had over four million – New York (8 million), London (7.2 million), Paris (4.9 million), Tokyo and Berlin (both 4 million). By 1960 there were sixteen cities over four million with the largest being New York (14.1 million) and Tokyo (13.5 million). In the 1980s there were twenty-six cities in the world with populations over five million. New York and Tokyo were both over 20 million and there were eight other cities larger than ten million (Peking, Buenos Aires, Cairo, Los Angeles, Mexico City, Sao Paulo, Shanghai and Seoul). The scale of the urbanisation in the world can be judged from the fact that in the early 1980s there were 230 cities with populations greater than one million – a twenty-five-fold increase in less than a century at a time when the world's population roughly tripled.

Although the urban population of the world as a whole has increased throughout the twentieth century, a new phenomenon emerged in the industrialised world in the second half of the century – a small, but noticeable decline in the importance of cities. In nearly all the countries of the industrialised world the number of people living in cities peaked at about 75–85 per cent of the population. The exact timing varied from country to country depending on the starting point for urban growth and the pace of change – Britain reached this level at the end of the nineteenth century, others much later. The population of London, not just in the inner city but in the suburbs too, began to decline in the 1950s and that trend has continued ever since. Paris experienced the same trend later – it lost 11 per cent of its population between 1968 and 1975. This drift of people away from the cities to the rural areas is also apparent in Germany, Canada and the Netherlands, and in Britain the proportion of the population living in cities has been falling since the 1960s.

In 1900 two-thirds of the world's urban population lived in Europe, North America and Australasia, now only about a third do so. The twentieth century has witnessed the urbanisation of the Third World, and this has happened at far faster rates than in the developed world in the preceding century. In the nineteenth century the fastest rate of growth in the urban population was 2½ per cent a year but in the twentieth century the Third World's equivalent annual growth rates were 3 per cent before 1940 and then 4 per cent (the latter figure is enough to double the urban population every eighteen years). In some countries, major cities have increased in size at even faster rates. In Nigeria the population of Lagos rose sixteen-fold between 1950 and 1985 and in Mauretania the population of Nouakchott increased forty-fold in the twenty years after 1965. Overall, the most rapidly urbanised area in the world has been Latin America with growth rates of over five per cent a year in the 1950s. In 1920 less than ten per cent of the population of Asia and Africa and only fourteen per cent of those in Latin America lived in cities with more than 20,000 people. By the 1980s about two-thirds of the people of Latin America lived in cities (not far short of European levels), some countries such as Argentina and Uruguay were as urbanised as Europe and only Haiti, Honduras and Bolivia remained predominantly rural. Asia and Africa though remain mainly rural – about a third of the population live in cities. But these percentage increases disguise very high absolute increases in urban numbers because of the high rates of population growth.

Migration to the cities of the Third World has not alleviated many rural problems in the way that it did in nineteenth century Europe, largely because of the continuing increase in the rural population and a tendency to focus scarce resources on the urban populace. Mortality in the cities is in most cases lower than rural mortality levels (unlike Europe in the last century). This has been brought about partly by the provision of higher standards of water and sanitation than in rural areas. In the Third World in the early 1980s 74 per cent of the urban population had access to some form of water supply (though this is officially defined as a tap no more than 100 yards away), compared with 39 per cent of the rural population, and for sanitation the figures were 52 per cent and 14 per cent respectively. This has meant that cities have become self-sustaining in terms of numbers rather than depending on continued migration from the countryside. Third World cities also tend to have better food supplies for political reasons (rather like ancient Rome, though without the circuses). The result is that they often dominate the economies of their countries – for example Abidjan in the Ivory Coast accounts for 70 per cent of all the economic activity in the country although only 15 per cent of the population live there. But in many other ways the cities of the Third World are very similar to those of Europe in the early stages of industrialisation. Rapid growth rates have placed immense strains on the infrastructure. Unemployment in many cities affects twenty per cent of the people and in some it is higher still. Cities also reflect the immense social inequalities found generally in developing countries, particularly in Latin America. In Lima twenty per cent of the families in the city earn just one-and-a-half per cent of the total income. Housing, however, is probably the most significant problem. In India about one-and-a-half million people live on the streets because, although many have jobs, they are so badly paid that they can not afford housing. Altogether in the Third World at least a third of the urban population, and probably more, live in illegal squatter settlements thrown up by the squatters themselves, usually on land designated as unsuitable for housing by the authorities, with few of the basic facilities such as sewage, water supply and schools available. Again this problem is a matter of poverty – houses are built but even those constructed by the state are too expensive for most people.

Developments in the last two centuries have meant the environment in which almost half the world's people are now living is urban. At the beginning of the period about ninety-eight per cent of the people in the world lived in the countryside, now only about half do so and in the industrialised world between two-thirds and three-quarters of the population are city dwellers. Large areas of countryside have been destroyed by the spread of houses, factories, roads and shopping centres across what were once fields and open spaces. Large quantities of energy and raw materials have been consumed in building and sustaining the cities and in moving millions of people to and from work each day. With their vast agglomerations of people on an unprecedented scale, cities have created their own, highly artificial environments. Cities have many benefits – they are usually the centres of cultural activity and have a much wider range of facilities than rural areas. Cities have, however, always created environmental problems and these have intensified in the last two centuries, new ones have developed and more people have been affected by them. The rapid growth of large cities has brought about major environmental deterioration in terms of living conditions, health and pollution (which will be considered in detail in the next two chapters). Although in some working class areas strong, but informal, means of community support developed, in general the flood of people into cities destroyed many community bonds or institutions without creating new ones capable of helping and sustaining the inhabitants. Cities, as the nineteenth century American philosopher Henry David Thoreau wrote, tend to be places characterised by 'millions of people being lonely together'.

In the industrialised world increasing wealth and better social provision have eliminated some of the worst aspects of urban life that are still found in the Third World. But in the twentieth century new and more complex problems have emerged. Public transport played a crucial role in the development of cities. However the twentieth century has been marked by the decline of public transport in many cities, particularly in Britain and the United States, and the increasing domination of the car. Not only has this transformed the suburbs by allowing them to spread over even larger areas away from railway lines and increased the length of commuter journeys, it has also altered the nature of the inner cities as the urban environment has had to accommodate ever increasing numbers of cars. Two-thirds of central Los Angeles is now occupied by streets, freeways, parking facilities and garages and a similar remaking of the urban environment has been repeated in many other cities. The overwhelming domination of the car in urban transportation has not made the system any more efficient or speedier. In 1907 the average speed of traffic in New York was 11½ miles an hour but by the 1960s this had fallen to about 6 miles an hour. In London traffic now flows as slowly as it did at the end of the nineteenth century, in Paris it is slower.

The economic decline of cities, particularly the inner sectors, has led to immense social pressures. The inner cities of Britain lost over 500,000 jobs in the 1960s, New York lost eleven per cent of its employment between 1969 and 1975 and the trend has continued in many cities in the last two decades. People in the inner cities have suffered from a bad environment, poverty, economic decline and social problems, caught in a vicious circle of continuing decay. In New York a quarter of the population has an income below the official poverty line, 90,000 people sleep on the streets every night, there are 500,000 drug addicts and only one in five babies born in Harlem is legitimate. In central Indianapolis the picture is much the same – 27 per cent of families live in poverty, 40 per cent have only one parent, 22 per cent are unemployed, 36 per cent of the houses lack proper sanitation and two-thirds of households do not own a car and therefore have to rely on a decaying public transport system. The picture is much the same in the centre of Britain's cities – in Islington in central London nearly half of the households in the late 1970s lacked their own hot water, bath or inside lavatory. A poor environment means that it can be very difficult to sustain other essential public services. In the black ghetto of Watts in Los Angeles the number of doctors per head is only a fifth of the national average. In Tokyo commuting and housing are the two main urban problems. Three million commuters a day have to depend on an inadequate transportation network built before 1940 and only slightly improved since then in order to get people to work. The average family lives in a block of flats with only a tenth of the space of a European flat, many with shared lavatories and kitchens. Nearly a third of these flats are officially designated as sub-standard even by Japanese criteria.

The rise of cities is a phenomenon linked to the exploitation of fossil fuels and industrialisation in the nineteenth century, together with the development of greater trade and more complex financial transactions on a national and eventually a worldwide scale. Despite increasing wealth in the industrialised world, cities have become areas where environmental problems, in many cases specific to urban life, are concentrated. These range from air pollution from vehicles, to poor living conditions exemplified by estates consisting of large tower blocks of flats with people crowded together with often limited living space (a marked characteristic of Japan and the Soviet Union), long commuting journeys often on inadequate public transportation systems, excessive noise and the multitude of social problems that flow from growing unemployment, social inequality and urban decline in the city centres. Most of the people who live in cities – about three-quarters of the population of the industrialised world and half of the people of the world as a whole – are now subjected to such problems on a daily basis.

15

CREATING THE AFFLUENT SOCIETY

Since the rise of settled societies some eight to ten thousand years ago the majority of the world's population have lived in conditions of grinding poverty. They have had few possessions, suffered from miserable living conditions and have been forced to spend most of their limited resources on obtaining enough food to stay alive. Although in all societies the elite have lived at a higher standard than the overwhelming mass of the population, they too only had access to a very limited range of goods and services for most of human history. However in the last two hundred years a sizeable minority of the world's population has achieved a material standard of living that would have been unimaginable for previous generations. But this relatively sudden and recent improvement has been obtained at a significant price – a vast increase in the consumption of the world's limited energy resources and raw materials, widespread pollution from the industrial processes involved and a variety of social problems. In addition, it has raised major questions of equity about the distribution of wealth within individual countries and about the comparative standards of living in the industrialised world and the Third World.

Gathering and hunting groups keep possessions to a minimum since these are a hindrance to their mobile way of life. They may wear a few pieces of jewellery but most of their household goods are simple, made from easily obtained materials, to be thrown away when necessary and quickly replaced if needed again. Modern studies have shown that these groups have little interest in acquiring more goods since they value their mobility more highly. The adoption of agriculture and the rise of settled communities changed this situation in two ways. First, agriculture required more goods to be made, especially to store and process food. Second, a sedentary way of life made it much easier to acquire more household and personal effects – they were no longer seen as a hindrance but a benefit. Some of the main evidence for the structure of early settled societies comes from analysis of the goods found in their burial sites. The earliest agricultural communities appear to have been relatively egalitarian but social differences increased fairly quickly to produce clear distinctions between the possessions of the religious and political elite and those of the mass of peasant farmers.

Until the last two centuries all societies in the world have been overwhelmingly agricultural. Average income was very low and most of the spare resources were devoted to elite consumption or directed into major public projects such as the great temples, palaces and pyramids of ancient societies or the cathedrals of medieval Europe. Limited trade and transport meant that regional and local self-sufficiency were vitally important and most people had little contact with a money economy. (This was one of the reasons why feudalism became so important in early medieval Europe and many other societies – the granting of land in return for military service was virtually the only way a military force could be supported.) People tried to be as self-sufficient as possible, even inhabitants of small towns kept their own animals and grew their own crops, and most local trade was barter – generally the exchange of farm produce for local crafts. Most goods that were produced were consumables and closely related to agricultural production – food, drink, clothes, candles and a few raw materials. As late as 1600, 80 per cent of England's exports were cloth and its four main imports were textiles, groceries, timber and wine. Trade was at a low level – most states did not have nationally agreed weights and measures and in early medieval Europe most of the continent's north-south trade was done in a few days at the fairs of Champagne. International trade was for the most part restricted to a few high value products. The range of goods available to all members of these societies was therefore extremely small.

In medieval and early modern Europe (and conditions in China and India were similar in this period) about 80 per cent of the expenditure of the mass of the population went on food but the diet was still poor. About half of this expenditure went on buying bread, which was often baked only every month or two (in the Tyrol two to three times a year and it was often cut using an axe). A rapid rise in food prices due to a poor harvest could quickly drive food expenditure to a hundred per cent of income and even that might not be enough to stay alive. In these conditions it is not surprising that occasional bouts of feasting, especially at major events such as harvest and wedding celebrations, when meat might be eaten, played a vitally important social role. Even in relatively prosperous times people might have no more than ten per cent of their income to spend on clothing, so that garments could become important items to be handed on to the next generation. For example the hospital regulations in Perugia in 1582 provided that the clothes of the deceased should not be usurped 'but should be given to lawful inheritors'.

Once food and clothing had been provided for, very little money was left for housing. The average peasant hut was made out of wattle and daub, with an earth floor, no windows or chimney and cooking was done on a spit or a pot over an open hearth. Few people had ovens, and bread (and meat, if available) would usually be baked communally. For bedding there might be heaps of straw or bracken on the floor. Living quarters were often shared with the few animals a peasant might own. Even in nineteenth-century England there was still dense overcrowding in rural areas and the conditions in Ireland were even worse. Conditions in the cities were worse still. In Florence in the 1630s houses in the poorest quarter contained about eight to ten people to a room, ten to twelve families in each house, making a total of about a hundred inhabitants, all without water and sanitation. Although the rich might avoid the worst of these conditions, the range of goods and services available to them was still highly restricted. Most of their wealth was spent on housing (which would be more spacious and built out of stone or timber but still lacking most modern facilities), better clothing and more elaborate food. They could also afford to employ servants, sometimes in large numbers – in 1393 the monastery of Meaux had twenty-six monks and forty domestic servants. The employment of a large number of servants remained a mark of social distinction until well into the twentieth century. In eighteenth-century European cities, on average about thirteen per cent of the population was engaged in domestic service.

Most people, though, lived either in a state of destitution or on the edge of it. They had no savings and so the slightest problem such as illness or unemployment would reduce them to starvation and begging. Little help could be expected from charity – the best estimate is that about one per cent of national wealth was devoted to charitable causes at this period, and that monasteries were giving between one and three per cent of their wealth to charity. Official returns in Florence in 1457 (when the 'Renaissance' was flourishing) showed that 82 per cent of the population were classified as either poor or destitute. Similar figures are recorded for the rest of Europe over the succeeding centuries. In 1698 at Vauban in France beggars made up 10 per cent of the population, near beggars 30 per cent and the very poor 50 per cent. In eighteenth-century France it has been estimated that about half the population was permanently destitute. In early eighteenth-century Cologne, there were 20,000 beggars out of a population of 50,000. In England in the 1690s a quarter of the population was described as 'cottagers and paupers' in a permanent state of poverty and unemployment – 'miserable people and (harvest time excepted) without any subsistence'. At times of poor harvest and bad trade about half the people would be reduced to this condition. As late as 1815 in Sweden it was estimated that half the population were either landless peasants or beggars. In these circumstances people could not always afford to keep all their children – in sixteenth and seventeenth-century Italian cities about ten per cent of all babies were abandoned on the streets and estimates from Paris in 1780 suggest a figure of about 8,000 abandoned children or nearly a quarter of all births.

Most of the population (about 90 per cent) worked in agriculture. Life expectancy was low, only about five per cent of the population was over sixty-five, whereas a third was under fourteen and so child labour was essential, particularly in the fields in the summer and during the harvest. The bulk of the population was illiterate, most children were lucky if they had some form of education between the ages of five and seven. The age for starting on apprenticeships varied, in some cases it was as low as seven but most apprentices were taken on at about ten or twelve years old. Children, orphans in particular, were vulnerable to exploitation – the cloth manufacturers of Leiden imported 8,000 orphans from Aachen, Julich and Liege in the thirty years after 1638 in order to keep wage levels down. The result was that adults were put out of work and the children died rapidly in the grim working conditions. Women worked too (about eighty per cent of the wool weavers in Florence in the early seventeenth century were female), especially in the rural areas where they did piecework in the home to supplement meagre agricultural earnings. But women were also employed in brickyards, arsenals and metal works. Work in industry for both sexes was only available in a few areas, and then often only intermittently, and wages were usually only just enough for subsistence – in the eighteenth century lace-making in the Massif Central (an intricate operation that almost always produced blindness eventually in the workers) paid about two sous a day at a time when that would buy about a pound of bread if the harvest had been adequate.

To some extent the standard of living for people fluctuated over time, depending mainly on the relationship between population and food supplies; there was no steady improvement in the human condition. In

1300 when Europe was severely overpopulated living conditions were very poor with food supplies overstretched and an excess of labour reduced the chances of finding work. Then with the severe population decline due to the Black Death, conditions improved for a while until numbers increased again to reach levels during the sixteenth century near to the medieval peak. There followed times of great hardship in most parts of Europe, made worse by the deterioration in the climate. From the seventeenth century onwards some areas of the continent did begin to see a rise in living standards as improvements in agricultural productivity, more trade and manufacturing and the expropriation of non-European resources increased wealth. The increase was small, very unevenly distributed and largely confined to the Netherlands, England and France. In the rest of Europe conditions probably continued to stagnate or even deteriorate.

By 1800 England and some parts of the continent had developed significant commercial and industrial enterprises and were on the verge of becoming industrial as opposed to agricultural societies. There is no doubt that large-scale industrialisation did, eventually, raise the material standard of living for the population at large (though far more for some than for others). However, this process of industrialisation, which requires substantial capital investment, often in conditions where it is difficult to mobilise the necessary resources, usually led initially to a deterioration in the standard of living for the majority of the population. This process can be illustrated by comparing the experiences of two very different societies – what happened under the essentially free market capitalism of nineteenth-century England and the state-directed, industrial expansion in the Soviet Union in the twentieth century. (The next chapter will also show how both types of society experienced many of the same environmental problems associated with industrialisation and its aftermath.)

The first stages of industrialisation in England in the early nineteenth century brought about the rapid rise of new manufacturing cities with an increasing proportion of the workforce employed in factories. But there is no conclusive evidence of any improvement in living standards for the bulk of the population before the late 1840s at the earliest. Throughout this period, because of a glutted labour market, about half of the industrial working class lived at or below subsistence level, surviving on casual, part-time work, and only a small elite of skilled craftsmen in steady jobs were able to improve their position. Many, such as the handloom weavers (about 500,000 people), suffered an almost complete collapse in their trade following mechanisation. Few workers had reserves of money or many possessions to pawn in times of recession when unemployment in some trades reached about 75 per cent. In the 1840s about 10 per cent of the population of England were still paupers (in the 1860s it fell to 5 per cent) and in some towns it was much higher – 20 per cent in Nottingham and at Clitheroe in Lancashire in 1842 during an industrial depression it was estimated that 2,300 people out of a total population of 6,700 were paupers. Living conditions in the industrial cities were squalid as workers flooding in to try and find jobs swamped the inadequate housing available. In Liverpool in 1790 one in eight of the population lived in cellars and conditions in the common lodging houses were even worse. In Manchester in 1833 there were about 20,000 people living in cellars (over ten per cent of the population). Not surprisingly mortality rates rose in the period 1810–1850 and only then began a slow decline. In 1840, 57 per cent of the working class children in Manchester died before the age of five (compared with 32 per cent in rural areas).

In the second half of the nineteenth century living conditions for the bulk of the population slowly improved but many still lived in almost permanent want and in sub-standard housing. In 1889 it was estimated that about a third of the population of London lived below the poverty line and were 'at all times more or less in want' and a survey in York in 1901 revealed the same proportion of the population living in poverty (by the 1930s this was about ten per cent). The diet of the poor was still seriously deficient. In 1800 boys recruited into the Royal Navy from the slums were, on average, eight inches shorter than their upper class contemporaries; in 1940 working class children were still four inches shorter than those attending public schools. In the late nineteenth century it was estimated that the poorest sections of the community had about half the calorie intake of the richest. In 1899 when 11,000 Manchester men tried to enlist in the army to serve in the Boer War, only 1,000 were deemed fit enough to be accepted. In 1914 an official survey estimated that over ten per cent of children had defective nutrition, and diseases such as scurvy, anaemia and rickets, all caused by poor diet, were common during this period. As late as the 1930s the British Medical Association calculated that a third of the British population did not have an income high enough to purchase the minimum diet recommended by the League of Nations to ensure good health.

Housing remained a severe problem. In the British census of 1901 for conditions to qualify as 'overcrowded' there had to be a household of at least two adults and four children living in two rooms without their own water supply and sanitation. Even on this restrictive definition 8 per cent of the population was officially designated as overcrowded and in the areas of greatest deprivation the figure was far higher – the London average was recorded as 16 per cent, (some boroughs such as Finsbury reached 35 per cent), Glasgow was 55 per cent and Dundee 63 per cent. Statistics from the other industrialising countries of Europe and North America reveal that conditions were similar – in New York for example the annual infant mortality rate rose from 120 per thousand in 1810 to 240 per thousand in 1870, when the legal requirement for new tenement blocks was to provide one lavatory for every twenty inhabitants and one tap per block and people on the Lower East Side were living at a density of 1,400 to the acre.

The peasants and proletariat in the Soviet Union went through the process of industrialisation at a later stage than the agricultural labourers and the working class in Britain, and the process was managed differently, but the immediate effects were very similar. The social strains in the Soviet Union were undoubtedly intensified because the leadership deliberately decided to undertake the initial phase of industrialisation at a speed unprecedented in the rest of the world and because they had the political power to enforce that decision. Russia had experienced fairly rapid industrial growth between 1860 and 1913 – industrial output rose at about five per cent a year. Following the disruption of war, revolution, civil war and the period of war communism the economy recovered in the more liberal NEP phase to reach 1913 levels of output again by 1927. Throughout the 1920s the debate within the Soviet leadership on industrialisation assumed that the investment capital required would, with little help from the west and in the absence of colonies to exploit, have to come from the agricultural sector. This was inevitable since eighty per cent of the population were peasants and farmers; the industrial working class, in whose name the revolution had been undertaken, only made up 3 per cent.

The first Five Year Plan of 1928 proposed a 236 per cent increase in industrial output and a 110 per cent increase in labour productivity. Increases on this scale could only be achieved by mass mobilisation of agricultural workers into industry. On the surface the first intense phase of Soviet industrialisation between 1927 and 1937 was extremely successful – iron output quadrupled, coal production rose three-and-a-half-fold, electric power generation increased seven-fold and the output of machine tools was seventeen times higher at the end of the period than at the beginning. The industrial labour force doubled in just five years between 1928 and 1932. However, the consequences for

those involved in the process were disastrous. The forced collectivisation of farms led to millions of deaths through starvation in the
countryside and the condition of the industrial workers and urban
dwellers was little better. Although there was unemployment of about
ten per cent in the NEP period in the late 1920s industrial workers had
their highest standard of living ever – real wages were at least ten per
cent higher than in 1913 and the average working day had fallen from
ten hours to seven-and-a-half. Rapid industrialisation after 1928
quickly produced a labour shortage and the need for greater productivity through the introduction of longer hours, a continuous working
week, increased output quotas, 'shock brigades', 'socialist competition'
and the 'deprivileging' of skilled workers. Not only did working conditions worsen drastically so did the standard of living. Food rationing
was introduced and by 1932 urban meat consumption was at a third of
its 1928 levels and even potato consumption fell in 1932. The living
standards of industrial workers fell drastically – their real wages in
Moscow were at 53 per cent of their 1928 level by 1932 and had only
recovered to 63 per cent by 1937. Even after the 1930s industrial output
continued to grow at about 9 per cent a year and although the Soviet
economy was about seven times bigger in the 1960s than it was thirty
years earlier, the living standards of the people had only recovered to
the levels of the late 1920s by the mid-1950s. Housing remained
woefully inadequate and although central planning had been successful
at increasing production in basic industries (though overall no better
than the unplanned economies of the nineteenth century) it failed
lamentably at producing consumer goods.

Industrialisation took a long time to improve the standard of living
for most people. Its more immediate impact was to drastically alter
their working patterns – here the changes in the free market economies
in the nineteenth century were slower to take effect but just as far
reaching as in the Soviet Union in the 1930s. In pre-industrial Europe
levels of industrial production and labour productivity were both low
and with demand also at a low level there was little incentive to change.
There were plenty of holidays scattered through the year, many
associated with religious festivals – the Carinthian iron industry only
worked about 100 eight hour shifts a year and in Paris, for example, in
1660 there were 103 holidays in the year. The tempo of work before the
introduction of the factory was also much more intermittent and in
industry the pace tended to vary during the week – on Mondays very
little work was done but towards the end of the week longer hours were
worked.

The growth of factory labour slowly changed this pattern. The essence of the new system was standardisation and discipline, especially time-discipline. Although not unknown before, clocking in to work was initiated on a large scale by Josiah Wedgwood at his factories in the Potteries in the eighteenth century. As early as 1700 the Crawley ironworks in Newcastle had drawn up a 100,000 word code of conduct for its employees to follow. In the 'putting-out' trades the self-employed workers retained some degree of choice about how and when they worked, but under the factory system the owner was able to dictate the hours and methods of work of the employees by using fines or the threat of dismissal to enforce the new rhythm of work. Such methods were first widely applied in the textile trades, although even here much of the work was still done in the home or in small 'sweated workshops'. In the mid-nineteenth century large areas of industrial output such as the metal trades of Sheffield and Birmingham were still organised on a small scale and most consumer goods were still handmade. As more employers turned to factory production to increase output they employed large numbers of women and children. The employment of women and children was not new: they had both worked extensively in virtually every society. Before the nineteenth century most female industrial labour had taken place in the home as part of the putting-out trades. By the mid-nineteenth century about 40 per cent of the female population was in work (although 40 per cent of them were in domestic service). Industrialisation in the Soviet Union also increased the number of women in work – they went from a quarter of the workforce in 1928 to half by the mid-1960s. In nineteenth century England about a third of all children under fifteen worked. Legislation sought to eliminate the worst abuses (not child labour itself), for instance by prohibiting children under eight working in mills or those under ten working underground. Child labour was not significantly reduced in the industrialised world until the introduction of compulsory education.

The factory system and large-scale production became the norm during the second half of the nineteenth century. Factories changed the nature of work significantly. The first machine tools (automatic lathes) were introduced in the United States in the 1840s and were widely used in Europe by the 1870s, although the real boom in their use was linked to the mass production of bicycles in the 1890s. Increasingly the use of machine tools fragmented jobs into simple, often repetitive tasks, that could be undertaken by semi-skilled or even unskilled labour. Jobs were therefore de-skilled, a process taken further by the introduction of assembly line techniques, epitomised by the Ford car factory in the early twentieth century. The consequence of growing mechanisation was that the pace of work was increasingly dictated by machines and by the managers of factories who wanted to make the best use of expensive equipment. The late nineteenth century was also to see the start of techniques to measure the performance and efficiency of workers and to set production norms. This was first done by Frederick Taylor at the Midvale Steel Works in Pennsylvania in the 1880s and 'Taylorism' or scientific management set the scene for the production methods of the twentieth century; they even fascinated Lenin who thought it should be the framework for the industrialisation of the Soviet Union.

For thousands of years, low agricultural productivity severely limited the amount of wealth created and with it the number of non-producers any society could support. The combined effect of increased agricultural output, greater productivity within industry stemming from a higher capital input (an American factory worker now produces five times more than his counterpart a century ago) greatly increased the number of non-productive (in agricultural and industrial terms) workers that could be supported. The twentieth century has, therefore, seen a massive growth in the tertiary economic sector, especially service areas such as finance, advertising and tourism. It has also supported a huge growth in other areas that have improved the quality of life for everybody – education (now compulsory in nearly all industrialised countries till the age of sixteen), health care and social care. In 1900, 25 per cent of the American workforce was engaged in tertiary occupations; by the 1960s it was 56 per cent.

Industrialisation has involved a succession of new technologies and industries that have changed the number and the type of goods available to society, and these in turn have impinged on the environment in many different ways. In agricultural societies trade and manufacturing were mainly limited to products derived from primary production such as foodstuffs and textiles. The first phase of large-scale industrialisation (which lasted until about the end of the nineteenth century) involved greater output of textiles and iron and steel, and it also introduced new technologies such as steam engineering, railways and heavy chemical production. In the earliest phases, however, the emphasis was on finding ways to produce textiles more quickly and more cheaply than before through increasing mechanisation and factory production. As late as 1900 food and textiles still accounted for over 40 per cent of all industrial production in both western Europe and the United States (they now account for less than 20 per cent). From the 1840s steam

engineering and in particular railways played a major role in industrialisation in Britain and other countries. In 1840 there were 45,000
miles of railways in the world but the figure had risen to 228,000 miles
forty years later.

By the late nineteenth century the industries that had formed the
backbone of the first wave of large-scale industrialisation were beginning to stagnate – indeed twentieth-century Europe and North America
have witnessed the steady decline of industries such as textiles manufactured from natural fibres and heavy industries such as shipbuilding in
relative terms, and in some cases, there has even been an absolute
decline. New industries that formed the second wave, such as chemicals
derived from organic materials, electrical engineering and car production, were developing at the end of the nineteenth century. These
industries were the key to the continued growth in output in the first
half of the twentieth century. In addition there was a rise in both the
output and variety of artificial fibres in place of natural fibres. The first
technological steps in this process were taken in the 1890s and both
cellulose fibre and rayon were being manufactured before 1914. Rayon
production increased markedly in the 1920s when it could be made for a
quarter of the price of silk. After the Second World War nylon
manufacture showed a similar rapid increase. After 1945 there was also
a phenomenal rise in plastic production. World production of plastics
has, on average, doubled every twelve years. By the 1970s it exceeded
the combined production of aluminium, copper, lead and zinc, and per
capita consumption had increased by over one thousand per cent since
1945. The second half of the twentieth century has been characterised
by the growth of new industries such as electronics, communications
and computers that form the third wave of modern industrialisation.

The massive upsurge in industrial output has been one of the most
striking features of human history in the last two centuries. Its increasing pace can be judged from the fact that world industrial production is
now fifty times greater than in the 1890s, and eighty per cent of that
growth has come since 1950. The world has seen an ever-increasing,
indeed almost bewildering variety, of products that industry can
conceive, design and persuade the public to buy. The technology and
machinery involved have often been highly sophisticated, but the basic
inputs remain what they have always been. At the heart of the industrialisation process has been a huge increase in energy consumption
(especially coal and oil) and the use of ever greater quantities of metals.

The development of metal-working technologies, although not a prerequisite for complex societies (those of pre-Columbian America had no metal tools), is an early feature of the rise of settled societies throughout Eurasia. Lead smelting was known as early as 6400 BC at Çatal Hüyük and copper smelting from about 3700 BC in north-west Iran – within a thousand years bronze was common across the whole of Eurasia from Britain to China. The much more difficult technical process of iron manufacture was known for some time before it was adopted on a major scale in Anatolia around 1200 BC by the Hittites, probably induced by an interruption in tin supplies from the east which they needed for bronze production. Within a few centuries iron was in common use for weapons and agricultural implements. But output remained small for another two thousand years, probably reflecting both limited demand and the production difficulties associated with small-scale furnaces and the need to use high grade ore because of the limitations of early smelting processes. In 1400, European production of iron was about 30,000 tons. China, the other major producer in the world, probably made about the same amount, and so total world production would have been substantially less than 100,000 tons a year. Between 1400 and 1700, European iron output rose about six-fold to reach nearly 200,000 tons a year (it was produced using charcoal and was therefore one of the main causes of the growing shortage of wood). Chinese production had increased very little and Britain's North American colonies made about 30,000 tons a year. At the beginning of the eighteenth century total world production of iron is unlikely to have exceeded 300,000 tons a year.

In the next three centuries a multitude of new uses for iron, and later steel (after the discovery in the mid-nineteenth century of how to make a harder alloy) formed the basis for most of the key products of modern industrial society – machines, railways, vehicles, buildings, ships, industrial plant, domestic appliances and many other consumer goods. What has happened to the output of iron and steel is therefore a good indicator of the scale of industrial production. The onset of the first stages of substantial industrialisation in Britain was marked by a rapid increase in iron output – production increased ten-fold between 1788 and 1830, from 68,000 tons a year to about 700,000 tons (twice as much as the whole world produced only a hundred years earlier). By the middle of the nineteenth century, world production was about 12 million tons a year (forty times higher than in 1700). Huge though this increase was, it pales into insignificance compared with what occurred over the next century. By 1980, world production of iron and steel had reached a combined total of 1,200 million tons (about 500 million tons of iron and 700 million tons of steel) – a one hundred-fold increase. The overall increase in production since the first rough estimates of world output are available in 1400 is a staggering 40,000-fold.

Industrial demand for other metals has also increased, especially in the twentieth century as new industrial processes have been developed. Between 1900 and 1960 more minerals were mined than in the rest of human history and output has continued to rise since then. Three-quarters of all the gold ever mined has been produced in the twentieth century. World production of copper, estimated at about 120,000 tons a year in the 1880s, rose rapidly with the development of the electrical industries and car production to reach about two-and-a-half million tons in the 1940s and eight-and-a-half million tons by the 1980s (a seventy-fold increase). The production of nickel, which is mainly used to harden steel, has increased from about 25 million pounds a year in the 1920s to 1,800 million pounds in the 1980s (a seventy-two-fold increase). Manganese consumption has increased eight-fold since the 1940s and zinc about three-and-a-half times in the same period. Aluminium was not produced until the late nineteenth century with the development of the electrolytic process to refine alumina from bauxite ore. Its many uses now range from household utensils and drinks cans to aeroplane parts. World production in 1895 was just 223 tons. By 1928 this had risen to 250,000 tons, then it expanded to 7 million in 1947, exceeding 20 million tons a year by the 1980s. Recycling of metals is significant in some areas, particularly copper and aluminium, where cost pressures give industry an incentive to re-use materials, but in most cases metals are still extracted, used and thrown away.

The massive increase in mining operations to produce metals on this scale has inevitably made a major and highly visible impact on the environment. About 70 per cent of the world's ore (95 per cent in the United States) is obtained by the most environmentally damaging of all methods – open-cast mining. This keeps costs down but it involves the digging of vast pits or the removal of whole mountain tops, the destruction of topsoil and the creation of large amounts of waste. This waste can cause problems other than the sight of large slag heaps: it can cause rivers to silt up and valleys to be filled in, it is often toxic and therefore creates an uncultivatable desert or leaches into water courses and poisons them. The history of mining has been characterised by exploitation of the richest and easiest seams and then moving operations on to new areas once these were worked out. In medieval Europe the Erzegebirge was the centre of mining activity but by the late fifteenth century all the best mines were exhausted and new sources of supply had to be found from further afield such as Swedish copper, Russian iron ore, and gold and silver from the Americas. As new technologies have made it possible to utilise lower grades of ore, new areas have been opened up for exploitation, and in some cases it has become possible to return to previously mined areas which had been abandoned as un-economic. The trend towards exploiting ever lower grades of ore has been particularly marked in the twentieth century. It has meant producing increasing quantities of waste and consuming increasing quantities of energy. For example in 1900 the minimum mineral content for workable ore was three per cent copper but by the late 1970s this had fallen to 0.35 per cent copper. What this means is that in order to obtain a ton of copper about 300 tons of rock has to be broken, transported and milled and then the same quantity of waste has to be disposed of. All of this activity requires a very high energy input – about four tons of coal (or its equivalent) to produce one ton of copper.

Increased industrial production and energy consumption have generated steadily increasing material wealth in society, and with it has come a transformation in the living standards of the population of the industrialised world. The vast expansion in the range and quantity of goods available is reflected in the development of shops and retail outlets. In medieval Europe the limited amount of trade that did take place was almost entirely local, conducted mainly at fairs and markets with a few pedlars touring the rural areas. Only in the largest cities was there enough demand and wealth to support any permanent retail outlets. In the sixteenth and seventeenth centuries large towns such as Paris and London witnessed the development of a few specialised shops; these dealt mainly with clothing and jewellery. Items such as furniture were normally made by craftsmen and sold direct. Shops in provincial towns developed even more slowly. But greater wealth gradually increased the amount and range of goods available. As late as the end of the nineteenth century most food was still sold in markets rather than in shops, normally brought direct from the farm by the producer. Shops remained highly specialised, linked to one particular trade and normally run by an individual proprietor.

In the last hundred years retailing has been transformed by changes affecting the goods sold and the ownership of the shops selling these goods. First, there has been increasing standardisation as items have been mass-produced by large manufacturers. The shopkeeper has therefore tended to become someone who sells products made and advertised by others. At its most extreme this trend has produced some products such as Coca-Cola, MacDonalds hamburgers or Kentucky

Fried Chicken which are promoted, recognised and sold all over the world. The second trend has been the rise of shops that are part of large chains. In Britain this began in the food sector with companies such as Liptons and Home and Colonial becoming established across the country in the late nineteenth century. This period also witnessed the development of large multiple networks selling a wide range of different products. The department store was a French invention (starting with Bon Marché in Paris in the 1860s) which spread rapidly across the world with stores such as Hermansky in Vienna and Tietz in Berlin. Many existing retailers such as Harrods (originally a grocer's shop) and Debenhams (originally a draper's) diversified and new stores such as Selfridges and the Army and Navy were also established. These new stores depended on a number of technical improvements such as gas (later electric) lighting and lifts plus an increasingly prosperous middle class able to afford the wide range of products being offered for sale. The twentieth century has seen this trend to bigger stores stocking a huge product range develop further with the rise first of the super-market and then, with increasing car ownership, of the out-of-town shopping centre and the hypermarket (again a French invention with chains such as Mamouth and Carrefour).

The twentieth century has witnessed the rise of a whole range of new industries to supply so-called consumer durables. Most of these indus-tries developed first in the United States, where greater wealth pro-duced a mass market early in the century. The 1920s marked the start of the consumer durable boom (expenditure on such items doubled during the decade) and refrigerators and washing machines became common in wealthier American homes. In Europe, the boom did not begin until the 1950s and in Japan, not until a decade later. In Japan, in the 1960s, the proportion of households owning refrigerators shot up from 5 per cent to 93 per cent; for washing machines the leap was from 29 per cent to 96 per cent and for televisions 16 per cent to 75 per cent). Virtual saturation point for these new products was soon reached – by the 1980s in West Germany 90 per cent of households had a telephone, 84 per cent a car, 83 per cent a refrigerator, 80 per cent an automatic washing machine and 70 per cent a colour television. However expendi-ture on consumer goods has been maintained at high levels through the development and introduction of new products. Since the 1970s the growth areas have tended to be in electronics – video recorders, video cameras, portable cassette players, personal computers, portable telephones and compact discs.

The new product that has had the greatest industrial and social impact in the twentieth century has been the car. At the beginning of the century there were only a few thousand cars in the world (in 1900 the United States had 8,000 and in Japan there were just sixty-two in 1909) and they were built in small quantities by several hundred firms (in 1908 there were over 250 American car manufacturers). The development of assembly line manufacturing techniques, epitomised by Ford's Highland Park factory in Detroit, greatly increased output and reduced prices – a Model T Ford cost 825 dollars in 1908 but only 345 dollars eight years later. The result was a boom in demand – car ownership grew from 79,000 in the United States in 1905 to ten million by 1921. By the 1920s US car ownership rates were already at levels not approached in Europe until the 1950s and four-fifths of the market was in the hand of three giant firms – General Motors, Chrysler and Ford. By 1930 there were 26 million cars in the United States and just over five million in the whole of Europe (Britain had one-and-a-half million). Car ownership in the United States continued to double roughly every twenty years, reaching over 120 million by the mid-1970s. In Europe the great boom was between 1950 and 1970, when the number of cars on the road quadrupled (in Britain it rose from two-and-a-half million just before the Second World War to 23 million by the 1980s). Across the world the ownership of cars and light trucks rose from 50 million in 1950 to just over 400 million by the 1980s, when over 33 million vehicles were being made every year. Car production now consumes more resources than any other industry. It uses 20 per cent of the world's steel production, 10 per cent of the aluminium, 35 per cent of the zinc, 50 per cent of the lead and 60 per cent of all natural rubber. In addition, over a third of all the world's oil consumption is accounted for by vehicles. In parallel, the rise of the car has also brought into being a whole range of subsidiary industries – road construction, petrol stations and service garages.

As greater affluence has spread through the industrialised countries there has been an increase in the amount of money spent on leisure activities. An early development in this field was the rise of mass spectator sports. In Britain professional football (which in the early twentieth century spread to the continent), to a lesser extent professional rugby and also cricket at a county and international level were soon attracting large crowds – several million every week at football matches and by 1923 100,000 at the Cup Final. In the United States the big attractions were baseball, American football and boxing – 130,000 spectators watched the Jack Dempsey and Gene Tunney heavyweight fight at Philadelphia in 1926. In addition to sport as a spectacle, hundreds of thousands of people were able to play competitive sports and new activities such as cycling in the 1890s and then golf and tennis became immensely popular. New, less active forms of entertainment were also growing in importance with the invention of new technologies. The late nineteenth and early twentieth century witnessed the rise of the cinema – by 1922 40 million tickets a week were being sold in the United States. After the First World War there was a boom in radio stations and ownership of sets. In 1922 about 100,000 households in the United States and 36,000 in Britain owned a radio set – a decade later the figures were 12 million and 3 million respectively (by 1939 UK ownership had tripled to 9 million sets). A similar very rapid expansion in ownership of television sets took place after 1945 – within a couple of decades across the whole of the industrialised world about 90 per cent of the population had at least one television and by the 1970s this was usually a colour set.

In the twentieth century there has been a major increase in the number and length of paid holidays for all workers, which, together with increasing wealth, has led to the development of a whole new industry – tourism. In the eighteenth century only the European elite could afford to spend several years travelling around the continent on the 'Grand Tour', admiring in particular the great classical sites of Italy. Slightly more people could take the waters at spas such as Bath, Harrogate, Marienbad and Carlsbad, or enjoy the sea air, but all travel was difficult, slow and expensive and foreign travel was confined to a small minority. The construction of the railway network changed the situation radically. Thomas Cook organised the first special excursion train, from Leicester to Loughborough, on 5 July 1841 with 570 passengers each paying one shilling. It was the start of a major boom in organised travel that developed as railways were built, new steamships were introduced, and people had more money to spend and more free time in which to spend it. Travel became tourism. At first the wealthier working class and the less well-off middle class were largely restricted to holidays at home in the developing seaside resorts and only the better-off could afford to venture abroad. Gradually more foreign travel was encouraged by developing the 'package' holiday. Firms such as Thomas Cook provided organised travel, featuring prepaid vouchers for hotels and facilities for currency exchange (the American Express travellers cheque started in 1891). At first the market was largely confined to the continent (Switzerland was a popular destination), but in 1869 Cook organised the first package tour to Egypt and Palestine and by the end of the century cruises and tours to the Near East were common both from Europe and the United States. As the trade developed so the number of hotels grew (at first many either owned by or tied to the new railway lines) as did the number of guides for travellers – the Michelin guide to hotels in France started in 1900 and the first AA guide to British hotels came out in 1911.

The rise of the car increased the range of holidays available and the demand for more facilities – by 1926 the United States had over 5,000 motor camps across the country, to accommodate tourists. As greater wealth began to reach those at the bottom of society new opportunities arose to provide cheap holidays – a trend exemplified by the development of 'holiday camps', which began in Britain in 1937 when Billy Butlin opened his first camp at Skegness. But it was the development of mass civil air transport after the Second World War, together with the vast increases in wealth in the industrialised world, that opened the way to mass tourism worldwide. The introduction of economy and tourist class on flights in the 1950s and the development of cheap charter flights widened the market still further. The growth in the tourism industry has been spectacular – in 1950 there were twenty-five million international tourists; by 1989 there were 400 million, spending an estimated £116 billion, occupying ten-and-a-half million hotel rooms and creating employment for sixty million people. Over 80 per cent of tourists come from the industrialised world (one quarter of them from West Germany) and almost three-quarters of them go to a European destination, with another 20 per cent bound for the Americas. Tourism is now a major source of income for many countries, providing a large part of the national wealth in some countries. The proportion of export earnings derived from tourism is over 30 per cent in Spain, Malta and Tunisia and over 25 per cent in Greece and Morocco. Tourism, at home and abroad, has become an accepted feature of the way of life of most people in the industrialised world.

The inhabitants of Europe, North America, Japan and Australasia now have a material standard of living that would have been unimaginable to their ancestors even a century ago. It has meant immense benefits in terms of better health care, better education, an easier and more comfortable way of life and a wider range of experiences. But it has also brought enormous problems. None of the industrialised countries has solved the problem of distributing the available wealth equitably and there remain large differences between people and regions within these countries, and the persistence of poverty amidst so much plenty creates more social tensions. Taking the industrialised countries as a whole, the poorest 40 per cent of their people receive only about 16 per cent of the total national income, which means a large part of their populations are excluded from many of the benefits of an increasingly affluent society. In Britain in the late 1980s ten million people (about 20 per cent of the population) lived in poverty, existing on less than half the average national wage. In the United States about twenty million people (almost 10 per cent of the population) are permanently hungry and about three million are homeless. There are also large differences in wealth between different regions within industrialised countries, as with the divide between the north and south of Italy or the south east of England and the rest of Britain. In the United States the average income in Mississippi is less than sixty per cent of that in Connecticut. In all these countries the inner cities are areas of major deprivation, often made worse by discrimination against ethnic minorities – the black infant mortality rate in some American inner cities is as bad as in parts of the Third World.

A major achievement of the industrialised economies has been to ensure that it is no longer true to say that the bulk of the population live in conditions of grinding poverty. The basic needs of the large majority of their citizens for food, shelter and clothing are now met. Even though these basic needs have been provided, and many more consumer goods supplied, the complex economic system that has developed has to be sustained. Democratically elected governments feel that they need to promise and encourage more economic growth as a way of maintaining their popularity. Companies who make these products also need to go on selling more goods and providing more services in order to survive. There are, therefore, strong political and commercial pressures to keep the economy growing and a number of factors help to maintain the desired state of increasing industrial output.

By the second half of the twentieth century production was mainly concentrated in the hands of large multinational corporations – the world's top 200 transnational corporations had an annual turnover of 3 million dollars, equivalent to a third of the world's gross wealth, and a single firm such as General Motors had a turnover greater than the national product of every Third World country except Mexico, India and Brazil. These corporations wield immense power; they control enough of the market in which they operate to have a decisive say in what goods are made and sold. Thus, for example, electrical companies have been reluctant to make long-life light bulbs (which also use less energy) because it would have reduced their turnover and profits from selling short-life bulbs. Companies also needed to develop new products to create new markets where none existed before or where perfectly adequate cheap alternatives were already available – for example, the development of the electric toothbrush. Companies therefore needed to spend large sums of money on advertising to create consumer desire for their products. Consumer spending was also boosted by the development of mechanisms to ensure easy access to credit so that people could buy more goods than their immediate income would provide. As early as 1926 three-quarters of all the cars sold in the United States were on credit terms.

Industrial production has also been maintained through in-built obsolescence. One facet of this is that many consumer goods are not designed to provide high levels of reliability. They require regular maintenance and some are deliberately designed so that they cannot be maintained but only replaced. Another aspect of built-in obsolescence is changing fashions so that there is strong pressure to replace goods regularly. In clothing a whole industry now depends on the deliberate promotion of frequent change in what was once a basic necessity. The car industry provides another example of these trends. In 1927 for the first time the number of replacement cars bought in the United States exceeded the number bought by new owners. With the market therefore facing a period of slower growth, American car manufacturers started to introduce annual styling changes to their models so as to increase pressure on customers to trade in their old cars and buy new models mainly for social and status reasons. A combination of changing fashions and a deliberate fall in reliability reduced the lifetime of cars and increased the turnover of car manufacturers. In 1955, 80 per cent of the cars made by General Motors, Chrysler and Ford were still on the road after nine years; by 1967 this figure had dropped to 55 per cent. The car industry is also a good example of another important way of boosting company profits by adding more 'value' to the product. Consumption has been increased by adding extra features to cars as standard fittings. At first these were items, such as heaters, radios and cigarette lighters, later came air conditioning, cassette decks and even compact disc players.

Conspicuous consumption has been a feature of all societies. One of the chief purposes of laws about the wearing of luxury clothing, the giving of large banquets and maintaining a vast array of servants in ancient and medieval societies (at a time when these were almost the only forms of conspicuous consumption available) was to confine display to a small group of people so that they could demonstrate wealth. As time went by the opportunities increased but the principle remained the same. Adam Smith noted in the eighteenth century:

> 'With the greater part of rich people, the chief enjoyment of riches consists in the parade of riches, which in their eye is never so complete as when they appear to possess those decisive marks of opulence which nobody can possess but themselves.'

In 1899, the American economist Thorstein Veblen, in his book *The Theory of the Leisure Class*, analysed the way in which rich people continued to accumulate wealth well beyond the point of rational wants and concluded that display was an important part of their expenditure. This phenomenon has become ever more widespread in the twentieth century. As increasing wealth has permeated through society, goods which were once only available to the few have become available to the many. Once they are readily available much of their symbolic value is destroyed and the rich need to possess new goods and signs of status in order to demonstrate their wealth. World tourism is a prime example of this trend. When large numbers of people are able to visit places which were once the prerogative of the rich then the wealthy have to travel further afield to more expensive and exotic locations in order to maintain the distinction. Much of the increased consumption in the twentieth century has been driven by these powerful social forces, aided and abetted by modern marketing methods and advertising techniques.

Rising expectations is another feature of modern industrialised societies. As these societies accumulated more wealth, their citizens came to expect and demand the provision of more public goods such as education, health care, street cleaning, libraries and social services. Greater productivity in agriculture and industry also meant that it was possible to support more of the population in these tertiary activities. By the second half of the nineteenth century large-scale provision of state-funded primary education was becoming common across the industrialised world and this later expanded into the secondary and university sectors. State-funded insurance and pension schemes were established by the early twentieth century. Later public provision of health care, housing and a vast array of services became common. The major problem that governments faced was that the demand for these services seemed to be inexhaustible – standards of provision were expected to rise and demands for new services were endless.

Cars and tourism provide striking examples of the way that growing affluence has brought not only many benefits but also major new problems and costs. For the individual, possession of a car has many attractions such as greater mobility, independence and personal convenience. At low levels of car ownership within society these benefits are apparent to all and they are one of the main motivating forces behind the increase in car numbers. As numbers rise, adjustments have to be made to accommodate the car – bigger and better roads are built, city centres are redesigned, public transport declines, shopping centres move to the fringes of the urban areas – thereby encouraging even more people to own cars at a time when the disadvantages of car travel in terms of congestion and pollution are becoming more apparent and finally it becomes difficult to manage without a car. The history of the motor car in the twentieth century reveals the transition from great expectations to major environmental problems.

At first the development of the car was hailed as beneficial for traffic in cities: people hoped it would reduce the task of road maintenance and the cost of cleaning up after the horses. It was also hoped that traffic chaos caused by roads clogged with horse-drawn traffic might be eased. (Modern cities are not the only ones to suffer from congestion – in Rome during the first century AD all vehicles except those owned by the state were banned from the streets during the day and in late nineteenth century London traffic speeds fell by 25 per cent in thirty years because of the increase in horse-drawn traffic.) With the rapid rise in car ownership it was soon apparent that existing roads in cities were inadequate. As early as 1903 a Royal Commission on traffic in London recommended parking restrictions and two new double-deck avenues across the city to intersect near the British Museum. Cities have had to adopt a number of methods to try and force an ever increasing volume of traffic through streets not originally designed for the purpose – including parking meters, multi-storey parking, one way streets, underpasses and tunnels. Some have given up this struggle and tried to redesign the city around the car, if necessary demolishing whole areas to build new urban motorways. Some have created traffic free areas or introduced selective bans on traffic in city centres. Such courses have dealt with the symptoms of the problem rather than its cause – the seemingly inexorable growth in car ownership.

As the number of cars in cities has increased, the provision of public transport (one of the main features of the rise of the city in the nineteenth century) has declined, caught in a vicious circle of declining usage, rising prices and slower speeds because of the congestion caused by other traffic. It was perhaps fitting that it was the city of Detroit in the 1920s, the home of the American car industry, which was the first to decide to widen roads rather than build an underground railway to provide better urban transport. The pattern was repeated in other American cities. Public transport reached a peak in the United States in 1945 then fell by two-thirds in the next twenty years as the car took over. In parallel, not only did ownership of cars increase, but so also did their use – doubling in per capita terms between 1946 and 1966 as people began to commute by car over greater distances. Other countries experienced the same pattern – in Australia every city apart from Melbourne lost its trams and trolley buses between 1950 and 1970, as car ownership quintupled. In the United States the car industry decided not to leave the decay of public transport to the vagaries of the market system and instead took action themselves to close down public transport and force people to use cars. In 1936 three corporations connected with the car industry (General Motors, Standard Oil of California and the tyre company Firestone) formed a new company called National City Lines whose purpose was to buy up alternative transport systems and close them down. By 1956 over a hundred electric surface rail systems in forty-five cities had been purchased and then closed. Their biggest operation was the acquisition, in 1940, of part of the Pacific Electric system, which carried 110 million passengers a year in fifty-six communities. Over 1,100 miles of track were ripped up and by 1961 the whole network was closed.

The social costs of increasing car ownership (in terms of congestion and the decay of public transport and city centre businesses as people moved ever further from the centre into new suburbs) were apparent in the United States very quickly as the American economy and society were reshaped around the car. The first widespread complaints about car parking in city centres were made in 1916 and by 1923 the first proposals were put forward to ban them from city centres. Other costs were also becoming clear. In 1924, 23,600 Americans (including 10,000 children) were killed and 700,000 injured in accidents involving cars. By the late 1960s increasing traffic resulted in 55,000 deaths a year and over four million injuries. Other countries experienced similar problems when their car ownership levels increased. (In the 1950s Europe reached the same ownership level as the United States in the 1920s). The main response of governments has been to spend more money on road construction, taking the easy way out to satisfy a powerful lobby and not risk antagonising the majority of their voters who were also motorists. (All western governments have spent far more on roads than public transport – the American government spends one per cent of its transportation budget on urban mass transit systems and 75 per cent on new roads). The United States introduced federal aid for state road construction in 1916 and five years later began building interstate highways. In Germany, an autobahn network was constructed in the 1930s and since the 1950s every west European government has built a system of motorways in addition to undertaking large-scale improvements to existing roads.

Transport policy is a good example of the difficulty of taking environmentally sound decisions within the modern economic system. Building more roads may be popular with motorists, the car industry and the construction lobby but the problem arises of how and when to stop. The energy and social costs of building roads and using them in preference to rail systems are enormous. The energy required in terms of steel and cement for road building is three-and-a-half times greater than that for an equivalent amount of railway construction and four times as much land is used. Overall railways are six times more efficient in energy terms at carrying passengers and freight than roads. Despite this, in every industrialised country the capacity of the rail system has been severely reduced since the 1950s – in the United States railways account for one per cent of all intercity traffic, cars for 85 per cent. In most industrialised countries cars now account for over 80 per cent of all passenger miles and the majority of these are made with only the driver in the car, which is highly inefficient in terms of energy consumption and congestion. Energy problems are made worse by the high fuel consumption of most car engines – between 1945 and the mid-1970s the average fuel consumption of American cars actually fell from seventeen miles per gallon to fifteen. Although this figure has since been improved following the rises in oil prices in 1973–4 and 1979–80, it is still lower than it need be, given technical developments in modern engines and it is a profligate way of using the most limited of all fossil fuel resources. The extensive pollution caused by cars is considered in the next chapter.

The rise of modern tourism has also brought with it a controversial blend of opportunity and blight. The eight-fold increase in international tourism in the last forty years has severely strained facilities and even destroyed the original attraction of the places that people came to see. In 1964 Hawaii received 15,000 tourists a year, a decade later the figure was three million. Spain now accommodates fifty-four million tourists a year (equivalent to almost the entire population of Britain). Other Mediterranean countries such as Greece and Turkey have gone through the same process of adjusting to mass tourism. The result has been the construction of large numbers of huge hotels, overcrowded beaches, the destruction of the local way of life and the development of synthetic 'local customs' to be shown to the tourists in resorts that are almost indistinguishable from each other. Venice has almost been destroyed as a living city by tourism. The resident population has fallen to less than 80,000 and the average age has risen to over fifty as the young have left to find work. The city is now little more than a museum, although a wonderful one. At times the number of visitors has risen to over 100,000, pedestrian movements have to be regulated along one way streets and entry restrictions imposed because of overcrowding. Tourism, apart from social problems, also causes direct environmental problems. The concentration of European tourism along the shores of the Mediterranean has resulted in major water quality problems: in some cases it is becoming difficult to find enough water for people to drink and sewage disposal is a major problem. Dumping it in the sea, often untreated, which is the usual 'solution', has simply meant that much of the Mediterranean is now unfit for bathing. These developments are seen in their most extreme form in Third World tourism, where luxury hotels, isolated from the country in which they are situated, are serviced by local people but bring few benefits to the local economy.

From a world perspective, the greater affluence of the industrialised world needs to be seen in the context of the overwhelming majority of the world's population that do not live in the wealthy countries. Until the last few hundred years there was little difference in the wealth of any of the societies of Eurasia (the pre-Columbian societies of the Americas were at a slightly lower level). The first settled societies and early empires such as Babylon, Egypt, Assyria, Persia, Macedonia, Rome, the Han in China and the numerous Indian states were all agricultural societies with roughly similar structures and dependent on much the same technology, and their relative wealth varied mainly according to the gains made from temporary success in war and the expropriation of the wealth of the defeated. Medieval China, India and Europe were also at roughly the same stage of development – still essentially agrarian with a relatively small industrial sector and limited trade – China was probably the wealthiest country in the world in the eleventh and twelfth centuries as its industrial sector expanded and technological advances were made but it had fallen back by the fifteenth century as stagnation set in.

The distribution of wealth in the world became increasingly unequal in the period after 1500. The expansion of Europe and its gradual extension of control over other territories led to the establishment of a world economic system that benefited Europe and the other parts of the industrialised world – the United States, Canada, Japan and Australasia. A considerable part of the wealth that was invested in commerce and industry in Europe after 1500 came from the newly founded colonies and it was the control exercised over the world's resources that underpinned the great industrial expansion of the nineteenth and twentieth centuries. The result was to create a highly unequal world. The 70 per cent of the world's population that lives outside the industrialised world accounts for just 15 per cent of global personal income. The per capita income of an inhabitant of one of the poorest countries in the world, Rwanda, is just one per cent of that of an American. This poverty is reflected in every area of life. On average a citizen of the industrialised world has a calorie intake 40 per cent higher than someone in the Third World, child mortality is 90 per cent lower and life expectancy 50 per cent longer. A rich European country such as Sweden has an infant mortality rate eighteen times lower than that of Ethiopia and a hospital bed for every sixty-seven inhabitants compared with one for every 5,538 people in Nepal. In Britain there are about thirty cars for every hundred inhabitants and in the United States fifty six – India has one car for every 800 people. These levels of wealth can only be sustained by a grossly unequal consumption of the world's resources. The United States contains roughly 5 per cent of the world's population but it uses 40 per cent of the world's mineral and 30 per cent of its energy resources. The average American consumes the same amount of resources every year as twenty-five Indians (and India is one of the wealthier countries of the Third World).

The problems of poverty tend to be nastier and more obvious than those of affluence. The fact that one part of the world has moved from a state of poverty to a state of affluence through industrialisation has, despite all the problems of affluence, encouraged the rest of the world to try to follow suit. However these countries have been attempting to achieve this within a world economy dominated by the industrialised countries. Only a few countries such as Singapore, Taiwan and South Korea have managed to move a considerable distance along the road. Others such as China, India and Brazil have major industrial sectors but their size, poverty and social problems have made industrialisation a very difficult process. The majority of countries in the Third World are still primarily agricultural, producing cash crops, minerals and timber for the industrial countries. The likelihood of these immensely poor countries industrialising seems remote.

Since the 1950s the industrialised world has been committed to a declared policy of providing aid to promote the economic development of the Third World and narrow the gap between rich and poor countries. It is a policy predicated on the idea that the correct economic course for the Third World is to follow the model of the industrialised countries and become even more closely integrated into the world trade system. Several decades of 'development aid' have singularly failed to narrow the gap. In 1950 the per capita wealth of the poorest countries of the world was about four per cent of that of the industrialised nations, by 1980 that figure had fallen to two-and-a-half per cent. In many areas of the world, particularly Africa, the social and economic position of the majority of the population worsened considerably in this period: per capita income in Africa fell every year from 1979 to 1990. Nearly 60 per cent of the inhabitants of the Third World (over 1 billion people) still lack basic human requirements such as adequate food, housing and drinking water. The World Bank officially estimates that about 800 million people (excluding those living in China) exist in conditions of absolute poverty (including twenty per cent of the world's children and that figure is increasing steadily) and that there are 800 million illiterate people in the world.

Throughout the period since the Second World War the economies of the industrialised world have continued to expand faster than those of the poorest, thereby increasing the gap between the two. The current UN target is that 0.7 per cent of national income of industrialised countries should be given in aid (a significant reduction from the original 1 per cent target). A few countries have met this aim but the overwhelming majority, including the United States, the world's wealthiest nation, have not – in Britain in the 1980s the proportion of national income going on aid actually fell from 0.52 per cent to 0.32 per cent. Much of the aid that has been given was mainly designed to help companies in the industrialised world – three-quarters of all Britain's bilateral aid in the 1980s was tied to the purchase of British goods and another 14 per cent was used to subsidise the prices of British firms competing for contracts in the Third World. Some of the deals that have been struck have had little to do with aid – in the mid-1980s £65 million of British aid was given so that India could buy helicopters from Westland, an ailing firm that needed government support. Each helicopter was worth more than the total of Britain's aid to Ethiopia, one of the poorest countries in the world suffering from acute environmental degradation. Most aid from the United States has gone to those countries judged to be of military and strategic importance and Britain's aid programme has paid for a £7 million hospital in the Falkland Islands and an £18 million naval repair yard in Gibraltar. As a result Gibraltar received as much aid as Ethiopia and aid to the Falklands was equal to £5500 per person and that to India just 15p.

The multilateral lending agencies, especially the World Bank (which accounts for a fifth of all the world's aid spending), have been wedded to large-scale construction projects which have provided work for multinational corporations. Although some of the aid agencies were, by the late 1980s, trying to move towards small-scale, environmentally sound forms of development, much of the aid that has been given since the 1950s has caused major social and environmental damage in the Third World. The World Bank supported Indonesia's transmigration programme, designed to relocate three-and-a-half million people from Java to the outlying islands, which was little more than military projects intended to swamp ethnic minorities and tribal peoples and so aid 'national security'. The building of large dams (which has taken up nearly half the World Bank's spending) has been particularly damaging. These large hydro-electric projects, designed to provide energy for industrialisation, have led to massive resettlement programmes – for example the Narmada valley project in India (comprising thirty large and 135 medium-sized dams and 3,000 irrigation projects) will make one million people landless (three-quarters of whom will receive no compensation). The lakes that have been created cause major land loss – the Volta dam flooded two million acres and Kariba over one million acres, much of it good agricultural land. They have spread disease – the schistosomiasis rate doubled after the Aswan dam was completed – and the fisheries that were established have often proved a failure. Even technically these dams were often a failure. Evaporation rates in tropical areas are very high so that much of the water is lost and deforestation of the surrounding slopes produces very high run-off and siltation rates – in India the Nizamsagar dam in Andra Pradesh lost two-thirds of its capacity, in China the Sanmenxia dam, which was completed in 1960, had to be abandoned four years later because the reservoir had silted up and the Laoying project even had to be abandoned before it was completed for the same reason.

The industrialised world has also been prepared to fund aid on strictly commercial terms. Latin American and Asian countries in particular were tempted to take out large debts with banks in the industrialised world in order to finance development. In the 1970s, when money was relatively cheap, this seemed a reasonable policy but the results turned out to be disastrous for the economies and peoples of the borrowing countries. By the mid-1980s Third World countries had a total debt of about one trillion dollars (less than half the national debt of the United States). By 1990 the total debt of African countries was $272 billion, almost equal to the total wealth of the continent and three times the value of its exports. The attempt to pay the interest on this debt, let alone the capital, was extremely difficult for three reasons. First, interest rates increased in the 1980s, thus raising the amount of money to be repaid. Second, the two oil price rises of 1973–1974 and 1979–1980 severely affected the majority of countries in the Third World which do not have their own supplies. Third, most of these countries remained dependent on a small number of commodities for their export earnings. The Third World's share of global trade has been falling (by a third between 1980 and 1986) and the real price of commodities has also fallen. Zambia for example remains dependent on copper for over 90 per cent of its export earnings. In 1975 the price collapsed and by the 1980s it was at a third of its level in 1966. Overall, primary commodity prices in the late 1980s were, in real terms, at two-thirds of their level in 1957. The payment of interest on these debts has taken up an increasing share of government budgets and export earnings and outweighs any benefits from aid. For most years in the 1980s the Third World transferred far more money to the industrialised world than it received in aid. For example between 1982–1986 the countries of Latin America paid 130 billion dollars in debt interest which, after taking account of aid, meant a net transfer of resources to the industrialised world of 106 billion dollars.

Not surprisingly in these circumstances many Third World countries experienced severe financial difficulties. This is nothing new – in the 1880s Egypt, which had borrowed large sums for economic development, including the construction of the Suez Canal, could not keep up the payments on its debts and Britain and France took over the country. In the 1980s assistance was normally only available through the International Monetary Fund, an organisation controlled by the industrialised world and committed to the continuation and expansion of the current structure of world trade. The IMF was been prepared to loan money to Third World countries to repay the interest on their debts to the private banks of the industrialised world under certain conditions. These involved accepting 'adjustment policies' designed to maximise export earnings and so keep up debt repayments. These policies usually consisted of devaluation of the currency, drastic cuts in government expenditure (especially on social services), elimination of food and consumption subsidies, privatisation of state industries, abolition of price controls, cuts in consumption, restrictions on credit, higher taxes and higher interest rates. They amounted to massive austerity programmes which placed the pressures of adjustment onto the poorest sections of the population who did not see many benefits from the projects financed by the loans. During the 1980s nearly fifty countries in the Third World had to accept such adjustment programmes.

A combination of external influences (including the type of 'development' programmes propounded by the industrialised countries, and the IMF's debt and austerity packages) and internal problems (such as corruption and the squandering of resources on armaments – between 1972 and 1982 Latin American arms imports rose at 13 per cent a year and Africa's by 18 per cent a year) undermined the fragile economies of the Third World. The effects can be seen clearly in the cases of Morocco and Zaire. Morocco, following an IMF and World Bank recommended programme in the 1950s, decided to concentrate its agriculture and exports on growing fruit and tomatoes primarily for the European market. This involved large-scale dam construction and irrigation systems (all on the land of large landowners) and meant a shift away from self-sufficiency in wheat production to reliance on imports. By 1984 the debt accumulated to pay for these projects (sixteen billion dollars) amounted to 110 per cent of Morocco's Gross National Product and the per capita production of wheat had fallen below the levels of the 1930s. Food imports, which took up most of the available limited foreign exchange reserves, rose 220 per cent between 1970 and 1983. Massive food subsidies kept prices at a level that could be afforded, and they also had the important subsidiary effect of keeping wages down and therefore exports cheap. When an IMF rescue package was required in order to allow Morocco to go on paying interest on its debts, food subsidies were cut (but not producer price subsidies) so that the weight of the economic adjustment was borne by the poorest. By the mid-1980s, of the 21 million Moroccans, 9 million were judged to be 'absolutely poor', nearly half the population was under fifteen but had very poor prospects because two-thirds of those aged between fifteen and twenty had no job and were not receiving any education either.

The case of Zaire illustrates the level of corruption and maldevelopment in some Third World countries, which in this case has been tolerated by an industrialised world heavily reliant on Zaire's mineral exports. The head of state, General Mobutu, and his family own shares in every foreign company operating in Zaire, receive a 5 per cent 'commission' on all mineral exports and the family company also produces a sixth of all Zaire's agricultural exports. As a result Mobutu and his close relations own eleven chateaux in France and Belgium, estates in four other countries and fifty-one Mercedes cars together with undisclosed wealth in Swiss bank accounts. Development aid received by Zaire has been channelled into prestige projects – for example the building of two runways and an air-conditioned terminal building at Kisangani airport, which has five flights a day. By the mid-1980s Zaire had accumulated debts of six billion dollars and when the IMF was called in, the 'adjustment package' in 1984 resulted in the sacking of 20 per cent of all teachers and a third of the staff working in higher education. At this time, the UN estimated that the population of the two main cities received only 60 per cent of the minimum calories required for a healthy life, 80 per cent of the population was in 'absolute poverty' and real wages were only 10 per cent of their level at the time of independence in 1960.

For the last eight or nine millennia settled societies have produced inequalities in wealth, but the differences were essentially internal. Before the expansion of Europe and the intensification of industrial output there were no major differences in wealth between the main agricultural societies themselves. The emergence of an affluent society has not changed the persistent historical fact of internal inequality (despite major changes in the standard of living for all the inhabitants of the industrialised world), but it has brought about a huge shift in the pattern of wealth distribution worldwide. Domination of an international economic system has enabled the industrialised countries to utilise the vast majority of the world's resources and develop unprecedented, high levels of consumption. One part of the world can now be dubbed 'affluent', while the great majority of the world's population still live, as they always have done in the past, in conditions of absolute poverty. The changes that opened the way to the higher levels of consumption also involved social and environmental penalties, some of which, notably a big increase in the amount and sources of pollution, are now affecting the whole world.

16
POLLUTING THE WORLD

Pollution has a long history. The creation of wastes has been one of the distinguishing characteristics of every human society. For thousands of years the chief struggle was over sanitary arrangements and the main challenge was to obtain unpolluted water supplies. These problems became ever more acute as human numbers and urban life increased, but widespread industrial production and the use of new technologies introduced new pollutants and brought new risks to human health and the environment. Contamination was at first essentially localised – generally confined to a city, river, waste dump or mine. By the late twentieth century pollution had increased to an unprecedented scale – affecting industrial regions, oceans, entire continents and even global regulatory mechanisms. Human understanding of the consequences of waste creation and disposal has always tended to lag well behind the release of pollutants into the environment. In earlier societies it is possible to find evidence of many of the features which characterise the response to contemporary pollution: fatalistic acceptance of pollution as an inevitable consequence of human activities; authorities balking at prevention or control measures; lack of foresight and technical understanding; the problem of allocating responsibility; a preference for short-term local fixes rather than long-term solutions and a failure of individuals or companies to take responsibility for their actions. Attempts to control pollution are as old as the problem itself but the response has usually been belated and inadequate with a poor record of co-operation and enforcement.

For archaeologists the wastes produced by prehistoric and historic societies are a great asset, a primary source of information about the earliest human communities. Many of the sites of the earliest cities in the Near East are built on huge piles of rubbish, known as tells, accumulated over the centuries. As archaeologists dig through the layers of discarded household refuse they find old pottery and tools, which help to identify different groups of people and the activities they undertook, and the charred remains of food and fossilised faeces (coprolites) together with plant and animal remains provide information about agricultural techniques and the diets of ancient societies. Even gathering and hunting groups accumulated large quantities of waste, particularly in caves which might be occupied for part of a year over many centuries. For example, the late Upper Paleolithic site of Gare de Couze in France consists of an area covering about 300 yards by 60 yards and archaeologists estimate that it contains between one and two million discarded stone tools. Most habitation sites contain large amounts of waste from the making of stone tools and the places where animals were killed and dismembered are usually littered with stone tools that had become blunt and were simply thrown away. Overall, however, the pollution produced by gathering and hunting groups was low level – their numbers were small, their possessions were few – and it was confined to very limited areas.

One of the most basic problems for every society has been to dispose of human excrement and urine whilst at the same time securing a supply of drinking water that it is not contaminated with these wastes. Failure to do so in most cases has been one of the major contributing factors to poor human health. The difficulty of separating the two functions, and of reconciling the needs of public health and personal convenience, is illustrated by the history of a small village in Cambridgeshire called Foxton, where a stream ran through the centre of the settlement and acted as both a sewer and a source of drinking water. The difficulty of regulating the use of the stream can be seen from the fact that by-laws for cleaning it out had to be made on eight occcasions between 1541 and 1698, which suggests that they were not being obeyed. The main problem though was the way that gutters, cess pits and what were described as 'other noysome sinks' were discharged into the stream. More by-laws to stop wastes being put into the stream except after 8pm on pain of a fine of twelve pence were issued in 1562, 1594, 1598, 1600, 1611, 1643, 1665 and 1698, which again suggests that the regulations were largely ineffective. In addition it was prohibited to do any washing in the stream or keep ducks and geese on it. Even if the various rules had been observed they would not have solved the problem for villages further downstream, which had to cope with the contents of the 'noysome sinks' of Foxton even if they were only discharged at night.

There are two closely related problems of water supply – the need to safeguard both quantity and quality. Gathering and hunting groups found their water from streams and springs, the location of which often dictated their camping sites, and by moving on fairly regularly they normally avoided any major pollution problems. The rise of settled societies meant that a reliable supply of water was essential and most settlements grew up around a stream, spring or well. For most small rural settlements throughout the world these are still the only source of supply (as they were in rural areas of the industrialised world until well into the twentieth century). Larger settlements needed more complex arrangements and the cities of the Indus valley such as Mohenjo-Daro and Harappa had, like many others of this period, fresh water tanks to store supplies and central baths, together with drains and lavatories to try and separate water supplies and sewage. But the increase in the size of settlements and the number of people needing water soon put a strain on what were often limited local supplies. Some of the first aqueducts to bring water in from outside the city were constructed in Greece as underground tunnels on Samos and at Athens and they were soon a familiar sight in their elevated form across the ancient Mediterranean from Spain and southern France to Carthage and Alexandria. By 312 BC the Romans decided that the river Tiber was too polluted to use as drinking water and constructed their first aqueduct. By the first century AD Rome depended on nine of these systems, which in total extended over 263 miles and supplied all the city's drinking water and 1,000 public baths. Many of the Roman aqueducts, which were impressive and enduring feats of civil engineering, continued to function long after the fall of the empire. The building of these centralised water supplies established a pattern that was to persist in virtually every city until the late nineteenth century – water was not normally provided for individual houses (unless they had their own wells) but was obtained from fountains and taps in public places.

The rise of cities in north and west Europe from the eleventh century led to the same sort of problems that had been faced by those in the Mediterranean and Near East thousands of years earlier. By the early thirteenth century the Thames was already polluted and in 1236 the first water was brought to the city of London from Tyburn spring (near what is now Marble Arch) in lead pipes. Other cities also laid water pipes, for example Zittau did so in 1374 and Breslau in 1479, but many of these were simply hollowed out logs, a method that was still employed on Manhattan Island until the nineteenth century. In 1610 the New River Company was established in order to supply clean water in pipes to London from the New river to replace steadily deteriorating Thames water. Other private water companies supplying the capital continued to draw raw water from the Thames and the first filtration plant was not built until 1869. Paris in the middle of the nineteenth century had to abandon taking water from the highly polluted Seine, switching in 1852 to using a large artesian well at Grenelle. As the new industrial cities emerged and population everywhere rose rapidly, maintaining an adequate and safe water supply became a severe problem. As early as the 1820s English industrial towns were building artificial reservoirs, a process taken much further in the second half of the nineteenth century and in the twentieth century with the construction of large artificial lakes, often many miles from the city – much of Birmingham's water for example is now obtained in central Wales. This had important aesthetic and other implications for the environment because of the flooding of whole valleys by the reservoirs. Between 1839 and 1847 a fifty-one mile long aqueduct was built to bring water to Marseilles and in the United States artificial, planned water supplies, which began in 1798 in Philadelphia, were being built across the country – between 1885 and 1893 a thirty mile long tunnel was built to provide New York's water supply.

Although through such developments much more water was being supplied to the great cities of the industrialised world, the fact that it was only rarely supplied to individual houses had a powerful, restraining effect on individual consumption. In eighteenth-century Paris water was taken round the city by 20,000 water carriers using buckets. In mid-nineteenth-century London out of 70,000 houses in the centre of the city 17,000 depended on their own wells and the rest relied on standpipes in the street, about one for every twenty or thirty houses, which normally supplied water for about an hour a day for three days a week. Coventry had running water in just 350 of its 7,000 houses. Few houses were built with bathrooms, indeed when Queen Victoria moved into Buckingham Palace in 1837 she found that there were no bathrooms in the building. As late as 1908 there were no bathrooms at 10 Downing Street. Even public baths were not always available – in 1842 Liverpool was the only town in Lancashire that had them. In the less developed parts of Europe this situation persisted well into the twentieth century. In Moscow in 1914 only 9,000 houses in the centre of the city had piped water, the rest relied on 140 wells. By 1926 only half the city's population had piped water and 250,000 people still depended on ponds and rivers of dubious purity for their supplies. In many parts of the industrialised world there is still plenty of sub-standard housing lacking its own water supply. In 1962 13 per cent of dwellings in Paris had no running water, neither did 10 per cent of those in the centre of

Tokyo and in the Soviet Union at the beginning of the 1960s 62 per cent of urban housing had no water supply of its own.

As population has increased, as better water supply systems have been built and as treatment methods have been improved, consumption has increased – global water use has quadrupled since 1940. But major problems of supply have begun to emerge. Fresh water is a scarce resource – less than 0.4 per cent of the water on earth is available in this form – and it is not evenly distributed across the globe, so that in some areas of low rainfall and increasing population such as north and sub-Saharan Africa and the Near East severe shortfalls are being experienced. As with other resources, it is the industrialised world that uses far more than the Third World. The average American consumes (including industry) 7,200 litres every day, the average Indian about 25 litres a day. Although industrial use is important, about three-quarters of the world's water supply is used to irrigate crops, especially in the Third World (in India over 90 per cent of water is used in this way) even though the majority of people are short of water. In many parts of the world the continual extraction of water from underground aquifers is at such high rates that resources are rapidly being depleted. One of the first places to notice this problem was London. When the fountains in Trafalgar Square were built in 1845 they drew their water using a well from the water table 112 feet below. By 1911 so much water had been taken for domestic and industrial use that the water table had fallen to 236 feet below the surface and the well supplying the fountains had to be abandoned. In Bangkok the water table has fallen by eighty feet since 1958 and is continuing to drop at over twelve feet a year. As this fresh water is extracted, sea water advances further inland at over 500 yards a year. In Tamil Nadu in southern India the water table has fallen over 100 feet in the last fifteen years. In the United States the giant Ogallala aquifer supplies water over an area stretching from South Dakota to northern Texas. Irrigation in the area quadrupled in the thirty years after 1945 and about half of the reserves have been consumed; in many areas little water remains – Oklahoma and Texas had lost 18 per cent of their irrigated farmland by the 1980s and 2,300 square miles in Colorado, Kansas and Nebraska had also gone out of production due to lack of water. Using modern technology Saudi Arabia has been able to irrigate large desert areas but this relies on underground aquifers which are being used up at a far faster rate than they are being replenished.

Although in the industrialised world the supply of large volumes of water has been achieved, its purity has been called into question again. The problem now is less that of pollution by human wastes but of

developments in modern industry and agriculture. These have produced contamination by industrial wastes and, in rural areas, the runoff into rivers of artificial fertilizers and pesticides, and not all these
pollutants are removed by modern filtration and treatment methods.
To a large extent the scale of the problem remains unknown, partly
because of the difficulty of detecting pesticide residues in water but
some alarming situations have been discovered. Twenty per cent of the
wells in California have pollution levels above official safety limits; in
Florida 1,000 wells have been closed because of contamination; in
Hungary 773 towns and villages have water that is unfit for consumption, in Britain ten per cent of aquifers are polluted above World Health
Organisation safety limits and in parts of both Britain and the United
States tap water cannot be given to new born babies because of high
nitrate levels. However in large areas of the Third World the problem
remains much the same as it always was. Here sixty per cent of the
people (a majority of the world's population) do not have access to safe
drinking water and 25,000 people die every day from drinking contaminated water. Official estimates suggest that 70 per cent of India's water
is polluted and forty-one out of the forty-four largest cities in China
have polluted groundwater.

Until the development of water treatment facilities in the latter part
of the nineteenth century virtually no city in the world had succeeded in
keeping its water supply clean and uncontaminated by human waste
and other rubbish. The persistent temptation was to dump waste of all
kinds into streams and rivers (and occasionally the sea) in the hope that
it would be carried away somewhere else, or be diluted. This failure was
symptomatic of a more general failure to find satisfactory ways of
disposing of human wastes and the other types of rubbish accumulated
by all settled societies. There is no doubt that someone living in the
industrialised world in the twentieth century who was transported back
in time to a city at any period earlier than about a century ago would be
horrified and overwhelmed by the smell. This came from piles of
rotting rubbish and human and animal excrement mixed with pools of
urine, which often blocked the streets or were occasionally swept into
the local stream or river to decompose there. The overall state of cities
was well summed up by the mother of the Regent of France, who
described Paris in the mid-seventeenth century as 'a horrible place and
ill smelling . . . one cannot linger there because of the stench of rotting
meat and fish and because of a crowd of people who urinate in the
streets'.

Most houses had no lavatory facilities at all and even in the richest palaces and castles of medieval and early modern Europe the lavatory was no more than a hole in the floor that discharged into the street, the moat or simply outside the wall of the building. The palace of Versailles was provided with portable commodes while visitors to the Louvre or Palais de Justice relieved themselves in corners, and the outside walls of the buildings were stained by chambermaids throwing the contents of commodes out of the windows. Town houses might be provided with a cess pit but normally with no sewer (there were a small number but they were little better than elongated cess pits since they were not flushed out by water). In town houses the cess pits were usually located in the cellars, which could create problems for neighbours as Samuel Pepys found out to his cost in October 1660 when he went to his cellar to look for a place to put in a new window: 'going down to my cellar to look, I put my foot in a great heap of turds, by which I find that Mr Turner's house of office is full and comes into my cellar, which doth trouble me.' Three years later the problem was still bad and Mr Turner had to extend his vault into Pepys' cellar to try to contain his cess pit.

Since people lacked their own lavatories they simply used any available open space. In eighteenth century Paris a row of yew trees in the Tuileries provided an open air toilet and when the authorities drove people away they simply used the Seine instead. City streets were also full of animal wastes, dead animals, refuse, and the leftovers of the butchering trade. In fourteenth century Paris about 300,000 animals a year were being slaughtered and the offal and carcasses were left to decay in the streets and streams. In September 1366 the butchers of Paris were forced to move out of the city and use a rural stream to dispose of their wastes. Although regulations and laws were often made to stop the dumping of rubbish in the streets (the English parliament did so in 1388 for example) they were usually ineffectual. Street cleaning, if it existed at all, was also primitive and small scale. At the end of the thirteenth century the Piazza del Campo in Siena, which was the civic centre, was kept more or less clean by five pigs which ate the refuse. In fourteenth century London there were just twelve rubbish carts for the whole city and even then they only tipped their loads into the Thames. In the American city of Boston in 1652 the town council issued an ordinance prohibiting the throwing of the 'entrails of beasts or fowls or garbage or carrion or dead dogs or cattle or any other dead beast or stinking thing' into the streets. It was obviously not effective because the city had to maintain a scavenging system to clean the streets but that had to be abandoned in 1720 because of the cost. Allahabad did have such a system in the nineteenth century which removed 100 tons of rubbish every day but it employed 638 sweepers and drivers and took up over half the city's budget. Few cities therefore could afford to do much to clean the streets and public places.

A visitor to Madrid in 1697 described the streets of the town as:

'always very dirty because it is the custom to throw all the rubbish out of the window. One suffers even more in winter because carts carry several barrels of water which are emptied into the streets in order to carry away the rubbish and let the filth run off; it often happens that one encounters torrents of this evil water which blocks one's way and poisons by its stench.'

The cities of the Near East were no different as a French traveller in Isfahan discovered in 1694 when he commented on the streets full of mud and noted that:

'This great filthiness is still further increased by the custom of throwing dead animals, together with the blood of those killed by butchers on to the squares and of publicly relieving oneself wherever one happens to be.'

Even when rubbish was removed from city streets it was often simply thrown over the walls of the town to decompose in a stinking pile. In 1512 when an English attack on Paris was feared, the garbage was so high against the city walls that it had to be dug away to make them defensible. When the French writer Jacques Caille visited Rabat in the early nineteenth century he reported that the city's waste was removed by just five or six donkey carts, which did not operate on holidays, in the winter or when it rained. The result was that:

'the streets of the city often show a layer of liquid mire more than ten centimetres deep. When waste matter has been removed it is thrown into the sea; or often it is simply heaped up at the gates to the city, where it forms a veritable cess pool.'

In some cities outside Europe and the Near East a more effective system operated. An English diplomat who visited Peking at the end of the eighteenth century was surprised to find that people did not throw their rubbish into the streets. Many Chinese cities had well organised systems whereby people left wastes in tubs outside their houses where they were emptied by teams of cleaners and used to manure paddy

fields. In Tenochtitlan, the Aztec capital, refuse collection was organised by large numbers of boats on the canals and the waste was taken to
be used as manure on the chinampas. The problem with using human
faeces as fertilizer or using irrigation canals as lavatories, as was the
custom in areas such as Egypt and Mesopotamia, is that it spreads
intestinal diseases, worms and flukes, very easily. In China, where it
was normal to use human waste as fertilizer, about 90 per cent of the
people in the early twentieth century suffered from worm infestation
and in 1948 a quarter of all deaths were due to faecal borne infections.

The rapid growth of industrial cities in the early nineteenth century
with their grossly overcrowded housing produced appalling sanitation problems. One of the worst places was the 'Potteries' of north
Kensington in London, an eight acre area originally dug out to provide
brick clay for the surrounding suburbs and then left to collect all the
sewage from the neighbourhood. It was full of open sewers and stag-
nant lakes (one covered an area of over an acre). In the early 1850s over
a thousand people lived there together with more than 3,000 pigs that
fed off the refuse. But London was in a generally disgusting state: in
1847 John Phillips, the engineer to the Metropolitan Commission of
Sewers, reported that:

'There are . . . thousands of houses in the metropolis which have no
drainage whatever, and the greater part of them have stinking
overflowing cesspools. And there are hundreds of streets, courts and
alleys that have no sewers . . . I have visited very many places where
filth was lying scattered about the rooms, vaults, cellar areas and
yards, so thick and so deep that it was hardly possible to move for it.'

Frederick Engels in his investigation into the condition of the working
class in Manchester in the 1840s described one area of the town near the
river Irk where 200 people shared one privy:

'In one of these courts, right at the entrance where the covered
passage ends is a privy without a door. This privy is so dirty that the
inhabitants can only enter or leave the court by wading through
puddles of stale urine and excrement.'

Improvements in the water supply and the invention of the water
closet merely had the effect of transferring the problem and intensifying
the accompanying stench. Although sewers could now be flushed
through with water (it was legal to connect water closets to surface

streams in England after 1815 and compulsory after 1847), this simply ensured that the rivers were turned into open sewers containing all the slowly decomposing waste products. During his tours of Manchester, Engels stood on the Ducie bridge over the river Irk and described the scene below:

'At the bottom the Irk flows or rather stagnates . . . [it] receives as well the contents of the adjacent sewers and privies. Below Ducie Bridge, on the left, one looks into piles of rubbish, the refuse, filth and decaying matter of the courts on the steep left bank of the river. [It] . . . is a narrow, coal-black stinking river full of filth and garbage which it deposits on the lower-lying right bank. In dry weather, an extended series of the most revolting blackish green pools of slime remain standing on this bank, out of whose depths bubbles of miasmatic gases constantly rise and give forth a stench that is unbearable even on the bridge forty or fifty feet above the level of the water.'

In London the sewers emptied into the river Fleet which carried their contents to the Thames, where the rubbish was left to float up and down on the tide in the centre of the city. During hot weather the smell caused by the decaying sewage spread over a wide area. In 1858 during what was called 'The Great Stink' the stench was so bad that sittings of the House of Commons had to be abandoned. Many water companies were still taking their water supply from the Thames and not surprisingly this was a major source of intestinal illnesses and outbreaks of cholera. In 1853 when the Lambeth Water Company moved its source of supply further upstream away from the most polluted area, the death rate in the area it supplied rapidly fell from 130 per 1,000 to 37 per 1,000.

The interlinked problems of sewage and water supply were not reduced to manageable proportions until the second half of the nineteenth century with the development of sewage treatment, better sanitary facilities in the home and more public conveniences linked to effective underground sewage systems, together with water purification and treatment works. By the early 1980s over half the population of the major industrialised countries were drinking water that had passed through water treatment plants. These were technological solutions enabling reasonable quality water to be produced from sources that were polluted by sewage. (These increasingly expensive and sophisticated biological and chemical methods maintaining water quality are now being affected by toxic chemical residues in drinking water.)

However these early improvements were slow to take effect. Before they did, towns adopted slightly different approaches to the problem. In Manchester, the city council was still disposing of over 100,000 cartloads of human excrement to local farmers in the second half of the nineteenth century. Halifax, on the other side of the Pennines, developed a dry sewage system where the excrement was dried in pits, ground up and sold to farmers.

Even a relatively prosperous country such as Britain during the nineteenth century was slow to introduce improvements because of the capital investment required to produce reasonably clean water and install better facilities in houses. As late as 1911 less than half the houses in Manchester had their own lavatory and in one part of the town 700 people shared thirty-three lavatories. Dundee in 1910 had only three hotels and two private houses with water closets (and even then they only worked with buckets of water). The rest of the town had to use about 1,000 privately owned dry privies and fourteen public conveniences and the waste was sold to local farmers. Not surprisingly a city such as Moscow had an even more primitive system until well into the twentieth century. The first sewer was not built in the city until 1898, and in 1905 only 6,000 houses were connected to the system. Before 1917 only eighteen cities in the whole of Russia had even a rudimentary sewage system. As late as 1960 two-thirds of urban homes in the Soviet Union were not connected to a sewer. In the 1980s nearly all Moscow's sewage was put into the Moscow river untreated. Since the sewage input is twice the volume of the normal flow of the river, the latter is little more than an open sewer. In Leningrad and Estonia 80 per cent of the sewage still goes into the rivers untreated. Improvements only came very slowly in other parts of the industrialised world. In Paris, in 1925, half the houses had no sewage system and until the 1960s half of the sewage went into the Seine untreated. Generally it was only with the destruction of much of the nineteenth century housing in the middle of the twentieth century that the overwhelming majority of people even in the prosperous countries of western Europe obtained a decent sanitation system. In Japan the situation remained far worse. As late as 1912 Tokyo still lacked even a rudimentary sewage system, and in 1974 over half the population did not possess mains drainage. In countries such as Britain and the United States it is still a widespread practice for untreated sewage to be dumped into the sea, often close to bathing beaches. At the end of the twentieth century sanitary problems persist, and some ideas are still current – for example the reluctance to take action because of the cost of treating the sewage before it is dumped in the sea and the belief that dilution is an effective solution.

In the Third World the situation closely resembles that of Europe in the nineteenth century. The colonial authorities were often reluctant to build sewage systems for the native inhabitants. Governor Lugard wrote of the Gold Coast: 'Such a community has no desire for municipal improvement. It neither appreciates nor desires clean water, sanitation or good roads or streets.' In Lagos, the capital of Nigeria, in 1916, street scavenging and piped water supply were limited to the European area. As many Third World countries lack the resources to build proper sanitation systems, descriptions of their cities have changed little over the centuries. A report on Hyderabad in the 1950s commented that:

'A high majority of the citizens commit nuisance promiscuously in open spaces . . . Public latrines are few and far between . . . [and] are not kept clean by the scavengers, and it is an annoying sight to see many a scavenger emptying his bucket full at some street corner.'

In Manila, untreated domestic sewage now makes up seventy per cent of the volume of the Pasig river. In total, eighty per cent of the people in the Third World (in other words an overwhelming majority of the world's citizens) have no sanitary facilities and therefore still suffer from the disease and squalor that this causes.

One problem that has largely disappeared from the streets of the industrialised world is the huge quantities of waste left behind by animals on their way to market and from the large number of horse-drawn vehicles. (Dogs are the main exception – in Britain they are responsible for 1,000 tons of excrement and three million gallons of urine fouling the streets every day). For centuries the streets of the main cities of the world were polluted with horse droppings and urine. Roads would be turned into rivers of liquid manure when it rained or in hot, dry weather large quantities of dried manure would blow about as dust. The flies which were attracted were also a major nuisance (as was the noise from the sound of horses' hooves and metal-wheeled vehicles on cobbled streets – hence the habit of laying straw on the streets in front of hospitals or houses where people were ill). Most cities had to employ a small army of crossing sweepers so that people could cross the roads in some comfort. In 1830 it was estimated that animals produced about three million tons of manure on the streets of British towns and most of it was not sold to farmers but simply piled up into rotting, stinking heaps. The great increase in horse-drawn traffic in the nineteenth century worsened the situation considerably so that by 1900 about ten million tons of manure were deposited on Britain's streets every year. Most of the horses were grossly overworked, few lasted more than two years and many died in the streets. In 1900 New York had to clear 15,000 dead horses a year from its streets and in 1912 Chicago had to deal with 10,000 a year. The problem was never solved – it disappeared when horses were replaced by cars, buses and lorries which caused a different form of pollution.

Apart from the smell and the piles of rubbish and human and animal excrement in the streets, one of the other distinguishing characteristics of most cities was the pall of smoke which hung over them. As with water, pure air is a basic need but it is not something that most societies have organised themselves to maintain even where the source of pollution is obvious. The earliest evidence of widespread air pollution comes with the transition from wood to coal burning, although wood burnt on open fires or in rooms without adequate chimneys, which was normally the case in pre-modern houses, causes considerable smoke, which can lead to eye diseases (still a major problem in the Third World). Not surprisingly it was in England, where the shortage of wood was most acute and was felt earlier than in other countries, that the first complaints about the pollution caused by coal smoke were made. In 1257 Queen Eleanor was driven from Nottingham Castle by smoke from the numerous coal fires in the town and thirty years later a commission of enquiry was set up to investigate complaints about smoke levels in London. In 1307 the burning of coal in London was banned but the edict was ignored.

It was the great increase in coal-burning in the sixteenth and seventeenth centuries that produced the first large-scale pollution problems in London. The city could be recognised at a distance by the huge pall of smoke hanging over it and it was at this time that the western parts of the city became the most fashionable quarter because the prevailing westerly wind normally kept the clouds of smoke away. In 1661 the problems of widespread contamination and the adverse effects on health were already noticeable as the diarist John Evelyn wrote his *Fumifugium* – an attack on the state of the capital city. He described it as more like:

'the face of Mount Aetna, the Court of Vulcan . . . than an Assembly of Rational Creatures and the Imperial Seat of our incomparable Monarch . . . For there is under Heaven such Coughing and Snuffing to be heard, as in London churches and Assemblies of People, where the Barking and the Spitting is uncessant and most importunate . . . It is this horrid Smoake which obscures our Churches, and makes our Palaces look old, which fouls our Clothes and corrupts the Waters, so as the very Rain, and refreshing Dews which fall in the several Seasons, precipitate this impure vapour, which, with its black and tenacious quality, spots and contaminates whatever is exposed to it.'

Provincial cities were suffering from the same conditions as London. Indeed as early as 1608 visitors to Sheffield were warned that they would be 'half choked with town smoke' and in 1725 when William Stukeley was in Newcastle he found that 'the perpetual clouds of smoke hovering in the air make everything look as black as London'. Even in Oxford the air was so bad in the eighteenth century that classical marbles brought back to England were damaged very quickly.

During the nineteenth century the problem worsened in every city as numbers increased and coal became almost the sole form of domestic heating and cooking. London, as the largest city in the world at this time, produced some of the worst conditions. In 1880 there were 600,000 homes in the central parts of the city with three-and-a-half million fireplaces, virtually all of them burning coal. London fog (or smogs as they became known) became an increasingly unpleasant experience and a health hazard. During the middle decades of the century the number of foggy days in the year tripled and the terrible fogs caused by the enormous quantities of smoke in the air became commonplace and the death rate from lung complaints rose sharply during each period of bad fog. In December 1873 there were about 500 deaths caused by a particularly severe fog and in just three weeks in February 1880 over 2,000 people died. This pattern was repeated remorselessly every year for decades as smoke pollution worsened. Between 1920 and 1950 the average number of hours of sunshine in central London was nearly twenty per cent less than in the outer parts of the city less affected by concentrations of coal smoke. It was the terrible smog of December 1952, when over 4,000 people died, that finally brought about action. The Clean Air Act of 1956 introduced controls on the types of fuel that could be burnt in the centre of cities and by 1970 the amount of smoke in the air over London had fallen by eighty per cent and the amount of December sunshine had increased by seventy per cent. The enforced use of smokeless fuels, the decline in domestic coal consumption and the greater use of electricity, gas and oil for heating and cooking have drastically reduced smoke concentrations in Britain, as in most cities in the industrialised world.

All industrial processes produce waste products, many of which are dangerous to life in any significant concentration. Pollution from industry and mining is known from a variety of early sources but its incidence was limited and its effects usually fairly localised whilst industrial output was on a small scale. Amongst the earliest industrial activities that produced significant pollution were the mining and refining of metal ores such as gold (which normally requires the use of highly poisonous mercury) and lead. The Roman writer Strabo commented on the need for lead smelting works to be equipped with chimneys 'so that the gas from the ore may be carried high into the air, for it is heavy and deadly'. Over a thousand years later in his *De Re Metallica*, a treatise on mining in Germany published in 1556, Georgius Agricola described a scene that could have been found anywhere in the great mining regions of central Europe at this time:

> 'the fields are devastated by mining operations . . . The woods and groves are cut down . . . then are exterminated the beasts and the birds . . . when the areas are washed, the water which has been used poisons the brooks and streams and either destroys the fish or drives them away.

Early industrial Japan was similarly affected by mining operations. In 1610 the Ashio copper mine, which was to produce almost half the country's copper, was opened. Within a few years there was widespread pollution which eventually, in 1790, led the government to close the mine. It was reopened after the Meiji restoration and the waste dumped, as before, into the Watarse river. Within a year the fish were poisoned as was farmland flooded by the river. People, plants and animals in the area died – within twenty years twenty-eight villages were badly affected and almost 100,000 acres of land contaminated.

Although the reliance on human, animal, water and wind power for early industry meant that the energy inputs were largely non-polluting, the waste products of the earliest industries produced numerous pollutants, particularly in water courses. The tanning of ox, cow and calf hides and the tawing of deer, sheep and horse hides produced large quantities of acid, lime, alum and oil which, together with the remains of the hides, were usually dumped into the local river or stream. Other industries, such as brewing, needed clean water and complained regularly about pollution further upstream, although breweries put their own wastes into the river. Other industries such as cotton dyeing and sugar refining also polluted water and as early as 1582 the Dutch authorities had to order linen bleachers not to dump their waste in the canals but to use separate disposal channels known as 'strinkerds'. Twenty years later, James I of England was issuing proclamations against the pollution caused by the starch makers in London. In 1627 there were complaints about the fumes from the alum factory at St Katherines near the Tower of London. Even the aristocratic part of town was not immune and in the early eighteenth century the Duke of Chandos was railing against the conditions at his new town house in Cavendish Square, which he claimed was 'poisoned with the brick kilns and other abominate smells which infect these parts'. In the sixteenth century, the Thames near London still contained barbel, trout, bream, dace, gudgeon and flounders but by the eighteenth century they were extinct, killed by the increasing pollution.

The concentrated phase of industrialisation that began in the late eighteenth century brought about a revolution in the scale, intensity and variety of pollutants released into the atmosphere. The use of coal to fuel the massive increase in industrial production, particularly of iron and later steel, formed the backbone of the first industrial revolution. The forty-six-fold increase in world coal consumption and the sixty-fold increase in iron production during the nineteenth century inevitably resulted, given the lack of any serious attempt to control emissions, in large increases in the amount of pollution. The burning of coal produces smoke and sulphur dioxide and the smelting of metals, together with the other early industrial processes, particularly chemical manufacturing, produces large quantities of various environmentally damaging gases and wastes. The first industrial revolution created areas of concentrated pollution and environmental degradation – ruined landscapes of chimneys belching smoke and poisonous gases, huge slag heaps of waste materials, water courses full of a cocktail of industrial wastes and surrounding areas of vegetation destroyed. People had to live and work in these conditions.

The first areas to suffer from extensive pollution were the great industrial cities. As early as 1750, before the great increase in industrialisation in Britain, the citizens of Burslem in the Potteries were described as groping their way through the dense smoke that covered the town. A major offender was the early chemical industry, which made large quantities of sodium carbonate for use in glass, soap and textile manufacture: an unwanted by-product was a huge amount of highly corrosive hydrogen chloride, which was vented out of the chimneys with no effective controls over emissions. The formation by the government of the Alkali Inspectorate in the early 1860s was a belated recognition of the extent of the problem but it also illustrated the early power of the industrial lobby, since regulations were not introduced until new, less polluting processes had been invented and brought into production. In 1875 Queen Victoria complained that the ammonia fumes from the local cement works were making Osborne House, her residence on the Isle of Wight, uninhabitable, but government inspectors found that they had no powers to close down the works. This largely unregulated industrialisation produced huge amounts of pollutants in every industrialised area from the Ruhr and Limburg regions on the continent of Europe to the Black Country of the English Midlands and the Monongahela valley near Pittsburgh which had 14,000 smokestacks belching fumes into the atmosphere. Some of these areas were turned into poisoned wastelands – a century of industrial production in the lower Swansea valley led to the destruction of virtually all the vegetation – and one observer on Tyneside in the mid-nineteenth century described an early scene of environmental degradation:

'The sturdy hawthorn makes an attempt to look gay every spring; but its leaves . . . dry up like tea leaves and soon drop off. Cattle will not fatten . . . and sheep throw their lambs. Cows too . . . cast their calves; and the human animals suffer from smarting eyes, disagreeable sensations in the throat, an irritating cough, and difficulties of breathing.'

Apart from putting pollutants into the atmosphere, industries also put their liquid wastes into the rivers. Rivers had received sewage and rubbish for centuries; what was new was not their use in this way but the concentration of industrial pollution with factories often built alongside rivers to facilitate the disposal of their wastes. These factories produced a potent cocktail of poisonous chemicals that killed off most life in the rivers and turned them into health hazards for the human population. Nearly every river in the industrialised areas of Europe and North America was used during the nineteenth century as a convenient dumping ground for every form of industrial waste. During the twentieth century most industrial countries have introduced some regulation of water and air pollution by industry. But pollution has not stopped. Governments generally have given greater weight to the requirements of economic growth and industrial profitability than to demands for stricter controls. In most cases industry has been able to obtain permission to release chemicals, producing a situation of regulated, rather than unregulated, pollution.

Many industrial areas in what were until the late 1980s the communist states of eastern Europe reveal what can happen when pollution control is minimal. The overriding priority given to the development of heavy industry by the communist governments of the Soviet Union and, after 1945, eastern Europe, together with an almost complete lack of interest in enforcing what limited environmental controls were available, has produced a major environmental catastrophe. Their experience provides an idea of what conditions in nineteenth-century western Europe and north America were like during their phase of early industrial expansion. One of the most devastated areas was that of East Germany, north Bohemia and upper Silesia (particularly around the towns of Most in Czechoslovakia and Katowice in Poland). In this region there is a large concentration of iron and steel plants, other metal industries and chemical plants, nearly all using poor quality lignite coal that produces large amounts of impurities and pollutants. Even the Communist government of Czechoslovakia was prepared to admit that the area around Prague was 'a disaster zone'. In Most, sulphur dioxide emissions twenty times higher than the World Health Organisation's (WHO) maximum recommended levels were recorded and school children have had to carry portable respirators. The Polish government has described upper Silesia as an 'environmental disaster area' where sulphur dioxide levels in the atmosphere are one hundred times higher than official safety levels and 170 tons of lead, 7 tons of cadmium, 470 tons of zinc and 18 tons of iron are dumped from the atmosphere onto the historic city of Cracow every year. On over a third of the days in the year there are smog conditions, almost two-thirds of the food produced in the area is contaminated and unfit for human consumption and 70 per cent of the water can not be drunk. A third of the rivers are devoid of all life, the Vistula is unfit even for industrial use over two-thirds of its length because it is so corrosive and offshore an area of 100,000 square kilometres of the Baltic is biologically dead from the poisons brought down by the rivers.

In the Soviet Union the great industrialisation drive since the late 1920s also produced grave pollution problems that have only received considerable publicity and attention in the era of glasnost. The USSR Academy of Sciences declared in 1989 that 16 per cent of the country, containing over 50 million people, suffered badly from industrial and chemical pollution and constituted 'an ecological disaster area'. Air quality in Moscow began to decline in the 1930s as industrialisation took off – trees started dying and their growth rates fell by 90 per cent. By the early 1960s according to official figures, emissions of sulphur dioxide and nitrogen oxides were reaching near lethal levels in some suburbs of the capital and by 1970 only 14 per cent of the factories in the worst pollution category had been fitted with any form of controls to reduce emissions. Although the state introduced regulations to limit pollution, the overwhelming pressure on industry was to maximise output and few resources were put into anti-pollution measures. About three-quarters of the industrial waste sludge produced in the Soviet Union is still dumped untreated into the rivers. At the Karaganda Central Ore Concentration Mill carbon monoxide levels were twenty times, and sulphur dioxide levels four times, higher than maximum permissible levels and at the copper smelters at Krasnoural'sk overall pollutant levels were ten times higher than the maximum theoretically allowed by the Soviet authorities. One particularly alarming example of the consequences of this large-scale industrial expansion and the lack of attention paid to controlling pollution is that an estimated 42 per cent of the milk produced in the Soviet Union contained dangerous chemicals.

Other countries which came late to industrialisation have followed much the same pattern. Japan adopted the western model of industrialisation and incurred its environmental problems. In Tokyo by the late 1960s three-quarters of the city's rivers were devoid of fish and the official report on the state of the Sumida river in 1972 reads like a description of the Irk and Irwell rivers in Manchester in the middle of the last century:

> 'As a result of the pollution, the famous events which once took place on the river – swimming, regattas and firework displays have vanished. The gases rising from the river corrode metals, blacken copper and silver ware and shorten the life of sewing machines and TV sets.'

In China, industry's share in the Gross Domestic Product rose from 10 per cent in 1952 to 43 per cent in 1984 and nearly all of this expansion was achieved using coal – production increased twenty-fold between 1949 and 1982. The type of coal used contains large quantities of pollutants and in some Chinese industrial cities sulphur dioxide levels are seven times higher than WHO recommended levels. In Brazil there has been only minimal control of pollution during the recent phase of industrial expansion. Cubatao near Sao Paulo has been described as the most polluted place on earth. Air pollution is actually at twice the level considered lethal by the WHO, there are no fish in the rivers and 80 per cent of the local flora has been destroyed.

For the last two centuries pollution has been treated as an inevitable concomitant of industrialisation, part of the price to be paid for the advantages derived from the goods produced and the wealth generated by industry. To varying degrees individual countries acted to limit the worst effects and began to set standards. The aim though was not to achieve clean air or pure water but to set maximum, permitted levels of certain pollutants, with penalties, usually quite small, for infringement, the aim was to keep the environmental and health risks at 'acceptable' levels. Nevertheless by the mid-twentieth century it was becoming clear that pollution was not just a national but an international problem. Indeed some of the measures taken to limit national pollution proved to be highly effective means of exporting the problem. Optimistic hopes that pollutants would be dispersed on the wind or the waves were bound sooner or later to fail if state after state followed the same route of trying to disperse its pollutants. A good example of the development of an international pollution problem is the history of acid rain, which is directly linked to basic industrial processes such as fossil fuel burning and metal production.

The phenomenon of acid rain was first identified in Manchester, one of the centres of British industrialisation, in the 1850s and explained in some detail by one of the earliest British pollution inspectors, Robert Smith, in his book *Acid and Rain*, published in 1872. At first, with low chimneys on most factories and power stations, acid rain was a localised phenomenon around the main industrial centres. But the ever greater consumption of fossil fuels and the expansion of industrial output, together with the misguided policy of building very tall chimneys (in an attempt to reduce local pollution levels by dispersing the pollutants), has turned acid rain into a worldwide problem, prevalent both around and downwind of the world's industrial centres.

The burning of fossil fuels and the smelting of sulphide iron ores are the main sources of sulphur dioxide. The burning of fossil fuel also oxidises nitrogen to produce nitrogen oxides. When these oxides escape into the atmosphere they are altered, through a complex series of processes, into sulphuric and nitric acids, which make precipitation unnaturally acid. Global sulphur dioxide production rose from about 10 million tons a year in 1860 to 50 million tons in 1910 and to over 150 million tons by the 1970s. About half of these emissions come from the twenty-four western industrialised countries who are members of the Organisation for Economic Co-operation and Development (OECD). The United States and Canada alone have been responsible for a quarter of the world's output of this one pollutant. Sulphur dioxide emissions from the OECD countries have been falling since the 1970s as cleaner technologies have been introduced but overall world production is still increasing, mainly in eastern Europe, the Soviet Union, China and other industrialising countries. The highest per capita output of sulphur dioxide now comes from what used to be East Germany and Czechoslovakia. The result of the fifteen-fold increase in global sulphur dioxide emissions over the last 130 years is that ninety per cent of the sulphur dioxide in the air over Europe now comes from human created sources and in just ten years the Sudbury copper and nickel smelter in Ontario, Canada emitted more sulphur dioxide than all the volcanoes (the main natural source) in the history of the earth.

Acidity is measured on a PH scale where 6.5 is neutral; the scale itself is logarithmic so that a reading of 5.5 is ten times more acid than 6.5. Normal precipitation is slightly acid (5.7), reflecting the presence of carbonic acid produced from the carbon dioxide that is naturally present in the atmosphere. However increasing amounts of sulphur dioxide and nitrous oxides in the atmosphere as a result of industrialisation have produced rain more acid than normal levels. Highly acid rain has been noted on a number of occasions, often as low as a PH of 2.1 (vinegar is 2.4) and once at Wheeling, West Virginia, in the heart of one of the most polluted areas in the United States, a PH of 1.5 (battery acid is 1) occurred.

Acid raid directly affects buildings by slowly destroying the stone work. One of Poland's most historic cities, Cracow, is now suffering severe damage caused by emissions from the Katowice industrial area and the great cathedrals of northern France such as Rheims, Beauvais, Tours and Orleans are badly affected. One of the major effects of acid rain on ecosystems has been the gradual acidification of streams, rivers and lakes, often with devastating effects on the fauna. A PH of 6.0 is the critical level; below this, animal life begins to be affected. The exact processes involved are complex but one of the most serious is the higher concentrations of heavy toxic metals at lower PH levels, in particular the precipitation of aluminium as aluminium hydroxide on the gills of fish, which reduces oxygen intake and causes major imbalances in internal salt levels. In water with a PH of 5.5 salmon are affected and molluscs are rare. Between 5.5 and 5.0 there is severe damage to eggs and larvae and snails can not survive below a PH of 5.2. Fish can not live much below a PH of 5.0 and at a level of 4.5 even the flora is badly affected. One of the problems for wildlife in streams and ponds is not just the normal level of acidity but the occurrence of bursts of very acidic conditions caused by heavy rainfall or the melting of the snow in spring. The inexorable poisoning of the water by acid rain can be traced in the example of Lumsden Lake in the La Cloche mountains near Killarney in Ontario, where careful scientific monitoring has taken place since the 1950s. At the start of the research in the early 1950s there were eight species of fish in the lake, by 1960 two were extinct, by 1965 recreational fishing had ceased, by the end of the 1960s five more species were extinct and the one remaining variety was rare – that died out in 1978.

Some of the greatest damage to rivers and lakes has occurred in eastern Canada and the north east of the United States, downwind of the main industrialised areas, and in Sweden and Norway, which receive their acid rain chiefly from Britain. In upstate New York in the Adirondack mountains the proportion of lakes with a PH of below 5.0 rose from 4 per cent to over half between 1930 and 1970 and most of these lakes had lost all their fish. Norway and Sweden suffer from acid rain levels as high as those of the most polluted areas of western Europe even though their national emissions of sulphur dioxide are some of the lowest in Europe. The thin soils and underlying granite rocks provide little neutralising or buffering capacity and so most of the acid passes directly into water courses, and the fact that half of the yearly precipitation falls as snow only increases these problems because of the high burst of acidity following the spring melt. In Sweden most lakes had a PH of about 6.0 in 1950 but by the 1980s many were below 5.0; in the western part of the country the lakes were a hundred times more acidic than they had been in the 1930s. In the southernmost counties of Norway fish stocks fell by a half in the forty years after 1940. After 1978 the Atlantic salmon disappeared from southern Norway because of the acidification of its spawning grounds. By the late 1980s in Scandinavia over 20,000 lakes were badly acidified and about a quarter of all the lakes no longer contained any life.

It was not until the 1980s, some 130 years after the problem of acid rain was first identified, that some steps were taken to try and reduce sulphur dioxide emissions. The principle of stopping transnational pollution was accepted at a UN Environment Conference in 1972, in an OECD report in 1977 and in an international treaty signed in 1979 but not ratified until 1985. No effective action was taken until 1984 with the formation of the '30 per cent Club' among some of the industrialised countries who agreed to make a 30 per cent cut in the 1980 level of their sulphur dioxide emissions by 1993. Some countries such as Austria, Switzerland and France did better than this and made cuts of over 50 per cent by the late 1980s. In 1988 the European Community agreed to a 60 per cent cut in emissions from large power stations by 2003. Although these cuts may alleviate a regional problem, in global terms their impact will be marginal, offset by the increasing industrialisation of countries such as China and India based almost entirely on coal-fired energy production.

The pollution caused by industrialisation in the nineteenth century in western Europe and North America, and later in eastern Europe and the Soviet Union, had a severe impact on the people who worked in those industries and also on the population in the surrounding areas. Early industrial processes had few, if any, safety procedures and many of the workers were exposed to conditions that disabled them or ensured an early death. A number of industrial diseases were first identified by Bernardino Ramazzini, the professor of practical medicine at the Universities of Modena and Padua between 1682 and 1714. He pointed out that potters suffered from trembling, paralysis and loss of teeth from the large amounts of lead in the glazes they used, glass-makers experienced ulcerated lungs and sores in the mouth from using borax and antimony to colour the glass and gilders and hatters were subject to mercury poisoning – hence the expression 'mad as a hatter' or 'the Danbury shakes' (named after the American centre of the hat industry). One of the other major causes of disability, illness and death was dust – this affected cutlery grinders and miners in particular. The great industrial expansion of the nineteenth century and the consumption of fossil fuel resources were built upon the labours of the workers in the coal mines, who suffered from high rates of pneumoconiosis – associated with inhaling large quantities of coal dust. Other trades had their own particular occupational diseases. Lead production works were probably the most dangerous places of all; only the very desperate would work there since it was virtually a death sentence but, in conditions of extensive poverty, enough employees could be found. Cotton mills were also unhealthy because of the large quantity of lint in the air, which gave rise to many cases of byssinosis, a lung disease. Exposure to coal and oil products also brought a markedly increased risk of contracting cancers. This was first noticed among boy chimney sweeps in 1775 and again in the 1870s when 'mule spinners' cancer' became common in the textile industry after a switch from animal lubricants (mainly whale oil) to mineral oils. In one coal tar dye plant in the United States over a quarter of the male work force employed between 1912 and 1962 contracted cancer.

Industrial pollution does not just affect the health of industrial workers. It also contributes significantly to poor health in the population at large, especially in the heavily industrialised areas. The conditions in the early industrial cities with their very high levels of pollution caused by extensive coal burning and heavy metals in the air, together with other pollutants, produced appalling living conditions and very high death rates. In Manchester in the 1840s almost 60 per cent of working class children died before the age of five (twice the rate in rural areas). Statistics drawn from parts of eastern Europe in the 1980s are probably comparable with the sort of effects that were experienced by the residents of industrial towns in the nineteenth century. The industrialised areas of upper Silesia have the highest infant mortality rate in Europe (44 in every thousand children die before their first birthday), three-quarters of all children aged ten need constant medical treatment and the childhood leukemia rate doubled in the 1980s. Over a third of all children in Katowice have symptoms of lead poisoning and overall cancer rates are 30 per cent higher and respiratory disease rates 47 per cent greater than the rest of Poland. It is now officially estimated that one in five of the Polish population face serious health hazards from high sulphur dioxide levels in the atmosphere. In Most in Bohemia the picture is similar – only just over a third of the children are free of illness, respiratory diseases are more than double the national average and life expectancy is four years lower than in the rest of Czechoslovakia. In Cubatao in Brazil, the situation is even worse as is shown from the fact that the number of children born with anacephalia (no brain) is twenty-five times higher than the national average.

Since the Second World War there has been a significant change in industrial processes and therefore in the type of pollution produced. In this period pollution levels have risen far faster than the increase in population or even the increase in material consumption in the industrialised world. Until about 1945 the overwhelming bulk of industrial pollution came from two main sources: the burning of fossil fuels and heavy industrial production such as iron and steel, other metals and chemicals. After 1945 industry increasingly manufactured synthetic chemicals, many of which are highly toxic and resistant to degradation by natural processes, so that they accumulate in the environment. Many of them have not been tested for their effects on animals or the environment, individually or in combination, and many are readily taken up by living organisms where they accumulate. Even if released in minute quantities, they can have catastrophic consequences for natural ecosystems. Modern industrial production has shifted towards more polluting products – plastics, detergents, synthetic fibres, fertilisers and pesticides in place of natural, less polluting products such as soap, natural fibres and organic fertilisers. For example, the switch from soap to detergent manufacturing has increased phosphate production twenty-fold (and used far more energy) – industry prefers detergents because the profit levels, if not the cleaning power, are far higher: on average about 30 per cent on soap but over 50 per cent on detergents. Detergent use has substantially increased phosphate contamination of water supplies. Phosphate levels in American water courses rose two-and-a-half-fold between 1910 and 1940 but another seven-fold in the next thirty years. In the twenty years after 1950 fibre use per person increased by 11 per cent but natural fibres fell from 80 per cent of the total to 45 per cent, and in the last twenty years this trend has continued. The scale of these changes can be judged by the figures for US synthetic chemical production, which has increased from one billion pounds weight in 1945 to 400 billion pounds in the 1980s.

The impact these new chemicals can have on the environment can be seen in two cases – pesticides and polychlorinated biphenyls (PCB's). Before the middle of the twentieth century farmers relied on natural products such as pyrethrum or chemicals with no long-term damaging effects such as 'Bordeaux' and 'Burgundy' mixtures for pest control. Since 1945 pesticide production has become a major industry – use has increased thirty-three-fold and is still rising at about twelve-and-a-half per cent a year. The first highly toxic pesticides used were organo-chlorines such as DDT, followed after the early 1950s by organophos-phates, which are far more toxic though less persistent than the organochlorines. For decades there was little control over their use and even by the 1980s only a few of the most toxic have been banned. Because only about 1 per cent of the amount of pesticide sprayed actually hits the pests they have to be highly toxic even in minute doses. Many of the compounds are carcinogenic and about 20,000 people die every year and about another 750,000 suffer serious health effects from their use. This toxicity affects wildlife and plants in the vicinity, agricultural workers applying the chemicals, local residents subject to spray drift and water supplies when the pesticides run off into streams and rivers and penetrate deep into ground water. Pesticides are often used in very high doses, and instructions about their application and the gap needed before harvesting are not always followed, leading to contamination of food. Their effectiveness is reduced over time; many pests have developed immunity – the number of pesticide resistant insect species increased from twenty-five in the mid-1950s to over 450 by the 1980s. Twenty-five out of the thirty-six pests that attack cotton are now resistant and there are twenty-four types of mosquito resistant to DDT. Some of the most harmful to all forms of wildlife such as DDT are banned in the industrialised countries but still used in many parts of the Third World – a third of all US pesticide exports are of types banned within the United States. The worst examples of misuse come from the Third World, where many people are unable to read the instructions or take safety precautions. Only 10 per cent of India's cropland is sprayed with pesticides but the country has the highest level of residues in the world and some babies are ingesting twenty times more than the maximum acceptable intake.

The increasing use of pesticides has not, in practice, reduced crop losses – they rose from 32 per cent to 37 per cent in the United States between the 1940s and the 1980s. Pesticides cause immense damage to ecosytems by killing both pests and harmless animals. Since the 1960s over 800 species of fauna in the Paris region have declined in numbers by between 60–80 per cent following the widespread use of pesticides but only 5 per cent of these species are harmful to cereal crops. The need to spray large quantities of pesticides in order to kill pests and the increasing number and frequency of sprays – apple crops in southern England are now sprayed on average over twenty times during the growing season – have produced large amounts of residues in food and water.

The production of PCBs illustrates the way in which industry is researching and producing new synthetic compounds whose effects on the environment are often not recognised at the time. By the time that the consequences are recognised it may be too late to avoid a major problem. PCBs are chlorinated hydrocarbons, closely related to DDT and other highly toxic chemicals and some of them are now recognised as the most carcinogenic compounds known to science. They have been used since the late 1930s as insulators in electrical products, particularly transformers, additives in paints and in 'carbonless' carbon paper. As early as 1936 chloracne (a very serious skin complaint) was identified among people who had handled PCBs and special industrial procedures were introduced for its manufacture, but not its disposal. Nevertheless production continued for nearly four decades until it was eventually banned in the United States and Japan in the mid-1970s and in the European Community a decade later under pressure from environmental groups. By then about two million tons had been made and about sixty-five per cent of the total is still in use. Disposal of just thirty-five per cent of world production has already caused major environmental and health problems. PCBs have been dumped in the oceans or left to rot in toxic waste dumps, where residues have contaminated water supplies. High temperature incineration is thought to be the only safe way of disposing of PCBs but even this process may leave residues in the atmosphere. They are very stable, suffer little biodegradation, are highly dangerous, even in miniscule doses, and tend to accumulate in the fatty tissues of animals. PCB contamination has been found in human milk across the industrialised world, and even small traces have resulted in birth defects. There have also been major instances of contamination – in 1968 in Japan 12,000 people suffered from terrible illnesses after eating contaminated cooking oil and in the Wadden Sea off the Netherlands about half of the seals are sterile because of PCB poisoning.

The risk of industrial accidents is not new but a number of factors have increased their likelihood, notably the greatly increased volume of world trade and the increased production of hazardous substances. The introduction of national and even international safety standards has not avoided a series of major disasters following accidents or as a result of inadequate safety standards. Many of the new industrial chemicals are based on petroleum products and this, together with the industrialised world's dependence on oil, has meant that enormous quantities of crude oil are transported around the world in large supertankers. An accident to one of these vessels can pollute a wide area of sea and shore. For example, in 1967 the *Torrey Canyon* ran aground off the coast of Cornwall and spilt 100,000 tons of crude oil and eleven years later the *Amoco Cadiz* broke up off the coast of Brittany releasing 200 million litres of crude oil and contaminating 180 miles of coastline. In 1989 the *Exxon Valdez* ran aground in Prince William Sound in Alaska and eleven million gallons of crude oil poured into the water polluting 1,000 miles of coastline. In every case beaches were polluted and large numbers of sea birds and marine animals were killed – the *Exxon Valdez* disaster killed 250,000 seabirds, at least 1,000 rare sea otters and an unknown number of other animals.

Incidents involving chemical plants have produced serious consequences for surrounding areas, for the workers and local residents. In 1976 an explosion at Seveso in northern Italy resulted in the release of the highly toxic chemical dioxin. Over 900 people had to be evacuated, many suffered from disfiguring skin diseases, and there was also an increase in birth defects in the area. The top eight inches of soil over an area covering seven square miles was so badly contaminated that it had to be removed and buried. In 1986 a fire at the Sandoz chemical plant at Basel resulted in thirty tons of pesticides, fungicides and dyes being released into the river Rhine. No life survived in the river for 120 miles downstream of the plant and at least 500,000 fish were killed. In 1984 at Bhopal in central India thirty tons of methyl isocyanate escaped from a storage tank into an adjoining slum area where 200,000 people lived. The death toll is still unknown. The minimum admitted is 2,300 people but the most likely figure is about 7–10,000 with up to 20,000 more severely disabled. Almost as dangerous, but much more difficult to estimate, are the risks to the workers and the people living around these chemical plants from prolonged exposure to even low dosages of highly toxic compounds, particularly in terms of the increased chance of contracting cancer – the US government estimates that about ten million workers in the country are exposed to eleven highly carcinogenic compounds.

An even more difficult task than ensuring the safety of toxic chemical production is to find ways of safely disposing of the waste produced, together with obsolete items containing dangerous substances. This is part of a wider problem of disposing of the increasing amount of waste produced by industrial societies and modern patterns of consumption. The trend in the latter half of the twentieth century has been towards increased packaging for goods (partly because distribution chains have become longer) and for containers and other products to become non-returnable. For example, in the United States beer consumption rose thirty-seven per cent between 1950 and 1967 but in the same period the number of non-returnable beer bottles increased by 595 per cent. Americans now throw away sixteen billion so-called 'disposable nappies' every year and the city of New York alone produces 24,000 tons of waste every day. Waste disposal or, more euphemistically, 'waste management' has become a major growth industry. With re-use and recycling still at very low levels (apart from in some metal industries such as copper), the options commonly adopted are to incinerate the waste (releasing pollutants into the atmosphere), to dump it into the oceans (damaging marine ecosystems) or to put it into landfill sites. The latter pose major problems – finding enough sites, dealing with non-degradable items and leaching from the dump into the adjoining soil and water causing contamination. Parts of the industrialised world are already finding it difficult to provide enough landfill sites for ordinary non-toxic waste and toxic waste poses even more difficult problems that have not been solved.

By the 1980s there were about 70,000 chemicals in use and new ones were being added at the rate of about 1,000 a year. The majority have not been tested for safety but the best estimates suggest that about half of these chemicals are either definitely or potentially harmful to humans. Since 1945 the amount of toxic waste requiring disposal has risen dramatically. In the 1940s the United States produced about one million tons of hazardous waste. Forty years later the total had risen to over 250 million tons a year – about two-thirds of the worldwide total of 375 million tons. According to the US government, 90 per cent of toxic waste is disposed of in an improper way. Until the 1970s there were few controls over toxic waste dumping in any industrialised society. The contents and even the location of many sites are unknown and some countries such as Britain still have no central agency to control dumping. There is also a risk of 'cocktails' of new chemicals being produced in the dumps. About eighty per cent of all toxic waste produced by the industrialised countries is put into landfill sites without adequate containment; many only have clay linings which in practice are permeable. In this area there have also been deliberate, dangerous and highly irresponsible attempts to export the problem. Some of the most dangerous waste is sent to eastern Europe and the Third World to benefit from more lax regulations and less public opposition. There it goes into sites with few safety procedures or is simply left out in the open.

Toxic waste dumps have become major hazards. One of the worst affected areas is in the north-east of the United States near Niagara Falls. There, over 200 dumps contain eight million tons of waste which is seeping into the water supplies for over six million people. Amongst the waste was Mirex, a pesticide used to kill fire ants in the southern United States. Over 2,000 pounds of the chemical leached through the soil and into Lake Ontario in the mid-1970s. It is so toxic and carcinogenic that the allowable level in water supplies under both American and Canadian law is nil. The sadly misnamed Love Canal, a dump used in the 1940s and later sold by the company responsible for filling it for one dollar plus an indemnity against any future liability, was used as the site for a school and nearly 250 homes. In 1978, after much local suffering and protest, the area was declared a disaster zone by the federal government and evacuated. In three separate incidents the Dutch authorities have had to demolish 500 homes and relocate 1,500 people from houses built on toxic waste dumps. In Britain large quantities of asbestos were dumped in sites around Hebden Bridge in Yorkshire – over seventy local residents have since died of asbestos related diseases. The Georgswerder dump in Hamburg exploded in

1984 and is still releasing over a hundred million cubic metres of gas a year.

Just as in previous centuries, much modern waste is dumped or discharged into rivers, lakes and oceans. Although the industrialised world has introduced legislation to limit discharges, many rivers are badly contaminated by a mixture of chemicals released from the industrial plants along their banks. As a result they may contain little, if any, animal life over long stretches. In some cases so much oil and chemicals have been poured into them that the rivers have actually caught fire. Such incidents have been reported on the Iset near Sverdlovsk (1965), the Ganges (1968), the Cuyahoga at Cleveland (1969) and the Volga (1970). In the Soviet Union the development of cellulose and paper plants along the shores of Lake Baikal, the largest freshwater lake in the world (the area contains 708 plants and animals not found anywhere else on earth, including the only freshwater seal) produced an environmental catastrophe. The water became so polluted that it could not be used in factory intakes without treatment. In just eighteen months in the late 1950s 383 tons of toxic chemicals were dumped in the lake, producing islands up to eighteen miles long and three miles wide of toxic sewage. The Great Lakes in North America, particularly Lake Erie, were also highly polluted with little life in them in the early 1960s, although the situation improved slightly later as stricter pollution controls were introduced.

Oceans have been treated as if they are so vast that any amount of waste can be put into them with impunity. Every year New York dumps nearly nine million tons of waste in the Atlantic off the mouth of the Hudson river. The result has been to create an area of black toxic sludge covering about a hundred square kilometres which supports no marine life at all. Each year an estimated six-and-a-half million tons of litter is thrown into the sea from ships, including five million plastic containers a day. (About one million seabirds die every year because of plastic pollution). In addition about six million tons of oil get into the seas; about one-and-a-half million tons of this come from ships flushing out fuel tanks. The oceans also have to absorb spoil from dredging, often containing very large amounts of toxic heavy metals, DDT and PCBs. The United States alone is responsible for sixty-seven million tons a year. Many states such as Britain and the United States also dump untreated sewage sludge and since the 1960s incineration of toxic chemicals at sea (which produces toxic gases and residues) has become widespread – 100,000 tons a year are burnt in the North Sea alone.

Since 1945 one of the most hazardous of all new technologies has been the production of energy from nuclear power. It provides only one per cent of the world's energy but produces one of the most dangerous forms of pollution. Although the world's population is exposed to background radiation from radioactive materials in the earth's crust and from extra-terrestrial sources, all forms of radioactivity are inherently dangerous. At high levels it is lethal within a short period and at lower levels there is an increased risk of cancers and genetic defects. There is no known safe dose – the nuclear industry works to exposure levels (both for workers and the public) which they hope will not produce an 'unacceptable' level of danger. The peacetime risk to humans comes in two ways – accidents leading to sudden intensive pollution and pro- longed exposure to lower levels of radioactivity among workers and the public.

Although theoretical calculations show that the chances of a nuclear accident are remote, in practice nuclear power has throughout its history suffered from serious accidents. In 1957 the core of one of the reactors at Windscale in north-west England caught fire and there was a major release of radioactivity across much of Britain. The number of people who died or contracted cancer as a result is unknown but over two million litres of contaminated milk were destroyed as a result. In the same year there was an explosion in a nuclear waste dump at Kyshytym in the Soviet Union, which heavily contaminated an area extending over 150 square miles. Thirty communities and 270,000 people had to be evacuated and about 10,000 people probably died as a result of the incident. At Three Mile Island in Pennsylvania in 1979 one of the reactors suffered a partial core meltdown and, although a catastrophic disaster was avoided without a substantial release of radio- active material, the work needed to contain the radioactivity within the plant, estimated to cost over one billion dollars, had not been completed a decade later and the reactor will have to be left permanently entombed in concrete.

The most disastrous of all nuclear power accidents occurred at Chernobyl in the Ukraine in 1986 and it illustrates the immense difficulty of dealing with such an accident and its aftermath. An explosion in one of the reactors released a gigantic cloud of radioactive debris that spread across Scandinavia and western Europe. Vegetable and animal sales were stopped across a wide area, and many of the reindeer of Lapland were slaughtered because they had eaten large quantities of contaminated lichen. When they were killed the animals were found to contain seven times more radioactivity than normal.

Four years after the accident sheep in parts of north-west England and Wales were still too radioactive to be eaten. About 21,000 people in western Europe are expected to die of cancer, and even more to contract the disease, as a result of the explosion. The effects in the immediate area were far worse and the full extent of the consequences had not become apparent four years later: 220 villages had to be abandoned and 600 towns and villages decontaminated. An area extending over 10,000 square kilometres was declared too dangerous for human habitation, though much of it remained occupied and farming continued. Over 150,000 people were evacuated but others were left in place after the Soviet authorities increased the 'safe dose' of radiation to fifty per cent greater than the lifetime dose allowed for workers in the nuclear industry. The health of at least 100,000 people in the Soviet Union is likely to be severely affected by the disaster.

Lower level exposure to radioactivity, although less spectacular than major accidents, has also been a source of many problems. The whole population of the world (but particularly the native inhabitants of the areas near the test sites) has been exposed to the fall out from 458 nuclear explosions in the atmosphere between 1945 and 1985 with an unknown toll in increased cancer deaths and genetic defects. The whole process of providing fuel and disposing of the waste is highly danger-ous. The mining of uranium, the fuel for nuclear reactors, is injurious to the health of the miners because of the radioactive dust. The very high lung disease rates experienced by the metal ore miners in the Erzegebirge region (in the Sudetenland) in the mid-sixteenth century were almost certainly caused by uranium in the rocks and in the twentieth century half of all uranium miners have died of lung cancer – a rate five times higher than that of the population as a whole. The next stage, the milling of uranium ore, causes about 4,000 deaths a year from lung cancer in the United States alone. Large amounts of radioactive waste are produced from a multitude of civil nuclear uses, from relatively low level items such as the clothes of the workers at nuclear installations, through isotopes used in hospitals, to highly radioactive materials such as reactor cores, which remain lethal for tens of thou-sands of years. There is no known safe method of disposing of this waste. Low-level waste is buried, like other toxic waste, in landfill sites but the most dangerous category is currently being stored above ground at the nuclear sites pending difficult political decisions about how and where to dispose of it. The term 'disposal' is even more inappropriate in this case than in other forms of pollution, given the difficulty (if not impossibility) of finding any method that can be guaranteed to be safe for the immense periods (perhaps 100,000 years) over which this highly radioactive material will remain dangerous.

Some attempts have been made to discharge or dump radioactive waste in the environment but they have all caused major problems. In 1949 the Soviet authorities started releasing liquid nuclear waste into the Techna river near Sverdlovsk. By 1952 it had reached Lake Karachai near Kyshytm, where the heat from the decaying radioactive material dried out of the lake and the radioactive bed of the lake had to be covered in concrete to stop wind erosion spreading the dangerous pollution any further. Until the mid-1980s the industrialised countries dumped some of the waste (mainly intermediate level) at sea – the total rose from 20,000 tons in 1967 to over 100,000 tons a year by 1983 – and radioactivity in the main dumping ground off the Spanish Atlantic coast rose seven-fold in this seventeen year period. Following concern at the dangers involved, especially corrosion of supposedly safe containers, international agreement was reached to stop dumping but no alternative method of 'disposal' has been found. The practice of reprocessing spent fuel to provide more fuel, which developed after the 1960s, only increases the amount of radioactive waste that requires disposal and encourages trade in highly dangerous materials around the world. Some of the material has leaked out into the environment. Between 1945 and 1973 422,000 gallons of radioactive material leaked out of storage tanks at the American nuclear site at Hanford. In a little over a decade after 1968 the British plant at Sellafield discharged 180 kilogrammes of plutonium (which is lethal in the minutest quantities) into the Irish Sea. Given these practices, and the difficulty of shielding the workers in the plants from low level radiation, it is not surprising that higher than average cancer rates have been experienced in members of the public living around many nuclear plants.

Another major cause of pollution which has been increasing rapidly since the Second World War is the internal combustion engine. This is a technology which has spread right across the globe (though the bulk of pollution comes from the industrialised world) and which has found multiple applications, with few controls or national policies to limit its use or the output of exhaust gases. All internal combustion engines produce a range of pollutants – carbon dioxide, carbon monoxide, nitrogen oxides, a range of toxic organic compounds and smoke. Once released into the atmosphere they produce different forms of air pollution, including peroxides (which irritate the eye) and ozone (which at ground level reduces photosynthesis in plants and makes breathing more difficult). In combination these exhaust gases react with sunlight to create 'photochemical smog' – a poisonous haze now found over most modern cities. Vehicle exhausts were also made more polluting by the addition of lead to fuel. By the 1920s the higher compression engines then coming into production required higher octane fuel to operate correctly. Instead of improving refining techniques to increase the octane rating of the fuel, the oil companies found it was easier and cheaper to add tetraethyl lead which produced the same result. The corporation that manufactured the tetraethyl lead was half owned by General Motors and there was therefore an incentive to keep increasing the compression ratios in car engines so as to increase the demand for fuel with lead additive. Between 1946 and 1968 the amount of lead used per vehicle mile in the United States rose by eighty per cent as more powerful and higher compression engines were introduced. Lead is poisonous and its effects include brain damage in children who breathe in vehicle exhaust fumes.

At first, cars, buses and lorries were welcomed as less polluting than the horses that fouled city streets during the nineteenth century. Significant problems began to emerge as the number of vehicles on the roads rose. The large-scale effects of vehicle pollution were first noticed in the United States, the first country with high levels of car ownership. The Los Angeles valley has a natural inversion layer, which results in air being trapped in the valley on many days in the year, causing concentrations of exhaust pollution to increase dramatically. In 1943 the first photochemical smog was noticed and within a decade the need for urgent action was clear. Although clean air controls were introduced on fires and the petroleum refining industry reduced its emissions by ninety per cent between the early 1940s and the late 1950s, no action was taken on vehicle exhausts. The number of cars continued to increase and the problem continued to worsen. By the late 1950s eye irritation was being experienced on half the days in the year and by August 1969 during a particularly bad period doctors had to warn residents not to play golf, jog or do anything that involved deep breathing. By the late 1980s photochemical smog affected over one hundred American cities, 80 million Americans lived in areas where ozone was above permitted levels and San Francisco suffered from photochemical smog and dangerous air on over 200 days a year. As car ownership increased in other countries so the same problems developed there. Smog became serious in Tokyo in the late 1960s and over 50,000 people were disabled by it in 1970–1972. In Mexico City, which like Los Angeles, has a natural inversion layer in the valley, there were 312 days of severe smog in 1988 and in early 1989 school children had to be kept at home for a month because of the high pollution levels. In Athens the pollution was severely damaging the historic monuments and in just two days in August 1984 over 500 residents had to be hospitalised because of the severe smog.

Controls on vehicle emissions have only been introduced belatedly. No government has been prepared to take action to limit car ownership directly and, at most, a few such as Venezuela and Greece have experimented with imposing restrictions on how vehicles can be used in the capital cities – usually on alternate days according to whether the number plates are odd or even numbers. Controls have therefore largely relied on technological fixes aimed at the symptoms rather than the root cause, and they were introduced only after considerable pressure from campaigning groups. In 1970 the Clean Air Act in the United States started the phasing out of lead additives, a process that did not begin in the European Community until the mid-1980s. This was not difficult technically since it merely required the petrol companies to produce a slightly modified product and adjustments to be made to vehicle engines. The reduction of exhaust gases is technically more difficult. Since 1975 all new American cars have had to be fitted with catalytic converters, which remove some of the most harmful chemicals in exhausts. Japan has also introduced restrictions but new cars will not have to be fitted with them in the European Community until 1993. Catalytic converters do not however affect the amount of carbon dioxide produced by vehicle engines. In other areas of the world relatively little has been done to reduce vehicle pollution.

The emergence of a new hazard in the form of photochemical smog illustrates one of the most alarming trends in pollution – the 'cocktail' effect. The increasing range of dangerous chemicals released by new industrial processes, the intensive application of pesticides and artificial fertilisers, and the ubiquity of vehicle exhaust gases coming on top of older pollutants such as sulphur dioxide and acid rain, have the potential to increase the damage done individually by any one of these pollutants. One of the most widespread manifestations of this effect is visible in damage occurring to many of the forests of North America and Europe, which have been seriously affected by a combination of atmospheric pollutants – acid rain, heavy metal deposition, nitrogen oxides and ozone (from vehicle exhausts) and various toxic chemicals. The complex way in which the latter can affect trees is demonstrated by the group of chemicals known as chlorocarbons, which include tetrachloroethylene (a dry cleaning fluid) and trichloroethylene (a lubricant). The production of chlorocarbons increased two-and-a-half-fold in the twenty years after 1960 and about seventy per cent of this production has escaped into the atmosphere. They can build up in the needles of pine trees, where they destroy the pigments necessary for photosynthesis. Tetrachloroethylene also reacts with ozone and ultra-violet light to produce trichloroacetic acid (TCA) which is a very powerful herbicide. Pollution levels can be judged from the fact that three year old pine needles on some trees in Germany had levels of TCA five times greater than plants that had actually been sprayed directly with TCA as a herbicide. As a consequence, needles which would normally live for about twelve years were dying after about three years.

Pollution has killed trees around industrial plants since the early nineteenth century through a combination of acid rain and heavy metal contamination. Most of the great industrial areas were rapidly de-forested and the same problems are still experienced across the world. In Norway fluoride emissions from aluminium smelters have killed all pines within a four mile radius, a desert surrounds the copper smelting plant at Copper Hill, Tennessee and no trees grow for twelve miles downwind of the magnesite brick factory at Satke in the Urals. Some of the first signs of widespread damage to trees not in the vicinity of industrial plants were identified in the San Bernadino forest eighty miles downwind of Los Angeles, where in the early 1960s excess ozone reduced growth rates by eighty per cent. Pine trees in the Great Smoky mountains showed the same problems and virtually stopped growing – on average between 1962 and 1983 they grew as much as they had done between 1958 and 1961. The situation in the United States worsened significantly and rapidly in the early 1980s. In Kentucky three quarters of the white pine trees had been damaged by 1984 and mature red spruce were losing ninety per cent of their foliage. On Mount Mitchell in North Carolina, where the hilltops are swathed in mist and fog containing very high levels of ozone and heavy metal particles, as well as acid levels a thousand times higher than normal rainfall, 78 per cent of the trees were still normal in 1984 but two years later 73 per cent were badly damaged and over 60 per cent had lost more than half their foliage. In the United States it appears to be pines that are the worst affected type whereas in Europe the damage has occurred in eleven species, including many deciduous varieties. The widespread damage to and death of trees, dubbed 'Waldsterben' in Germany, became evident in the early 1980s. In West Germany 8 per cent of the conifers were damaged in 1982, 50 per cent by 1984 and 87 per cent two years later. In Switzerland over a third of the forests are affected (up to half in many cantons) and in Britain about two-thirds of all conifers have been damaged. In eastern Europe, with its very high levels of pollution, damage is even more extensive – in Poland three-quarters of all forests are affected (about 100 million trees), in East Germany 83 per cent. Overall more than 20 million acres of forest in Europe had been damaged by the mid-1980s (an area equivalent to a third of the British Isles).

During the last two centuries pollution has increased dramatically in volume as more countries have industrialised and the size of industrial output has expanded, and it has also become more dangerous with the increasing use of complex, artificial chemicals. Its effects have spread from the immediate vicinity of industrial plants and cities through transnational pollution such as acid rain, to the diffusion of poisons into the most remote areas of the world. The ease with which modern chemicals can spread can be illustrated by two examples. When in 1983–4 the East Germans sprayed DDT (a pesticide banned in many other countries), residues were detected over a 1,000 mile range from north of Stockholm to the south of France. Samples taken in West Germany showed DDT levels four times higher than normal and in neighbouring Poland contamination increased ten-fold. In 1978 islands on Lake Superior showed traces of pesticides that had only been sprayed onto cotton crops in the southern United States over a thousand miles away.

Increased pollution has had a devastating impact on wildlife around the world because of the way natural ecosystems and food chains work. Artificial compounds such as pesticides or PCBs can only be broken down very slowly, if at all, and they therefore tend to accumulate in living creatures. Organisms at the bottom of a food chain may only have ingested a minute quantity but higher up the chain, as these organisms and animals at lower levels are eaten and their pollutants are passed on, concentrations rise rapidly. The effects this can have are illustrated by what happened when the Clear Lake area of California was sprayed with DDT in 1949, 1954 and 1957 in an unsuccessful attempt to eliminate gnats. The insecticide was sprayed at a concentration of one fiftieth of a part per million. The level of DDT found in plankton was 250 times greater than in the water, in frogs it was 2,000 times more, in fish 12,000 times and in the grebes who fed on the fish 80,000 times greater. As a result the grebes at the top of the food chain had 1,600 parts per million of DDT in their bodies; their eggshells became so thin that they cracked under the weight of the bird and of the 1,000 pairs of grebes in the area not one hatched a chick between 1950 and 1962. It was the implications of this ecological disaster, which had been repeated elsewhere with other chemicals, that led Rachel Carson to write *Silent Spring*. The controversy surrounding her revelations led, despite strong opposition from the chemical companies involved, to the eventual banning of DDT in the industrialised countries although it is still used in the Third World. Similar effects have been seen with the use of many other chemicals – for example the spraying of grassland in Scotland with dieldrin led to the deaths of many golden eagles at the top of the food chain. Other highly toxic chemicals have spread around the world. For example, even the relatively small amounts of PCBs that have so far been disposed of have been detected in Antarctic penguins and also dolphins and seals in the Indian Ocean. In some cases the level of contamination has been sixteen times higher than that which would be required to classify the animals concerned as toxic waste in the industrialised world. Even minute quantities of PCBs are carcinogenic and also cause major birth defects.

Evidence of industrial pollution has been found all over the globe in places far away from the original sources. Traces of heavy metals in peats, lake sediments and ice sheets show that by 1700 pollutants released by the metal industries of Britain and central Europe were reaching most parts of Scandinavia. In cores taken from the Greenland ice cap lead levels began to rise after 1800 and have grown twenty-four-fold in the last two hundred years (quadrupling since 1940 because of higher vehicle emissions). Even cores from the Antarctic ice sheet, supposedly the last wilderness on earth and even more remote from the industrial centres of the northern hemisphere, show that lead levels have quadrupled since the eighteenth century. A comparison of bodies from a well preserved Inuit grave on Greenland dating from about 1450 shows that the levels of heavy metals in the bodies of contemporary Inuit are much greater than five hundred years ago – mercury contamination is four times, copper four-and-a-half times and lead eight times higher.

Pollution has not only spread to every part of the world but, by the second half of the twentieth century, it had begun to affect the global mechanisms that make life on earth possible. Ozone depletion and global warming are probably the most serious pollution threats the world has ever faced. At ground level ozone is a pollutant that reduces plant photosynthesis by about twenty per cent and makes breathing more difficult for humans. However, in the stratosphere (twelve to

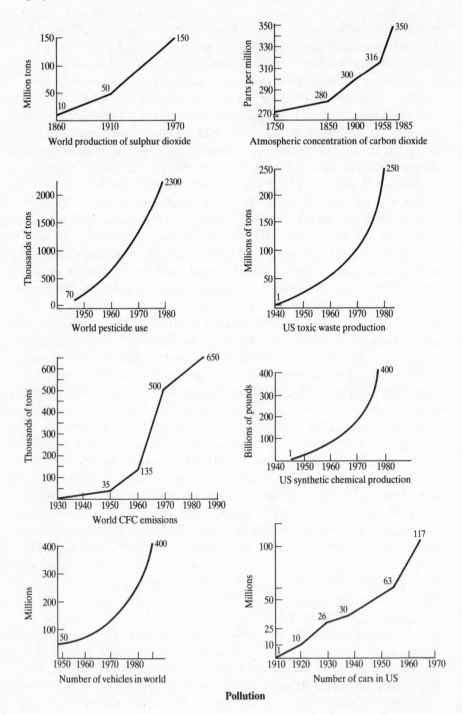

World production of sulphur dioxide

Atmospheric concentration of carbon dioxide

World pesticide use

US toxic waste production

World CFC emissions

US synthetic chemical production

Number of vehicles in world

Number of cars in US

Pollution

eighteen miles above the earth) the ozone layer absorbs ultra-violet radiation, which is harmful to nearly all forms of life, and severely reduces the amount reaching the earth's surface. This protective ozone layer is being destroyed by artificial chemicals called chlorofluorocarbons, or CFCs. These gases are very stable and can survive in the atmosphere for up to a hundred years without breaking down. They gradually rise into the stratosphere, where the ultraviolet radiation splits away one of their chlorine atoms and starts a complex series of chemical reactions that break down the protective ozone. A single chlorine atom can destroy up to 100,000 ozone molecules.

CFCs were invented in the 1920s (by Thomas Midgely, the same scientist who first suggested tetraethyl lead as an additive for petrol) and were adopted in many industrial processes because they were non-poisonous, did not burn and did not react with other substances. They were used to clean electronic circuit boards, as refrigerants, in car air-conditioning systems, to make expanded foam containers which were good heat insulators and as propellant gases in spray cans. CFCs were cheap to produce and their use expanded rapidly; their low cost and apparent safety meant there was little incentive to minimise waste or make any special arrangements for their disposal. About a third of the CFCs in car air-conditioners were lost through 'routine' leakage and over half during servicing. When old fridges were scrapped the gases were simply let out into the atmosphere. About three-quarters of the CFCs in the atmosphere come from spray cans, a use that began in 1950 – by the early 1970s Americans alone were using about one-and-a-half billion spray cans a year powered by CFCs. Emissions of CFCs into the atmosphere rose rapidly from 100 tons in 1931 to 35,000 tons a year in 1950, 130,000 tons in 1960, 500,000 tons in 1970 and to 650,000 tons a year by the mid-1980s. Nearly all CFCs have been used by the industrialised world – American consumption is eight times higher than the world average – but use is increasing in the Third World; for example the number of people owning fridges in Peking rose from 3 per cent of the population to 60 per cent in the ten years before 1985 and all the machines used CFCs.

Emissions of CFCs have increased and with them concentrations in the atmosphere (the levels doubled in just ten years after 1974). As a consequence, levels of chlorine have also increased at about 5 per cent a year (doubling every fourteen years), from 0.6 parts per billion in the late 1950s to 4 parts a billion by 1989. Between 1979 and 1986 4 per cent of the world's ozone was destroyed but in the higher latitudes near the poles the figure was over 6 per cent. The most spectacular fall in ozone levels occurred over the South Pole, where the conditions in winter were ideal for large-scale destruction. A 'hole' in the ozone layer was first noticed in 1982 but by 1989 about half of all the ozone over Antarctica had been destroyed and the resulting hole in the spring months covered an area equivalent to the continental United States. In the stratosphere, where most of the destruction takes place, about 95–97 per cent of the ozone was destroyed. When the 'hole' drifted north in the summer (to as far as 45°S) ozone levels fell by 12 per cent over Melbourne in 1987, by 15 per cent over Macquarie island in 1987–90 and to 20 per cent below 1979 levels over New Zealand. In the northern hemisphere a severe thinning of the ozone layer was evident by the late 1980s over Scandinavia, Siberia, Canada and Greenland.

A thinning of the ozone layer allows more ultraviolet radiation to reach the surface of the earth, where it has deleterious effects on human health and plant and animal life. The best estimates suggest that for every one per cent reduction in ozone the number of human non-malignant skin cancers increases by four per cent, malignant cancers by one per cent and eye cataracts by one per cent. By the late 1980s warnings were issued in Australia not to sit in the sun during periods when the ozone 'hole' was drifting over the country. Some plants such as soybeans, one of the major crops in the world, are easily damaged by ultraviolet radiation as are the phytoplankton in the top few inches of the oceans, which form the base of oceanic food chains.

Environmental pressure groups pointed out the dangers in CFC use in the early 1970s but industrial interests denied any linkage with the ozone layer and governments failed to take action. Only under growing pressure and the unmistakable evidence of the Antarctic 'hole' did action begin to emerge in the 1980s although most was achieved by a successful consumer boycott of CFC powered spray cans. In 1978 the American government banned the use of CFCs in spray cans, some other countries followed suit but no international action was taken until 1987 with the Montreal Convention. This was a weak agreement between the industrialised countries that allowed production to increase by 10 per cent above 1986 levels (in practice for sale in the Third World) and then provided for a cut of 20 per cent by 1994 and a target of a total cut of 30 per cent by 1999. Growing public awareness of the scale of the problem forced governments to hold a further conference in London in 1990. That led to a worldwide agreement to reduce CFC emissions by 50 per cent by 1995 and 85 per cent by 1997 and to phase out their use by 2000 (some countries such as West Germany and Sweden have announced plans to phase out production by the early 1990s).

However because of the immense stability and long life of CFCs it will be well into the twenty-first century before any significant benefits are obtained. Although CFC emissions started to fall in the 1980s, atmospheric concentrations have continued to rise. Continued production during the 1990s, release of CFCs already used in fridges and airconditioners and the drift of already released CFCs into the stratosphere will continue to deplete the ozone layer for decades. Latest estimates suggest that 18 per cent of the ozone layer above the northern hemisphere will be destroyed by 2000 resulting in significantly increased cancer and cataract rates. CFC concentrations are unlikely to fall back to 1986 levels before 2030. It is also possible that the rate of ozone destruction may increase faster than the rate of CFC accumulation in the stratosphere from past emissions. In addition some of the substitutes that will be used for the two main types of CFC have similar though less intense effects. Destruction of the ozone layer is therefore likely to continue at least until the latter half of the twenty-first century, posing a continued threat to human health and with other as yet undiscovered knock-on effects on delicate ecosystems.

Without greenhouse gases in the atmosphere to trap outgoing terrestrial infra-red radiation, the average temperature on the earth would be about $-18°C$ and too cold for life. These gases, primarily carbon dioxide and methane, maintain the temperature at about $15°C$. However, in the last two hundred years human activities have added extra quantities of existing greenhouse gases – carbon dioxide, methane and nitrous oxide – and introduced new ones in the form of CFCs. The effect of these additions has turned the greenhouse effect from a vital life-sustaining mechanism into what is probably the world's most threatening environmental problem – global warming. The major human contribution to the greenhouse gases has been carbon dioxide. It is a form of pollution that has been building up over the last two hundred years since fossil fuels became central to sustaining the industrialised world's way of life. Annual consumption of coal is now over one hundred times greater than it was in 1800 and annual oil consumption has increased more than two hundred-fold in the twentieth century. Fossil fuels are burned to provide energy for industry and to generate electricity, they are used in homes for heating and cooking and in vehicles (the latter produce 20 per cent of global carbon dioxide emissions and are the fastest growing source). All these activities release carbon dioxide into the atmosphere. The destruction of the tropical forests also has the effect of increasing carbon dioxide levels, not only because trees and plants are burned but also because there are fewer plants and trees to absorb carbon dioxide during photosynthesis. It is estimated that when carbon dioxide is produced, about half of it is absorbed in various natural 'sinks', in particular the oceans, and the remainder accumulates in the atmosphere. The net result of these various human activities is that the amount of carbon dioxide in the atmosphere has risen by a third in the last two hundred years – from about 270 parts per million in 1750 to 350 parts per million in the late 1980s. About half of this increase has occurred since the 1950s – carbon dioxide emissions rose from 1.6 billion tons a year in 1950 to 5.4 billion tons in the mid-1980s. Global use of fossil fuels is rising at about 4 per cent a year (which means a doubling every sixteen years) and carbon dioxide is increasing in the atmosphere at about 0.5 per cent a year. Carbon dioxide has provided by far the greatest volume of greenhouse gas emissions and contributed about two-thirds of the total warming effect so far.

The second major source of greenhouse gases is methane, which has been produced in a number of ways. Because of the need to feed the growing population, there has been, in the last two hundred years, a big increase in the number of paddy fields in south-east Asia and methane is released from the decaying vegetation and manures that sink to the bottom of the paddy fields. Another contributory factor has been the increase in the number of domesticated animals, which all have bacteria in their guts which produce methane as a waste product. Large scale destruction of the tropical forests has also increased the world's population of termites, which feed on decaying wood and which also produce methane as a waste product. The number of paddy fields in the world is increasing at about 0.7 per cent a year while the number of cattle doubled between 1960 and 1980 and is continuing to rise at about 1 per cent a year. The combined effect of all these processes has been to increase the amount of methane in the atmosphere by about 135 per cent since the eighteenth century; the current rate of increase is about 1 per cent a year. The third and fourth sources of greenhouse gases are the CFCs that have accumulated in the atmosphere since the 1930s and emissions of nitrous oxide, coming partly from the increasing use of nitrate fertilisers and also from vehicle exhausts. Methane only makes up about 1.7 parts per million of the atmosphere but is responsible for about 17 per cent of the greenhouse effect because it is about twenty times more effective than carbon dioxide at absorbing infra-red radiation. CFCs are only in the atmosphere as trace gases but still make up about 12 per cent of the greenhouse effect because they are many thousand times more potent as absorbers of infra-red than carbon dioxide. Nitrous oxide is found only in a low level in the atmosphere but contributes 5 per cent of the greenhouse effect because it is 120 times more potent than carbon dioxide.

In 1896 a Swedish scientist, Svante Arrhenius, was the first to forecast a rise in global temperatures from the burning of fossil fuels. His warning was largely ignored for decades. Environmentalists first warned of the potential problems in the 1960s but it was not until the 1980s that the scientific community began to accept the reality of global warming. The scientific problem lies in identifying to what extent climatic changes may be attributed to artificially induced global warming and in forecasting the likely consequences. The earth's climate is subject to both long-term changes (the Milhankovic effects, which are the primary determinants of the ice ages and warm interglacials) and smaller, short-term fluctuations caused by factors such as sunspots, dust in the atmosphere and natural variability. Meterological observations suggest that in the course of the twentieth century global temperatures have increased by 0.5°C, with the 1940s being warmer and the 1950s and 1960s cooler than the average. The 1980s were the warmest decade since records began and they also contained six out of the ten warmest years in the period 1860–1989. 1990 was the warmest on record. Research has also revealed that the amount that glaciers have retreated during the last century and the extent of the rise in sea levels are also in line with what would be expected as a result of a global warming of 0.5°C. The increase in temperature is consistent with the estimates of the overall increase in greenhouse gases, and it has been estimated that there is only about a one per cent chance that this is a random fluctuation. The human induced increase in greenhouse gases is already equivalent to all the short-term natural variability in the climate caused by volcanic activity and sunspot cycles, and of course it is only pushing in one direction. The warming of the earth's atmosphere also has important feedback effects. As the tundra regions, which are widespread in the northern hemisphere near the poles, become warmer and the permafrost melts, they release methane and therefore multiply the greenhouse effect. As the atmosphere warms it can also hold more water vapour, which itself absorbs infra-red radiation, although this effect may be partly offset by the increase in cloud cover reflecting more of the sun's heat back into space.

The greenhouse gases that have been put into the atmosphere over the last few decades have yet to make their full impact on global temperatures. It is virtually certain that gases already emitted will cause a further 0.5°C rise in global temperatures by the early twenty-first century. With emissions likely to go on increasing with continued industrialisation, more vehicles on the roads, more animals and more paddy fields, temperatures are likely to continue to increase. One of the reports by the UN Intergovernmental Panel on Climate Change (IPCC), set up in the late 1980s in response to growing scientific and public alarm about the implications of global warming, estimates that emissions of greenhouse gases will be equivalent to a doubling in current levels of carbon dioxide in the atmosphere by 2030. This, according to the panel of experts, is likely to produce a temperature rise of between 1.5–4.5°C, with 2.5°C the most likely outcome, above pre-1850 levels by 2030. An overall global increase of this magnitude disguises much larger variations likely to be experienced in some parts of the world depending on exactly how the world's climatic systems adapt to the higher temperatures – in northern high latitudes in winter, temperatures may increase by about 8°C. This sort of increase in global temperatures would mean that the earth will be as warm as it has ever been in the last 120,000 years (at the peak of the last interglacial, which was one of the warmest during the succession of ice ages and inter-glacials that have occurred since humans have existed) and possibly even warmer.

The IPPC reports predict that the consequences of global warming on this scale will be profound for the whole of the world. Climatic patterns are likely to alter drastically but unevenly. Global precipitation is likely to increase by about 10 per cent but some areas will be much drier, others much wetter – scientific modelling of the earth's weather systems is not sophisticated enough to predict changes in detail. The most likely outcome is that the earth's vegetation belts will shift towards the poles, but in an uneven way. The Great Plains of North America together with the Mediterranean region may become drier and, as in other climatic optima such as the warm spell around 1000–1200 AD, crops could be grown nearer to the poles than in the recent past but on an even larger scale. The real difference between previous periods of global warming and the experience now envisaged for the period up to 2030 and beyond will be not just the magnitude of the change (more than that ever experienced before by settled societies) but the rate of change.

In the past during the descent into ice ages or the ascent into interglacials, the average global temperature has not fallen or increased by more than about 0.5°C a century. The IPCC projections suggest warming at about three to six times this rate. Natural vegetation zones, which in the past have been able gradually to shift in response to changing climatic conditions, will almost certainly be unable to adjust to changes at this speed. There is no guarantee that if the conifers of the great taiga of Northern Europe and America die off they will be replaced by decidous trees better adapted to the warmer climate. Although in agriculture it would, in theory, be feasible to adjust to new crops, different techniques and changed seasonal conditions, the uncertainties involved and the scale of the problem would in practice create enormous difficulties for both farmers and governments. Changes in rainfall and temperature will cause severe problems of water supply, especially in areas already suffering from shortages. There are no direct historical parallels to draw on in assessing the likely impact on human populations. Among the worst affected are likely to be the poorest living in the most marginal areas and with the most fragile food supplies. The social effects could involve large-scale migration, social disruption and widespread starvation. Some low-lying countries and regions will face the problem of severe flooding as rising temperatures expand the oceans and cause glaciers and ice sheets to melt. A 2.5°C rise in temperature is likely to cause sea levels to rise significantly across the world, although the effects will vary from area to area. Among the areas most at risk of coastal flooding and salt water infiltration into drinking water are the Nile Delta and Bangladesh, and low lying islands such as the Maldives could even disappear altogether. Ocean currents could also shift in unpredictable ways leading to further changes in temperature and rainfall across the globe.

Dealing with the problem of global warming will cause severe economic, social and political problems. Human societies have never faced an environmental problem on this scale and of this complexity before. Because the output of greenhouse gases is so closely linked to industrial output, energy consumption and other factors such as car ownership, the problem of reducing emissions is essentially one concerning the future of industrialised societies and the nature of their consumption of energy and resources. For societies apparently committed politically, structurally, psychologically even, to the idea of economic growth and higher levels of consumption this particular form of pollution represents a fundamental challenge. It has already raised the question of equity between the countries of the world and their respective claims to further economic expansion. Carbon dioxide emissions have been overwhelmingly the responsibility of the industrialised world. Almost half of these emissions have come from just eight countries – the United States has been the largest single contributor with 17 per cent of the global total, the Soviet Union next with 12 per cent and then the most industrialised countries (Japan, Germany, Britain, France, Italy and Canada) with another 17 per cent. India and China currently contribute 10.5 per cent between them (though their past contribution is much less). Because of their huge populations, in per capita terms they rank well below any of the major industrialised countries (about a twelfth of the level of the United States) and even below countries such as Colombia and Thailand. Since the primary responsibility for the problems posed by global warming lies elsewhere, it is not surprising that countries still engaged in the process of industrialisation have objected strongly to the idea of accepting targets for emissions that would have the effect of holding back, and possibly even ending, their plans to industrialise. But, without a global agreement, any measures to limit emissions from the industrialised world are likely to be offset by increases elsewhere in the world. An attempt to cut global emissions by 50 per cent by 2030 could be offset by current Chinese plans to expand its industrialisation programme over this period and increase its energy consumption six-fold (two-thirds of it coming from coal). These plans, if implemented, would still produce levels of consumption far lower than those of the industrialised world.

Ecosystems all over the world have now been affected to varying degrees by pollution of various types. Even Antarctica has been polluted, so far-reaching has been the spread of industrial pollutants. Evidence about how resilient plants, animals and humans are to the risks and long-term stresses associated with pollution is still accumulating. It is, however, already apparent that the effects of pollutants have become more threatening. Actions have been taken with very little thought for the consequences, particularly in the case of highly toxic chemical and CFC production. The output of greenhouse gases is likely to have the greatest and most widespread effects of all the pollutants so far produced by humans. After ten thousand years of settled societies and only two hundred years of substantial industrialisation, human activities and the pollution they generate threaten irreversible changes on an unprecedented scale to the world's climatic system.

17
THE SHADOW OF THE PAST

The foundations of human history lie in the way in which ecosystems operate. All living things on earth, including humans, form part of these complex webs of interdependence between the different plants and animals constituting a food chain stretching from the photo-synthesisers at the bottom through the herbivores to the carnivores at the top. Because of the decreasing energy efficiency of the food chain, the number of creatures that can be supported at each level gets pro-gressively smaller. When the direct ancestors of humans first emerged, probably in East Africa about 2 million years ago, they operated mainly as herbivores, but they were also carnivores – scavenging dead animals and undertaking a small amount of hunting. Their numbers therefore were limited by the ability of the local ecosystems to support animals operating towards the top of the food chain.

Human history is, at one level, the story of how these limitations have been circumvented and of the consequences for the environment of doing so. Overwhelmingly the most important departure from basic ecological constraints has been the increase in human numbers far beyond the level that could be supported by natural ecosystems. The first steps were the gradual spread of humans around the world and their adoption of techniques that enabled them to dominate terrestrial ecosystems. This depended on a number of special attributes stemming from their greatly increased brain size – speech, social co-operation and the development of various technologies (very simple at first) to further the process of adaptation to a wide variety of habitats. At this stage people lived by gathering and hunting food and their impact on the environment was, apart from a few instances such as the extinction of large mammals at the end of the last ice age, generally limited by their way of obtaining food, their mobile way of life, their lack of posses-sions and their relatively small numbers. But numbers did creep upwards very gradually, perhaps to about four million people by about

10,000 BC. The pressure from rising numbers did not abate and these groups broke through ecological constraints by the adoption of agriculture. It was not a sudden process; initially it involved little more than a more intensive use of existing ways of obtaining food. But the end result was to disrupt or destroy natural ecosystems, since all farming involves creating an artificial environment to grow selected plants and tend domesticated animals.

This was a watershed in human history, a shift from a way of life that had prevailed for two million years. It helped in a way to solve the problem of how to feed an increasing number of people, but in doing so it opened the way to further growth in population. Agriculture, once adopted, proved a generally effective method of supporting an ever larger number of people by bringing more land into cultivation and using more intensive means of cultivation. Human history for the last 10,000 years has been shaped by this agriculture-based boom – a rise in numbers from four million to five billion. Behind this overall trend were some significant fluctuations and some individual cases of agricultural failure, societies which in the end failed to sustain the particular artificial habitat they had created and come to rely on, where the superstructure proved too much for the foundations. Until the late eighteenth century the overall rate of population growth was generally slow because of the difficulty of matching food output with human numbers. Nevertheless, as more land was brought into cultivation, more people could be fed. It is only in the last two hundred years, with improvements in health, higher agricultural output and the increasing importance of commerce, industry and services, that the world's population expanded rapidly. By the 1980s the earth had to support about ninety million extra people every year – an increment the same size as the total population only 2,500 years ago. These people have had to be fed, accommodated, clothed and provided (to a varying extent) with goods and services. Even if per capita consumption had not increased, this huge rise in numbers was bound to place increasing demands on the earth's resources. Most of these demands were driven by basic human needs. As more land was needed to grow food, more natural ecosystems were destroyed. Timber was needed to construct houses and wood was required for cooking and heating and so forests were gradually cleared. Metal ores were wanted to make both tools and luxury items and so the earth's mineral resources were consumed. People had to be clothed and so land had to be cultivated for crops such as cotton, animals kept to provide wool and leather and wild animals trapped for their skins and fur.

The increasing demand for resources resulting from the growth in numbers not only placed strains on the environment, it also forced the development of more complex techniques requiring more effort. Agriculture illustrates this process very well. Gathering and hunting involves a relatively low level of effort in order to obtain an adequate and varied diet. The adoption of agriculture required more work such as sowing, weeding, watering, harvesting and storing. Domesticated animals required such things as tending, milking, shearing, pasture, winter feed, fencing and shelter. In return for that greater effort a higher output of food could be obtained from a smaller area, although, because farming depended on a small range of crops, agricultural societies in fact faced a greater risk of inadequate food supplies compared with gathering and hunting groups. Different types of agriculture involve very different levels of effort to obtain food. The one requiring least work is swidden or 'slash and burn' since it dispenses with weeding and fertilising and the only tool required is a digging stick. It seems likely that only pressure from growing numbers (which reduced the scope for fallow periods when the forest cover could regenerate and soil fertility recover) forced people towards establishing permanent fields and taking on the additional task of clearing grassland and ploughing. Paddy fields and irrigation also require higher levels of effort. Modern intensive methods, although less labour intensive, require even more inputs in the form of machines, fertilisers, pesticides, energy and resource consumption in order to achieve the high levels of output needed to feed a larger population.

The same sort of results stemming from increasing population pressure can be seen in the case of clothing. The first humans were able to clothe themselves using the skins of animals they had killed or scavenged. As numbers rose, this was no longer possible and textiles were made from natural fibres such as flax, cotton and wool. This required using land for cultivating crops or for animal grazing as well as the extra effort of spinning and weaving the raw materials. These sources, together with hunting and trapping wild animals for fur, provided enough clothes for centuries. Rapidly rising population in the nineteenth century, the need to use more land to grow food rather than other crops and the wholesale destruction of many populations of fur-bearing animals placed an increasing strain on these resources. Only the development of ways of manufacturing artificial fibres from chemicals has enabled the world's population to be clothed in the twentieth century. But these more complex manufacturing techniques use more resources and energy.

The same sequence of increased demands leading to shortages, the adoption of new technology and the use of new resources can also be seen in the case of writing materials. Given a low productivity agriculture where finding enough food for humans was a difficult task, medieval Europe (and China too) could support only a small number of animals because of the difficulty of feeding them, especially in winter. The amount of parchment and vellum (from animal skins) that could be produced was therefore strictly limited. As demand for writing materials increased, it was necessary to substitute what was widely regarded as an inferior product, paper, made mainly from wood pulp. The consequence was that more trees were felled (and in the twentieth century large monocrop plantations of pines and eucalyptus created) to support an industry with a wide range of paper products and rapidly increasing output. Similarly shortages of wood supplies in Europe led to the increasing use of what was regarded as an inferior fuel – coal, which required greater effort to mine and transport than wood and which was more difficult to use in many industrial processes. As energy demands have continued to increase, even more technologically complex processes such as offshore oil production have had to be developed.

From one perspective this invention of new techniques and more complicated production processes and the utilisation of more resources can be viewed as *progress* – the increasing ability of human societies to control and modify the environment to meet their needs through sheer ingenuity and a capacity to respond to challenges and to engage in problem solving. From an ecological perspective, the process appears as a succession of more complex and environmentally damaging ways of meeting the same basic human needs.

It was the first great transition in human history – the adoption of agriculture and the consequent rise of settled communities – that set human society on this path. It allowed more people to be fed, though often numbers were out of line with the capacity of the agricultural system, perennially exposed to the vagaries of the weather and climatic changes, thus leading to widespread malnutrition and recurrent famine. The second great transition in human history – the use of fossil fuel energy sources and the spread of industrialisation – marked a massive leap in the process of using more of the earth's resources to support far more people, making it possible to provide some of them with far more food and goods than had ever been available before. For the first time in human history energy was freely available enabling industrial output, and with it the rate of consumption of the earth's resources, to increase to unprecedented levels. It has been estimated that the *extra* industrial output produced in the world *each* decade after 1950 is equal to the whole industrial output of the world before 1950. Within less than two hundred years after 1800 the world's population increased five-fold, requiring a vast increase in agricultural output and the destruction of large areas of previously untouched natural ecosystems as well as using far more intensive ways to farm the already highly modified ecosystems that made up existing agricultural land. A large proportion of this increased population has been concentrated into cities, where numbers have risen from about twenty-five million people to over two billion. The amount of pollution caused by human activities has increased faster than the rise in population and the level of industrialisation. Its nature has also changed since 1945 with the increasing production of non-natural products, often toxic in minute quantities, which cannot be broken down by natural ecosystems.

The effects of the first great transition were experienced in virtually every part of the world – agriculture was adopted separately in different places and distinctive settled societies developed in the Near East, China, the Americas and elsewhere. The second great transition was different. It was a process dominated from the start by a part of the world – Europe, then North America and then Japan. The reasons for this lie mainly in the establishment of their increasing control over the rest of the world in the centuries after 1500. This control took a number of different forms – European settlement, colonies and colonial trade, followed by the United States and later Japan operating a different, but still very effective, form of domination through trade. Since 1945 these countries have been able to ensure their continued domination of the world's economy not just because of their overwhelming political, military and economic power, but also through international institutions and control over aid and surplus food distribution. Until the last four or five centuries all societies in the world depended almost entirely upon the resources they could obtain from within their immediate area – trade was limited and transport was poor. Since 1500 Europe and the industrialised countries have had access to the resources of the whole world, first to provide a wider variety of food, then important staples and second to provide a source of raw materials (and also markets) for continued industrial expansion.

The expansion of Europe can be viewed as the gradual establishment and expansion of empires and the bringing of 'civilisation' to less fortunate peoples. From an ecological perspective, it seems more like a wave of destruction spreading across the world. The settlement of North America exemplifies this process. At the leading edge of the frontier the indigenous inhabitants were brought under European influence and, eventually, control, starting with the activities of traders and trappers. They were dispossessed of their land by settlers and pushed further westwards, where the process was repeated until they were reduced to a sad remnant of a once flourishing people. As the fur trappers and hunters extended their activities, they exterminated many species such as the beaver, bison and passenger pigeon, either totally or over a wide area. The settlers cleared the natural forests and established fields. With so much land the tendency was for agriculture to expand to meet the space available – moving on as poor practices rapidly exhausted the soil and left it susceptible to erosion. As productivity declined, degraded land was abandoned and the frontier of cultivation moved further west. At the same time timber companies were also cutting down the forests and mineral prospectors and companies were developing mines to extract metal ores and coal. Industries developed and with them large, sprawling cities that spread across the countryside.

The process of moving from a pre-industrial society to an industrialised one has been dubbed *development*. As with the idea of progress, it has been acclaimed not only as desirable but inevitable if more people are to be supported and the seemingly insatiable desire for higher material standards is to be met. The global framework of institutions and trading patterns created by those nations which went down the path first, and their related mental framework, revolving around the ideas of modern economics and the imperative of maximising GNP, fostered a climate in which the goal of development is accepted worldwide. Today the tide of destruction can be seen sweeping across the Amazon region of Brazil, a country with vast natural resources, which is energetically pursuing the course of development. It is, in a more concentrated form, the same process of change that took several hundred years to accomplish in Europe and which was replicated later in a select number of other countries.

Amazonia, the largest area of tropical forest on the earth and inhabited by some of the last remaining gathering and hunting peoples, was too remote and difficult to exploit on a large scale until the 1960s. Then the region was opened to settlement with the building of roads into the tropical forest – the population along the Brazilia-Belem road rose from 200,000 when it opened in 1960 to two million a decade later. The Indian tribes suffered immensely in the wake of a series of intrusions into their traditional lands: including first gold prospectors, then land speculators and landless peasants, ranchers, loggers and civil engineers building roads and dams. The gold prospectors (100,000 people were trying to find gold in 1988 as part of the military Calha Norte programme to settle the area along the northern borders of Brazil) use mercury to obtain the gold and this pollutes the water over a wide area. To provide land for settlement and cultivation and, above all, for huge cattle ranches, large forest areas are burnt, even though the grass which grows after clearance of the forest is too poor to support animals for more than a few years. Peasant settlers are encouraged to move into the area in order to relieve the pressure for land reform in the rest of the country (over 80 per cent of the farmland in Brazil is owned by less than 5 per cent of the population). In Rondonia (the western part of the Amazon) 70–80,000 new settlers arrive every year and a third of the forest had been cleared by the late 1980s. The rate of forest destruction is increasing rapidly. In Para state about 18,000 square kilometres were destroyed in the century before the mid-1970s. Between 1975 and 1986 180,000 square kilometres were destroyed. Probably about a fifth of the tropical forest in the Amazon has been destroyed and about fifty million acres a year are added to the total. Industrial development in the region is now underway and will increase the scale of destruction still further. For example, the Grande Carajas project in the north east of Brazil will affect one sixth of Brazilian Amazonia (an area the size of Britain and France combined) with a series of plantations, ranches, mines and heavy industry. Dams will flood large areas to provide hydroelectric power for new industries. 11,500 square miles of forest will be cleared for cattle ranching and 21,000 square miles for plantations to grow export crops. A bauxite mine will produce eight million tons a year (mainly for Japan) and the estimated eighteen billion tons of iron ore in the region (some of the highest grade left in the world) will form the basis for an iron-smelting industry. No pollution controls are planned and the smelters will be fuelled by cutting down the forest to make charcoal – an estimated ten million acres every year.

A political, social or cultural history of the twentieth century, and particularly the last few decades of the century, might well record a growing disillusion with the consequences of development and detect a trend towards a greater interest in the idea of conservation and protection of the environment. This has involved the injection of environmental topics into both domestic and international politics together with the growth of public campaigning to obtain policy changes in areas affecting the environment such as agriculture, industrial regulation, pollution and development aid. However such currents of thought have not displaced the basic philosophy, engrained in western thought for the last two thousand years, that sees a separate 'natural world' for humans to exploit, and the economic approach that sees (or claims to see) continued industrialisation and further economic growth as a prerequisite for any environmental improvements. Nor have greater awareness and campaigning on environmental issues led to significant changes in practice. In recent decades there has been an increase in the number of measures, both domestic and international, introduced to try to limit damage to the environment, including important international agreements on acid rain and CFC emissions. Yet many of the measures by their nature – accepting wildlife conservation in specific areas, licensing pollution up to certain levels, let out clauses for 'scientific' whaling, setting targets without allocating resources to ensure they are implemented, giving a small amount of help for organic, less intensive farming while continuing with huge subsidies for more intensive farming – could be more readily interpreted as ways of shoring up the existing economic system than the first steps towards something new and different. There have been some achievements and in some cases (for example, pollution from coal smoke in major cities) conditions are undoubtedly better than they would otherwise have been.

However, compared with the scale of the problems, many measures are little more than cosmetic. Set against the powerful momentum induced by continued population growth, the need for more land to grow food and the in-built requirement of the world's industrial system to expand, the results of these measures on a world scale have been barely noticeable. It is clear that the process of industrialisation is a continuing one. Just as agricultural production has become steadily bigger and more intensive so industrialisation is taking the same path. The process has been under way for thousands of years since the first potters and metal workers, the introduction of the first water power sources two thousand years ago and the increasing use of machinery in Europe and China after about 1000. The great burst of industrialisation from the late eighteenth century is only the most intensive phase of that development so far. There is also no sign of the industrialised world ceasing to grow while the rest of the world catches up or of any large scale transfer of resources that might help to make that possible. Those who refer to the 'post-industrial society' are focusing on a sociological phenomenon of a relative decline in heavy industry and factory production in favour of services and high technology industries. As industrial productivity increases, more of the population can be supported in tertiary activities but industrial production persists, indeed it continues to expand and therefore the amount of resources and energy consumed increase too. De-industrialisation may apply to some regions within a country but not to modern society as a whole.

What do past experiences suggest about the stability and sustainability of human society as it has developed in the industrialised world and in the partly industrial but still mainly agricultural Third World? Contemporary societies are subject, as a result of past developments, to a number of pressures affecting the quality of life for many of their citizens, stemming from unequal access to wealth and food, resource shortages, pollution, health problems and shortened life expectancy. Yet both human beings and societies are remarkably tolerant and resilient. For thousands of years humans have lived with the consequences of various forms of environmental degradation without necessarily incurring social breakdown. In some cases societies have succumbed to environmental pressures but the decline and eventual collapse were usually prolonged (in Mesopotamia it came about gradually over at least a thousand years) and generations living through this process would probably not have been aware that their society was facing long-term decline. Even where the collapse came relatively rapidly (as on Easter Island and with the Maya), the import of the preceding period of rising problems may not have been fully apparent to those alive at the time.

The environmental problems now facing the world stem from a variety of pressures that have developed over long periods of time, some restricted to specific areas whilst others affect the whole world. Over this same period the political history of the world has produced a large number of highly unequal states all asserting the right to independence and national sovereignty, yet at the same time obliged to operate within a wider international system. Relations within that system, as in the past, are characterised as much by competition and conflict as by co-operation. This means that, given the highly unequal distribution of the world's wealth and power that has evolved in the last five hundred years, it is extremely difficult to deal with problems that cut across national boundaries and with those that entail significant financial and social costs. The effects of the various pressures on the world (whether they are interpreted as evidence of growing global breakdown or not) have been, and will continue to be, experienced by different countries and different regions in radically different ways, thus reinforcing the difficulties inherent in evolving coherent international strategies or even compatible national ones. Past experience suggests that these pressures will continue to be felt in four main areas – growing strains on resources, unequal development and distribution of food and wealth, a growing weight of numbers and the threat from the outputs of industrial society in the form of pollution. In each of these areas the shadow of the past falls across all modern societies as they try to find solutions.

The ability to utilise more resources and energy has always been essential for the continuation of industrial society. In 1972 the Club of Rome published a controversial book *Limits to Growth*, which forecast a collapse in industrial output and uncontrollable decline in population within a century largely as a result of the exhaustion of resources and energy supplies. The computer models on which the study was based, and the assumption of continued exponential growth in production, have proved to be unreliable. The experience of the 1970s and the 1980s showed that the main immediate threats to the world did not come from a shortage of resources or even a shortage of energy, although at some time these non-renewable resources are bound to be exhausted. Apart from one or two specialised minerals, known reserves of metals are estimated as sufficient for at least a century and in most cases even longer. New reserves are likely to be discovered (as they have been in the past) and recycling and substitution of materials can be increased. Past experience suggests that these processes will require additional energy in order to utilise lower grades of ore and this, together with the continuation of the increasing demand elsewhere in the system for energy and oil-based products, which has been apparent for several hundred years, is likely to cause problems. The world's known coal reserves are sufficient for several centuries. On current projections proven reserves of oil might only last to the first quarter of the twenty-first century though the total exploitable reserves on the earth are still unknown. World consumption of oil is seven times higher than in 1940 but known reserves have been growing even faster, by about two per cent a year more than consumption. During the great fossil fuel boom alternative energy sources have been largely ignored with the exception of high technology programmes and there is considerable scope in this area to develop new sources of energy. As far as resources generally are concerned, the main problems in the foreseeable future are likely to be accessibility and whether the experience of the past two hundred years of a relative abundance of energy at low prices can continue. A looming global crisis and social breakdown brought on by the world running out of raw materials and energy in the immediate future now seems less likely (although these problems, and therefore the future of industrialised societies, will have to be confronted at some point in the future). The serious and immediate pressures are now coming in the form of the degradation and destruction of some of the other vital resources on which societies depend: global environmental regulators, soil, water, air and biodiversity.

Over the last two hundred years the industrialised countries have reached levels of consumption and affluence (and experienced the problems that go with this growth) that would have been unimaginable to previous generations. This has been achieved by consuming the great majority of the world's energy supplies and resources (and creating a similar proportion of the world's pollution). The United States contains about 5 per cent of the world's population yet it consumes 30 per cent of the world's energy and 40 per cent of its other resources. The other side of the coin is that more than 55 per cent of the world's population still live in rural areas and remain, as their ancestors were, directly dependent on agriculture for their livelihood. About half of the people of the world (two-and-a-half billion) are undernourished, twenty per cent (about one billion) live in absolute poverty and lack basic necessities such as clean water, sanitation and proper housing, and only slightly fewer are illiterate. Even if current European and American levels of consumption were to be stabilised, it must be extremely doubtful whether the rest of the world (over 80 per cent of the people on the earth) could ever repeat the process of industrialisation and attain these levels. The number of people in the world is expected to be six billion by the end of the twentieth century. If they were to live at current European (not American) levels of consumption, it would require a 140-fold increase in world steel production together with a similar increase in other key materials. It is unlikely that there are enough mineral or energy resources on the earth to sustain this level of production and the consequences of doing so in terms of pollution would probably be catastrophic. Likewise to feed the whole of the world on the diet enjoyed by the average American, and using the same level of inputs into agriculture, would require all the world's current oil production and exhaust known reserves within not much more than a decade. But the non-industrialised world aspires to industrialisation on the western model and some countries are firmly set on this road. This raises major problems of equity as to whether the Third World could, or should, be prevented from industrialising because of the possible consequences in terms of resource consumption and pollution, when the current problems of unequal development and pollution are mainly the responsibility of the industrialised world.

For the last ten thousand years the weight of human numbers has been a crucial factor in determining the ability of societies to feed their citizens and provide an adequate standard of life. The industrialised world (having moved out of its period of rapid population growth in the nineteenth century) is having to adjust to lower birth rates and unbalanced age structures while, elsewhere, the continuation of two centuries of extremely rapid population growth is producing major strains in the Third World. The population of the world in the late 1980s was 5 billion and it will, given the number of young people and the likely birth rate, rise to about 8 billion by 2025 and even higher later in the century. 95 per cent of this growth will occur in the Third World, where the pressure on scarce resources and limited land is already most intense. In the 1980s the total amount of land in the world devoted to agriculture expanded at only 0.1 per cent a year and the amount of arable land actually declined because of the effects of past agricultural expansion – soil erosion, desertification and salinisation. After ten thousand years of agriculture about 11 per cent of the world's surface is now used for growing crops and there is little land left suitable for agriculture – what remains is either too steep (as in the Andes), too acid, too dry (as in most of Africa) or in the tsetse fly area of Africa where trypanosomiasis (sleeping sickness) is rife. About a quarter of the world's surface has been taken over for grazing animals and although arable land could extend into this area, the net increase in food production would be small and past experience suggests that these soils, if ploughed, are likely to suffer from severe soil erosion very quickly. The only other land that could be used for agriculture lies in the tropical forests where the soils are poor and produce crops only for a limited time, and where it is apparent that the consequences of clearance will be environmentally catastrophic. It is therefore extremely unlikely that the world will be able to feed, let alone provide the other resources to support, the estimated growth in population without a radical restructuring of the pattern of world food consumption that has evolved in the last five centuries since the expansion of Europe. If this does not take place, the current levels of malnutrition, hunger, starvation and death are likely to rise among the poorest of the world's people.

The fourth area where stresses and strains have been increasing for the last two centuries is the unwanted outputs of the industrial system. In particular developments in the second half of the twentieth century have raised the question of the extent to which societies can pollute the environment with impunity. Experience suggests that societies can tolerate appalling conditions on a localised scale, for example those found in the heavily industrialised areas of nineteenth-century Britain and the United States, and in parts of eastern Europe in the mid-twentieth century, albeit at a cost of shortened lives, more illness and general environmental degradation. Even dramatic local disasters such as the deaths of thousands of people at Bhopal or the vast radioactive fallout after the Chernobyl explosion can occur without any major changes in industrial society happening as a consequence. However, the volume of pollution in the twentieth century, which has so far been largely produced by the industrialised world, is still on the increase in these countries and will go up even more as other countries, in particular China, India and Brazil, attempt to become industrialised in turn. Many of the pollution problems faced by western Europe, North America, Japan and later by eastern Europe – smoke pollution, heavy metals in the atmosphere, sulphur dioxide emissions from burning fossil fuels and acid rain – will become even more widespread. Industrial discharges into rivers and seas will increase. Even more dangerous will be an increase in the range and volume of highly toxic chemicals produced and allowed to escape into the atmosphere and water. Not only animals in these ecosystems will suffer – it is likely that the higher rates of cancer in the industrialised world in the twentieth century are partly caused by the massive increase in chemical pollutants and these rates may, therefore, continue to rise. The threat to the ozone layer from CFC emissions in the last sixty years is likely to increase for some decades and remain substantial well into the twenty-first century despite the agreement reached in London in 1990.

The greatest stresses within the global system though stem from the output of greenhouse gases as a direct consequence of the concentrated burst of industrialisation in the last two hundred years. Serious attempts to control emissions would raise fundamental questions about the way of life that has evolved in the industrialised world and also of equity between the industrialised nations and the rest of the world. It is now virtually inevitable, even if strict controls are introduced quickly, that global temperatures will rise to a level never before experienced by settled societies or even in the last 100,000 years and possibly longer. The production of food will be disrupted; the latest UN estimates suggest a 10 per cent fall in output and a 70 per cent reduction in American grain exports, which will intensify the problem of feeding the world's rapidly growing population. Even more worrying is the rate of global warming, which will almost certainly be far above natural rates in the past and too fast for natural ecosystems to adapt, causing widespread damage. Every ecosystem in the world will certainly be affected by human produced pollution, but in unpredictable ways. Global warming is therefore a demonstration, for the first time on a world-wide scale, of the results of ignoring, as settled societies have done for most of their history, vital ecological constraints. The consequences for life on earth and humanity will be profound.

Instead of seeing the environment as the foundation of human history, settled societies, especially modern industrial societies, have acted under the illusion that they are somehow independent from the natural world, which they have generally preferred to see as something apart which they can exploit more or less with impunity. Ever since the first great transition which began 10,000 years ago, and particularly in the last two centuries, humans have put increasing pressure on the earth's environment – in defiance of basic ecological principles. They have destroyed climax ecosystems to create agricultural land leading to environmental damage such as widespread soil erosion. Through a combination of hunting and farming they have driven individual animals to extinction and severely reduced the population of others. Either deliberately or accidentally they have introduced new animals and plants and thereby disrupted ecosystems, often with unpredictable results. (The release of genetically engineered organisms would carry the process of intervention and the risk of harmful consequences to a new level.) Over the last two hundred years human societies have become dependent on fossil fuel energy resources. A pricing system continues to operate that takes no account of the fact that these are irreplaceable assets in which future generations have a vital interest. The unwanted outputs of the industrial system have been dumped into the world's ecosystems, neglecting the fact that these wastes cannot be 'disposed of' in a closed system such as the earth. The waste products produced by industry have not disappeared when they were discharged into the environment. At best they were diluted but, more frequently, the problem was merely delayed or transferred, as in the case of CFCs polluting the upper atmosphere. Industrial wastes have polluted the earth on an increasing scale and with increasing toxicity. The effects have also been felt over a wider area until global mechanisms that make life on earth possible – the ozone layer and the regulation of global temperatures – have been affected, the ultimate reminder that the earth is a closed system.

Environmental problems are nothing new. However with the expansion of Europe to dominate much of the globe, the rapid growth in the world's population, the increase in the cultivated area at the expense of natural ecosystems and the rise of highly industrialised societies, the scale of environmental problems has increased and they are more complex in nature. The world now faces a series of interrelated crises caused by past actions – deforestation, soil erosion, desertification, salinisation, increasing loss of wildlife and plants, grossly unequal distribution of food, wealth and basic human amenities, increasing levels of pollution (and damaging new cocktails and 'chain reactions'). Another challenge facing modern societies is the sheer speed of change. If this book were to give a chronologically accurately weighted account of human history then of its 407 pages, 405 pages would have to be devoted to gathering and hunting communities, 2 pages to agricultural societies and just a couple of lines to modern industrialised societies.

The fact that a breakdown has not so far occurred does not guarantee that it will not happen. Many societies in the past believed that they had a sustainable way of life only to find some time later that it was not so and that they were unable to make the social, economic and political changes necessary for survival. The problem for all human societies has been to find a means of extracting from the environment their food, clothing, shelter and other goods in a way that does not render it incapable of supporting them. Some damage is clearly inevitable. Some depradation is tolerable. The challenge has been to anticipate or recognise at what point the environment is being badly degraded by the demands placed upon it and to find the political, economic and social means to respond accordingly. Some societies have succeeded in finding the right balance, some have failed.

In this wider perspective it is clearly far too soon to judge whether modern industrialised societies, with their very high rates of energy and resource consumption and high pollution levels, and the rapidly rising human population in the rest of the world are ecologically sustainable. Past human actions have left contemporary societies with an almost insuperably difficult set of problems to solve.

GUIDE TO FURTHER READING

General

Ehrlich, P. R., Ehrlich, A. H. & Holdren, J. P., *Ecoscience: Population, Resources, Environment*. (San Francisco, W. H. Freeman, 1977)

Goudie, A., *The Human Impact: Man's Role in Environmental Change*. (Oxford, Basil Blackwell, 1981)

Grigg, D. B., *The Agricultural Systems of the World: An Evolutionary Approach*. (Cambridge, Cambridge University Press, 1974)

Simmons, I. G., *Changing the Face of the Earth: Culture, Environment, History*. (Oxford, Basil Blackwell, 1989)

Thomas, W. L. (ed), *Man's Role in Changing the Face of the Earth*. (Chicago, Chicago University Press, 1956)

Worster D., (ed) *The Ends of the Earth: Perspectives on Modern Environmental History*. (Cambridge, Cambridge University Press, 1988)

Wilkinson, R. G., *Poverty and Progress: An Ecological Model of Economic Development*. (London, Methuen, 1973)

Chapter 1: The Lessons of Easter Island

Heyerdahl, T., *Aku-Aku: The Secret of Easter Island*. (London, Allen and Unwin, 1958)

Jennings, J. D., *The Prehistory of Polynesia*. (Cambridge (Mass), Harvard University Press, 1979)

Metraux, A., *Easter Island*. (London, Andre Deutsch, 1957)

Chapter 2: The Foundations of History

Colinvaux, P., *Why Big Fierce Animals Are Rare*. (Princeton, Princeton University Press, 1978)

Lovelock, J., *Gaia: A New Look at Life on Earth*. (Oxford, Oxford University Press, 1979)

Lovelock, J., *The Ages of Gaia: A Biography of Our Living Earth*. (Oxford, Oxford University Press, 1988)

Odum, E. P., *Fundamentals of Ecology*. (Philadelphia, W. B. Saunders, 1971)

Chapter 3: Ninety-nine per cent of Human History

Butzer, K. W., *Environment and Archaeology: An Ecological Approach to Prehistory. (Second Edition).* (London, Methuen, 1972)

Clark J. G., *World Prehistory in New Perspective (Third Edition).* (Cambridge, Cambridge University Press, 1977)

Dennell, R., *European Economic Prehistory: A New Approach.* (London, Academic Press, 1983)

Gamble, C., *The Palaeolithic Settlement of Europe.* (Cambridge, Cambridge University Press, 1966)

Lee, R. B. & De Vore, I., *Man the Hunter.* (Chicago, Aldine, 1968)

Sahlins, M., *Stone Age Economics.* (Chicago, Aldine, 1972)

Chapter 4: The First Great Transition

Adams, R, McC., *The Evolution of Urban Society: Early Mesopotamia and Prehispanic Mexico.* (London, Weidenfeld and Nicolson, 1966)

Clutton-Brook, J., *The Walking Larder: Patterns of Domestication, Pastoralism and Predation.* (London, Unwin Hyman, 1988)

Cohen, M. N., *The Food Crisis in Prehistory: Overpopulation and the Origins of Agriculture.* (New Haven, Yale University Press, 1977)

Ferrill, A., *The Origins of War: From the Stone Age to Alexander the Great.* (London, Thames and Hudson, 1985)

Gledhill, J., Bender, B. & Larsen, M. T., *State and Society: The Emergence and Development of Social Hierarchy and Political Centralisation.* (London, Unwin Hyman, 1988)

Harris, D. R. & Hillman, G. C., *Foraging and Farming: The Evolution of Plant Exploitation.* (London, Unwin Hyman, 1988)

Higgs, E. S., (ed), *Papers in Economic Prehistory.* (Cambridge, Cambridge University Press, 1972)

Higgs, E. S., (ed), *Palaeoeconomy.* (Cambridge, Cambridge University Press, 1975)

Megaw, J. V. S., *Hunters, Gatherers and the First Farmers Beyond Europe.* (Leicester, Leicester University Press, 1977)

Sanders, W. T. & Price, B. J., *Mesoamerica: The Evolution of a Civilisation.* (New York, Random House, 1968)

Ucko, P. J. & Dimbleby, G. W., *The Domestication and Exploitation of Plants and Animals.* (London, Duckworth, 1969)

Ucko, P. J., Tringham, R. & Dimbleby, G. W., *Man, Settlement and Urbanism.* (London, Duckworth, 1972)

Chapter 5: Destruction and Survival

Butzer, K. W., *Early Hydraulic Civilization in Egypt: A Study in Cultural Ecology.* (Chicago, Chicago University Press, 1976)

Carter, V. G., & Dale, T., *Topsoil and Civilization* (Norman (Okl), University of Oklahoma Press, 1974)

Culbert, T. P., (ed), *The Classic Maya Collapse*. (Albuquerque, University of New Mexico Press, 1973)

Hughes, J. D., *Ecology in Ancient Civilizations*. (Albuquerque, University of New Mexico Press, 1975)

Rzoska, J., *Euphrates and Tigris: Mesopotamian Ecology and Destiny*. (The Hague, W. Junk, 1980)

Chapter 6: The Long Struggle

Braudel, F., *Capitalism and Material Life 1400–1800*. (London, Weidenfeld and Nicolson, 1974)

Crosby, A. W., *The Columbian Exchange: Biological and Cultural Consequences of 1492*. (Westport (Conn), Greenwood, 1972)

Elvin, M., *The Pattern of the Chinese Past*. (London, Eyre Methuen, 1973)

Gribbin, J., *Climatic Change*. (Cambridge, Cambridge University Press, 1978)

Grigg, D. B., *Population Growth and Agrarian Change: An Historical Perspective*. (Cambridge, Cambridge University Press, 1980)

Ladurie, Le Roy, *Times of Feast, Times of Famine: A History of Climate since the Year 1000*. (London, Allen and Unwin, 1972)

Lamb, H. H., *Climate, History and the Modern World*. London, Methuen, 1982)

McEvedy, C. & Jones, R., *Atlas of World Population History*. (London, Allen Lane, 1978)

Post, J. D., *The Last Great Subsistence Crisis in the Western World*. (Baltimore, Johns Hopkins University Press, 1977)

Rotberg, R. I. & Rabb, T. K., *Climate and History*. (Princeton, Princeton University Press, 1981)

Rotberg, R. I. & Rabb, T. K., *Hunger and History: The Impact of Changing Food Production and Consumption Patterns on Society*. (Cambridge, Cambridge University Press, 1985)

Smith, T. C., *Agrarian Origins of Modern Japan*. (Stanford, Stanford University Press, 1959)

Walter, J. & Schofield, R., (ed), *Famine, Disease and the Social Order in Early Modern Society*. (Cambridge, Cambridge University Press, 1989)

Watson, A. M., *Agricultural Innovation in the Early Islamic World: The Diffusion of Crops and Farming Techniques 700–1100*. (Cambridge, Cambridge University Press, 1983)

Wigley, T. M. L., Ingram, M. J. & Farmer, G., *Climate and History: Studies in Past Climates and their Impact on Man*. (Cambridge, Cambridge University Press, 1981)

Woodham-Smith, C., *The Great Hunger*. (London, Hamish Hamilton, 1962)

Chapter 7: The Spread of European Settlement

Bater, J. H. & French, R. A., *Studies in Russian Historical Geography, Volume 1*. (London, Academic Press, 1983)

Bley, H., *South-West Africa under German Rule 1894–1914*. (London, Heinemann, 1971)

Hagan, W. T., *American Indians*. (Chicago, Chicago University Press, 1979)

Hemming, J., *The Conquest of the Incas*. (London, Macmillan, 1970)

Hemming, J., *Red Gold: The Conquest of the Brazilian Indians*. (London, Macmillan, 1978)

Hoskins, W. G., *The Making of the English Landscape*. (London, Hodder and Stoughton, 1955)

Hughes, R., *The Fatal Shore*. (London, Collins, 1987)

Moorehead, A., *The Fatal Impact: An Account of the Invasion of the South Pacific 1767–1840*. (London, Hamish Hamilton, 1966)

Rackham, O., *The History of the Countryside*. (London, J. M. Dent, 1986)

Smith, C. T., *An Historical Geography of Western Europe Before 1800*. (London, Longmans, 1967)

Wagret, P., *Polderlands*. (London, Methuen, 1968)

Chapter 8: Ways of Thought

Capra, F., *The Turning Point: Science, Society and the Rising Culture*. (London, Wildwood, 1982)

Glacken, C. J., *Traces on the Rhodian Shore: Nature and Culture in Western Thought from Ancient Times to the end of the Eighteenth Century*. (Berkeley, University of California Press, 1967)

Passmore, J., *Man's Responsibility for Nature: Ecological Problems and Western Traditions*. (London, Duckworth, 1974)

Polanyi, K., *The Great Transformation*. (New York, Octagon, 1980)

Pollard, S., *The Idea of Progress: History and Society*. (London, C. A. Watts, 1968)

Thomas, K., *Man and the Natural World: Changing Attitudes in England 1500–1800*. (London, Allen Lane, 1983)

Chapter 9: The Rape of the World

Busch, B. C., *The War Against the Seals: A History of the North American Seal Fishery*. (Montreal, McGill–Queen's University Press, 1985)

Cherfas, J., *The Hunting of the Whale*. (London, Bodley Head, 1988)

Crosby, A. W., *Ecological Imperialism: The Biological Expansion of Europe 900–1900*. (Cambridge, Cambridge University Press, 1986)

Hall, S., *The Fourth World: The Heritage of the Arctic and its Destruction*. (London, Bodley Head, 1987)

Innis, H. A., *The Fur Trade in Canada*. (Toronto, University of Toronto Press, 1956)

Jackson, G., *The British Whaling Trade*. (London, A&C Black, 1978)

Martin, J., *Treasure of the Land of Darkness: The Fur Trade and its Significance in Medieval Russia*. (Cambridge, Cambridge University Press, 1986)

Ritchie, J., *The Influence of Man on Animal Life in Scotland*. (Cambridge, Cambridge University Press, 1920)

Schorger, A. W., *The Passenger Pigeon: Its Natural History and Extinction*. Madison, University of Wisconsin Press, 1955)

Veale, E. M., *The English Fur Trade in the Later Middle Ages*. (Oxford, Oxford Univeristy Press, 1966)

Wishart, D.J., *The Fur Trade of the American West 1807–1840*. (London, Croom Helm, 1979)

Chapter 10: Creating the Third World

Binder, P., *Treasure Islands: The Trials of the Ocean Islanders*. (London, Blond and Briggs, 1977)

Dean, W., *Brazil and the Struggle for Rubber*. (Cambridge, Cambridge University Press, 1987)

Geertz, C., *Agricultural Involution: The Process of Ecological Change in Indonesia*. (Berkeley, University of California Press, 1963)

Klee, G. A., *World Systems of Traditional Resource Management*. (London, Edward Arnold, 1980)

Lanning, G. & Mueller, M., *Africa Undermined: Mining Companies and the Underdevelopment of Africa*. (Harmondsworth, Penguin, 1979)

Tucker, R. P. & Richards, J. F., *Global Deforestation and the Nineteenth Century World Economy*. (Durham (N.C.), Duke University Press, 1983)

Ward, R. G., *Man in the Pacific Islands: Essays on Geographical Change in the Pacific Islands*. (Oxford, Oxford University Press, 1972)

Williams, M. & Macdonald, B., *The Phosphaters: A History of the British Phosphate Commissioners and the Christmas Island Phosphate Commission*. (Carlton (Va), Melbourne University Press, 1985)

Wolf, E. R., *Europe and the People Without History*. (Berkeley, University of California Press, 1982)

Wolf, R. D., *The Economics of Colonialism: Britain and Kenya 1870–1930*. (New Haven, Yale University Press, 1974)

Chapter 11: The Changing Face of Death

McKeown, T., *The Origins of Human Disease*. (Oxford, Basil Blackwell, 1988)

McNeill, W. H., *Plagues and Peoples*. (Oxford, Basil Blackwell, 1976)

Chapter 12: The Weight of Numbers

Blaikie, P. & Brookfield, H., *Land Degradation and Society*. (London, Methuen, 1987)

Caulfield, C., *In the Rainforest*. (London, Heinemann, 1985)

Eckholm, E., *Losing Ground: Environmental Stress and World Food Prospects*. (Oxford, Pergamon, 1978)

George, S., *How the Other Half Dies: The Real Reasons for World Hunger*. (Harmondsworth, Penguin, 1977)

Grigg, D. B., *The World Food Problem 1950–1980*. (Oxford, Basil Blackwell, 1985)

Pearse, A., *Seeds of Plenty, Seeds of Want: Social and Economic Implications of the Green Revolution*. (Oxford, Oxford University Press, 1980)

Sen, A., *Poverty and Famines: An Essay on Entitlement and Deprivation*. (Oxford, Oxford University Press, 1981)

Warnock, J. W., *The Politics of Hunger*. (London, Methuen, 1987)

Worster, D., *Dust Bowl: The Southern Plains in the 1930s*. (New York, Oxford University Press, 1979)

Chapter 13: The Second Great Transition

Albion, R. G., *Forests and Sea Power: The Timber Problem of the Royal Navy 1652–1862*. (Cambridge (Mass), Harvard University Press, 1926)

Cipolla, C. M., *The Economic History of World Population*. (Harmondsworth, Penguin, 1962)

Daniels, G. H., & Rose, M. H., *Energy and Transport: Historical Perspectives on Policy Issues*. (London, Sage, 1982)

Foley, G., *The Energy Question*. (Harmondsworth, Penguin, 1976)

Gimpel, J., *The Medieval Machine: The Industrial Revolution of the Middle Ages*. (London, Gollancz, 1977)

Maczak, A. & Parker, W. N., (eds), *Natural Resources in European History*. (Washington DC, Resources for the Future, 1978)

Schurr, S. H. & Netschert, B. C., *Energy in the American Economy 1850–1975*. (Baltimore, Johns Hopkins University Press, 1960)

Thompson, F. M. L., *Victorian England: The Horse Drawn Society*. (London, Bedford College, 1970)

Thompson, F. M. L., *Horses in European Economic History: A Preliminary Canter*. (Reading, British Agricultural History Society, 1983)

White, L., *Medieval Technology and Social Change*. (Oxford, Oxford University Press, 1962)

Chapter 14: The Rise of the City

Chudacoff, H. P., *The Evolution of American Urban Society*. (Eaglewood Cliffs (N.J.), Prentice-Hall, 1975)

Dyos, H. J. & Wolff, M., *The Victorian City: Images and Reality*. (London, Routledge, and Kegan Paul, 1973)

Hall, P., *The World Cities*. (London, Weidenfeld and Nicolson, 1977)

Hohenberg, P. M. & Lees, L. H., *The Making of Urban Europe 1000–1950*. (Cambridge (Mass.), Harvard University Press, 1985)

Kornhauser, D., *Urban Japan: Its Foundations and Growth*. (London, Longmans, 1976)

Lowder, S., *Inside Third World Cities*. (London, Croom Helm, 1986)

Mumford, L., *The City in History: Its Origins, Its Transformations, and Its Prospects*. (London, Secker and Warburg, 1961)

Sjoberg, G., *The Preindustrial City*. (New York, Free Press, 1960)

Sutcliffe, A., (ed.), *Metropolis 1890–1940*. (London, Mansell, 1984)

Wheatley, P., *The Pivot of the Four Quarters: A Preliminary Enquiry into the Origins and Character of the Ancient Chinese City*. (Chicago, Aldine, 1971)

Chapter 15: Creating the Affluent Society

Davis, D., *A History of Shopping*. (London, Routlege and Kegan Paul, 1966)

Flink, J. J., *The Car Culture*. (Cambridge (Mass.), MIT Press, 1975)

Galbraith, J. K., *The Affluent Society*. (London, Hamish Hamilton, 1958)

Hirsch, F., *Social Limits to Growth*. (London, Routledge and Kegan Paul, 1977)

Kuromiya, H., *Stalin's Industrial Revolution: Politics and Workers 1928– 1932*. (Cambridge, Cambridge University Press, 1988)

Chapter 16: Polluting the World

Ashby, E. & Anderson, M., *The Politics of Clean Air*. (Oxford, Oxford University Press, 1981)

Ashworth, W., *The Late, Great Lakes: An Environmental History*. (New York, A. A. Knopf, 1986)

Boyle, S. & Ardill, J., *The Greenhouse Effect*. (London, Hodder and Stoughton, 1989)

Commoner, B., *The Closing Circle*. (London, Jonathan Cape, 1972)

Goldman, M. I., *The Spoils of Progress: Environmental Pollution in the Soviet Union*. (Cambridge (Mass.), MIT Press, 1972)

Goldsmith, E. & Hildyard, N., *The Earth Report: Monitoring the Battle for our Environment*. (London, Mitchell Beazley, 1988)

Gribbin, J., *The Hole in the Sky: Man's Threat to the Ozone Layer*. (London, Corgi, 1988)

Huddle, N., Reich, M. & Stiskin, N., *Island of Dreams: Environmental Crisis in Japan*. (New York, Autumn Press, 1975)

McCormick, J., *Acid Earth: The Global Threat of Acid Pollution*. (London, Earthscan, 1989)

McKibben, B., *The End of Nature*. (London, Viking, 1990)

Wylie, J. C., *The Wastes of Civilization*. (London, Faber and Faber, 1959)

INDEX

Aachen, 318
Abidjan, 311
Aborigines, 19, 21, 22, 33, 35, 44, 65, 130, 136–7
Abu Hureyra, 39
Abu Simnel, 86
Academy of Sciences (USSR), 363–4
acid rain, 365–8, 380
Adam and Eve, 143–4, 148
Addis Ababa, 75
additives, food, 250
Adige valley, 126
Adirondack mountains, 367
Adriatic Sea, 275
Afghanistan, 76
Africa: bushmen, 19, 20–1, 22; cities, 311; deforestation, 257, 258; desertification, 264; disease, 235–6; European exploration and colonisation, 127, 128, 129, 137–40; extinct animals, 162; food imports, 252; food shortages, 253; geological history, 9; *Homo erectus*, 18–19; land ownership, 251; living standards, 341; minerals, 216–17; new crops, 111, 112, 113; plantations, 206, 211–12; population, 92–3, 242; slave trade, 197–8; water supply, 350
see also East Africa; North Africa; West Africa
Agen, 109
Agricola, Georgius, 360
agriculture: cash crops, 201–2; colonial, 199–214; energy efficiency, 291–2; environmental impact, 68–87; famines, 103–9; fertilizers, 218–21, 247; and global warming, 390–1; horses, 271–2; improved productivity, 109, 114–15, 245–8; influence on development of society, 54–5, 57–65; influence of weather, 98–102; irrigation, 55–7, 59, 68–9, 70–3, 264–5, 350; labour, 268; limits to growth, 404; new crops and animals, 110–14; pesticides, 370–1; plantations, 195–6, 201–14; and population growth, 88–98, 243–4, 394–5; soil erosion, 258–63; and spread of disease, 225–7; swidden system, 47, 49, 80, 121, 227, 395; Third World, 250–3; transition to, 37–52; water pollution, 351

aid, foreign, 341–3, 345
Aids, 235–6
air pollution, 358–60, 361–2, 379–80, 381–2
air travel, 332
Akkadian empire, 63, 72
Alabama, 208
Alaska, 30, 35, 129, 184, 287, 372
Aleutian Islands, 34, 135
Alexander the Great, 120
Alexandria, 348
Algeria, 138, 256
Alkali Inspectorate, 361
Allahabad, 352–3
Alps, 101
Altamira, 28
aluminium, 286, 327, 366
Amarillo, Texas, 260
Amazon, 133, 140, 209–10, 257, 398–9
American civil war, 209, 232
American Express, 331
American war of independence, 279
Amoco Cadiz, 372
Amorites, 72
Amsterdam, 229, 309
An-Yang, 61
Anatolia, 43, 46, 58, 66, 326
Andes, 51, 131
Andra Pradesh, 342
Anglo-Saxons, 124
Angola, 197, 216
animals: continental drift, 9–10; destruction of, 161–70, 174–5; diseases, 103, 105, 225–6, 235; energy efficiency, 292; evolution, 10; extinctions, 34–5, 193; fur trade, 177–82; hunting, 33–4, 182–6; introductions, 110, 170–3; man's attitudes to natural world, 141–9, 151; manure, 357–8; medieval agriculture, 95, 102; methane production, 388; pastoralism, 263–4; rearing systems, 247–8; source of power, 270–4; transition to agriculture, 38–40, 44–52
Antarctic: fishing, 176–7; geological history, 9; ozone layer hole, 386; pollution, 383, 392; seal hunting, 184; whaling, 189–90, 191
Antioch, 78
Apache, 131

Apollo cave, 28
Appalachian mountains, 129, 134, 171
apprenticeships, 318
aqueducts, 348
aquifers, 350-1
Aquinas, Thomas, 144-5
Arabs, 72, 198
Aragon, 123
Aral Sea, 265
Araucanians, 131
archaeology, 346-7
Archangel, 278
Arctic, 10, 18; hunting, 22, 31; Inuit, 19, 23, 36; walruses, 185; whaling, 187-8
Arena, 1
Argentina, 311
Argonne, 122
Aristotle, 76, 142, 145
Arkwright, Joseph, 273
Arles, 124-5
Army and Navy Stores, 329
Arrhenius, Svante, 389
Asante, 198
Ashio copper mine, 360
Asia: cities, 310-11; debt, 342; energy efficiency, 291; extension of agricultural land, 244, 251; food shortages, 253; intensification of agriculture, 251-2; irrigation, 264; plantations, 205-6; population growth, 242; *see also* south-east Asia; south-west Asia
Asia Minor, 77, 161
Assam, 206, 208
Assyria, 67, 339
Astor, Jacob, 181
Astrakhan, 128
astronomy, 65, 79
Aswan dam, 86-7, 342
Atacama desert, 264
Athens, 76, 296, 348, 380
Atlantic Ocean: continental drift, 8; fisheries, 176-7; pollution, 375; radioactive waste, 378; seal hunting, 183-5; whaling, 188, 189
atmosphere: air pollution, 358-60, 361-2, 379-80, 381-2; damage to ozone layer, 385-7; global warming, 387-92, 405-6
Attica, 76
Audubon Society, 192
aurochs, 162
Austin, Thomas, 171, 172
Australia: Aborigines, 19, 21, 22, 44, 65, 130, 136-7; cities, 301; convicts, 198; deforestation, 256; desertification, 264; destruction of wildlife, 165-7; extension of agricultural land, 244; extinct animals, 35; food exports, 245; fur trade, 182; geological history, 9; indentured labour, 199; introduced wildlife, 170-2, 173-4; ozone layer hole, 386; phosphate extraction in Pacific, 218-21; rock art, 28; seal hunting, 183; settlement of, 29-30, 128,

129, 136-7; soil erosion, 262; transport, 337; whaling, 188
Austria, 282, 367
Auvergne, 102, 106
Azores, 127, 195
Aztecs, 63, 67, 112, 128, 129, 130, 131, 230, 301, 354

Baalbeck, 78
Babylonians, 58, 65, 72, 339
Bacon, Francis, 148
Baffin Bay, 187-8
Baghdad, 72-3
Bahia, 132, 278
Baikal, Lake, 375
Baku, 287
Balkans, 47, 112, 113, 127
Baltic, 114, 123, 175, 179, 232, 279, 363
Banabans, 218-21
bananas, 212
Bangkok, 350
Bangladesh, 254, 263, 391
Banks, Joseph, 136, 166
Barbados, 197, 206
Barcelona, 231
barley, 43-4, 49, 62, 71, 85
Basel, 373
Bass Rock, 165
Bass Strait, 137, 183
Bath, 303, 331
Bayer, 302
Bayonne, 109
Beale, John, 148
beans, 113
Bear Island, 185
bears, 163
Beauce, 122
Beauvais, 366
beavers, 161, 163, 179, 180, 181-2
Bedfordshire, 164
beef, 214, 257
Beemster, Lake, 125
bees, 171, 173
Belgian Congo, 216
Belgium, 106, 162, 216, 246, 283, 301, 302
Belize, 50, 78, 82
Benelux countries, 240
Bengal, 104, 108, 254
Benguela railway, 216
Berbers, 77, 195
Bering Sea, 184
Bering Strait, 30
Berlin, 249, 285, 300, 302, 304, 305, 306, 309
Berlin Conference (1884-85), 139
Berwick, 177
Besançon, 162
Bhopal, 373, 405
Bialowieza forest, 162
Bible, 143-4
Biebosch marsh, 125
Biharis, 206

birds: destruction of, 162, 163, 164–5, 166, 167, 168–70, 193; introductions, 172–3
Birmingham, 302, 323, 349
birth control, 23
birth rates, 241–2, 404
Biscay, Bay of, 187
bison, 30, 33, 162, 168, 171, 174–5
Black Country, 302, 308, 362
Black Death, 97, 123, 224, 229–30, 300, 319
Black Sea, 27, 128–9, 296
Blue mountains, 167
Boccaccio, Giovanni, 229
Bochum, 302
Boer war, 232, 320
Bohemia, 104, 363, 369
Bolivia, 51, 218, 311
Bon Marché, 329
Boston, 285, 304, 306, 309, 352
Brabant, 97, 121
brain, human, 24, 35
Brandenburg, 122
Brasilia, 300
Brazil, 9, 166, 222; cash crops, 252; coffee, 203, 211; crops, 112, 113; deforestation, 256; exploitation of Amazonia, 140, 398–9; extension of agricultural land, 244; feather exports, 167; Indians, 21, 128, 132–3; pollution, 364–5, 369; rubber, 209–10; slavery, 270; sugar cane, 206; whaling, 188, 197, 198
bread, 237, 249, 250, 316
Breslau, 348
Britain: acid rain, 367; adulterated food, 250; agricultural improvements, 114–15, 247; air pollution, 358–60, 361–2; astronomy, 65; cars, 330; cities, 299, 300–2, 306–7, 310; climatic changes, 100, 101; coal, 281–4; cocoa trade, 211–12; colonies, 128, 202–4; conurbations, 308; cotton industry, 207; death rates, 233, 235; deforestation, 122; destruction of wildlife, 163–5; disease, 229–30, 231; drainage projects, 124, 126; early population, 120; electricity, 291; famines, 105–6; fishing, 175, 176; food imports, 115, 245; food shortages, 98; foreign aid, 341–2; fur trade, 178; and global warming, 392; horses, 272, 273–4; ice ages, 27; and the Irish potato famine, 107; iron and steel, 326–7; labour, 268; leisure activities, 330; living standards, 317, 318, 319–21, 333, 340; loss of natural habitats, 255; manure, 357–8; natural gas, 288; new crops, 113; nuclear accidents, 376, 378; pesticides, 371; phosphate extraction in Pacific, 218–21; pollution, 375–6, 382, 404; population growth, 240–2; rabbits, 110; sanitation, 356; settlement of, 33; settlement of Australia, 136–7; shops, 329; slave trade, 197–8; soil erosion, 259; tea imports, 208; timber shortages, 278–9, 280–1; timber trade, 215; tourism, 332; toxic wastes, 374, 375; transport, 312; water power, 274, 275; water supply, 348–9, 351; whaling, 187, 190; wildlife conservation, 192–3; windmills, 277; wood consumption, 277
British Honduras, 215
British Medical Association, 320
British Phosphate Commission, 219, 220
Brittany, 122, 255, 372
Brooke Bond, 214
Bruges, 268
bubonic plague, 227, 228–30, 235
Buckingham Palace, 349
buckwheat, 102
Buddhism, 152
Buenos Aires, 173, 245, 309
Bureau of Mines (US), 290
Bureau of Soils (US), 260
Burgundy, 121, 178, 280
Burma, 50, 199, 209, 215
Burslem, 361
Burundi, 214
bushmen, 19, 20–1, 22, 102, 225
Butlin, Billy, 332
Byzantine empire, 120, 127, 178, 297

cable cars, 304
Cadbury's, 211–12
Caille, Jacques, 353
Cairo, 232, 309
Calcutta, 232, 254
calendar, Mayan, 79–80
Calha Norte programme, 399
California, 173, 176, 184, 185, 188, 351, 382–3
Calvin, John, 145
Cambridgeshire, 122, 347
camels, 171, 271
Canada, 22, 32, 129, 181, 182, 244, 247, 279, 365, 366, 367, 386, 392
Canary Islands, 127, 195–6, 212
Canberra, 300
cancer, 236, 238–9, 368, 373, 376, 377, 378, 386, 405
cannibalism, 104, 105, 106
Canton, 228, 301
Canvey Island, 126
Cape of Good Hope, 127, 197
Cape Verde Islands, 195
capercaillie, 163
carbon dioxide, 378, 380, 387–8, 392
Carey, H. C., 147–8
Caria, 77
Caribbean, 52, 112, 128, 197, 198
Carinthia, 322
Carlsbad, 331
carnivores, 12, 21–2
Caroline Islands, 31, 219
Carpathians, 27
Carrefour, 329
cars, 156, 291, 305, 312–13, 330, 334, 336–8, 379–80
Carson, Rachel, 383

Carthage, 77, 120, 348
cash crops, 201–2, 208–14, 240, 251, 252,
  256–7
Caspar, Wyoming, 30
Caspian Sea, 177
Castille, 123
Çatal Hüyük, 46, 66, 326
Catalonia, 196
catalytic converters, 380
Catherwood, Frederick, 79
cattle, 44, 47, 170–1, 226, 237, 248, 249,
  257, 388
cave paintings, 28, 66, 117
Cebu, 256
cedars of Lebanon, 76
Central America, 128, 212, 231; see also
  Mesoamerica
cereals, 39, 43–4; see also rice; wheat etc.
Cetacean Research Institute, 191
Ceylon (Sri Lanka), 197, 199, 203, 206, 208,
  211, 214
CFCs (chlorofluorocarbons), 385–7, 388,
  405, 406
Champagne, 316
Chandos, Duke of, 361
charcoal, 121, 277, 280–1, 326, 399
Charlemagne, Emperor, 32, 120
Cheng-Chou, 61
Cheng Ho, 127
Chernobyl, 376–7, 405
Cherokees, 134, 149
Chesapeake Bay, 259
Cheshire, 164
Chesowanja, 24
Cheviots, 163
Chiaravalle abbey, 124
Chicago, 234, 250, 260, 304, 309, 358
chicken, 110
children: employment, 318, 323; infanticide,
  23, 242; mortality rates, 225, 232–3, 234,
  235
Chile, 131, 166, 170, 183, 188, 218, 264
chillies, 113
Chilterns, 122
China, 32, 59, 208; acid rain, 368;
  agricultural improvements, 245;
  astronomy, 65; cities, 296, 297, 298, 299,
  301; coal, 285; deforestation, 74, 255;
  disease, 227, 228, 231, 233; early cultures,
  26, 60–1; earthquakes, 9; energy
  efficiency, 291; European colonisation,
  129, 130; exploration, 127; famines, 103;
  food consumption, 102; food shortages,
  253–4; food supply and population
  growth, 93–5; and global warming, 392;
  hydroelectricity, 342; indentured labour,
  199; intensification of agriculture, 251;
  iron production, 326; irrigation, 264;
  labour, 268, 269–70; lack of colonial
  territories, 116; living standards, 339–40;
  new crops, 112; pollution, 364, 366;
  population, 91–3, 242, 243–4; rubbish

disposal, 353–4; sewage, 354; slavery, 269;
  soil erosion, 258, 262; Taoism, 152;
  transition to agriculture, 37, 41–2, 49–50;
  water power, 275–6; water supply, 351;
  windmills, 276; wood consumption, 278
chlorine, 385
chlorocarbons, 380
cholera, 226, 232, 233, 234, 355
Christianity, attitudes to natural world, 142,
  143–7, 151–2
Christmas Island, 173
Chrysler, 330, 334
Chuang Tsu, 149
Cicero, 143
Cistercians, 122
CITES, 193
cities: air pollution, 358–60, 361–2; and
  deforestation, 74, 75; development of, 46,
  295–314; disease, 226, 227; Mayan, 81;
  rubbish disposal, 351–2; sanitation, 354–8;
  suburbs, 303–8, 312; Third World,
  310–12; traffic problems, 306, 312–13,
  336–7
citrus fruit, 111
Clark, 181
class, food surpluses and, 57–8
Clean Air Act (Britain), 359–60
Clean Air Act (USA), 380
Clear Lake, 382–3
Cleveland, 375
climate: Aral Sea area, 265; and crop
  failures, 98–102; cyclical changes, 10–11,
  99–102; and deforestation, 258; and
  ecosystems, 14; and famines, 106; global
  warming, 387–92, 405–6; ice ages, 10, 11,
  26–9, 99, 389, 391; and transition to
  agriculture, 41
Clitheroe, 320
clothing, 29, 317, 334, 335, 395
Club of Rome, 402
coal: air pollution, 358–60, 361, 364; as
  energy source, 281–5, 290; formation of,
  9; and greenhouse effect, 387; reserves,
  293, 402
Coca-Cola, 329
cocoa, 211–12, 214
coffee, 202, 203–4, 205, 211, 214, 256
coke, 281
Cologne, 297, 318
Colombia, 392
Colombo, 197
Colorado, 30, 260, 350
Colorado beetle, 174
Columbus, Christopher, 128, 130, 170, 171,
  231
Comte, Auguste, 151
Condorcet, Marquis de, 150
Congo, 216
Connecticut, 333
conservation, wildlife, 192–3
Constantinople, 127, 297, 298–9
consumerism, 329–30, 334–5

continental drift, 8–9
conurbations, 308–9
convicts, 198
Cook, Captain James, 1, 135, 136, 137, 166
Cook, Thomas, 331–2
Cook Islands, 135
Copan, 79
copper, 327, 328, 343
Copper Hill, 381
coppicing, 74
Cordoba, 299
Corn Laws, 107, 115
Cornwall, 275, 372
Cort, Henry, 281
Cortes, Hernando, 197, 230
Costa Rica, 129, 214, 257
cotton, 205, 207–8, 256, 259
Courland, 123
Coventry, 349
Cowley, Abraham, 148
Crecow, 363, 366
craftsmen, 65
Crawley ironworks, 323
creation myths, 143–4, 145
credit, 334, 343–4
Cree Indians, 32
Crete, 9, 120
Crewe, 302
Crimea, 229
Crimean war, 232
crop rotation, 95–6
crusades, 126
Cuba, 198, 206, 213
Cubatao, 364, 369
Cuyahoga river, 375
Cuzco, 301
Cyprus, 111, 127, 195, 196, 232
Czechoslovakia, 363, 366, 369

Da Gama, Vasco, 231
Dacia, 162
Dahomey, 198
dairy products, 237–8, 249
Dakotas, 260
Dalmatia, 278
dams, hydroelectricity, 342
Danube, river, 47, 123
Darby, Abraham, 281
Dartmoor, 100
Darwin, Charles, 142, 148–9, 173
Davis Straits, 183, 187
DDT, 370, 371, 375, 382–3
death rates, 225, 232–5, 241, 311, 320, 321, 333, 340, 369
Debenhams, 329
debt, 223, 342–4
Deeping St James, 164
deer, 110
deficiency diseases, 113, 225, 236, 320
deforestation, 33, 47, 69–70, 73–8, 82, 253–8; and climate, 258; Easter Island, 5–6; in Europe, 121–2, 124; and

greenhouse effect, 388; soil erosion, 257–8; tropical forests, 257–8, 398–9
Del Monte, 214, 249
Delft, 309
Dempsey, Jack, 330
Denmark, 47, 246, 279
Denmark Strait, 101
Denpr basin, 179
Derbyshire, 163
Descartes, René, 147, 148
desertification, 264
deserts, 14
detergents, 370
Detroit, 330, 337
development, 398–9
Devon, 275
diet see food
dioxin, 372
diseases, 224–39; animal, 103; deficiency diseases, 113, 225, 236, 320; epidemics, 95, 103, 106, 224; industrial, 368–9; infectious, 225–6, 233–4, 235–6, 240; parasitic, 225, 226, 354; plague, 91, 97, 123, 224, 227–30, 235; of plants, 174; spread by European explorers, 135
Dnestr valley, 47
dogs, 44, 226
Domesday Book, 122, 124, 274
Dordogne, 28
Dordrecht, 309
drainage, 124–6, 255
Drake well, Pennsylvania, 286
droughts, 258, 260–1
drugs, 233–4
Duffield forest, 280
Dumfries, 109, 178
Dundee, 321, 356
'dust bowls', 260–1
Dutch East India Company, 201
Dutch East Indies, 211

eagles, 163, 164
earth, variations in orbit and tilt, 10–11
earthquakes, 8–9
East Africa, 199, 202–3, 206, 211, 232
East Germany, 363, 366, 382
East India Company, 208
East Prussia, 123
Easter Island, 1–7, 32, 401
eastern Europe, pollution, 363, 366, 369, 374, 382, 404–5
Ebro delta, 126
economics, 153–9, 222, 333
ecosystems, 11–17, 393–4; gatherers and hunters' impact on, 32–3; global warming and, 405–6; impact of early agriculture, 68–87
Ecuador, 51, 212, 252
Edo see also Tokyo, 297, 298, 301, 307
education, 318, 324, 335
Edward I, King of England, 178
Edward II, King of England, 104

Egypt: agriculture, 55, 83–7, 111, 112;
cities, 296; debt, 223, 343; development of
society, 59–60; disease, 227; extinct
animals, 161; living standards, 339;
population growth, 242; sewage, 354;
slavery, 269; tourism, 331; transport,
271; warfare, 66, 67; water power,
274
Elamites, 72
Elbe river, 122
Eleanor, Queen, 358
electricity, 267–8, 285–6, 291
electronics, 329–30
Elizabethviloed (1421), 125
emigration, 116, 129
Empedocles, 149
Ems, river, 125
energy, 267–94; animal, 270–4; coal, 281–5,
290, 294; efficiency, 291–2; electricity,
285–6, 291; gas, 284–5, 288; human,
268–70; hydroelectricity, 286, 288, 342;
natural gas, 288, 290–1; nuclear power,
289, 376–8; oil, 286–8, 290, 293;
photosynthesis, 11–12; renewable sources,
294; reserves, 402; steam power, 283–4,
290; transport, 338; water, 274–6; wind,
276–7; wood, 277–81, 283–4, 293
Engels, Frederick, 151, 157–8, 354, 355
England see Britain
Epicureans, 143
epidemics, 95, 103, 106, 224
Erie, Lake, 177, 375
Eritrea, 75
erosion see soil erosion
Erzgebirge, 123, 327, 377
Eskimos see Inuit
Essex, 165
Estonia, 356
Ethiopia, 75, 84, 103, 104, 108, 111, 128,
254, 258, 340, 341
Etruscans, 120
Euphrates, river, 70, 73
Eurasia, 34–5
Europe: agriculture, 41, 46–8, 110–13,
246–7, 248; Black Death, 229–30; cars,
330, 337–8; cities, 299–303; climatic
changes, 99–102; coal, 281–3;
consumerism, 329; creation of Third
World, 194–223; destruction of wildlife,
162–5; disease, 227, 229–30, 231–2, 238;
electricity consumption, 286; emigration
from, 129; exploration and colonisation,
55, 127–40, 397–8; famines, 103–8;
fishing, 175–6; food consumption, 102–3;
food supply and population growth, 95–8;
forced labour, 269; fur trade, 177–80; ice
ages, 26–8; metal-working, 326; oil, 288;
population, 91–3, 240–2, 243–4; poverty,
316–19; seal hunting, 182; settlement of,
26–9, 117–27; soil erosion, 258; timber
shortages, 278–80; tourism, 331–2;
transport, 271–2; water power, 274–6;

ways of thought, 141–60; whaling, 187;
windmills, 276–7
European Community, 248, 249, 368, 371,
380
Evelyn, John, 358–9
evolution, 10
exports, food, 244–5
extinctions, 33–5, 161–70, 174–5, 193
Extremadura, 78
Exxon Valdez, 372

factories, 302–3, 323–4, 362
Falkland Islands, 183, 342
famines, 88–9, 97–9, 103–9, 254
Faroes, 189
fashion, 334
Fellarich, abbot of, 123
Fens, 124, 126
fertilizers, 68, 87, 116, 218–21, 247, 251–2
feudalism, 154, 316
Ficino, Marsilio, 146
Fiji, 199, 213, 215, 219, 221
Finland, 104, 121, 179
fire, 24, 33
Firestone Rubber Company, 206, 210, 337
First World War, 128, 164, 232, 235, 272
fish, 175–7, 248, 292, 366–7
Flanders, 96, 97, 120, 125, 154, 179
Flinders Island, 137
floods, 125, 263, 391
Florence, 299, 300, 317, 318
Florida, 166, 170, 255, 351
fodder crops, 110, 114
fog, 359
food: calorific value, 102–3; and disease, 224,
225, 234–5, 236–8; famines, 103–9;
food-processing industry, 249–50;
gathering and hunting groups, 20–36;
imports, 115, 244–5, 252; influence on
development of society, 54–5, 57–65;
influence of weather, 98–102; limits to
production, 404; pesticide residues, 371;
and population growth, 88–98, 243–4;
shortages, 253–4; surpluses, 54–5, 57–8;
Third World countries, 213, 214;
transition to agriculture, 37–52
Food and Agriculture Organisation, 177
food chains, 12, 16, 382–3, 393
food riots, 106, 109
Ford Motor Company, 330, 324, 334
foreign aid, 341–3, 345
forests: ecosystems, 13–14; and global
warming, 387–8; pollution damage, 381–2;
rainforests, 14–16, 216; soil, 15; timber
extraction, 215–16, 277–8; see also
deforestation
Fort York, 181
fossil fuels, 9, 267, 282–5, 290, 292, 293–4,
338, 365, 387–8
fossils, 18
Foxton, 347
France: acid rain, 366, 367; agriculture, 96;

cave paintings, 28, 66, 117; cities, 301, 302; coal, 282; colonies, 138, 209, 212; deforestation, 121–2; disease, 229, 231; drainage projects, 124–5, 126; early population, 120; famines, 103, 104, 106; food consumption, 102; food shortages, 98, 109; forced labour, 269; fur trade, 180, 181; and global warming, 392; horses, 272, 273; ice ages, 26, 28; infant mortality, 225; life expectancy, 103; nuclear power, 289; population growth, 241; poverty, 317–18; sanitation, 351–2; shops, 329; soil erosion, 258, 259; timber shortages, 280; tourism, 332; water power, 274–5; water supply, 348

Francis I, King of France, 162–3
Francis of Assisi, 145–6
Franks, 121
French Revolution, 109, 150
Freud, Sigmund, 149
Friends of the Earth, 193
fur trade, 177–82
Fyans, Captain Foster, 167

Galapagos Islands, 192
Gambia, 213, 258
Ganges, river, 227, 375
Garden of Eden, 143, 145, 148, 149
Gare de Couze, 347
Garonne, river, 275
gas, 284–5, 288, 290–1
gasoline, 287
gathering and hunting groups, 18, 19–36; attitudes to natural world, 152–3; communal property, 154; damage to ecosystems, 32–5; diseases, 224, 225; food supply, 20–3; hunting, 21–2, 33–5; pollution, 347; possessions, 315; spread of, 26–8, 29–32; tools, 24–6, 28–9; transition to agriculture, 38–42, 52–4
Gauguin, Paul, 136
General Motors, 330, 333, 334, 337, 379
Genesis, 143–4
genetic engineering, 406
Genoa, 278, 296
Georgia, 172, 208, 259
Georgswerder dump, 374
Germanic peoples, 122–3
Germany: African colonies, 138–9; agriculture, 112, 246; cars, 338; CFCs, 386; cities, 302, 310; consumerism, 329; conurbations, 308–9; electricity, 286; food consumption, 102, 103; forced labour, 269; fur trade, 178, 179; and global warming, 392; horses, 272, 274; pollution damage to trees, 381, 382; population, 120, 240; soil erosion, 258; tourism, 332; whaling, 187, 189; wildlife, 162; see also East Germany
Ghana, 212, 218, 257
Ghent, 299
Gibraltar, 342

Gidjingali Aborigines, 22
Gilbert Islands, 188, 220
glaciers, 101, 389
Glasgow, 321
global warming, 387–92, 405–6
Goa, 128, 278
goats, 44, 173, 226, 237
God, 143–7
Godthaab Fjord, 100
Godwin, William, 150
gold, 194, 216, 327, 360
Gold Coast, 357
Gondwanaland, 9
Gorakhpur district, 215
Gran Canaria, 195
Grand Banks, 175
Grand Canal (China), 93, 268, 269
Grand Rapids, 169
'Grand Tours', 331
Grande Carajas project, 399
grasslands, 14, 15, 22
great auks, 162
Great Barrier Reef, 166, 192
Great Lakes, 177, 375
Great Ouse, 126
Great Plains, 167, 171, 181, 256, 260, 390
Great Smoky mountains, 381
Great Wall of China, 269
Greece, 150; agriculture, 47; air pollution, 380; city states, 120; colonies, 297; food shortages, 109; philosophy, 142–3; slaves, 270; soil erosion, 76–7; tourism, 332, 338; water supply, 348; wildlife, 161
'Green Revolution', 251–2
Greenland, 100, 101, 187, 383, 386
Greenpeace, 193
Grenelle, 349
Gross National Product (GNP), 156–7
Guadalquivir, river, 101
Guanches, 195, 196
guano, 116, 218, 247
Guatemala, 50, 78, 79, 82, 214
guilds, 154
Guinea, 195, 197, 218, 257
Guti nomads, 72
Guyana, 199

Haarlem, 126, 309
haciendas, 205
Hacilar, 66
Hadrian, emperor, 77–8
Hadza, 19, 21, 33
The Hague, 309
Haiti, 255, 258, 311
Hale, Sir Matthew, 146
Halifax, 356
Hamburg, 299, 303, 374
Hampshire, 120
Han empire, 91, 93, 94, 111, 298, 339
Hanford, 378
Hanseatic League, 179, 299
Harappa, 60, 348

Harlemmermeer, 125
Harrods, 329
Harrogate, 331
harvest, failure of, 98–9
Haussmann, Baron, 306
Hawaii, 2, 32, 34, 64, 135, 199, 215, 262, 338
heart diease, 236, 237
Hebden Bridge, 374
Hebrides, 185
Henderson, Hazel, 159
Henry VIII, King of England, 178
herbicides, 247
Herculaneum, 9
Hermansky, 329
Hereo, 139
Herodotus, 76
Hertfordshire, 164
Hesiod, 143, 149
Heyerdahl, Thor, 2
Hickeringill, Edmund, 164
Himalayas, 50, 215, 262–3
Hindus, 297
Hispaniola, 230
Hittites, 326
Hobart, 188
Hobbes, Thomas, 19
holidays see also tourism, 322, 331–2
Holland, 125, 300, 301
Holstein, 122–3
Home and Colonial, 329
Homo erectus, 18–19, 26
Homo sapiens, 19
Homo sapiens sapiens, 19, 28
Honduras, 50, 78, 311
Hong Kong, 222
Hopewell furnace, Pennsylvania, 277
Hormuz, 128
Horn of Africa, 108
horses, 48, 171, 270–2, 273–4, 304, 357–8
House of Commons, 285, 355
housing, 311–12, 317, 320–1
Howes, Edmund, 280
Hsiang valley, 94
Hudson river, 180, 375
Hudson's Bay, 22
Hudson's Bay Company, 180–1, 182
Hungary, 27, 120, 122, 351
Huns, 48
hunter-gatherers see gathering and hunting
    groups
hunting: big-game, 167; birds, 169; for furs,
    177–82; seals, 182–5; for sport, 164, 167;
    walruses, 185; whaling, 186–92
Hyderabad, 357
hydroelectricity, 286, 288, 342

ice ages, 10, 11, 26–9, 99, 389, 390
Iceland, 100–1, 162, 176, 189, 191, 235
Ieyasu, Tokugawa, 298
Ijsselmeer, 126
Ile-de-France, 120, 122
Illinois, 261

imports, food, 115, 244–5, 252
Incas, 2, 112, 128, 129, 130, 131, 230, 270,
    301
indentured labour, 198–9
India, 111, 112, 222,; acid rain, 368;
    attitudes to natural world, 152; cities, 296,
    297, 298, 311; coal, 285; deforestation,
    255, 256; disease, 227, 228, 232; early
    man, 26; European colonies, 127, 128,
    130; food consumption, 102; food exports,
    214; food shortages, 253; foreign aid,
    341–2; and global warming, 392;
    indentured labour, 199; intensification of
    agriculture, 251; irrigation, 264; living
    standards, 339, 340; new crops, 112, 113;
    pesticides, 371; pollution, 373; population,
    92–3, 242; rice, 49–50, 93; soil erosion,
    258; tea plantations, 206, 208; timber,
    215; water supply, 350, 351
Indian Ocean, 9, 31–2, 127, 128, 183, 383
Indianapolis, 313
Indians, North American, 40, 130, 133–4,
    153, 168, 169, 171, 180, 181, 225, 231
Indians, South American, 21, 130–3, 398
Indicopleustus, Cosmas, 144
Indo-China, 94, 209
Indonesia, 26, 32, 106, 140, 200–2, 216, 342
Indus valley, 59, 60, 73–4, 227, 271, 295,
    296, 298, 348
'Industrial Revolution', 272, 275, 276, 282–4,
    361
industry: in cities, 306; coal supplies, 281–5;
    electricity consumption, 286; industrial
    diseases, 368–9; industrialisation, 319–20,
    321–8, 400–1; pollution, 360–9; water
    power, 275–6
infant mortality, 321, 333, 340, 369
infanticide, 23, 242
infectious diseases, 225–6, 233–4, 235–6, 240
influenza, 226, 230, 235
infra-red radiation, 387, 388–9
insect pests, 174, 371
interglacial periods, 11
internal combustion engine, 287, 378–80
International Monetary Fund, 343–4, 345
International Whaling Commission (IWC),
    190–1
Inuit, 19, 23, 36, 100, 383
Inverness, 178
Inverness-shire, 163
Iran, 43
Iraq, 43
Iraq, 265
Ireland, 104, 106–8, 113, 114, 116, 163, 176,
    178, 241, 317
Irish Sea, 378
Irk, river, 354, 355, 364
iron, 326–7, 361, 399
Iroquois, 133
Irrawaddy delta, 215
irrigation, 55–7, 59, 68–9, 70–3, 84–7,
    226–7, 264–5, 350

Irwell river, 364
Iset river, 375
Isfahan, 353
Isin, 71
Islam, 32, 111–12, 120
Israel, 39
Italy, 154, 174; agriculture, 111; bird
  hunting, 165; cities, 299; deforestation,
  77; disease, 231; drainage projects, 124,
  126; early population, 120; and Ethiopia,
  128; famines, 97; fur trade, 178; and
  global warming, 392; industrialisation,
  282; pollution, 372; poverty, 318; timber
  shortages, 278; tourism, 331
Ivory Coast, 206, 212, 214, 216, 257, 311

Jainism, 152
Jaktorowa forest, 162
Jamaica, 201, 206, 245
James I, King of England, 361
Jamestown, 133, 172
Jan Mayen Island, 184
Japan, 194, 208, 222; cars, 330; cities, 297,
  298, 307, 309, 313; climatic changes, 99;
  consumerism, 329; deforestation, 74–5;
  disease, 231, 232; early cultures, 40, 44,
  61–2; fishing, 176; and global warming,
  392; indentured labour, 199;
  independence, 130; industrialisation, 284;
  irrigation, 264; pollution, 360, 364, 371;
  population growth, 242; rice, 93;
  sanitation, 356; water power, 276;
  whaling, 186, 188, 189, 191
Japanese Joint Whaling Company, 191
Jarmo, 45
Java, 18, 93, 140, 200, 202, 211, 251, 342
Jebel Sahaba, 66
Jericho, 46, 66
Jesuits, 132
Jews, 297
Jomon culture, 40
Jordan valley, 43, 265
Juan Fernandez Islands, 166, 183
Judaism, 143–4, 145, 152
Julianehaab, 100
Julich, 318
Jura, 27, 162
jute, 205

Kadesh, battle of, 67
Kalahari desert, 103
Kama region, 278
Kamchatka, 127, 129
Kansas, 260, 350
Kansas City, 306
Kant, Immanuel, 149
Karachai, Lake, 378
Karaganda Central Ore Concentration Mill,
  364
Kariba dam, 342
Karnak-Luxor, 59
Katanga, 216

Katowice, 363, 366, 369
Kazakstan, 262, 265
Kazan, 128, 179
Kempen, 282
Kent, 120, 280
Kentucky, 172, 381
Kentucky Fried Chicken, 329
Kenya, 129, 138, 202–4, 211, 238, 252
Kerguelen Island, 183, 185
kerosene, 287
Keynesian economics, 155, 156
Khuzistan, 44, 55
Kiev, 178, 179
Kikuyu, 203
Killarney, Ontario, 367
Kisangani airport, 345
Kish, 57, 71
Kobe, 309
Kola peninsula, 176
Korea, 61, 93
Krasnoural'sk, 364
krill, 177
Kwangtung, 94
Kyoto, 298
Kyshytm, 376, 378
Kyushu, 62

labour: children, 318, 323; in early societies,
  66, 268–9; forced labour, 269–70;
  indentured, 198–9; servants, 317; slavery,
  195–8, 269, 270; unemployment, 311, 313;
  women, 318, 323
Labrador, 185, 187
La Cloche mountains, 367
Lagash, 57, 66, 71, 295
Lagos, 310, 357
lakes, pollution, 366–7, 375
La Mancha, 78
Lambeth Water Company, 355
Lancashire, 276, 302, 320, 349
The Lancet, 250
land ownership, 54–5, 154–5, 251
land reclamation, 124–6
landfill sites, 373–4, 377–8
Lanzarote, 195
Laoying dam, 342
Lapland, 376
La Rochelle, 181
Larsa, 71
Lascaux, 28
Latin America, 102, 182, 204, 205, 213, 214,
  244, 250–1, 271, 310–11, 342
Laurasia, 9
Laurentian shield, 30
La Venta, 62
Lawrence, 276
lead pollution, 360, 379, 380, 383
League of Nations, 138, 320
Lebanon, 76
Leiden, 309, 318
leisure activities, 330–1
Lenin, 157–8, 324

Leningrad (St Petersburg), 300, 309, 356
Leopold, King of the Belgians, 216
Lepanto, battle of (1576), 270
leprosy, 226, 228
Leptis Magna, 77
Leutwein, 138
Levant, 39, 111, 127
Lever Brothers, 302
Leverkusen, 302
Lewis, 181
Liberia, 206, 210, 217, 257
Libya, 77
Liège, 318
life expectancy, 103, 225, 233, 318
lighting, 268, 284–6
Lima, 311
Limburg, 282, 362
Limits to Growth, 402
Lincolnshire, 126, 164, 165
Liptons, 329
Lisbon, 9, 197
'Little Ice Age', 99–100, 112
Liverpool, 320, 349
living standards, 315–45
Livonia, 104, 123
loess, 49, 74
London: adulteration of food, 250; air
    pollution, 358–60; disease, 229–30, 236;
    'Green Belt', 306–7; growth of, 297, 299,
    300, 302, 303, 309, 310; housing, 321;
    lighting, 285; milk sales, 249; pollution,
    361; poverty, 313, 320; rubbish disposal,
    352; sewers, 354, 355; shops, 328;
    suburbs, 304, 305; tobacco trade, 207;
    trade in wildlife, 165, 167, 179; transport,
    273, 313, 336; water supply, 276, 348–9,
    350; wildlife, 163
Lord Howe Island, 167
Lorraine, 122
Los Angeles, 306, 309, 313, 379, 381
Louisiana, 168, 208
Love Canal, 374
Low Countries, 299
Lowell, 276
Lugard, Governor, 357
Lumsden Lake, 367
Lyon, 109, 229

MacDonalds hamburgers, 328
Macedonia, 339
machinery: agricultural, 246; horse power,
    273
Macquarie Island, 183, 185, 386
Madagascar, 32, 34, 111, 189, 197
Madeira, 172, 195
Madrid, 300, 353
Maimonides, 145
Maine, 279
maize, 51, 62, 63, 88, 112, 113, 114, 203,
    236
Malabar coast, 215
Malacca, 128

Malawi, 211
Malaya, 199, 203, 206, 210
Maldive Islands, 391
Malta, 332
Malthus, Rev. Thomas, 151, 158
Mamouth, 329
Manaus, 210
Manchester, 302, 320, 354, 355, 356, 364,
    365, 369
Manchester (USA), 276
Manchuria, 235
Manhattan, 168, 305, 348
Manila, 357
manioc, 113
manure, 94, 95, 268, 357–8
Maoris, 33, 34
Marakanda, 297
Maremma, 126
Marienbad, 331
markets, 154–5
manioc, 113
Marquesas Islands, 2, 32, 215
marriage, and population growth, 97
Marseilles, 101, 230, 297, 349
Marshall Islands, 31
marshes: creation of, 77; drainage, 124–6,
    255; raised fields, 82, 83
marsupials, 9–10
Marx, Karl, 151, 157–8
Marxism, 155, 158
Maryland, 197, 207
Mas Afuera, 1, 166, 183
Masai, 39, 138, 203
Massachusetts, 168, 276, 304
Massif Central, 259, 318
Mastodon Mill, 276
Mauretania, 217, 310
Mauritius, 166, 199
Maurya empire, 296
Maya, 62, 65, 78–83, 269, 296, 401
meat, 214, 244–5, 253, 257, 292
Meaux, monastery of, 317
Mecklenburg, 122–3
medicine, 233–4
Mediterranean, 32; cities, 299, 300;
    deforestation, 75–7; disease, 227–8, 229;
    early cultures, 120; extinct animals, 161–2;
    global warming, 390; mules, 271; new
    crops, 111, 112, 113; population, 92; soil
    erosion, 258; tourism, 339; transition to
    agriculture, 47, 48; water supply, 348;
    whales, 187; windmills, 277
Mekong delta, 209
Melbourne, 337, 386
Melville, Herman, 136
Melville, Captain Thomas, 166
Memphis, 59
Merrimack river, 276
Mesoamerica, 59; agriculture, 37, 41–2,
    50–2, 112; astronomy, 65; cities, 296, 297;
    development of society, 62–3; slavery,
    269; warfare, 67

Mesopotamia, 76, 111, 401; agriculture, 55–6; cities, 56–8, 295–6; destruction of environment, 69–73; development of society, 56–8, 65; disease, 226, 227; sewage, 354; slavery, 269; technology, 58–9; transport, 271; warfare, 66–7; wildlife, 162
metal-working, 58, 66–7, 325–7, 360
methane, 387, 388–9
Mexico, 78; agriculture, 50; desertification, 264; development of society, 62–3; development of society, 62–3; disappearance of Aztecs, 130; disease, 230, 232; 'Green Revolution', 251, 252; minerals, 194, 216; native food crops, 39, 50; wildlife, 170
Mexico, Gulf of, 287
Mexico City, 63, 301, 309, 379
mice, 172
Michelin guides, 332
Michigan, 168, 169–70
Michigan, Lake, 177
Michoacan, 170
Micronesians, 31
Midgely, Thomas, 385
Midvale Steel Works, 324
Milhankovic effects, 10, 389
milk, 249
Mill, John Stuart, 149, 151, 155
millet, 49, 61, 74, 113
mills, 274–7
Mindinao, 197
minerals, 216–18
mining, 282–3, 327–8, 360
Minoan culture, 9, 120
Mirex, 374
missionaries, 130, 131, 135
Mississippi river, 181, 283–4
Mississippi (state), 208, 333
Mitchell, Mount, 381–2
Mobutu, General, 344
Mohawk river, 276
Mohenjo-Daro, 60, 295, 348
Moissac, 109
monasteries, 122
Mongols, 48, 73, 95, 123, 127, 228
mongongo nuts, 20, 21
monocrops, 247
Monongahela valley, 362
Montauban, 109
Monte Alban, 296
Montpellier, 280
Montreal Convention (1987), 386
Morocco, 76, 218, 332, 344
mortality rates, 225, 232–5, 241, 311, 320, 321, 333, 340, 369
Moscow, 128, 179, 306, 307, 322, 349, 356, 364
Moselle river, 110, 122
Most, 363, 369
Mughal empire, 297
Muhammad, Prophet, 111

mules, 271
multinational corporations, 214, 217–18, 333–4, 342
Murray-Darling basin, 167
Muscat, 232
Muscovy Company, 185
Mycenae, 120
myxomatosis, 172

Nahal Oren, 39
Nama, 139
Namibia, 139
Nandi, 203
Nanking, 298
Nantucket, 187
Naples, 297, 300
Napoleonic wars, 106, 279
Nara, 298
Narbonne, 126
Narmada valley project, 342
Natal, 199
National City Lines, 337
National Parks, 192
Natufian culture, 45–6
natural gas, 9, 288, 290, 293
Nauru, 218–20
Navaho, 131
Nazis, 269–70
Nebraska, 260, 350
'Neolithic Revolution', 37–8
Nepal, 263, 340
Netherlands: agricultural improvements, 114; cities, 310; climatic changes, 101–2; coal, 283; colonies, 206, 210; conurbations, 309; and Indonesia, 200–1; land reclamation, 114, 125–6; natural gas, 288; pollution, 361, 372; seal hunting, 182; slave trade, 197; toxic wastes, 374–5; whaling, 187; windmills, 277
Netsilik Inuit, 22, 23
Nevada, 225
New Delhi, 300
New England, 133, 168, 169, 172, 187, 197, 279
New Guinea, 21, 29–30, 32, 33, 44, 52
New Hampshire, 276, 279
New Mexico, 260
New River Company, 348
New Romney, 124
New South Wales, 171, 173, 262
New York, 174, 245; horses, 274, 358; infant mortality, 321; lighting, 285; milk supply, 249; population, 301, 303, 309; slaughter of passenger pigeons, 169; starlings, 172; suburbs, 305, 306; traffic speed, 313; underground railway, 304; waste disposal, 373, 375; water supply, 349
New York State, 133, 168, 173, 180, 259, 367
New Zealand: agricultural improvements, 246; deforestation, 33, 256; food exports, 245; introduced wildlife, 170–1, 173; ozone layer hole, 386; phosphate extraction

New Zealand – *cont.*
  in Pacific, 218–21; settlement of, 3, 32, 34,
  128, 129; whaling, 188
Newcastle, 281, 323, 359
Newfoundland, 175, 176, 183–4, 187
Newton, Isaac, 147
Niagara Falls, 286, 374
Nicaragua, 130
nickel, 327
Nicopolis, battle of (1396), 127
Nigeria, 257, 287, 296, 310, 357
Nile Delta, 391
Nile valley, 46, 59, 83–7, 161, 162
nitrous oxide, 387, 388–9
Nizamsagar dam, 342
Noah, 144
nomads, 39, 263–4
Norfolk, 120
Norfolk Broads, 124
Normandy, 97, 275
Normans, 122
North Africa, 55, 59, 77, 102, 112, 264
North America: cities, 301; destruction of
  wildlife, 35, 166, 167–70; disease, 227,
  230–1; fishing, 177; fur trade, 180–2;
  geological history, 9; introduced wildlife,
  170, 171, 172–3; iron production, 326;
  native animals, 10; new crops, 113;
  population, 92–3, 243; seal hunting,
  183–4; settlement of, 30–1, 128, 129,
  133–4, 397–8; slave trade, 198; timber
  exports, 279; whaling, 187–8; *see also*
  Canada; United States of America
North Cape, 176
North Carolina, 197, 208, 259–60, 381–2
North Sea, 176, 287, 288, 375
Northern Ireland, 235
Northern Rhodesia, 216
Northill, 164
Northumbria, 100
Norway, 100, 102, 116, 189, 191, 279, 367,
  381
Nottingham, 320, 358
Nouadhibou, 217
Nouakchott, 310
Novgorod, 179
Nubia, 66
nuclear power, 288, 376–8
nuclear weapons, 377
Nullarbor desert, 171
Nuremburg, 276

O'ahu, 64
Oaxaca, 50
Oberfalz, 277
obsolescence, 334
occupational diseases, 368–9
Ocean Island, 218–21
Oceana County, 169
Oceania *see* Pacific Ocean
oceans *see* sea
Oder, river, 123, 127

Ogallkala aquifer, 350
Ogodai, 127
Ohio, 133, 168, 170, 249
oil: consumption by cars, 338; as energy
  source, 267, 285, 286–8, 290, 293;
  formation of, 9; and global warming,
  387–8; pollution, 372, 375; reserves, 402;
  and Third World economics, 343; whale
  oil, 186, 189, 190, 285, 287
Okhotsk, 129
Oklahoma, 134, 260, 261, 290, 350
Olduvai Gorge, 26
olive trees, 75, 76, 101
Olmecs, 62
Oman, 111
Omayyad empire, 120
Ontario, 366, 367
Ontario, Lake, 374
open-cast mining, 327–8
Ophuls, William, 174
Organisation for Economic Co-operation and
  Development (OECD), 365, 366, 367
Orkneys, 162, 185
Orleans, 366
Orongo, 4
Orslosa, 105
Osaka, 298
Osborne House, Isle of Wight, 362
ospreys, 163
Ostia, 77
Otmoor, 124
Ottoman empire, 126, 128, 179, 270, 297
Ovambo, 139
ox transport, 270–2
oxford, 359
ozone, 378, 380, 381, 383, 385
ozone layer, 385–7, 405

Pacific Electric, 337
Pacific Islands Company, 218–19
Pacific Ocean, 8; European colonisation, 130,
  134–7; fishing, 176; indentured labour,
  199; population, 92–3, 243; seal hunting,
  183, 184; settlement of, 2–3, 31–2;
  walruses, 185; whaling, 188
packaging, 373
paddy fields, 93–4, 388
Paestum, 77
paintings, cave, 28, 66, 117
Pakistan, 251
Palenque, 79, 81
Palermo, 299
Palestine, 43, 45–6, 331
palm oil, 212
Panaetius, 142–3
paper, 396
Para state, 399
parasitic diseases, 225, 226, 354
Paris, 165, 297; abandoned children, 318;
  food riots, 109; holidays, 322; lighting,
  285; pesticides, 371; population, 97, 299,
  300, 309, 310; sewage, 351–2, 356; shops,

328, 329; suburbs, 305–6; underground railway, 304; waste disposal, 353; water power, 274, 275; water supply, 349; wolves, 162
Pasig river, 357
passenger pigeons, 168–70, 174
pastoralism, 39, 263–4
Pataliputra, 296, 298
PCBs (polychlorinated biphenyls), 370, 371–2, 375, 382, 383
Peisistratus, 76
Peking, 93, 269, 296, 301, 309, 353, 385
pellagra, 114
Pennsylvania, 133, 278, 286, 324, 376
Penrith, 106
Pepys, Samuel, 229–30, 352
Persia, 111, 162, 297, 339
Peru, 59; agriculture, 51–2, 112; animals, 62, 170, 172; cities, 296; conquest of Incas, 131; destruction of environment, 78; disease, 230, 231; indentured labour, 199; minerals, 194, 216; mules, 271; slavery, 197; whaling, 188, 189
Perugia, 317
pesticides, 247, 251–2, 351, 370–1, 373, 374, 382–3
Peter the Great, Tsar, 300
petrol, 379, 380
pheasants, 110
Philadelphia, 303, 309, 331, 349
Philip II, King of Spain, 278
Philippines, 199, 213, 215–16, 251, 256, 258
Phillips, John, 354
philosophy, 141–3
Phoenicians, 76
phosphates, 218–21, 247, 370
photochemical smog, 379–80
photosynthesis, 11–12, 381, 385, 388
Phrygia, 77
phylloxera, 174
pigeons, 168–70, 174
pigs, 44, 170, 226, 248
Pittsburgh, 303, 362
plague, 91, 97, 123, 224, 227–30, 235
plankton, 383, 386
plantations, 195–6, 201–14
plants: continental drift, 9; exports, 167; extinctions, 193; and global warming, 391; introductions, 173–4; pests and diseases, 174; photosynthesis, 11–12; transition to agriculture, 38, 39–40, 43–52; ultraviolet damage, 386
plastics, 325, 375
plate tectonics, 8
Plato, 76–7, 143
ploughs, 96, 260
Po valley, 111, 124
Poitevin marshes, 124
Pokrovskiy, M. N., 158
Poland, 27, 162, 276, 278, 280, 363, 366, 369, 382
pollution, 16–17, 346–92, 404–5; acid rain,

365–8; air, 358–60, 361–2, 378–80, 381–2; 'cocktail' effect, 380–1; damage to ozone layer, 385–7; global warming, 387–92, 405–6; industrial, 360–9; internal combustion engine, 378–80; nuclear, 376–8; PCBs, 370, 371–2; pesticides, 370–1; waste disposal, 351–3, 373–6; water, 265, 347–8, 351, 360–1, 362
Polynesians, 2–7, 32, 52, 64, 218–20
Pompeii, 9
Pontine marshes, 77, 126
population: early humans, 24, 36; food supply and growth of, 37, 88–98; growth of, 120–1, 240–3, 394–5, 404; and imported food, 115; and transition to agriculture, 42
Port Nelson, 181
Port Sunlight, 302
Porto Santo, 172
Portugal, 123, 127–8, 131–2, 137, 172, 195, 196–7, 206, 211, 278
potash, 277–8
potato blight, 107
potatoes, 52, 106–7, 112–15, 174
Potosi, 131, 197
Potteries, 308, 323, 361
pottery, 40, 46
poverty, 254, 311–12, 313, 315, 317–20, 333, 340–1
power stations, 286, 291
Prague, 363
Prestbury, 164
Pribilof Islands, 135, 184, 185
prickly pear, 173–4
Prince William Sound, 372
processed food, 238, 249–50
progress, 149–51, 160, 396
Provence, 97, 101
Prussia, 106, 300, 301
public transport, 337–8
Puerto Rico, 201, 206
Punjab, 255, 265
Puritans, 133
pygmies, 19
Pyrenees, 102

Qadan culture, 66
Quakers, 133
Queensland, 173, 199

Rabat, 353
rabbits, 110, 171–2
radioactivity, 376–8
Radisson, Pierre, 166
railways, 244, 273, 283, 285, 304, 305–6, 325, 331, 338
rainfall, 102, 258; acid rain, 365–8, 381
rainforests see forests
Rajasthan, 255, 263–4
Ramazzini, Bernardino, 368
Rambi Island, 219, 221
Ramessid dynasty, 86

Randstad, 309
Rano Raraku, 4, 5
Rarotonga, 135
rats, 166, 172
Ravenna, 77
Ray, John, 146
recycling, 16, 327, 373
red kites, 163
Red River, 181
Reformation, 145
refrigerated transport, 244, 245
reindeer, 27–8, 39, 377
religion, 57–8, 65, 141–2, 143–7, 151–2
retailing, 328–9
Rheims, 366
Rhine, river, 47, 373
Rhineland, 277
Rhode Island, 284
Rhodes, Cecil, 221–2
Rhone, river, 101, 126
Ricardo, David, 155, 221
rice, 49–50, 88, 93–4, 111, 112, 200, 201,
    202, 208–9, 251, 254, 291
Richard II, King of England, 178
Riga, 123, 279
rinderpest, 103
Rio de Janeiro, 211
riots, food, 106, 109
rivers: acid rain pollution, 366–7; pollution,
    355, 362, 375; silt, 263; water power, 275,
    276
roads, 336–7, 338
Robec, river, 274
Rocky mountains, 30, 35, 181, 182
Rogers, Woods, 166
Roggeveen, Admiral, 1
'Roman Bank', the Wash, 124
Roman empire, 150, 339; agriculture, 55,
    111; deforestation, 77–8; disease, 228;
    drainage projects, 124; extinct animals,
    161, 162; food shortages, 109; fur trade,
    177; philosophy, 142; population, 91, 120;
    slaves, 270; towns and cities, 297, 299,
    303; vineyards, 48; water supply, 348
Rome, 154, 162, 296, 297, 303, 336, 348
Romney Marshes, 124
Rondonia, 399
Ross Sea, 189
rotation systems, crops, 95–6
Rotterdam, 309
Rouen, 275
Royal Navy, 278–9, 284, 320
Royal Society for the Protection of Birds,
    192–3
rubber, 202, 203, 204–5, 206, 208, 209–11
Ruhr, 282, 302, 308, 362
Russia (pre-1917): climatic changes, 101;
    disease, 232; expansion of, 123–4, 128–9,
    135, 177; extension of agricultural land,
    244; famines, 108; fur trade, 178–80; oil,
    287; rinderpest epidemic, 103; sanitation,
    356; seal hunting, 182, 184; timber

exports, 279; windmills, 276; wood
    consumption, 278; see also Soviet Union
Russo-Japanese war, 232
Ruxton, Frederick, 181
Rwanda, 340

Saale river, 122
Saginaw, 168
Sahara desert, 264, 271
Sahel, 108, 263, 264
St Albans, 104
St Domingue, 206
St Helena, 173
St Lawrence river, 180, 183, 185
St Petersburg (Leningrad), 300, 309, 356
Saint-Simon, Comte de, 151
Sal Luis, 132
Salem, 168
Salford, 284
salmon, 31
Salonica, 126
salt: salinisation of soil, 68–9, 70–3, 84–5,
    86, 264–6; salt works, 278, 280
Samarkand, 297
Sami, 39
Samoa, 2, 32
Samos, 348
San Bernardino, 381
San Francisco, 379
San Salvador, 50
Sandoz, 373
sanitation, 226, 234–5, 311, 347, 351–8
Sanmenxia dam, 342
Santiago, 170
Santo Domingo, 130, 197
Sao Paulo, 309, 364
Sargon of Agade, 72
Satke, 381
Saudi Arabia, 264, 350
Saxony, 301
Scandinavia, 27, 101, 113, 279, 283, 376,
    383, 386
Schumacher, E. F., 159
science, 147–8, 159–60
Scotland, 100, 101, 109, 162, 163, 164, 178,
    179, 383
sea: ecosystems, 14; fishing, 175–7; land
    reclamation, 124, 125; pollution, 372,
    375–6; radioactive waste, 378; rise in sea
    level, 389, 391; sewage dumping, 356–7;
    whaling, 186–92
seals, 23, 31, 182–5
Seattle, Chief, 153
Second World War, 272
Seine, river, 274, 349, 352, 356
Selfridges, 329
Sellafield, 378
Seoul, 309
Serengeti park, 192
serfdom, 269
servants, 317
Severn, river, 100

Seveso, 372-3
Seville, 101, 111, 297, 299
sewage, 234, 339, 347, 351-8
Shang dynasty, 61
Shanghai, 309
share cropping, 205
sheep, 44, 170-1, 226, 237
Sheffield, 302, 323, 359
Shensi province, 9
Shetland, 162
shipping, 244-5, 270, 278-9, 284
shops, 328-9
Shoshoni, 131
Shuruppak, 57
Siane tribe, 21
Sib eria, 30, 129, 177, 179-80, 288, 386
Sicily, 77, 196
Siena, 352
Sierra Club, 192
Silesia, 104, 123, 363, 369
silt, Nile floods, 84-7
silver, 131, 194, 197, 216
Sinclair, Upton, 250
Sind, 111
Singapore, 222, 340
sisal, 203, 205
Skegness, 332
'slash and burn' see swidden agriculture
slavery, 111, 130-2, 137, 195-8, 205, 207,
    208, 269, 270
Slavs, 122, 196
Slovakia, 280
slums, 303
smallpox, 226, 228, 230, 233, 235
Smith, Adam, 155, 221, 335
Smith, Robert, 365
smog, 359, 363, 379-80
smoke pollution, 358-60, 361-2
soap, 370
socialism, 157
society, agriculture's influence on, 54-5,
    57-65
Society Islands, 3
Socrates, 142
soil: creation of, 15; erosion, 6, 68, 69, 74-8,
    82-3, 257, 258-63; fertility, 95-6; loess,
    49; Nile floods, 84-7; in rainforests,
    15-16; salinisation, 68-9, 70-3, 84-5, 86,
    264-6
Solon, 76
sorghum, 112
South Africa, 28, 138, 140, 216-17, 236, 264
South America: cattle herds, 170; cocoa
    plantations, 211; deforestation, 257;
    disease, 230-1; extinctions, 35; geological
    history, 9; guano deposits, 218; introduced
    wildlife, 173; mules, 271; native animals,
    10; population, 92-3, 243; railways, 244;
    settlement of, 30-1, 129, 130-3; Spanish
    conquest, 128
South Australia, 171, 172
South Carolina, 197, 207, 208, 209

South-East Asia: cities, 298; deforestation,
    257; diesease, 232; European colonies,
    127, 128; paddy fields, 388; plantations,
    204, 208-11; slave trade, 197; transition to
    agriculture, 49-50, 52
South Georgia, 183, 189
South Korea, 222, 251, 340
South Pole, 386
South Shetland Islands, 183, 189
South-west Africa: European colonisation,
    138-40
south-west Asia: irrigation, 55-7; transition
    to agriculture, 37, 41-8
Southern Rhodesia, 138
Southwell, Sir Robert, 248
Soviet Union, 55; agricultural improvements,
    247; cities, 306-7, 313; economics, 157,
    158; famines, 108; forced labour, 269-70;
    and global warming, 392; ice ages, 27;
    industrialisation, 321-2, 323, 324;
    irrigation, 265; natural gas, 288; nuclear
    accidents, 376-7, 378; oil, 287, 290;
    pollution, 363-4, 366, 375; sanitation,
    356; soil erosion, 258, 261-2; water
    supply, 349-50; whaling, 191; see also
    Russia
soybeans, 49
Spain: agriculture, 112; and the Canary
    Islands, 195-6; cave paintings, 28, 66;
    cities, 300; colonies, 130-1; exploration,
    127, 128; food exports, 245; fur trade, 178,
    179; ice ages, 28; overgrazing, 78;
    reconquista, 123; slave trade, 197; timber
    shortages, 278; tourism, 332, 338; water
    supply, 348; whaling, 187
Spanish Armada, 278
Sparta, 296
speech, development of, 24
Spencer, Herbert, 148-9, 151
spices, 201-2
Spitzbergen, 185, 187
sports, 330-1
Squamish tribe, 153
squatters, 311-12
Sri Lanka (Ceylon), 197, 199, 203, 206, 208,
    211, 214
Stalin, Joseph, 307
Standard Oil, 337
starlings, 172-3
starvation, 88-9, 97-9, 103-9, 254
steam power, 283-4, 290
steel, 326-7
Stephens, John, 79
Stoics, 142-3
stone tools, 19-20, 24, 26, 28-9, 347
Stow, John, 281
Strabo, 360
Strzelecki, Count, 137
Stukeley, William, 359
subsidies, agricultural, 248
suburbs, 303-8, 312
Sudan, 264

Sudbury smelter, 366
Sudeten mountains, 123
Sudetenland, 377
Suez Canal, 205, 209, 214, 343
sugar cane, 111, 195, 199, 201, 205, 206–7, 213, 237, 256
Sui dynasty, 93
sulphur dioxide, 361, 363, 365–8, 369
Sumatra, 206, 210
Sumer, 57–8, 63, 69–72, 265
Sumida river, 364
sun: photosynthesis, 11–12; sunspots, 10, 389; variations in earth's orbit and tilt, 10–11
Superior, Lake, 166, 382
Surinam, 197
Sussex, 120, 165, 278, 280
Sutherland, 164
Sverdlovsk, 375, 378
Swansea, 362
Sweden, 47, 105, 121, 235, 242, 279, 280, 318, 328, 340, 367, 386
swidden agriculture, 47, 49, 80, 121, 227, 395
Swindon, 302
Switzerland, 174, 332, 367, 382
Sydney, 136, 137, 166, 172, 262
syphilis, 231, 232
Syria, 39, 43, 45–6, 76, 78, 265
Szechwan, 94

Tahiti, 135–6, 213
taiga, 14
Taiwan, 222, 340
Tamil Nadu, 350
Tamils, 206, 208, 210
T'ang dynasty, 32
Tanzania, 192, 238
Taoism, 152
Tapuia Indians, 132
Tasmania, 29, 33, 137, 140, 188
Taxila, 298
Taylor, Frederick, 324
'Taylorism', 324
tea, 201–2, 205, 208
Techna river, 378
technology: gathering and hunting groups, 24–6, 28–9; Mesopotamia, 58–9; see also industry
Tehuacan, 50
television, 331
Tell es-Sultan, 46
temples, 57, 62–3, 65, 296
Tenasserim, 215
Tennessee, 381
Tenochtitlan, 63, 67, 230, 301, 354
teosinte, 51
Teotihuacan, 63, 78, 80, 82, 269, 296, 297
Tethys Sea, 9
Texas, 208, 260, 261, 350
textile industry, 324–5
Thailand, 50, 209, 392

Thames, river, 101, 185, 276, 348–9, 352, 355, 361
Thar desert, 255
Thera, 9
Third World: agriculture, 250–3; cities, 310–12; creation of, 194–223; debt, 343–4; disease, 234–5; energy consumption, 292; food shortages, 253–4; foreign aid, 341–3; and global warming, 392; living standards, 341; pesticides, 371; population growth, 242, 404; sanitation, 357; tourism, 339; toxic wastes, 374; water supply, 350, 351
'30 per cent Club', 368
Thoreau, Henry David, 312
Three Mile Island, 376
Tiber, river, 348
Tibet, 276
tidal mills, 275–6
Tierra del Fuego, 183
Tietz, 329
Tigre, 75, 254
Tigris, river, 70, 73
Tikal, 79, 81, 82
timber see wood
tobacco, 202, 205, 207, 238, 256–7, 259
Tokugawa period, 75, 297, 298
Tokyo see also Edo, 9, 297, 307–8, 309, 313, 350, 356, 364, 379
Toltecs, 63
Tomatoes, 113
Tomboro volcano, 106
Tomsk, 129
Tonga, 2, 32
tools: stone, 19–20, 24, 26, 28–9, 347; transition to agriculture, 40
Torrey Canyon, 372
Toulouse, 109, 275
tourism, 331–2, 335, 338–9
Tours, 366
towns, development of, 46; see also cities
toxic wastes, 374–5, 377–8
trade, development of, 154–5
Trafalgar Square, London, 350
Trajan, Emperor, 162
transport: animal power, 270–4; cars, 156, 312–13, 336–8; development of wheel, 271–2; of food, 244–5; public, 337–8; railways, 244, 273, 284, 285, 304, 305–6, 325, 331, 338; shipping, 244–5, 270, 278–9, 284; suburbs and, 303–4; tourism, 331–2
trees: air pollution, 381–2; diseases, 174; see also forests
trichloroacetic acid (TCA), 381
Tring, 164
Trinidad, 199
Tristan da Cunha, 183
tuberculosis, 226, 227, 233, 234
Tula, 63
tundra, 14, 18, 27, 389
Tunisia, 218, 332

Tunney, Gene, 330
Turkey, 207, 233, 258, 340
Tuscany, 97, 103, 196, 299
Tuscany, Duke of, 126
Tweed, river, 177
Tyneside, 362
typhus, 230, 232
Tyrol, 316

Uganda, 84, 211, 238
Ukraine, 128, 129, 262, 376–7
ultraviolet radiation, 385, 386
Umma, 57, 66
UN Intergovernmental Panel on Climate
    Change (IPCC), 390
underground railways, 304
unemployment, 311, 313
United Brands, 214
United Fruit Company (UFC), 212
United Nations, 177, 220, 341, 345, 367, 405
United States of America: acid rain, 365,
    366, 367; agricultural improvements, 246,
    247; agricultural surpluses, 248; air
    pollution, 379–80; beef imports, 214, 257;
    cars, 330, 334, 337–8; cities, 301, 303,
    306, 307; consumerism, 329; conurbations,
    309; cotton, 207–8; deforestation, 256;
    desertification, 264; disease, 232, 236, 239;
    energy consumption, 292–3; energy
    efficiency, 292; extension of agricultural
    land, 244; food consumption, 253; food
    processing, 249, 250; foreign aid, 341, 342;
    and global warming, 392; horses, 273–4;
    immigration, 115; industrialisation, 283–4,
    323–4; irrigation, 264, 265; leisure
    activities, 330–1; living standards, 333,
    340; loss of natural habitats, 255; natural
    gas, 290; nuclear accidents, 376, 378; oil,
    285, 286, 287, 288; pesticides, 371;
    plantations, 205; pollution, 370, 375–6,
    381–2, 404; population growth, 243;
    railways, 244, 338; rubber trade, 210–11;
    sanitation, 356; seal hunting, 182, 184;
    settlement of, 133–4; slavery, 198, 207,
    208; soil erosion, 258, 259–61; suburbs,
    303–5; timber extraction from Philippines,
    215–16; tobacco, 207; tourism, 332;
    transport, 312–13; waste disposal, 352,.
    373, 374; water power, 276; water supply,
    349, 350, 351; whaling, 187–8; wildlife
    conservation, 192–3; wood consumption,
    277–8
Upanishads, 152
Ur, 57, 69–70, 71, 72, 295
Ural mountains, 129, 179, 381
uranium, 377
Uruguay, 173, 311
Uruk, 57, 58, 59, 71, 295
Utrecht, 309

vaccination, 233, 235
Valencia, 101, 275

Valladolid, 300
Van Buren County, 169–70
Vauban, 317
Veblen, Thorstein, 335
vegetables, 102, 112
vehicle pollution, 378–80
Venezuela, 223, 287, 380
Venice, 179, 196, 275, 278, 296, 299, 300,
    339
Vermuyden, Cornelius, 126
Versailles, 352
Vesuvius, 9
Victoria, Queen of England, 349, 362
Victoria (Australia), 171, 182, 262
Vienna, 122, 309
Vietnam, 50, 251
Vijayanagar, 297
Vikings, 32, 100, 120, 178–9
vineyards, 174
Virginia, 172, 207, 208, 259
Vistula, river, 47, 363
vitamins, 113
volcanoes, 8–9
Volga river, 124, 127, 128, 129, 375
Volta dam, 342
Voltaire, 148
Vosges, 122

Wadden Sea, 126, 372
Wahlstatt, battle of (1241), 127
Wainfleet, 165
'Waldsterben', 382
Wales, 163, 281, 282, 302, 349, 377
Wallace, Mackenzie, 86
walruses, 185
warfare, 58, 66–7, 272
The Wash, 124, 126
Washington, 300, 306, 309
waste disposal, 351–8, 373–6
Watarse river, 360
water: acid rain pollution, 366–7; drinking
    water, 234, 235, 311, 339, 347–51, 355–6;
    hydroelectricity, 286, 288; irrigation, 59,
    68–9, 70–3, 264–5, 350; Nile floods,
    84–7; paddy fields, 93–4; pollution, 265,
    347–8, 351, 360–1, 362; power5, 274–6,
    282
Wayne County, 168
Weald, 122, 280
wealth, 335, 339–40
weapons, 66–7
weather see climate
Wedgwood, Josiah, 323
weeds, 173
West Africa, 206, 212, 216, 227, 257,
    258
West Germany see Germany
West Indies, 199, 205, 206–7
Western Isles, 162
Westland, 341
whale oil, 186, 189, 190, 285, 286, 287
whales, 166, 186–91

wheat, 43–4, 49, 62, 71, 85, 88, 101, 111, 214, 251–2, 260
wheel, invention of, 58, 66–7
Wheeling, West Virginia, 366
White Highlands, 129
Whitney, Eli, 207
Wieliczka, 280
wildlife: attitudes to, 141–60; conservation, 192–3; destruction of, 33–5, 161–70, 174–5, 193; introductions, 170–4; pollution, 382–3; see also animals; plants
Wiltshire, 120
wind power, 125, 276–7
Windscale, 376
Windsor Castle, 277
Winnebagos, 134
Wollo, 254
wolves, 162–3
women, employment, 268, 318, 323
wood: air pollution, 358; as fuel, 267, 268, 277–8, 279–81, 283–4, 293; paper production, 396; shortages, 278–81, 326; timber extraction, 215–16; see also forests
Woolley, Leonard, 69–70, 79
World Bank, 341, 342, 344
World Helath Organisation (WHO), 351, 363, 364, 365

World Wide Fund for Nature, 193
Worlidge, John, 164
worms, 354
Worthing, 165
writing, invention of, 58–9, 60, 65
writing materials, 396
Wylye, river, 274
Wyoming, 30

Xenophon, 76, 142, 143, 149

yams, 52
Yangtse river, 49, 93, 94, 227
Yellow river, 49, 74, 227
Yellowstone National Park, 192
Yokohama, 307
York, 320
Yorkshire, 126, 276, 282, 302, 375
Yoruba, 296
Ypres, 276

Zagros mountains, 43, 44, 45, 72
Zaire, 344–5
Zambia, 217, 343
Zanzibar, 111, 127
Zeeland, 125
Zittau, 348
Zuider Zee, 125, 126

Linda ♀〰

<u>Dr. Shilling</u> on MAYA Culture

CBC. Gabaro Feb 2ⁿᵈ 1994

<u>David Feedell</u>   Anthropologist

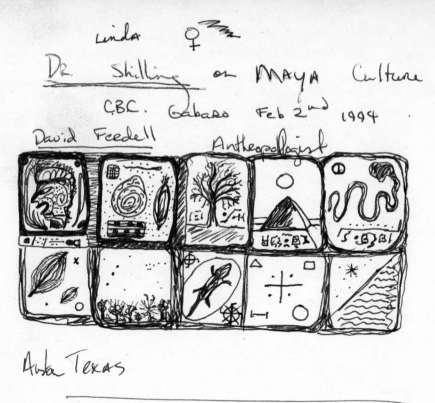

Anta Texas

MAYA COSMOS 3000 years
of Shaman Past